SECURING PEACE IN EUROPE

Woodrow Wilson Center Series

The Woodrow Wilson International Center for Scholars was chartered by the U.S. Congress in 1968 as the living memorial to the nation's twenty-eighth president. It serves as the country's key nonpartisan policy forum, tackling global challenges through independent research and open dialogue. Bridging the worlds of academia and public policy, the Center's diverse programmatic activity informs actionable ideas for Congress, the administration, and the broader policy community.

The Woodrow Wilson Center Series shares in the Center's mission by publishing outstanding scholarly and public policy-related books for a global readership. Written by the Center's expert staff and international network of scholars, our books shed light on a wide range of topics, including U.S. foreign and domestic policy, security, the environment, energy, and area studies.

Conclusions or opinions expressed in Center publications and programs are those of the authors and speakers and do not necessarily reflect the views of the Center staff, fellows, trustees, advisory groups, or any individuals or organizations that provide financial support for the Center.

Please visit us online at www.wilsoncenter.org.

Lucian Kim, *Putin's Revenge: Why Russia Invaded Ukraine*

Kevin J. Middlebrook, *The International Defense of Workers: Labor Rights, U.S. Trade Agreements, and State Sovereignty*

Margarita M. Balmaceda, *Russian Energy Chains: The Remaking of Technopolitics from Siberia to Ukraine to the European Union*

Abraham M. Denmark, *U.S. Strategy in the Asian Century: Empowering Allies and Partners*

Samuel F. Wells Jr., *Fearing the Worst: How Korea Transformed the Cold War*

Donald R. Wolfensberger, *Changing Cultures in Congress: From Fair Play to Power Plays*

William H. Hill, *No Place for Russia: European Security Institutions Since 1989*

Securing Peace in Europe

STROBE TALBOTT, NATO, AND RUSSIA AFTER THE COLD WAR

Stephan Kieninger

Columbia University Press

New York

Columbia University Press
Publishers Since 1893
New York   Chichester, West Sussex
cup.columbia.edu
Copyright © 2025 Columbia University Press
All rights reserved

Library of Congress Cataloging-in-Publication Data
Names: Kieninger, Stephan author
Title: Securing peace in Europe : Strobe Talbott, NATO, and
Russia after the Cold War / Stephan Kieninger.
Other titles: Strobe Talbott, NATO, and Russia after the Cold War
Description: New York : Columbia University Press, 2025. |
Series: Woodrow Wilson Center series | Includes bibliographical references and index.
Identifiers: LCCN 2025009666 (print) | LCCN 2025009667 (ebook) |
ISBN 9780231217729 hardback | ISBN 9780231217712 trade paperback |
ISBN 9780231561877 ebook
Subjects: LCSH: United States—Foreign relations—1993–2001 | Talbott, Strobe |
Foreign ministers—United States | North Atlantic Treaty Organization |
United States—Foreign relations—Europe | Europe—Foreign relations—United States |
United States—Foreign relations—Russia (Federation) | Russia (Federation)—
Foreign relations—United States
Classification: LCC E885 .K54 2025 (print) | LCC E885 (ebook) |
DDC 973.929—dc23/eng/20250508
LC record available at https://lccn.loc.gov/2025009666
LC ebook record available at https://lccn.loc.gov/2025009667

Printed and bound by CPI Group (UK) Ltd, Croydon, CR0 4YY

Cover design: Chang Jae Lee
Cover image: Stephen Jaffe/AFP © Getty Images

GPSR Authorized Representative: Easy Access System Europe, Mustamäe tee 50,
10621 Tallinn, Estonia, gpsr.requests@easproject.com

For Valentina

Contents

Foreword   ix
Javier Solana

Preface: Formative Years and Journalism   xiii
List of Abbreviations   xxxi

INTRODUCTION   1
I   U.S. Foreign Policy and the European Security Mess   10
II   Engaging Russia and Enlarging NATO   44
III   Building a New Security Architecture   77
IV   The NATO-Russia Founding Act and Its Aftermath   112
V   Russia's Financial Crisis and the End of Reform   136
VI   The Kosovo War as a Game Changer   160
VII   Putin and the Crisis of U.S.-Russia Relations   194
CONCLUSION   223

Acknowledgments and Note on Sources   237
Notes   245
Archives and Interviews   305
Bibliography   311
Index   331

Foreword

JAVIER SOLANA

I first met Strobe Talbott in 1993 when, as Spanish minister for foreign affairs, I visited Washington, DC, to establish contact with my counterpart Warren Christopher and the State Department of the newly elected Clinton administration. Since then, Strobe and I have shared a great deal, both on a professional and a personal level. From the negotiations that led to the NATO-Russia Founding Act of 1997, the first NATO enlargement after the dissolution of the Soviet Union and the rise of the post–Cold War order, our paths have been defined by the events that led a rapidly changing world into the twenty-first century.

But of course, this is not a book about my relationship with Strobe. It is a book about Strobe Talbott, the towering figure in the State Department, that from his many positions within the department—including ambassador-at-large on the newly independent states, special adviser to the secretary of state, and then deputy secretary of state—successfully steered the Clinton administration through one of the most consequential geopolitical shifts of the twentieth century as the Soviet Union, and the Warsaw Pact, crumbled. As a diplomat, Strobe Talbott was appointed to do one of the most difficult jobs at a particularly difficult time in global history.

As I look back to those days, I cannot think of a more qualified person to carry out the job than Strobe. As I started to get to know him, Strobe instantly struck me as a very intelligent person who was knowledgeable about many topics, an attribute that I would quickly associate to his

Figure 0.1 President Bill Clinton and Strobe Talbott meeting President Boris Yeltsin of Russia in Vancouver, Canada, April 3, 1993. U.S. interpreter Peter Afanasenko is in the center. Clinton Presidential Library.

voracious reading and the enormous personal library he has at his house in Washington. In addition to being a great thinker, Strobe Talbott is a prolific writer. Having read a number of his books, I can say fairly that quantity has clearly in no way compromised quality.

Perhaps the one thing that enabled Strobe to make such a difference in the State Department was his deep knowledge of Russian society, its history, and its culture. After having studied Russian literature at Yale University and as a Rhodes scholar at Oxford University alongside Bill Clinton, he then spent more than twenty years working with *Time* magazine, where he followed the State Department, the White House, and, perhaps most important, Russia and eastern Europe. As I understood at the time, Strobe would be present at virtually every single meeting or telephone call between Clinton and his Russian counterparts and would frequently act as translator whenever Russian was being spoken.

During the process of negotiating the NATO-Russia Founding Act with my counterpart Yevgeny Primakov, one of my main and essential contact points was Strobe, as well as his colleagues at the State Department. Strobe and I were driven by one clear objective: to integrate both central Europe and the former republics of the Soviet Union into the institutions of the Euro-Atlantic community. This would prove to be a monumental task that would require many conversations as well as a significant dose of tenacity.

Strobe and I agreed strongly on the idea that personal relations matter a great deal in diplomacy, which this book captures so well. Between myself, Strobe, Russian Deputy Foreign Minister Yuri Mamedov, and eventually Russian Foreign Minister Yevgeny Primakov, the long conversations in the Talbott's house in Washington allowed us to build the necessary trust and familiarity and test ideas on how our visions for the European security architecture could be carried out. Personal touch, building trust and supporting Boris Yeltsin as he navigated a complicated domestic political scene were the cornerstone of NATO's approach toward Russia.

Eventually, the turn of the century would send us onto new paths. In 2000, Strobe left the State Department, and continued his academic career as director of the Brookings Institution. Strobe, with the assistance of his collaborators Bruce Jones, Carlos Pascual, and James Steinberg, to name a few, would turn the Brookings Institution into the first-class think tank that it is today.

Given Russia's invasion of Ukraine in February 2022 and the revisionist account of history that justified it from the Kremlin's perspective, this book could not have been a timelier one. To justify the Russian invasion of Ukraine, Putin and his regime have held on to the historically erroneous idea that NATO enlargement made the invasion of Ukraine inevitable. Therefore, the historical rigor and detail of this book makes it especially timely. Through an extensive array of archival materials, this book helps dispel the Kremlin's dominant narrative that NATO and the United States bullied their way through NATO enlargement.

This is a timely, insightful, and detailed book that captures the remarkable contribution of one of the indispensable diplomats of the post–Cold War period. I hope that you will enjoy learning about Strobe's fundamental role in the State Department during the Clinton years. I can assure you that it is a story worth reading.

Preface

Formative Years and Journalism

On Saturday, January 2, 1993, Strobe Talbott and his wife Brooke Shearer visited President-elect Bill Clinton at Hilton Head, a retreat in South Carolina where the Clintons usually celebrated New Year's Eve. Before breakfast, Talbott and Clinton went jogging on the beach. As they had done many times before, they discussed Russia.[1] It was just three more weeks until the onset of Clinton's administration, and Talbott was already slated to join the State Department as Clinton's key Russia expert. Being a diplomat had never been Talbott's ambition. He was a journalist who had worked at *Time* magazine for more than two decades. "Journalism is the only profession I ever aspired to," Talbott used to say. "It was a biographical fluke that presented me with this extraordinary opportunity."[2] The fluke was that Talbott and Clinton had been housemates and Rhodes scholars at Oxford in the late 1960s when Clinton witnessed Talbott's enormous capacity for analysis and meticulous writing.

At the time, Talbott began to make a name for himself as a Russia expert when he helped edit and translate the first volume of Nikita Khrushchev's memoirs.[3] In the summer of 1969, he interned for Jerrold Schecter, the head of *Time*'s Moscow Bureau, who managed to procure Khrushchev's memoirs and smuggled them out of the Soviet Union.[4] In November that year, Schecter presented Talbott with a pile of Russian typescripts to translate. "After reading several pages," Talbott recalled, "I knew that I had in my hands one of the most fascinating and unusual documents ever to emerge from the Soviet Union."[5] When Talbott started translating parts of the material in Oxford, Clinton sustained him with plates of scrambled eggs, biscuits, and cups of coffee.[6] Talbott recalled that "the venture was all hush-hush, but since I was doing much of the work just upstairs from Clinton's room on Leckford Road, I took him into my confidence. He savored being in on a secret project. He was a night owl. I was a morning person. But during that spring, he adjusted his schedule to mine, often getting up early to fry eggs for breakfast. I'd take a break from my work and sit with him in the kitchen, regaling him with tales of Kremlin skull-duggery that I'd gleaned from the thick stack of transcripts strewn around my room."[7]

In January 1993, twenty-four years later, Clinton and Talbott still discussed Russia as they jogged along the beach that morning. Clinton expressed concern that the country could return to its imperial past. He knew he might have to face this scenario if Russian President Boris Yeltsin were to surrender to his Communist Party opponents in the Supreme Soviet, who were keen to oust him. Another challenge was the state of the Russian economy and America's financial support to keep it going. Clinton was determined to seize the historic opportunity for Russia's integration. He worked on a comprehensive strategy and did not want to be the president who lost Russia. At the same time, he knew that most of his voters expected him to focus on domestic U.S. issues. Clinton and Talbott thought Russia needed internal reform and external assistance to overcome its problems.[8] After the January 2 run on the beach, Talbott's essential question to Clinton was whether he "was willing in principle to commit American resources and his own time and energy and leadership capital to the Russian problem." In response, as Talbott noted, Clinton said, "yes, he was if he can be convinced that it will, at a minimum, head off disaster and/or, at a maximum, make that place a going concern of 10 or so years. I realize that for the time being at least, this is an exercise in damage limitation—of making sure that it doesn't all blow up in my face," Clinton added.[9]

Clinton and Talbott pursued a liberal internationalist U.S. foreign policy and believed that cooperation among nations was essential to project security in an increasingly interconnected and globalized world.[10] Their blueprint for U.S. leadership hinged on the adaption and expansion of the institutions that enhanced the prosperity and security of the West after the end of World War II, including the United Nations, NATO, the European Community, the International Monetary Fund, the World Bank, and the General Agreement on Trade and Tariffs. "Uniquely in the history of Great Powers," Talbott said, "the United States defines its greatness not as an ability to dominate others but as an ability to work with others in the interest of the international community."[11] After the end of the Cold War, Talbott saw the necessity of integrating the newly emerging countries of the East and the South, and he endorsed the establishment of new international organizations, including the Asia-Pacific Economic Cooperation Forum, the North Atlantic Free Trade Association, the World Trade Organization, and the Kyoto Protocol on Climate Change.[12] Talbott recalled that "Clinton was diametrically opposed to Charles Krauthammer's concept of the 'unipolar moment,' which held that the United States had a several-decade window of opportunity to get its way unilaterally—unencumbered by the need for consensus-building and compromises—before the world became multipolar. Clinton just believed the opposite: what we had in the wake of the Cold War was a multipolar moment—and opportunity to shape the world through active leadership by the institutions Clinton admired and Krauthammer disdained."[13]

When Talbott joined the Clinton administration in 1993, he could not anticipate that he would work at the State Department for eight years. In 1993, he started as the ambassador-at-large and special adviser to Secretary of State Warren Christopher on the newly independent states of the former Soviet Union. Beginning in 1994, he served as deputy secretary of state for seven years until the end of the Clinton administration in 2001. At the outset, Talbott played a crucial role in the negotiations on the trilateral agreement with Ukraine and Russia that led to Ukraine's nuclear disarmament and its accession to the Non-Proliferation Treaty as a nonnuclear weapons state. Talbott fostered engagement with Russia and worked on the transformation of NATO's mission and the enlargement of the alliance in the context of a larger goal—a reordering of the European and Euro-Atlantic security architecture after the Cold War. In 1995, among other things, Talbott worked for Russia's inclusion in the International Peace Force to implement the Dayton Peace Accords after the end of the war in Bosnia. In 1996, he began to craft regional security frameworks to stabilize Ukraine and the Baltic countries, given that they did not make NATO's first enlargement round. In 1997, Talbott worked feverishly on the conclusion of the NATO-Russia Founding Act, a pivotal document to strengthen the new partnership with Moscow. In the summer of 1998, Talbott set up an important Clinton visit in Moscow amid Russia's financial crisis. In 1999, he helped save the U.S.-Russia partnership when it almost collapsed over the war in Kosovo. Finally, after Yeltsin's resignation, Talbott was one of the first Western interlocutors who identified the dangerous sides of Russia's new president, Vladimir Putin.[14]

In the post–Cold War world, it was challenging to find a general framework to address vital foreign policy questions, including globalization, international trade, and the emergence of new threats such as the revival of ethnic violence, nuclear proliferation, and religious extremism. It was challenging to build a new order when foreign policy could no longer be explained on a bumper sticker. Clinton grew increasingly tired of constant references to the post–Cold War era, thinking the term was "agnostic, provincial, backward-looking." Worse still, "it was an admission that while everyone knew what was finished, no one knew what had taken its place, to say nothing of what would or should come next. He didn't want his presidency to coincide with an age of uncertainty."[15] As a bottom line, the Clinton administration was determined to pursue a policy of democratic enlargement that would promote democracy, self-determination, and international law. "The successor to a doctrine of . . . containment must be a strategy of enlargement of the world's free community of market democracies," National Security Advisor Anthony Lake argued.[16] Talbott, too, wanted the United States to be a force for good in the new era. He very much saw the United States as an indispensable nation. "If the United States leads, the world will be a safer place for Americans to live, work, travel, and trade," Talbott thought. "We believe that we face historic opportunities—not just to combat threats and enemies from abroad, but also to build a world that promotes our interests and reflects our ideals."[17] Throughout his eight years in office, Talbott helped establish security architectures and communities in which a web of international institutions would provide stability to transcend purely national notions of security and statehood. Talbott thought that a lasting global peace necessitated postnational security policies and a turn away from the traditional concepts of geopolitics and the balance-of-power approaches of the past.

Over the long term, he envisaged the world as a "global nation" beyond the traditional Westphalian definition of statehood and sovereignty. In the 1992 *Time* magazine essay "The Birth of a Global Nation," Talbott wrote that "the best mechanism for democracy, whether at the level of the multinational state or that of the planet as a whole, is not an all-powerful Leviathan or centralized superstate, but a federation, a union of separate states that allocate certain powers to a central government while retaining many others for themselves."[18] When Talbott entered government, his views were tempered by his official experiences. After the end of the Cold War, newly emerging states hesitated to abandon their recently gained sovereignty. The wars in the Balkans revealed that boundaries were often contested. At the same time, ethnic conflicts reaffirmed the importance of integration and international institutions to project stability over the long term. Talbott thought that European integration and the emergence of the European Union were role models in this endeavor. They provided a bulwark against retrogression and backsliding into old patterns of nationalism and geopolitics that had destroyed Europe twice in the twentieth century.

After the end of the Cold War, the European Union's deepening and opening were essential to pivot Europe toward a rules-based order and a system that had to include the countries that had suffered from communism during the Cold War. Talbott had always endorsed the enlargement of the European Union and was appalled about the inability of the Bush administration to come to terms with the ethnic wars in the Balkans.[19] He knew that armed conflicts in Europe's periphery could undermine the security of the entire continent. Europe's transformation was a matter of the heart for Talbott. In the 1970s, in his early days as a journalist, he had personally witnessed the fate of the people who suffered from communist dictatorship. From 1971 to 1973, he lived in Yugoslavia and traveled to all parts of the country as a journalist for *Time* magazine. He had been to all the battlegrounds of the wars in Bosnia and Kosovo. He spoke several Slavic languages and knew the particularities of Europe's east and southeast as he had traveled these regions on many occasions for *Time* magazine.

All of this gave Talbott credibility and trust in his contacts with policymakers in the region. He spoke from experience and had personal connections to people and places. In March 1998, for instance, when he visited Bucharest University and gave a speech on the U.S. strategic partnership with Romania, he reminisced about his first visit to communist Romania in 1973.[20] Recalling the bad old days and his interview with Romanian dictator Nicolae Ceausescu, Talbott emphasized the unique chance to overcome the shadows of the past once and for all times—through Romania's accession to NATO and the European Union, joint peace missions, regional cooperation, and economic integration. Moreover, Talbott was friends with Romanian President Constantinescu, who used to be a visiting member of the faculty at Duke University in North Carolina and participated in a bilateral U.S.-Romanian educational exchange program in the early 1990s. The emergence of civil society and the integration of postcommunist states such as Romania was a matter of personal importance for Talbott. In his 1998 address at Bucharest University, Talbott emphasized that "we are building a complex but coherent structure of organizations and associations in which our children and grandchildren will make their homes and in which they will be able to live safely, freely, and prosperously. This construction job requires us to adapt existing institutions where possible and to establish new ones where necessary."[21] Talbott thought institution-building was the only durable method of integration, quoting Jean Monnet's maxim that "nothing is possible without men, but nothing lasts without institutions."[22]

The relevance of world governance was instilled by Talbott's parents, Nelson "Bud" Strobridge Talbott Jr. and Josephine "Jo" Talbott. They were both active members of the World Federalist Organization, a nonpartisan organization formed in the 1930s to mobilize support for free institutions among all peoples and effort to cooperate to keep the peace. "That loomed fairly large," Talbott recalled. "I was very close to my parents, and as I got older, they introduced me to Toynbee as a historian and the *Saturday Review*, and Norman Cousins, who was an advocate of world federalism and that kind of thing."[23] Born in 1946 into a patrician family in Ohio, Talbott grew up in the shadow of the early Cold War. He saw gruesome pictures of the victims of Hiroshima and Nagasaki on the cover of *Life* magazine. He witnessed the oppression of the Hungarian freedom fighters in 1956 at the age of ten, the launch of Sputnik, and the flight of Yuri Gagarin at age eleven. "So, as a child," Talbott recalled, "one thing after another, either in history just before I was born, family associations, my own coming to terms with the upside and downside of the era in which we were living, all kind of pointed me in a particular direction which is world peace and the threats to world peace, the principal threat being Soviet communism."[24]

In the early 1960s, Talbott went to Hotchkiss, the eminent prep school in northwest Connecticut. In October 1962, he was at chapel in school the day the then headmaster, Bill Olsen, told the students about the Cuban missile crisis. "We got down on our knees and prayed that the world wouldn't blow up," Talbott reminisced.[25] He credited that morning with his decision to study Russian with Clint Ely, the master teaching Russian at the school.[26] It was pretty simple: If one was interested in international affairs, then the central issue for U.S. foreign policy was the U.S.-Soviet relationship. In

1964, Talbott went to Yale to pursue his passion for Russian studies. He wanted to be "at the cutting edge of world history," his friend Grisha Freidin said.[27] At Yale, Talbott was chairman of *Yale Daily News*, the oldest college daily newspaper published in the United States. His fellow student, Daniel Yergin, ran against Talbott for the position of chairman. Talbott won. "His natural leadership was evident," Yergin recalled, "and he took leadership."[28] Studying at Yale was a matter of family tradition. Talbott's father graduated from Yale in 1943, and his grandfather had captained the Yale football team (class of 1915). Talbott's former roommate David Detweiler recalled that "during his freshman year Talbott kept a journal, 'in part to record how well he was doing. In the front of it he had a picture of his father and his grandfather, on a fishing trip they took every year. And each had a string of fish. In Strobe's script underneath it, he had written, 'Get the point?' . . . The point Strobe got was he needed to catch some big fish, too.'"[29]

While at *Yale Daily News*, Talbott editorialized against the Vietnam War and participated in antiwar rallies.[30] Yet he was already a diplomat at heart when he emphasized the need for U.S. peace initiatives in an interview with *New York Times* columnist James Reston in 1967, saying that he was "interested to see if there are new means and attitudes by which this university, and hence the university community in general, can make discussion less polemical and more meaningful and at the same time help the search for peace."[31] In 1968, Talbott submitted his senior thesis on the nineteenth-century Russian poet and diplomat Fyodor Tyutchev. Meanwhile, Talbott pursued a long-distance relationship with Brooke Shearer, the sister of his friend and fellow Russia student Derek Shearer. Talbott carried out his courtship in letters. "It was all correspondence. He wrote a lot," Brooke Shearer once said, smiling.[32] Finally, in 1968, Talbott obtained a bacherlor's degree in Russian studies from Yale. After that, he went to Oxford for a three-year Rhodes scholarship.

Clinton's and Talbott's friendship and their decades-long conversation about Russia began in September 1968. They first met in Philadelphia when they joined their fellow Rhodes scholars, taking a bus to New York City and traversing the United Kingdom aboard the SS *United States*. Talbott and Clinton instantly liked each other. "My first conversation of any substance with him was during the ocean crossing," Talbott recalled, "and the subject was the Soviet Union, the giant, alien, antagonistic country that had preoccupied U.S. foreign policy all our lives."[33] In Oxford, Talbott studied under the supervision of Max Hayward, a lecturer and translator of Russian literature who worked at the British Embassy in Moscow in the early Cold War and translated Boris Pasternak's novel *Doctor Zhivago*, among others. Having Hayward as his tutor, Talbott wrote a thesis on Vladimir Mayakowsky, a Russian poet and playwright who wholeheartedly endorsed the Bolshevik Revolution and later on committed suicide by the onset of Stalinism. In December 1968, after three months of intense studies at Oxford, Talbott visited the Soviet Union for the first time over the long Christmas holiday traveling across both Germanies and Poland by train to Moscow. "The city was muffled in snow," Talbott noted, "the buildings better heated than those in Oxford and foreign visitors in the dead of winter rare enough for me to make friends, especially among younger people who were eager for any contact with the West. . . . On my return to Oxford, I described the adventure to Clinton, who started thinking about making a similar journey at Christmas time a year later."[34]

At a relatively young age, Clinton and Talbott aspired for something big in the future. Talbott recalled that Clinton would have won if one had surveyed the cohort of Rhodes scholars and said who in the group might be president of the United States one day. "A totally unprovable proposition, but I'm certain of it," Talbott said. "You just knew that Bill Clinton was going to be a politician and that he was going to probably be President."[35] Talbott himself was also predestined to achieve great things. Back in the 1970s, his *Time* magazine colleagues used to say that he would either become secretary of state or the editor-in-chief of *Time*, his former colleague Philip Taubman recalled.[36] The publication of the Khrushchev memoirs in 1970 gave Talbott special status at *Time*. In his late twenties and early thirties, he radiated a gravitas like someone in his fifties. "He was one of those old young men," said Evan Thomas, who worked with Talbott at *Time*.[37] "All grown-ups loved Strobe!" recalled Steven Weisman, a Yale classmate and former deputy foreign editor at the *New York Times*.[38]

Friends and colleagues thought "there was a powerful logic to Talbott's trajectory."[39] He rose through the ranks at *Time*, turning from diplomatic correspondent to Washington bureau chief and finally to the magazine's editor-at-large and foreign affairs columnist. Talbott was a big foot pursuing access journalism. He was friends with several policymakers in the Jimmy Carter and Ronald Reagan administrations, including Carter's secretary of state, Cyrus Vance, and President Reagan's arms control negotiator, Paul Nitze. Talbott's 1979 book *Endgame: The Inside Story of SALT II* originated from discussions with Vance who endorsed the idea to write an in-depth article on the conclusion of the negotiations, which Talbott then turned into a book.[40] In the 1980s, Talbott wrote two sequels and two further books on U.S.-Soviet relations, all of which brought critical acclaim. In the two sequels, *Deadly Gambits* and the *Master of the Game*, he used Paul Nitze's career as a prism to analyze the knitty-gritties of arms control in the late Cold War.[41] "He was the only journalist who could discuss these treaties with as much specificity as the assistant secretaries who were in charge of them," said Bruce Jackson, who served in the Pentagon under Reagan.[42]

Talbott first saw Nitze in the early 1960s when the latter was honored at Hotchkiss, shortly before Talbott left the school, for his accomplishments in the Kennedy administration. When Talbott was a teenager, Nitze was about forty years his senior and had graduated from Hotchkiss in 1924. In adult life, Talbott first spoke with Nitze after the publication of *Endgame* in 1979. "Nitze invited me to his office," Talbott wrote, "and led me through his copy of the book page by page, explaining with great patience and in great details, but also with relentless and reproving certitude, what he viewed as the shortcomings of my analysis."[43] At first sight, it seemed surprising that Talbott chose Nitze as his subject. Whereas Talbott was oriented toward accommodation with the Soviets, Nitze had a reputation as a hawk and a Cold Warrior. Yet Nitze changed over time and thought it was essential to work out arms control problems with the Soviets—a critical assumption that he and Talbott shared. Although Nitze left the government in 1974 and criticized the strategic arms control process in the Ford and Carter administrations, he was willing to return as a negotiator in the Reagan years. Talbott admired Nitze for his attempt to seek a compromise solution in the Geneva arms control talks on intermediate nuclear forces in the early 1980s. In 1982, Nitze had his *Walk in the Woods* with the Soviet ambassador, Yuliy Kvitzinsky, to find a U.S.-Soviet trade-off on the question of intermediate-range nuclear weapons in Europe.[44]

Writing *Endgame, Deadly Gambits,* and the *Master of the Game*, Talbott benefited from unique access to key people at the White House, the State Department, and the Pentagon. Working on *Deadly Gambits*, for instance, Talbott impressed Paul Nitze with meticulously detailed knowledge about the *Walk in the Woods* and how Secretary of Defense Caspar Weinberger and the Pentagon torpedoed a potential U.S.-Soviet compromise on intermediate-range nuclear weapons. In December 1982, Nitze recalled

how he had breakfast with Talbott and *Time* editor-in-chief Henry Grunwald the other day.

> Nitze marveled about Talbott's treatment of the *Walk in the Woods*
> and said, "what happened during all that he's got now in a piece of
> paper which is 65 pages long? And he has got it right. . . . He knows
> so much more about it than I. . . . I have got all the memoranda and
> all the documentation that is connected with it. But what he has that
> I don't have, didn't have until I saw this, was what the reactions were
> of everybody in town. . . . All my enemies, and all their intrigues and
> what they said to everybody else. And here it all is in black and white.
> He had pretty darn well everything that concerned what I did, pretty
> damn accurate. . . . I find this absolutely fabulous."[45]

Talbott had fantastic sources. He managed to keep the trust of key decision-
makers as he assured them that he would only use their insights once a
particular negotiation was over and their information would no longer
affect the outcome. Nitze was, of course, one of Talbott's key sources. Talbott often visited him to learn additional details and verify information.
"Strobe Talbott has got all this," Nitze said. "It is extraordinary how people talk to him. There is hardly a thing that he doesn't have and then he
comes in and talks to me about it and says I learned this, this, this, and the
other. Well, I prefer to have him have it accurate rather than have it inac-
curate. So then I fill in further details for him. Now he has got it letter
perfect."[46]

At the same time, Talbott and Nitze differed in their perceptions of the
Soviet Union. Nitze thought that Talbott was "clearly prejudiced, he looks
with rosy glasses on everything that might help an agreement, might help
accommodation with the Soviet Union. He looks skeptically at anything
which looks with cold and fishy eyes at what the Russians are doing. He
admits that that is his starting point, that's what he wants, he thinks that's
what should happen. That makes him more of an advocate of a point of
view than an objective observer. But that doesn't mean that he closes his
eyes to facts. He hasn't been unfriendly to me so far," Nitze noted.[47]

Talbott's audience was aware that *Deadly Gambits* had a political purpose.
Published in 1984, the book was a manifesto favoring arms control. Talbott
said "at the most basic level, avoiding nuclear war is what Soviet-American

relations are all about. . . . Arms control can be a very complex, esoteric subject. I have tried to bring a human dimension to it by describing the forceful personalities who shape policy on both sides of the negotiating table."[48] Given the stalemate in U.S.-Soviet relations, the book was an issue in the 1984 presidential election campaign. The candidate of the Democratic Party, Walter Mondale, recommended it twice in his second television encounter with President Reagan. "We have this arms race underway," Mondale said, "and a recent book that just came out by perhaps the Nation's most respected author in this field, Strobe Talbott, called 'Deadly Gambits,' concludes that this President has failed to master the essential details needed to command and lead us, both in terms of security and terms of arms control. That's why they call the President the Commander in Chief."[49] Mondale's reference to *Deadly Gambits* revealed the book's broad appeal, policy relevance, and innovation as a pioneering contribution to the literature on nuclear arms policymaking.

Writing *Deadly Gambits*, Talbott added to the rise of a new genre. "We are in the presence of something more than journalistic history; this is novelistic journalistic history," John Draper wrote in an enthusiastic book review in the *New York Times*. Draper argued that *Deadly Gambits* "does to journalism what Truman Capote did to the novel in 'In Cold Blood' and Norman Mailer did in 'The Executioner's Song.' . . . The novels of Capote and Mr. Mailer were essentially biographical, focusing on the lives of single persons. Mr. Talbott's book is ostensibly historical, dealing with a large cast of important official characters and a subject of singular moment. The two subjects are incommensurable, yet their treatment has been converging."[50]

In the second Reagan administration, Talbott found another fascinating issue that became a matter of public debate: the Reagan administration's Strategic Defense Initiative (SDI). Like Nitze, he saw it as undermining deterrence and nuclear peace.[51] As a journalist, Talbott wanted to facilitate a new enlightened public debate on space weapons and technology. In 1986, for instance, he proposed convoking a conference on SDI to produce "a coherent, focused and expert debate for the benefit of correspondents and editors and, through a special report in the magazine, for *Time's* readers."[52] Taking place in June 1986, the gathering was a success, assembling several key Reagan administration officials, including Nitze, Assistant Secretary of Defense Richard Perle, and SDI Director General

James Abrahamson of the Air Force. Hitherto, policymakers had only spoken about SDI on background. At the conference table, Nitze and Perle spoke on the record and even revealed differences in their assessments. Moreover, Talbott worked intensely on U.S.-Soviet relations and the ensuing arms control summits between President Reagan and Soviet Secretary General Mihail Gorbachev. He reported in detail about their Reykjavik summit in October 1986 when Reagan and Gorbachev came close to finding an agreement on the abolition of nuclear weapons.[53]

Given the improvements in U.S.-Soviet relations, Talbott thought about writing a sequel to *Deadly Gambits*: Nitze was the perfect subject. In the early Cold War, Nitze had proposed a massive U.S. military buildup to counter the Soviet threat in National Security Council Paper NSC-68 of 1950. In the changing circumstances of the 1980s, however, Nitze was determined to work things out with the Soviets at the arms control negotiation table as President Reagan's special adviser and the State Department arms control tsar.[54] Nitze epitomized the "Reagan Reversal" and a turn from confrontation toward U.S. engagement with the Soviet Union in the late Cold War.[55] Talbott thought Nitze symbolized "the continuity of arms control efforts into the Reagan administration in spite of so-called revolutionary approaches."[56] Talbott had Nitze's support in writing *The Master of the Game*. Both had regular meetings, and Talbott often called and turned in written requests for assistance to Nitze's office. In the autumn of 1986, Talbott began to share draft book chapters with Nitze, asking him to check the accuracy of its historical and contemporary parts.[57] Moreover, Talbott conducted meticulous interviews with Nitze, sharing the transcripts and asking for materials when Nitze spoke about his previous career.

In December 1987, Talbott did a profile of Nitze in *Time* magazine after the conclusion of the landmark Intermediate-Range Nuclear Forces Treaty. It included a quote that portrayed the seventy-nine-year-old Nitze as a tough competitor who played tennis against much younger opponents: "My body does what I tell it."[58] Nitze found the phrase unamusing and wrote Talbott a letter of complaint. "I was originally displeased by the text of the profile. It seemed to me incompetent and unprofessional. It is represented as being a profile; however, its main interest is built around the sharpest available quotes from my well-known critics."[59] In response, Talbott wrote Nitze a long letter emphasizing that the profile was intended differently. Its focus was on facts, Talbott argued. "I've tried very hard and am continuing to try, go get the facts right," Talbott wrote.

Beyond the facts lie judgments. There we've had our differences. Our acquaintance began with a deep difference in judgment about SALT II, although I was grateful for the way you dealt with me on that subject. Since I am working on a project about you, your career, your thoughts and motivations, I feel under a particularly powerful responsibility not only to get the facts right but to make sure that my judgements—independent as they must always be, critical as they will sometimes be—are based as much as possible on a clear understanding of your own. . . . I admire you, Paul. I admire much, though not all, what you have done; I admire all of what you are doing and intend to do. And I think you're going to succeed. Which is why I'm hanging in there on this project and hope that despite setbacks like this week's, you will, too.[60]

Nitze was not resentful at all. He held Talbott in high esteem and invited him and Brooke to a dinner dance he gave in January 1988. Moreover, both had regular lunches in the following months when Talbott finished the *Master of the Game* while Nitze was negotiating strategic arms reductions with the Soviets. Essentially, based on interviews with Nitze and plenty of people from the national security community, Talbott wrote a journalist's history of negotiations that was still in the making. In 1988, Talbott agreed with Nitze that he would not publish the book if Nitze thought it would interfere with the possibility of a serious negotiation with the Soviets. As the U.S.-Soviet talks were stalemated, Talbott sensed he could go ahead.[61] In the summer of 1988, Nitze noted that Talbott "was really very good about it. He said that he would not publish this book until I told him he could. He said that he would expect me to tell him whenever I'd come to the conclusion that there was really no longer any chance of getting it done during this administration. . . . If I feel there's no chance during this administration, then I can't really hold him to this commitment."[62] Finally, Talbott published *The Master of the Game* in late 1988 and overtook Nitze, who released his memoir *From Hiroshima to Glasnost* in 1989.[63]

Talbott's books on arms control and U.S.-Soviet relations brought critical acclaim and facilitated new associations in academia and the think tank world. Beyond his job as a journalist, Talbott was affiliated with the Council on Foreign Relations and Stanford University's Center for International Security and Cooperation, fostering new ties between the U.S. and Soviet academic and policymaking communities.[64] In 1984, for instance, he wrote *The Russians & Reagan* for the Council on Foreign Relations. In addition to his tasks at *Time*, he finished the two-hundred-page book in ninety days, his editor Robert Legvold recalled.[65] In 1987, Talbott and Michael Mandelbaum of the Council published a new book on Reagan and Gorbachev.[66] Talbott was fascinated by how their personalities played off great forces, sensing that their diplomacy made a real difference in international affairs. In 1989, Talbott and Michael Beschloss decided to write a book about U.S.-Soviet relations in the following three years without anticipating the fall of the Berlin Wall and the demise of the Soviet Union. In *At the Highest Levels*, the focus was on the partnership between George Herbert Walker Bush and Mikhail Gorbachev in ending the Cold War.[67] Later on, as Clinton's foreign policy adviser, Talbott would continue to emphasize the pivotal relevance of personality and leadership diplomacy relative to structures and constraints in international relations. After Bush's and Gorbachev's first summit meeting in December 1989, Talbott highlighted the potential of a closer partnership with Gorbachev, arguing that "the West ought to realize that much of its fear of the Soviet Union was also misplaced."[68] Finally, in December 1991, Talbott and Beschloss had a unique chance for a last interview with Gorbachev, expecting his resignation in due time.[69]

In 1991, Clinton occasionally consulted Talbott about foreign policy and the Soviet Union in particular. In August 1991, during the 1992 presidential election campaign run-up, for instance, Clinton was on the phone with Talbott to get his assessment of the coup against Gorbachev in Moscow. In his diaries, Talbott noted how Clinton said that "his principal concerns are, a) whether the cold war is back on (cuz he senses that if it is, his chances of being president are zilch) and b) that he not say anything that will make the situation worse or that will undercut Bush." During the election campaign, Clinton quizzed Talbott about potential candidates for the position of secretary of state. Talbott thought out of the box and did not suggest Warren Christopher, the number one candidate within the Democratic Party. Instead, he proposed Richard Holbrooke as a capable and younger representative of the Democratic foreign policy establishment. In addition to Holbrooke, Talbott made the case for the Republican Winston Lord, who had worked closely with Henry Kissinger and had been president of the Council on Foreign Relations and the U.S. ambassador to China in the 1980s. Clinton was open-minded, valued Talbott's advice, and approached Lord on a joint briefing in New Haven, saying, "Strobe says you're someone

I should know."[70] Clinton appreciated that Talbott had his own mind and was not just waving the flag for the Democratic Party.

Although Talbott stayed out of the campaign, Clinton called him occasionally. In the autumn of 1992, Clinton rang to talk about his position on the establishment of the North American Free Trade Agreement (NAFTA), an institution that promised to create the world's largest free-trade zone but was unpopular domestically and could cost Clinton votes in Ohio and Michigan. In his diary, Talbott noted, "Bill gets on and says he wanted to make sure I'd been aware that he'd come out in favor of NAFTA. Clearly wanted congrats for having done the right thing. . . . I gave him the wanted chuck under the chin," Talbott added.[71] From Clinton's perspective, his election and Talbott's appointment did not change their relationship. They continued the kind of conversations they had been pursuing during the previous twenty years.[72]

In 1993, at age forty-six, Talbott had a unique chance to use his expertise and talents on behalf of the Clinton administration. He was uniquely qualified and determined to excel in his new job. He hit the ground running and adapted in no time when he arrived at the State Department. His former deputy, Richard Kauzlarich, recalled that Talbott needed about seventy-two hours to become proficient in his new job in terms of substance.[73] Regarding bureaucratic procedures, Talbott relied on his assistants Victoria Nuland and Eric Edelman for guidance. As Foreign Service officers, they steered Talbott through the interagency and interdepartmental processes and sometimes appeared to be naysayers when they argued for more patience and caution.[74] Talbott assembled all the necessary ingredients to make for a good start. At the same time, he kept reminding himself that he was not in all of this for careerist reasons. "I'm not trying to do a good job in order to get a better job afterward," he noted. "I'm in it to do a good job, period—or at least to get credit for trying."[75] With regard to his career plans, Talbott did not rule out the possibility of returning to *Time* after a few years in government. "If I stay two years, three years, four years—I can leave with my head held high; and if I've done respectably," he thought, "I'll be perfectly hirable for something next—including going back to *Time* and *Time Inc*, if there's anything there worth going back to."[76] It goes without saying that Talbott's friendship with Clinton was helpful in the day-to-day government business. Everyone knew Talbott had the president's trust. But Talbott never bragged about their friendship. He never called the president by his first name in the presence of others. In his memoranda and letters to Clinton, he usually called him Chief. Regarding his status in the circle of Clinton's advisers, Talbott said that he was "by no means the only person in his circle who's known him a long time. I do not have any sense of having a unique position or even a primary position."[77]

He did not see Clinton daily, either. Talbott was in the Oval Office when Clinton spoke with Yeltsin; he was in all of their eighteen meetings except the one in Budapest in December 1994, which went badly and almost cost Talbott his job. At the time, Talbott was preoccupied with the aftermath of the UN-authorized U.S. military intervention in Haiti and could not accompany Clinton. After that, he never missed a Clinton-Yeltsin meeting again. A team player, Talbott worked closely with Secretaries of State Warren Christopher, Madeleine Albright, and Clinton's national security team at the White House. Talbott's influence in Washington was also rooted in his broad international networks and his ability to engage with people from diverse backgrounds worldwide. Talbott's style was "deeply intellectual and carried a spirit of inquiry" his former Chief of Staff John Bass recalled.[78] An out-of-the-box thinker, Talbott was not constrained by conventional wisdom and generally accepted theories. His diplomacy was about the art of the possible, driven by relentless curiosity and optimism. Bass recalled that "Talbott did not care about titles. He put emphasis on good ideas no matter who brought them up."[79] He mentored a generation of young Foreign Service officers who worked on his staff and rose through the ranks. Talbott trusted his coworkers and gave people at the working level a chance for input. At the outset, it was an effort to improve morale in the State Department. Over time, Talbott's management style made a difference and broadly strengthened the foreign service. Talbott's former chief of staff, Victoria Nuland, recalled that he believed in the compatibility of family and work life and was one of the few men who dared to leave the office earlier to attend his sons' soccer games. Moreover, Talbott encouraged Nuland to bring her toddler to important Saturday meetings on U.S.-Russia relations, which took place in the Talbott kitchen. "It was like family," Nuland said.[80]

Indeed, in all of this, Talbott's family was the anchor in his life. Strobe, Brooke, and their sons Devin and Adrian lived in Washington's Cleveland Park area. Their home and kitchen were the hub for many discussions on world politics.[81] In the 1970s, Brooke also worked as a journalist when *Time* magazine sent Talbott to Belgrade as their correspondent.[82] Strobe and

Brooke worked together at every stage of their careers. Brooke had achieved a position of her own on Washington's political stage and worked for Hillary Clinton in the 1992 presidential campaign and later as director of the White House fellows program and in the Department of the Interior, responsible for the U.S. National Park Service and its international activities. In 1998, for instance, Shearer helped the authorities in Georgia to set up a national park system based on the example of the U.S. national parks. After their work in the Clinton administration, in 2001–02, they went to New Haven. They started the Yale Center for the Study of Globalization and the Yale World Fellows Program before Talbott took over as president of the Brookings Institution in 2002. Back in Washington, Brooke worked on the International Center for Research on Women board, a nongovernmental organization focusing on women's health and empowerment. Brooke and Strobe complemented each other. She was playful, fun-loving, and a corrective to his brainy and scholarly image.

Brooke often called Strobe in the evenings when he was still at work while she was already setting the stage for visitors at their Cleveland Park home. On Thursday, February 4, 1993, Talbott received such a call when he was still at his transition office at 7:45 p.m. "If you want to have dinner with the president, you better get home," Brooke said.[83] Talbott quickly closed up work and jumped into a taxi to rush home. When he approached his place, he saw flashing lights and police everywhere given that Clinton was due to arrive soon. A female Secret Service agent stopped Talbott when he wanted to enter the house. Clinton arrived at 8:30, played saxophone, and finally stayed for dinner, even though he first said he would leave relatively soon.[84] Russia's problems were again on Clinton's mind. He was concerned about Yeltsin's inclination to side with the Serbs in the Bosnian War and lamented that his last phone conversation with Yeltsin did not go well. In his diary, Talbott noted that Clinton "complained about Yeltsin talking too much, badgering him on who would be ambassador and when he would commit to a meeting—but despite all that, still asks the key encouraging question, 'should I set something aside in the budget for Yeltsin?' I give him an emphatic yes, do a short version of my argument for macroeconomic assistance."[85]

Talbott felt that Clinton's engagement with Yeltsin was essential to help democracy in Russia survive when the reformers in Moscow were in retreat and the country's economic crisis was worsening. Russia's continuing economic misery made ordinary citizens turn against Western recipes for reform and economic shock therapy. In 1992, millions of Russians stood in line for food at grocery stores and supermarkets while a few oligarchs amassed enormous fortunes.[86] Millions lost their jobs when Yeltsin decided to trim the subsidies and central bank loans that had previously allowed big military industries to stay in business. After the end of the Cold War, the West could have provided more financial assistance to the new Russia. However, there was no Marshall Plan aid and there was not enough money.[87] When Clinton's term started in January 1993, plenty of Russia's reformers had already been thrown out of the government. In December 1992, the anti-Yeltsin Russian Congress of People's Deputies refused to confirm the reformist Acting Prime Minister Yegor Gaidar as prime minister, leading to Viktor Chernomyrdin's appointment as a compromise figure.[88]

Russia's new entrepreneurs funneled billions of dollars out of the country—they bought raw materials at discount prices and sold them at world market prices in the West, generating huge profits and directing them to overseas bank accounts. "We have created a class of communist-capitalists," said Alexander Rudenko, a leading St. Petersburg businessman. "The state still has a monopoly over the export of basic goods. The economic conditions have been created in which people who are well-connected can steal like crazy."[89] At the same time, there was reason for hope. The new Russia was indeed making some progress.[90] Presidential and parliamentary elections were free and fair. Russia avoided armed conflicts with its neighbors and withdrew former Soviet military forces from the Baltics and the former Warsaw Pact states.[91] The disintegration of the Soviet Union did not produce a Yugoslavia writ large. In terms of Russia, Talbott believed that "we don't have anything like decisive influence, but we do have some influence"—and he emphasized that "there is great urgency in our using whatever influence we do have to bolster Yeltsin and keep his policies moving in the right direction."[92] The years to come would reveal where Russia was headed.

Abbreviations

ABM	Anti-Ballistic Missile (Treaty)
BALTBAT	Baltic Batallion
CEE	Central and Eastern Europe
CFE	Treaty on Conventional Forces in Europe
CFR	Council on Foreign Relations
CIA	Central Intelligence Agency
CIS	Commonwealth of Independent States
CL	Clinton Library
CSCE	Conference on Security and Cooperation in Europe
CTBT	Comprehensive Test Ban Treaty
CTR	Cooperative Threat Reduction (U.S. Program)
DC	District of Columbia
DoD	Department of Defense
EAPC	Euro-Atlantic Partnership Council
EC	European Community
EU	European Union
FSB	Federal Security Service (Russian domestic intelligence service)

FSU	Former Soviet Union
G-7	Group of Seven
G-8	Group of Eight
IFOR	Implementation Force
IMF	International Monetary Fund
JCS	Joint Chiefs of Staff (U.S.)
KFOR	Kosovo Force
KGB	Committee for State Security (Soviet Union)
MAP	Membership Action Plan
NAC	North Atlantic Council (NATO)
NACC	North Atlantic Cooperation Council (NATO)
NATO	North Atlantic Treaty Organization
NIS	newly independent states (post-Soviet states other than Baltics)
NPT	Non-Proliferation Treaty
NSC	National Security Council
OSCE	Organization for Security and Cooperation in Europe
PfP	Partnership for Peace
PJC	Permanent Joint Council
SACEUR	Supreme Allied Commander Europe (NATO)
SFOR	Stabilization Force
SHAPE	Supreme Headquarters Allied Powers Europe
START	Strategic Arms Reduction Treaty
UK	United Kingdom
UN	United Nations
UNGA	United Nations General Assembly
UNSC	UN Security Council
USSR	Union of Soviet Socialist Republics, also Soviet Union
WTO	World Trade Organization

SECURING PEACE IN EUROPE

Introduction

In this book, I use Talbott's diplomacy as a lens to detail the Clinton administration's statecraft to simultaneously engage Russia and to open NATO to new members and new missions as elements of a new Euro-Atlantic security architecture. Engaging Russia has always preceded the steps to open NATO. In the spring of 1993, for instance, Clinton backed up Yeltsin during Russia's constitutional crisis when NATO enlargement was not even firmly on the agenda of international affairs. Later on, Clinton sought accommodation with Russia before NATO debated the who and when and how of NATO enlargement. In 1998, Clinton went out of his way and visited a battered Yeltsin amid Russia's financial crisis. Clinton and Talbott exhausted all opportunities to work with Russia. "Maximizing the positive, minimizing the negative," was the precept of their Russia diplomacy, as Clinton recalled.[1] In this book, I argue that Clinton's statecraft rebuts Russian President Vladimir Putin's claims that the West exploited Russia's weakness after the end of the Cold War. In fact, the Clinton administration and its NATO allies constantly extended a hand to help Russia.[2] However, Russian policymakers were never comfortable with the emergence of the post–Cold War security system. They complained about not being treated as an equal by the West, and Putin has often emphasized the reputed humiliation Russia had suffered in the face of "broken promises" by the West, including an alleged one to not enlarge NATO beyond the borders of a reunited Germany. For more than twenty years, the grievance story has been used as a catalyst for the revival of Russia's new imperialism, providing the pretext for Russia's war of annihilation against Ukraine.[3]

In this book, I go beyond the myopic NATO enlargement versus Russia narrative. I look into Strobe Talbott's efforts to square the circle and open NATO to new members and missions while devising ways to include Russia in the new security system and the new missions through joint peacekeeping forces such as in Bosnia. I repel claims that NATO enlargement was done too quickly or without attention to Russian concerns. Neither was Talbott too focused on Russia. Using his perspective, I depict the multitude of diplomatic tracks that the Clinton administration established to open NATO and to pursue a strategic partnership with Russia and Ukraine—both within a new security architecture and a system of new institutions that Talbott envisaged. This book is in conversation with Mary Sarotte's *Not One Inch*, which covers similar ground but comes to different conclusions. Sarotte overstates the urgency and the importance of the NATO enlargement track when she writes that after the end of the Cold War, "the United States realized that it could not only win big, but bigger. Not one inch of territory need to be off-limits to NATO."[4]

In fact, the administration of George H. W. Bush had been cautious and slow in opening NATO's door to new members and expanding NATO's missions into peacekeeping.[5] NATO enlargement was not on the agenda until 1993, and no consensus was established that the alliance should engage in peacekeeping activities.[6] The immediate aftermath of the Cold War saw much more pressing foreign policy issues, such as the danger of loose Soviet nuclear weapons, the war in Bosnia, and humanitarian interventions in Somalia and elsewhere. NATO's principal decision in favor of enlargement emerged only in 1994, NATO engaged "out of area" in the Balkans only in 1995, and Russia joined the alliance in maintaining the peace. No master plan for NATO's enlargement was established until the mid-1990s. After the fall of the Berlin Wall in 1989, it took ten years for NATO to accept three new members, which it did in 1999. Initially, the initiative for enlargement did not even come from the Clinton administration. Others blazed the trail, including policymakers from Central Europe such as Lech Walesa, Vaclav Havel, and German Defense Minister Volker Rühe.[7]

Moreover, Sarotte's book deemphasizes the importance the Clinton administration attached to the evolution of the strategic partnership with Russia and the broader context in which it evolved. NATO's opening was just one piece in the rise of the post–Cold War order: It was never seen in isolation and only made sense in connection with the enlargement of the European Union, the renewal of the transatlantic partnership, the strengthening of the Organization for Security and Cooperation in Europe (OSCE) and the emergence of regional security frameworks to bolster the stability of the countries that could not join NATO instantly.[8] NATO enlargement was never seen as the only game in town—but it was essential to keep the United States engaged as a European power—and it gave the new aspiring members in the East the same sense of security that the old NATO members in the West enjoyed in NATO. Equal security was a precondition for the enlargement of the European Union and the long-term success of the economic transitions in central and eastern Europe. Hence it was not enough to merely provide the aspiring NATO members with some sort of associated membership under Partnership for Peace (PfP), as Sarotte argues when she writes that PfP's "incremental approach did not require Washington either to draw a new line through post-Cold War Europe or to leave Ukraine and most other post-Soviet republics to their own devices."[9]

Actually, the rationale of NATO enlargement was to create a Europe whole and free without dividing lines and to make sure that NATO's opening was part of a larger process to improve everyone's security in Europe. Talbott helped build partnerships with those who did not make the first round of NATO's opening. He crafted "strategic homes" for Romania and the Baltic countries while preparing them for eventual NATO membership and building a new NATO-Ukraine partnership.[10] Moreover, the Clinton administration did not abandon PfP, as Sarotte argues when she writes that the Clinton administration relinquished PfP because "it succeeded a little too well."[11] Instead, Clinton was proud of PfP as it "has proven to be a bigger deal than we expected—with more countries and more substantive cooperation. It has grown into something significant in its own right."[12] Moreover, Talbott worked for the stabilization of Europe's so-called periphery to foster the EU accession of Turkey at a time when reformist policymakers in Ankara were determined to lead Turkey into the EU. Later, he worked with Russian and European counterparts to end the Kosovo War and set the stage for efforts to integrate the Western Balkans into the European and Euro-Atlantic mainstream.[13]

This book shows how these issues fit within the larger puzzle of recrafting the post–Cold War security system and reinventing the U.S. role in it.[14] A lot of Talbott's diplomacy was, as he would often say, "architectural." He envisaged a new Europe resembling a dense web of interlocking institutions and mechanisms to project stability and peace. The purpose was to have a safety net and several lifelines and cornerstones to build an irreversible structure to sustain a crisis. Talbott saw the post–Cold War security structure as "a complex set of Venn diagrams—overlapping organizations and groupings, different in their missions and memberships, but sharing an underlying premise of openness to each other and to the task of making a virtue out of interdependence."[15] Talbott's book *The Great Experiment* includes a diagram of the Euro-Atlantic security institutions; it's a solar system of thirteen colored overlapping circles with the names of countries grouped according to the institutions to which they belonged, including the OSCE, the PfP, the Euro-Atlantic Partnership Council, the Council of the Baltic Sea States, the South European Cooperation Initiative, and the Conventional Forces Treaty in Europe, among others.[16]

Talbott wanted to integrate Russia and its neighbors into the network of institutions to align the former Soviet space with the West. The post–Cold War years offered a unique window of opportunity to turn the new Russia into a true partner because it would be prosperous, democratic, and peaceful for the first time in history. Promoting democracy in Russia was rooted in the Kantian idea that democracies do not fight each other. Clinton made this case early in his first major foreign policy speech on Russia before the American Society of Newspaper Editors: "If we can help Russia to remain increasingly democratic, we can leave an era of standoff behind us and explore expanding horizons of progress and peace," Clinton said.[17] At the same time, Talbott and Clinton were realists about Russia, its future, its problems, and the scope of its long-term relationship with the West. Talbott was utterly aware of Russia's search for identity and purpose in times of economic misery and widespread disorientation. Although Talbott was a strategic optimist, he fully acknowledged the imperfections of Russia's reforms and the country's internal problems:

In many ways, Russia is a self-liberated country, but it's also in many ways an unhappy, confused, and angry one. That's partly because almost every good thing that has happened there over the past decade—and there are many—has had its dark underside. For example, the implosion of the monolithic police state has left a vacuum of the kind that nature—especially human nature—abhors. In place of the old, bureaucratized criminality, there is a new kind of lawlessness. It's what my friend and colleague, Bronislaw Geremek, has called "the privatization of power" and it has quite literally given a bad name to democracy, reform, the free market, even liberty itself. Many Russians have come to associate those words with corruption and with the Russian state's inadequacy in looking after the welfare of its citizens. For all these reasons, Russia's first decade as an electoral democracy has been a *smutnoye vremya* or "time of troubles."[18]

Russia's troubles were a key issue at the start of Talbott's tenure. The first chapter of this book recounts how Clinton used Talbott's advice in the context of Russia's 1993 constitutional crisis and the first Clinton-Yeltsin summit in Vancouver in April 1993. Moreover, Talbott helped Clinton address many European security problems, including the war in Bosnia, the nuclear disarmament of Ukraine, and NATO enlargement—all pieces of a larger puzzle and all related to Russia's role in the newly emerging security architecture. Given Russia's domestic turmoil, Talbott argued for a slow approach to NATO enlargement. In the autumn of 1993, his advice was to focus on PfP with the countries in the East to win time for the stabilization of Russia and the emergence of a NATO-Russia partnership. PfP emphasized bilateral cooperation programs between NATO and aspiring new member states and did not instantly extend NATO's Article 5 guarantees on collective defense to them. It envisaged NATO's opening at the end, rather than the beginning, of a long-term process. Finally, the first chapter recounts Talbott's promotion to deputy secretary of state in the aftermath of the flawed U.S. military interventions in Somalia and Haiti in the autumn of 1993. Clinton turned to Talbott to organize the reshuffle of his foreign policy team. In private conversations with Talbott, Clinton discussed ideas for dismissing Secretary of State Warren Christopher and the potential appointment of General Colin Powell from the Joint Chiefs of Staff to build more of a bipartisan foreign policy.

Chapter 2 delves into the constant U.S.-Russia conflicts over the shape of the post–Cold War order, recounting misunderstandings on NATO enlargement and the role of PfP. Although Clinton saw it as a waystation in the NATO enlargement process, Yeltsin believed it was a way to postpone or avoid enlargement. Rather than debating these essential questions, Clinton and Yeltsin deliberately avoided them to focus on the less controversial trying to solidify U.S.-Russia relations. The discrepancy in perception led to Yeltsin's outburst at the December 1994 OSCE Summit in Budapest when he referred to the dangers of a "cold peace" in Europe. Talbott was among those who took most of the blame. He had advocated the meeting but could not participate because his involvement in the stabilization of Haiti kept him away. Starting in January 1995, Talbott began to reassert his role as the principal manager of the U.S.-Russia relationship. He began to elaborate on an outline for a new NATO-Russia charter to give Russia more of a role and a stake in the transformation of Europe, yet short of NATO membership and a veto or co-decision-making for Moscow. Talbott advised Clinton to maintain a gradual approach to NATO's opening to give Russia's domestic stabilization more time. In May 1995, Clinton convinced Yeltsin that NATO's decision on new alliance members would only be taken after Russia's presidential election in the summer of 1996. Meanwhile, the focus would be on PfP activities, such as the joint multinational NATO-Russia peacekeeping mission in Bosnia and Herzegovina and the Stabilisation Force (SFOR). Although SFOR strengthened the U.S.-Russia partnership, Russia also preferred to work bilaterally with the United States rather than place its peacekeeping forces under NATO command.

The third chapter depicts the start of a new phase in the making of Europe's new security architecture in 1995 when Talbott began to work on broader schemes for Europe's transformation. Beyond NATO enlargement, Talbott turned to the age-old European trouble spots that threatened to undermine Europe's security, including Ukraine, the Baltics, Turkey, and the Caucasus. He aimed to project a new sense of regional security and stability to "extend the Europe of the institutions to the Europe of the map," as Richard Holbrooke put it.[19] In contacts with policymakers from Kyiv, Talbott discussed Ukraine's role and place in Europe's security architecture including its wish for closer association with NATO and the European Union. Given NATO's preparations for enlargement, Ukraine switched from a policy of nonalignment to a more openly articulated desire to join the institutions of the West against the backdrop of increasing Russian pressure for integration in the former Soviet space. Moreover, Talbott intensified his work on Baltic security. He established a new concept of postnational security in the region, under which the states on the shores of the Baltics would feel secure enough to cooperate with each other and with Russia regardless of their nationality. However, Talbott's concepts were not met with approval in Moscow given the revival of traditional Russian foreign police precepts assuming that Russia needed a sphere of domination over its neighbors under the new foreign minister, Yevgeny Primakov. Talbott was concerned about the potential return of imperialism in Russian foreign policy, but argued for strategic patience to buy time for the arrival of a younger and hopefully more liberal cohort of Russian policymakers. The unfinished Russia project was among the main reasons Talbott stayed on in President Clinton's second term.

Chapter 4 examines Talbott's contributions to the negotiations on the NATO-Russia Founding Act of May 1997. On the positive side, the Founding Act indicated Russia's grudging tolerance of NATO enlargement. The Founding Act established the Permanent Joint Council (PJC) as a new NATO-Russia consultation mechanism in terms of joint peacekeeping missions, counterterrorism operations, and confidence-building military measures. On the downside, the Founding Act was merely a "conditional peace" and an "interim arrangement."[20] Confrontation and war between NATO and Russia could not be entirely excluded. NATO and Russia could not find consensus on the norms and rules governing the post–Cold War order in Europe. Moreover, the chapter looks into NATO's July 1997 Madrid summit and the Allied decision to open NATO's door to Poland, the Czech Republic, and Hungary. Meanwhile, Talbott helped bolster the security of those that did not make NATO's first enlargement round, including the Baltics and Romania, through the conclusion of bilateral charters and strategic partnerships. In July 1997, NATO and Ukraine concluded a new charter to institutionalize their strategic partnership. Although it signaled Ukraine's ambitions to join NATO, the charter did not provide a clear membership perspective, nor did it include the kind of robust security guarantees that policymakers in Kyiv demanded as protection against future Russian aggression.

Chapter 5 investigates Talbott's efforts to stop the downward spiral in U.S-Russia relations against the backdrop of Russia's 1998 financial crisis and Moscow's missile technology sales for Iran. In the spring of 1998, Clinton was able to convince Yeltsin to issue catch-all legislation to ban Russian supplies for the regime in Teheran. Clinton also managed to reassert himself domestically against the Republicans in Congress, who saw Russia as a lost cause and argued in favor of disengagement and less cooperation. Talbott fought hard to maintain a proactive Russia policy in Washington. His advice for Clinton was to continue the partnership with Yeltsin's Russia and to reach out to the younger generation of reform-oriented policymakers in Moscow, including Boris Nemtsov and Sergei Kiriyenko. However, Russia's financial collapse in the summer of 1998 triggered the end of its reform project. Most ordinary people in Russia blamed Western economic recipes for their misery when inflation skyrocketed and led to social unrest, large-scale protests and strikes among workers, and a drastic fall in real wages. In August 1998, amid the crisis, Talbott visited Moscow. He spoke with the entire Russian leadership and managed to secure the convocation of the Clinton-Yeltsin summit in Moscow in early September 1998, even though Clinton himself was weakened in the wake of the Monica Lewinsky affair. It was important for Clinton to show up, but the coalition of Communists and nationalists in the Russian Duma forced Yeltsin to appoint the antireform Primakov as the new prime minister.

The sixth chapter recounts Talbott's diplomacy to end the Kosovo War in 1999. At the outset, it looks into his efforts to avert war in 1998 when the Clinton administration pursued a two-track approach to address the Kosovo crisis—a diplomatic track to defuse tensions and a military track to help stabilize Kosovo's neighborhood. NATO was trying to apply a carrot-and-stick strategy toward Milosevic. This approach was backed up by the threat of freezing assets and a potential ban on investments in Yugoslavia. However, Milosevic did not meet NATO's benchmarks and deadlines. When NATO started bombing Yugoslavia in March 1999, Talbott wanted to control the Russian reaction. He stepped forward with creative proposals to include Russia in the diplomacy to end the war. In parallel to NATO's bombing campaign, Talbott searched for a diplomatic solution and teamed up with Finnish President Martti Ahtisaari and former Russian Prime Minister Viktor Chernomyrdin. The trick of Talbott's Kosovo statecraft was the combination of dialogue and the use of force. NATO was bombing Yugoslavia while Chernomyrdin and Ahtisaari spoke with Milosevic in search of a solution. The trilateral scheme worked. Yugoslav forces withdrew from Kosovo in June 1999. Even though the Kosovo War did not blow up the U.S.-Russia partnership, it made cooperation much, much more difficult against the backdrop of a nationalist groundswell in Russia culminating in Vladimir Putin's appointment as prime minister in August 1999 and the start of the second Chechen War later that year. In June 1999, Putin was flatly lying to Talbott when he promised that Russia's peacekeeping forces would not be deployed in Kosovo unilaterally and ahead of time as part of the international peacekeeping effort. As things turned out,

Putin sided with the military and the Russian hawks in a gambit for power, signaling that the hard-liners gained the upper hand.

The last chapter depicts the U.S.-Russia relationship in Putin's tenure as prime minister and president. It recounts the start of Russia's second war in Chechnya and the deterioration of relations between Washington and Moscow. It also depicts Talbott's assessment of Putin's personality as a Jekyll and Hyde figure and a dubious statesman. Through numerous personal meetings, Talbott identified Putin's dangerous sides, his gimmicks, his abilities for manipulation, and his willingness to undermine Yeltsin's reform legacy. Talbott sensed that Putin began to use nationalism and neo-imperialism to abandon Russia's reform trajectory in an effort to build an autocratic regime for the long haul. The more Talbott interacted with Putin, the more clearly he sensed that Putin's Russia was at odds with the West. Although the deterioration of relations and the new Cold War were not preordained, Talbott saw a variety of indicators suggesting Russia's return to its imperial past, including Putin's moves against the free press, the revival of Russia's ambitions in its near abroad, and the comprehensive personnel changes that brought Putin's KGB people to positions of power. Talbott's advice to Clinton was to show reserve and to deny Putin the kind of warm relationship that Clinton had cultivated with Yeltsin. During the last year of his tenure at the State Department, Talbott was growing disenchanted with the way Putin pursued Russia's foreign policy at the expense of the United States. Yet Talbott thought Russia could not make it alone and needed some cooperation with the West.

CHAPTER I

U.S. Foreign Policy and the European Security Mess

The Start of Clinton's Russia Policy

Bill Clinton won the 1992 elections, promising to address America's economic problems. However, after the end of the Gulf War in 1991, Clinton could not just focus on domestic issues at a time when Russia's turmoil and the Bosnian War emerged as new foreign policy challenges. Both signaled that the end of the Cold War had not resolved Europe's security issues. The violent dissolution of Yugoslavia revealed that the European Community had failed to stabilize its immediate neighborhood. The United States had to play a vital role in making the new Euro-Atlantic security order.[1] When Clinton entered office, there was no blueprint.[2] The struggle to create post–Cold War Europe had only just started. The revolutions of 1989 had redrawn Europe's borders, and its nations sought for ways to overcome old divisions. The challenge for Clinton was to expand old and tested institutions and establish fresh ones to create a new and secure Europe. In late October 1992, a week before the presidential election, Talbott wrote Clinton a letter arguing that "global interdependence makes any form of isolationism not just undesirable but impossible. Quite simply, with the old order in shambles and with only one surviving superpower, the world isn't going to leave you alone to devote all your energies to the home front."[3] Clinton could not afford to join the widespread "post-victory blues" after the end of the Cold War.[4]

The relationship with Russia was among the first issues the Clinton administration had to confront. Two weeks after the election, Talbott and Clinton met privately at the Hay Adams Hotel in Washington, DC, to discuss Russia. They thought about a response to a letter from Russian President Boris Yeltsin in which the latter was yearning for additional Western support and a personal meeting with Clinton. Most of Clinton's advisers recommended that the invitation to a summit should not be accepted at such an early time. Clinton asked Talbott for his assessment when they went over Yeltsin's message. "His letter reads like a cry of pain," Clinton said. "You can just feel the guy reaching out to us, and asking us to reach out to him. . . . We've got to try to keep Yeltsin going."[5] Then, suddenly, Clinton asked Talbott to be the U.S. ambassador in Moscow. Talbott declined. His family was thriving in Washington. His sons were sixteen and twelve, and he did not want to take them out of their lives in Washington. In his diary, Talbott added that Clinton "didn't belabor the matter; said he understood; asked if I was ruling myself out for working for him in some other capacity. I said no, of course not."[6]

Three weeks later, on December 13, Clinton had Secretary of State designate Warren Christopher call Talbott. Christopher had not come up with a specific job offer yet. He and Clinton looked for ways to use Talbott's expertise on Russia and the states of the former Soviet Union. In his memoirs, Clinton recalled that "Strobe and I had been discussing Russian history and politics for almost twenty-five years. . . . He had a fine analytical mind and a fertile imagination behind his proper professorial façade, and I trusted both his judgment and his willingness to tell me the unvarnished truth."[7] Clinton and Christopher sought an operational role for Talbott, but they did not want him to get bogged down with administrative work in the State Department's European Bureau. Instead, Christopher and Talbott agreed to establish a new position to cut into existing bureaucratic structures to pursue a more coordinated U.S. policy toward Russia and the former Soviet states. The idea was that Talbott would take over responsibility for Russia and the Newly Independent States (NIS) from the European Bureau (EUR). After the end of the Cold War, the traditional scheme of handling Russia in EUR no longer made sense. The problems of Russia and the NIS were too manifold and urgent and had to be dealt with by a new entity. After another phone call with Christopher on December 15, Talbott put his job description on paper. In it, Talbott outlined his proposal for the designation of an ambassador-at-large and special adviser to the secretary of state for Russia and the new independent states (S/NIS).

Talbott's objective was to establish a more coordinated U.S. policy toward Russia and the rest of the fourteen newly independent states. He would report directly to the secretary of state and be the secretary's principal adviser on all aspects of U.S. policy toward the NIS. The position would "combine advisory responsibility with operational authority," as Talbott put it. "Whoever holds this post should do more than just write memos and second-guess the bureaucracy. Rather, the post itself should be structured and empowered in a way to assure that policy, politics and operations will all come together."[8] Initially, Secretary of Labor Robert Reich, who had been in Talbott's and Clinton's Rhodes scholars cohort at Oxford and knew both of them well, came up with the idea that Talbott could be working as "tzar" in the State Department.[9] On December 17, 1992, Talbott called Clinton to make sure that the new position in the State Department was where the president wanted him to be. Clinton confirmed and said he wanted to build up the State Department. Talbott was all for it and wanted to ensure that the idea would come from the president "insofar as the job would have 'presidential imprimatur.'" In his diary, Talbott noted that Clinton was "very emphatic, saying yes, absolutely—and it's up to me to make sure it's seen that way."[10] In January 1993, Clinton informed Yeltsin that Talbott would be the critical person in Russian affairs. Unhampered by other administrative responsibilities, Talbott could focus on the key issues in U.S.-Russia relations, and Clinton promised Yeltsin that this arrangement would be "good for both you and me."[11]

Thus Talbott left *Time* magazine after twenty-one years and became the ambassador at large and special adviser to the secretary of state on the newly independent states of the former Soviet Union. He reported directly to the secretary and carried one of the longest titles in the federal government. Initially, Talbott had a small staff of nine, including Victoria Nuland and Eric Edelman, two youngish and talented Foreign Service officers who would rise to become undersecretary of state and undersecretary of defense in their later careers.[12] Talbott's job was challenging in many ways. Initially, he had a uneasy relationship with Warren Christopher. In 1992, Talbott thought Clinton should choose someone from the younger generation, such as Richard Holbrooke or perhaps even the Republican Winston Lord.[13] Yet it seemed that Christopher was the favorite candidate within the Democratic Party. He had been deputy secretary of state in the Carter administration and was passed over in 1980 when Cyrus Vance resigned, and President Carter preferred Senator Edmund Muskie over Christopher. Another asset was that Christopher brought plenty of foreign policy experience. He had the kind of deep diplomatic background that Clinton and his young team lacked so far. Christopher was of an older generation and had carried high government positions in the 1960s when he was Under Secretary of State George Ball's special envoy to trade talks in Tokyo in the Kennedy years and deputy attorney general in the Lyndon Johnson administration.

Regarding Russia, Christopher was more cautious and against an early Clinton-Yeltsin meeting that Talbott favored. The first minor disagreement between Talbott and Christopher occurred on February 23, 1993, when both discussed the question of the venue for the envisaged Clinton-Yeltsin summit. Talbott was fine with the Russian suggestion to convene it in Helsinki as the Finns were used to international summit diplomacy. Christopher disagreed and got rather sharp with Talbott "in front of others—saying, in effect, why should we let ourselves be dictated by the Russians' convenience when our obligation is to our own president?"[14] Talbott stood his ground, arguing that Helsinki would be necessary to beef up Yeltsin. But this was not the way Christopher thought. "Chris thinks in strictly political—as opposed to policy—terms; he sees himself as very much a lawyer with one client, and that's the President," Talbott noted.[15] Moreover, Christopher hesitated to use the terms *partnership* and *cooperation* as labels for U.S.-Russia relations. His preference was to use the neutral term *assistance*. "Chris is already uncomfortable with Clinton's being so far out in front supporting Yeltsin [and thought that] he shouldn't go to Moscow unless it is 'winnable,'" Talbott noted. "Throughout this episode, I'm thinking in terms of the effect of what we do on Yeltsin, Chris of its effect on Clinton. That's not bad. We all work for Bill Clinton after all, not Yeltsin; but at a minimum it sets up a dialectic between Chris and me," Talbott observed.[16]

On March 15, Talbott wrote his first memo for Clinton after the president had called him late the night before. The previous day, Clinton had discussed the need for more comprehensive Russia aid with former President Richard Nixon. He wanted his foreign policy team to think bigger regarding support for Russia's reformers. At Clinton's request, Talbott wrote a memo titled "A Strategic Alliance with Russian Reform" that he discussed with Christopher before the latter forwarded it to the president. The key message was that "it should be U.S. policy not just to prevent the worst but also to nurture the best that might happen in the former Soviet Union. . . . The meltdown of the Soviet Communist system has so far been relatively bloodless. That in itself is nothing less than a miracle—the greatest political miracle of our era. Doing what we can from outside, marginal and modest as it may be, to keep that miracle going is the greatest single task facing American foreign policy in the years to come."[17]

Talbott thought Clinton's support was essential given Russia's worsening internal situation against the backdrop of the parliamentary impeachment vote against Yeltsin. Domestic opposition to Yeltsin's reform program had been mounting throughout 1992 when inflation was skyrocketing and heavy taxes were enacted. The Supreme Soviet and the Russian Congress of People's Deputies clashed with Yeltsin on several issues. Eventually, they refused to confirm his candidate for prime minister, Yegor Gaidar, the increasingly unpopular architect of Russia's market liberalization. Finally, on March 20, 1993, Yeltsin gave a televised address in which he declared he had signed a new law under which he was entitled to govern with extraordinary power and to rule by decree. Moreover, he announced the gathering of a referendum on April 25 that would decide the timing of new legislative elections, a new constitution, and public confidence in the president.[18] Three days later, Russian parliament speaker Ruslan Khasbulatov called for Yeltsin's impeachment after Russia's Supreme Court ruled that Yeltsin had violated the constitution. The standoff between Yeltsin and his opponents resembled the situation of August 1991 when hard-liners attempted to topple Gorbachev.

Clinton was determined to support Yeltsin at this critical juncture. On March 22, he assembled his national security team and discussed the implications of the Russian situation in a Saturday emergency meeting at the White House. Clinton started by emphasizing his support for Yeltsin. He argued that Yeltsin was "breaking the impasse, he's not suspending civil liberties and taking his case to the people, which is a time honored tradition."[19] Clinton and Talbott sensed that Russia's constitutional crisis revealed that democratic procedures were new and untested. "It's a fledgling democracy there, with a lot of anti-democrats trying to topple a democratic leader," Talbott argued. Clinton did not waver when some of his domestic advisers and Christopher hesitated to back up Yeltsin. "I'm not worried about backing a loser as long as he's the right loser. I've lost plenty of times myself," Clinton argued. Christopher's primary concern in the discussion was that Clinton could leave the impression of being naïve by backing a disaster in Russia. Moreover, Christopher was opposed to the idea that Clinton would call Yeltsin as a way of supporting him. "This is definitely Chris the cautious uncle speaking; there's something very close to patronizing in his tone toward Clinton," Talbott thought.[20]

Finally, the Clinton-Yeltsin summit was on. It was scheduled to take place in Vancouver on April 3 and 4. However, whether Yeltsin would still be in office by early April was unclear. On March 28, he narrowly survived an impeachment vote in parliament that fell 72 short of the 689 votes needed for a two-thirds majority to oust him. Until then, the Clinton administration was still working on contingency plans in case Yeltsin was toppled. On March 27, Talbott and National Security Advisor Anthony Lake went through various scenarios. The cancellation of the summit was still a possibility. Another scenario was that Clinton could send either Vice President Al Gore or Christopher to Moscow. Talbott did not like the alternatives. "All these strike me as too clever by half, they'd look as though they were an attempt to hedge our bets, cover our asses, etc.," he noted.[21] Talbott's advice was to convene the summit between Clinton and Yeltsin, period. On March 28, after Yeltsin's victory over his domestic opponents, Clinton called Talbott to discuss preparations for the meeting. Talbott was out for dinner with his family and friends on Sunday evening at 7:30, eating pizza, when his beeper went off. He took Clinton's call in the basement of the pizzeria.

During their conversation, Clinton's main concern pertained to the size of the U.S. financial assistance package to Russia. He wanted to give more than President Bush but had to explain the necessity for aid to the American people and Congress. Talbott noted, "he's got two concerns, one that he'll be beat up by the Republicans for doing too little . . . two that he'll be beat up for doing too much in a time of stringency. Doesn't want to end up as 'George Bush junior.'"[22] Moreover, during their Sunday evening conversation, Clinton and Talbott searched for new diplomatic channels to help stabilize relations with Russia. Talbott floated the idea for the establishment of the Gore-Chernomyrdin Commission. Kozyrev had presented the proposal in Washington the previous week. It promised to bolster his difficult position as a reform-oriented and pro-Western policymaker in Moscow. Clinton liked the idea instantly. "Given Yeltsin's erratic streak," he wrote, "the Presidential connection was an uncertain flywheel in the machinery of U.S.-Russian relations. It would help to have another channel at the second-highest level."[23] Clinton agreed that he would propose establishing the commission at the summit.[24]

Talbott also established a new diplomatic channel that promised to help solidify U.S.-Russian relations. His contact person on the Russian side was Deputy Foreign Minister Georgy "Yuri" Mamedov. The two set up the so-called strategic stability group as a new consultation mechanism. Christopher suggested its establishment at his initial meeting with Kozyrev in Geneva on February 25, 1993, when he designated Talbott as the Clinton administration's representative to conduct the strategic stability dialogue with Russia.[25] The goal was to have closer contacts, more trust, and increased predictability in the day-to-day business of U.S.-Russia relations.[26] During the following eight years, Mamedov was indispensable to Talbott. They had countless meetings and were often able to find creative solutions for intricate problems, including arms control, NATO enlargement, and all sorts of challenges in the U.S.-Russia relationship. Mamedov was straightforward and honest, giving Talbott a sense of explanation and understanding when things went wrong or Russian decisions took longer. Thus he helped Talbott to read and interpret Yeltsin's and Kozyrev's diplomacies, including their occasional zigzags and unpredictability. Relative to other U.S. government agencies and Russia experts, Talbott often had an edge in terms of the information and analysis he received from Mamedov. All of this bolstered Talbott's position as the number one Russia explainer in Washington. The contact with Mamedov had already been established during the transition period in December 1992 when Secretary of State James Baker's adviser Dennis Ross told Talbott about Yeltsin's requests for an early summit meeting with Clinton. Ross praised Mamedov as the "ablest, shrewdest and most creative diplomat on the Russian side. . . . You folks are going to inherit a lot of problems with the Russians," Ross said, "and you'll probably get into a few of your own. Mamedov is the one guy over there you can work with. He's in the solution business."[27] The rash establishment of these channels helped to set U.S.-Russia relations on a promising trajectory.

In addition, Clinton was aware of the need to explain the strategy of his Russia diplomacy in public. In April 1993, shortly before the Vancouver meeting with Yeltsin, Clinton gave a major speech elaborating on the need to engage the new Russia as a partner in the emergence of the post–Cold War order. During the Cold War, no U.S. president had met his Soviet counterpart just ten weeks after inauguration. In 1993, though, things were different, Clinton argued. The Cold War was gone. Russia was not an enemy but a partner, and Yeltsin was the best bet for the long-term success of Russia's peaceful transition. On April 1, 1993, in an address before the American Society of Newspaper Editors in Annapolis, Maryland, Clinton said, "the end of the long, twilight struggle does not ensure the start of a long peace. Like a wise homeowner who recognizes that you cannot stop investing in your house once you buy it, we cannot stop investing in the peace now that we have obtained it," Clinton argued. "Nowhere is that engagement more important than in our policies toward Russia and the newly independent states of the former Soviet Union. Their struggle to build free societies is one of the great human dramas of our day. It presents the greatest security challenge for our generation and offers one of the greatest economic opportunities of our lifetime. That's why my first trip out of the country will be to Vancouver, to meet with President Yeltsin."[28] In terms of Russia aid, Clinton often referred to the rationale of the Marshall Plan. The best policy prescription was to support and embrace Yeltsin the way President Truman had handled the Germans after World War II.[29]

On April 3 and 4, 1993, the Vancouver summit offered a chance to set the course. It was the starting point for the close personal relationship between Clinton and Yeltsin. Their meetings went beyond courtesy. Both called each other by their first names instantly. Mutual sympathy came at first sight.[30] "I liked him," Clinton recalled, adding, "he was a big bear of a man, full of contradictions—compared with the realistic alternatives, Russia was lucky to have him at the helm."[31] Yeltsin was even more enthusiastic. In his memoirs, he wrote that he "was completely amazed by this young, eternally smiling man who was powerful, energetic, handsome."[32] In terms of substance, Yeltsin appreciated Clinton's readiness for assistance. He thought that the $1.6 billion aid package in support of Russia's reform program made for a good start. Moreover, Yeltsin appreciated the U.S. purchase of highly enriched uranium from Russia, Ukraine, and Kazakhstan, which was worth $12 billion. Psychologically, it did not give Yeltsin the same feeling as just asking for funds. He had something to offer in return, namely, fissile materials from the reduction of twenty thousand Soviet-era nuclear warheads that would be converted for nuclear power generation and then sold to the United States as fuel for some one hundred reactors producing nearly 20 percent of domestic electricity under the label "Megatons to Megawatts."[33]

The success of the Vancouver summit sent a strong signal. Clinton was determined to support Yeltsin for the long haul. He frequently emphasized that "the message of the meeting is that we're not constrained by the budget—we've got to think big."[34] Talbott's concern was that Clinton could appear to be too accommodating. The president had a different view, arguing that "Yeltsin's already working plenty hard at home. I'll get further with him if I don't add too much to his troubles."[35] Clinton did not bother about Yeltsin's drinking habits either. When his advisers complained about Yeltsin's intake, Clinton countered, "I've seen a little of this problem in my time," referring to his experience with his alcoholic stepfather. "At least Yeltsin's not a mean drunk," Clinton said.[36] The success of the Vancouver summit bolstered Talbott's position. Vancouver was not just important in terms of U.S.-Russia relations. It was also a precedent in terms of the way Clinton conducted foreign policy. He very much wanted to be a hands-on president. He was willing to negotiate himself and determined to engage in personal diplomacy—and Talbott could provide the kind of practical advice that Clinton sought. He had the president's trust. Clinton often called or visited the Talbott family at home. He could speak his mind when Talbott was around and when they were discussing foreign policy. It seemed that the relationship with Christopher was different for various reasons. Christopher was of another generation and twenty years older with a different background. His formal style had little in common with the habits of the baby-boomer generation to which Clinton, Talbott, and most of their advisers belonged. After a Saturday national security meeting, Talbott noted that "Chris is very much the odd man out—older by far than anyone else, dressed to the nines, the only nod to it's [sic] being Saturday is that he's tweedy rather than pinstripe; but still has a starched color and of course a tie."[37]

No Solution to End the War in Bosnia

After the end of the Cold War, Europe's security was a mess. Relations with Russia were just one problem in a larger puzzle. The war in Bosnia was perhaps Clinton's most urgent foreign policy challenge. It emerged after the violent breakup of Yugoslavia and mainly took place in Bosnia and Herzegovina when its multiethnic population of Muslim Bosniaks, Orthodox Serbs, and Catholic Croatians engaged in bitter fighting and ethnic cleansing in a quest to redraw borders. The Serbs and Croats wanted to extend the territories of their countries; the Bosnian Muslims were determined to establish their own state in Bosnia and Herzegovina.[38] The war threatened to undercut the rest of the efforts to stabilize Europe's post–Cold War security system. Clinton struggled with the absence of suitable options and sought Talbott's advice, although Bosnia was outside the latter's portfolio. The president knew that Talbott was very much in favor of U.S. military action to end the war. In several *Time* magazine articles, Talbott warned about the potential expansion of the war into Kosovo and Macedonia and the conflagration of the entire Balkans.[39] He was shocked by the inability of the West to stop the genocide and advocated NATO's use of military force to end the war. "There must now be a decisively more powerful external force, one that goes far beyond the U.N.'s current peacekeeping mission," he wrote in August 1992. "What is needed is an all-out peacemaking effort, also authorized by the U.N. but armed and manned largely by NATO and led by a U.S. that can thereby truly cure itself of the Vietnam syndrome."[40] However, Christopher and Secretary of Defense Les Aspin thought that U.S. airstrikes would involve the risk of a quagmire and a new Vietnam. Clinton himself was reluctant to resort to military force. Still, he felt an increasing need for U.S. leadership, sensing that the war in Bosnia tested America's willingness to be the leader of the free world.

On April 25, 1993, Clinton called Talbott late at night to ask for advice on Bosnia. It was Talbott's birthday. He was asleep already, got up again, and argued in favor of a more muscular U.S. approach, saying that "there was an argument for doing something very tough; there were, all across Eurasia, cases of such instability and civil war and bigger countries tempted to aggrandize their territory at the expense of neighbors on the basis of ethnic diasporas and tempted to carry out ethnic cleansing. Therefore, it was extremely important for us—the world community—to firmly establish the principle that such was not permissible."[41] It seemed that Talbott thought about opening NATO to new missions not just in the Balkans but also with an eye to broader challenges of instability across Europe. Talbott knew it was impossible to build a secure new European home as long as the Bosnian War threatened its foundation. Richard Holbrooke used to say that "you couldn't expand or enlarge NATO and bring in new members, on one hand, while NATO failed to deal with the fire right in the middle of its area."[42] In April 1993, Talbott's thinking foreshadowed much of the action that NATO took to end the war in 1995. While on the phone with Clinton, he argued that "we've got to take out the Serbian military; that means mostly airstrikes, but against air bases etc. in Serbia as well as against artillery installations in Bosnia. It also means leading an international force afterward to keep everyone from everyone else's throats afterward," Talbott said.[43] Moreover, Talbott emphasized the need for Russia's inclusion in a multilateral political track to achieve a lasting peace settlement. In 1993, however, it was unclear how the military and political tracks could be combined into a comprehensive effort to end the war.

When Clinton and Talbott rang off on April 25, Talbott called Deputy National Security Advisor Samuel "Sandy" Berger to tell him about the call. Talbott started by saying he knew that his advice for Clinton differed significantly from the counsel the president got from leadership personnel at the White House and the Pentagon working full time on Bosnia and former Yugoslavia. Berger then reviewed the options that Clinton had to end the war. Option 1 was to enforce a ceasefire with multilateral troops on the ground. This scenario was impossible for various reasons, namely, opposition from Congress, the European allies, and Russia. Option 2 involved air strikes, a lot of NATO airpower, and ground troops to enforce a peace agreement. Talbott favored it.[44] However, in 1993, the time was not ripe for such an approach because critical allies, including France, Germany, and the United Kingdom, preferred to maintain NATO's Operation Deny Flight to enforce the UN no-fly zone over Bosnia and Herzegovina.[45] Finally, option 3 focused on lifting the arms embargo to provide the Muslims in Bosnia and Herzegovina with weapons and the right to defend themselves. This approach would mean something like parity but would also trigger a further escalation of the fighting.

In 1993, it seemed that option 3 was the most straightforward course of action and the smallest common denominator in the Clinton administration. There was no need for U.S. leadership and NATO's military involvement. Talbott's problem with option 3 as the preferred approach was that "it's like squeezing the balloon—if you intensify the civil war in Bosnia, you provoke the Serbs to intensify their activity against Kosovo and Macedonia, which is where the whole thing has the worst danger of going regional/international."[46] Given the lack of good options, Bosnia could destroy Clinton's presidency. Initially, Clinton could not deliver on his forceful campaign rhetoric to stop the war. In 1993, he was unwilling to make Bosnia a critical foreign policy priority either. After the end of the Cold War and the U.S. victory in the Gulf War, U.S. public opinion was against new military commitments in the Balkans. Thus, Clinton tried to persuade his European allies to support forceful military action. In

May 1993, Clinton decided to send out Christopher to vital European capitals with the proposal to lift the arms embargo and to threaten air strikes. Christopher's mission was a setback. All European allies came out against "lift and strike" for various reasons.[47] Helmut Kohl was searching for a polite way to say no when he posed several crucial questions. "What had to happen in the critical phase between the adoption of the decision and the supply of weapons? What could be achieved with airstrikes in this context? What exactly had to happen with the UN troops on site? This was certainly a crucial issue for Great Britain and France," Kohl said.[48]

The war in Bosnia was, of course, a vital issue for Russia. It was a running sore in the evolving U.S.-Russia relationship at a time when economic assistance and partnership were meant to be in the foreground. Policymakers in Moscow wanted to avoid a leading NATO role in the Balkans. The problem for Clinton was that even Yeltsin and the liberal Kozyrev did not dare to confront those in Russia who sided with Milosevic. Talbott recalled that "Russian liberals knew that Milosevic was a scoundrel and that to defend him was disgraceful, but they feared that Western military action would set off a new cold war in the Balkans and, closer to home, set up a xenophobic backlash in Russia."[49] Hence Yeltsin and Kozyrev did all they could to avoid even the threat of force against the Bosnian Serbs. There was no movement in the Russian position when Talbott visited Moscow to discuss Bosnia in May 1993. Talbott noted that "the Russians appear preoccupied with the question of what to do, and uncertain whether military action is a worse option than doing nothing."[50] Russian Minister of Defense Pavel Grachev was working from screwed data that suggested military parity between the Serbs and the Muslim side in Bosnia. Kozyrev's concern was that providing arms for the Muslim side would precipitate a Serbian surge and an escalation of the war.

Talbott tried to convince Kozyrev and Grachev that it was in their interest to support a threatening military posture toward the Serbs because this was perhaps the only credible way to avoid an escalation of the war. However, Kozyrev cut Talbott off during his presentation, saying, "you know, it's bad enough having you people tell us what you're going to do whether we like it or not. Don't add insults to injury by also telling us that it's *in our interest* to obey your orders."[51] For now, Yeltsin was not prepared to do anything on Bosnia. His primary concern was to avoid new peace initiatives that his domestic opponents could interpret as disadvantageous for the Yugoslav side. The Clinton administration did not manage to get Yeltsin around by arguing that the halt of ethnic cleansing was also in Russia's interest given the manifold ethnic problems in its neighborhood. Talbott thought that "we've got to make him [Yeltsin] see that what he faces around the periphery of the FSU [Former Soviet Union] has Yugo-type risks, and we've got to work with him on a variety of things, like Russians in the Baltics and peacekeeping in the CIS, to keep together on this."[52] Kozyrev's sharp response in May 1993 revealed Russia's reluctance to accept this advice from the United States.

The war in Bosnia did not just burden relations with key allies and new partners such as Russia. It also led to tensions within the Clinton administration and strained Talbott's relationship with National Security Advisor Anthony Lake, who was in charge of Bosnia policy and did the daily national security briefings, confronting Clinton with lousy news about Bosnia every morning.[53] Moreover, Lake did not see Russia as a pivotal foreign policy issue. He wanted to shift the president's attention away from Europe and focus on the problems of the developing countries instead.[54] In his diaries, Talbott noted that "here's a guy who has spent much of his professional life trying to get the U.S. to pay attention to the 3rd world, to break out of the east–west axis and be more active North–South. He'd seen the cold war distort and thwart that other agenda many times; he'd hoped the end of the cold war would permit the U.S. finally to adopt a more global, south-looking approach; now here we were, in the post–Cold War era, and still obsessed with Russia. Still devoting most of our foreign aid budget to Russia! It just wasn't fair."[55] Lake was in a difficult position. The "insatiability" of Talbott's team bothered him. In September 1993, Talbott wrote Lake a letter to clarify things. "This is Bill Clinton's policy we're trying to carry out; the American people hired him to be a world leader, not just to fix the economy, stupid; and he'll derive political benefit from being seen and heard to be out front and clearly identified with it," Talbott wrote.[56]

Russia's Domestic Instability Again

In July 1993, the World Economic Summit in Tokyo offered Clinton a chance to meet Yeltsin in person for the second time. The summit was mainly about Russia aid and produced another assistance package of $3 billion to develop private industry in Russia. The key message was that

Russia did get help from the Group of Seven (G-7)—unlike in 1991 when Gorbachev got nothing at the G-7 meeting in London, and unlike 1992 when Yeltsin received less than expected at the G-7 summit in Munich.[57] In the summer of 1993, Clinton got something in return from Yeltsin— Russia abstained from selling missile engine parts to India, something very dear to Clinton—and facilitated his nuclear nonproliferation policy. In a letter to Clinton, Talbott emphasized that the president's Russia state-craft began to pay dividends. Talbott wrote, "you have convinced Yeltsin that you are serious about support for his program—that you really are committed to helping Russia make it into the 21st century as a great power and as a member of the community of democracies; that is why he has decided to swallow hard, pull out of the India deal, and join the Missile Technology Control Regime, despite the brutal opposition he faces from his military-industrial complex and from the parliament. . . . No American President has ever had as much influence over a Russian leader as you do now."[58]

Clinton's Russia policy had a good start. His channel with Yeltsin worked well. Moreover, Congress approved Clinton's $2.5 billion assistance package for Russia. Alas, new challenges emerged. Russia's constitutional crisis was not over yet. Clinton knew Yeltsin's domestic troubles, but did not expect an escalation of the conflict between Yeltsin and the Supreme Soviet. On September 21, 1993, everyone was surprised by Yeltsin's announcement to suspend the parliament and his call for elections on December 12. Right after Yeltsin's address, Ruslan Khasbulatov, the chairman of the Supreme Soviet, convened an emergency session at the parliament to organize a vote to remove Yeltsin from office. Clinton was scheduled for an ad hoc phone call with Yeltsin. When he arrived at the White House, Talbott gave him a brief heads-up summarizing the situation. "If this turns out badly, you'll have a new Russian counterpart tomorrow, and it'll be a whole new ball-game. No more win/win—it's back to win/lose. Think August '91. Yelt-sin's going for broke."[59] Clinton was determined to back up Yeltsin and reiterated his support in a public statement.[60] Yeltsin was combative and fervently believed he would win it again.[61] On September 25, 1993, troops from the Interior Ministry surrounded the White House in Moscow. Tanks opened fire. Russian Vice President Alexander Rutskoi and Khasbulatov were arrested.[62] Yeltsin ruled by decree. Clinton's instinct was to go all out to save Yeltsin. Talbott's advice was for Clinton to emphasize that Yelt-sin had to play by the rules of the constitution. "We don't want to treat the old Soviet constitution as the Ten Commandments, but it's the only one Russia's got, and 'constitutional rule' is essential to what we're supporting there. There are constitutional ways for a parliament to fire a president, but not the other way around. You've got to tell him he can't destroy democracy in order to save it," Talbott said.[63]

The events in Moscow signaled that Russia's future and Yeltsin's role were still contested. In the autumn of 1993, Yeltsin was focused on getting the Duma's approval for the new constitution. It foresaw even more authority in the hands of the executive and the president. "Even many reformers worry about establishing a new Russian democracy so heavily tilted toward presidential power," wrote U.S. Deputy Chief of Mission James Collins from Moscow.[64] Moreover, Collins was concerned whether the December 1993 Duma elections would be free and fair even though ninety-two parties were registered. Russia's electoral system favored large parties with substantial funding, given the strict registration rules for new parties and the short time remaining until the convocation of the election. When Christopher visited Moscow in October 1993, he stressed the importance of the Clinton administration's attachment to free and fair elections and a free press. He announced that the United States would send election observers and emphasized his concern about a decree banning opposition newspapers in Russia.[65] Despite these concerns, Clinton and his foreign policy team assumed that there was "no choice" other than to back Yeltsin. Talbott thought that Yeltsin's policy went in the right direction. "Yeltsin is okay," Talbott said when his family visited the Clintons at Camp David in November 1993. "Yes, there was a lot of conventional wisdom gathering to the effect that he was a dictator and an imperialist, but that was bullshit. He had shown his democratic credentials several times, but Russian democracy wasn't going to be like ours." Clinton agreed. Talbott noted that "Bill said he didn't have any worries either. He was very comfortable with the policy and where it was going."[66]

However, the result of the December 1993 Duma elections was a disaster for Yeltsin and a bitter pill for the Clinton administration. The nationalist Liberal Democratic Party of Vladimir Zhirinovsky emerged as the winner and received 23 percent of the vote. The Communist Party of Gennady Zyuganov reached 12 percent. Yeltsin's party, Russia's Choice, headed by Yegor Gaidar, garnered only 15 percent.[67] Yeltsin had a hard time trying to stabilize the country. The votes for Zhirinovsky and Zyuganov resulted from widespread poverty, unemployment, and unrest after the shock of rapid economic reforms. Russia remained in search of orientation and needed more time to consolidate. Yeltsin tried to put the best spin on the election disaster when he spoke with Gore in mid-December 1993. Yeltsin said, "Zhirinovsky's lead was exaggerated, the twenty-five percent that went to Zhirinovsky on the party list of the election will really turn out to be only twelve and one half percent in the whole Duma."[68] The results came as a shock at the end of a promising year. Talbott was in Moscow with Gore when the disastrous news came in. On December 13, Clinton called Talbott and started to ask about the election: "What's going on over there in Russia? I thought you had that thing under control," Clinton joked. His interpretation was that "this looks like a classic anti-incumbency deal, only multiplied by about 100 cuz they're new to the process and cuz things are so tough for the average person."[69] Talbott was shocked and felt he was at a loss. Would this be the end of Russian reform? "In the midst of all this, I had a truly sick feeling in my stomach," he noted. "So much of our policy was invested in the proposition that Russian democracy would essentially support the Russian reform. *Newsweek*'s Mike Elliot was in the process of closing a profile on me that I knew was going to pick up on the idea that those who came into Russian studies via art/literature/culture/etc. were more inclined to give the Russians the benefit of the doubt on their basic political/national character; it was quite true."[70]

Clinton did not give up on Russia. Instead, he was determined to work with Yeltsin and endorse further U.S. economic assistance programs.[71] Yeltsin promised that "there is no room for extremism or fascism in the new parliament."[72] However, Zhirinovsky's triumph had bold domestic consequences. Yeltsin stopped Russia's economic and financial reform project and returned to an approach that combined state interventionism and central planning. In January 1994, Yeltsin fired the architects of his economic reform policy—Yegor Gaidar, Boris Fyodorov, and Ella Pamfilova. Russia's reformers were alarmed and sensed that the country might relapse into a new age of authoritarianism at home and imperialism abroad. Was Yeltsin still a reformer? The liberals in Russia were not sure. "Russia, instead of moving along the axis of time, will continue spinning in the Western-versus-Slavic circle codified in Russian thought by the early nineteenth century Petr Chaadayev," wrote Yury Afanasyev, the liberal rector of Russian State University in Moscow.[73] Talbott was equally upset and concerned over Russia's potential return to a traditional Soviet foreign policy. In a January 1994 letter to Yuri Mamedov, Talbott pointed out that "worries about the possible 'Sovietization' . . . of the Russian economy are fueling concern over a perceived similar trend in Russian foreign and security policy."[74]

Ukraine's Nuclear Disarmament

Russia's potential retrogression had enormous implications for Ukraine. Although the dissolution of the Soviet Union had been remarkably peaceful, economic misery and the rise of nationalism could still turn the former Soviet space into a large Yugoslavia. In addition to the question of the presence of the Russian navy in the Crimean peninsula, the nuclear legacy of the Soviet Union was a critical problem in relations between Russia and Ukraine.[75] Following the disintegration of the Soviet Union, most Ukrainian policymakers did not want to abandon the nuclear weapons it inherited on its territory, including 130 liquid-fueled SS-19 intercontinental ballistic missiles tipped with six warheads each and forty-six solid fuel SS-24 missiles with ten warheads. In addition, there were about three thousand tactical nuclear weapons, approximately six hundred air-launched cruise missiles, and forty-two strategic bombers on Ukrainian territory.[76] Many in Ukraine thought the newly independent country needed the weapons as a deterrent against Russian intimidation and aggression. "Ukraine was not going to easily give up nuclear weapons like Kazakhstan and Belarus. Russia was not the kind of state to trust," Ukraine's former deputy foreign minister and later foreign minister Boris Tarasyuk recalled.[77] Ukrainians saw the security of their country in danger, fearing that Russia would not accept Ukraine's sovereignty. In July 1993, for instance, Ukrainian Defense Minister Kostyantyn Morozov complained about Russia's imperial ambitions. "Russia is artificially exacerbating the economic situation in Ukraine so that the people will go for reunification with Russia," he said in a meeting with U.S. Secretary of Defense Les Aspin and Talbott. "Moscow, via the Transnistria Republic, is trying to take Moldova, using Abkhazia to take Georgia, Crimea to take Ukraine."[78]

If Ukraine wanted to join the West, it could not retain the nuclear weapons it inherited. Ukraine did not have access to nuclear warhead technology. The weapons on its territory were still Russian because only Russia could command and control them. Tarasyuk recalled that "if Ukraine had decided to keep nuclear weapons on its territory, it would have faced the necessity of Russia's help to maintain them. So, to be truly independent, Ukraine had to abandon the nuclear weapons on its territory."[79] After extensive internal debates, Ukrainian policymakers cooperated with the Bush and Clinton administrations.[80] However, tensions between Moscow and Kyiv jeopardized Clinton's aim to help build a new security architecture between Russia and the rest of the former Soviet republics. In January 1993, Talbott noted in his diaries that Clinton wanted "a policy that takes account of all the former republics, that deals holistically or gestalt-like with Russia in its relations with the other republics; feels that policy till now has tended to treat Russia a vacuum, or to pit the issue of the other republics (especially Balts and Ukraine) against the issue of Russia; goal: a true commonwealth; peace and cooperation between Russia and the new abroad."[81] The key to this rationale was the relationship between Russia and Ukraine. The aim was to broker an agreement on the denuclearization of Ukraine and Russia's recognition of Ukraine's sovereignty and territorial integrity, including Western security guarantees.

Talbott played a crucial role in the Clinton administration's diplomacy toward Ukraine and chaired a newly established interagency group managing relations toward the newly independent states. He oversaw the Clinton administration's policy review toward Ukraine based on the premise that its nuclear disarmament was the precondition for broadening the U.S.-Ukrainian relationship.[82] In the spring of 1993, Talbott helped find a solution when the Ukrainians were still hesitant to abandon the inherited nuclear arms.[83] In mid-May 1993, Talbott went to Kyiv and offered financial help to return the weapons to Russia and technical assistance for their dismantlement in exchange for Russian assurances of Ukraine's independence underwritten by the United States. The Clinton administration was willing to provide financial assistance from the U.S. Cooperative Threat Reduction program established under the leadership of Senators Sam Nunn (D-GA) and Richard Lugar (R-IN) when the Soviet Union disintegrated.[84] Ukraine's President Leonid Kravchuk was concerned that the Clinton administration favored Russia at the expense of Ukraine. "You should have good relations with Russia, but don't put all your eggs in one basket and don't give the Russians a blank check," Kravchuk argued.[85] Talbott very much argued for a broader relationship. In late June 1993, he used a testimony on Ukraine before the Senate Foreign Relations Committee to underscore Ukraine's geopolitical role as a key U.S. partner, emphasizing that the Clinton administration would pursue its relationship with Ukraine on its own merits independent of its ties with Russia.[86]

In July 1993, at the margins of the G-7 summit in Tokyo, Yeltsin agreed to launch a trilateral process to address the question of nuclear weapons in Ukraine. Clinton quickly agreed.[87] In late July 1993, Talbott started trilateral talks with Mamedov and Tarasyuk to broker a solution. The nuclear weapons would be dismantled in Russia, and Ukraine would obtain payments for the commercial value of the highly enriched uranium in the nuclear warheads.[88] The initial round of talks with the Ukrainian side did not go well.[89] Tarasyuk approached Talbott with requests for the conclusion of a legally binding treaty stipulating Western security guarantees in return for Ukraine's complete nuclear disarmament. Moreover, Tarasyuk demanded that Ukraine's eligibility for NATO membership be mentioned in a bilateral U.S.-Ukraine charter. Talbott rejected both requests. A legal treaty would require the consent of the U.S. Senate for ratification. NATO Article 5–type guarantees were out of the question because granting them would trigger more such requests from other post-Soviet states.[90] In his diaries, Talbott noted, "we have a long 45-minute-wrange on security guarantees/treaty, etc; it's real discouraging; they just keep worrying the issue like a bone. They're also trying to get NATO membership mentioned in the charter. I hit them pretty hard w/ what I see as the basic problem—they want to be members of NATO and can't be. It's pretty close to a bust."[91] Talbott's no reflected the Bush and Clinton administration's resistance to new commitments to Ukraine. Eventually, Ukraine secured a package of existing assurances from the UN Charter and the Helsinki Final Act. The Clinton administration engaged in a diplomatic process with Ukraine and Russia, resulting in the Budapest Memorandum of December 1994, under which Ukraine agreed to transfer the nuclear warheads to Russia for elimination. In return, Ukraine received security assurances from the signatories—the United States, Russia, and Britain all pledged to respect Ukraine's territorial integrity and inviolability of its borders and to refrain from the use or threat of military force. "Although the assurances themselves were not new, their packaging in a Ukraine-specific document was symbolically and politically important to Kyiv as it sought to bolster its sovereignty," Steven Pifer recalled.[92]

However, the Budapest Memorandum was disappointing from Ukraine's perspective because it did not include legally binding security commitments and merely entailed general promises of nuclear weapon states not to use or threaten to use nuclear weapons against non-nuclear-weapon states.[93] The agreement did not stipulate any enforcement mechanism to make the agreement stick and protect Ukraine over the long term.[94] "It failed to deter Russian aggression because it imposed no immediate cost for its violation," Mariana Budjeryn wrote. "The political assurances it provided rested on the goodwill and self-restraint of the guarantors, an arrangement that can work between allies but not potential adversaries."[95] Although the security assurances were inadequate and could neither avert Russia's military seizure of Ukrainian territory in Crimea and Donbas in 2014 nor Russia's full-scale war against Ukraine that began in 2022, it would not have made sense for Ukraine to keep nuclear weapons in the 1990s because the country did not have access to nuclear weapons technology—and retaining the weapons meant that it would remain reliant on Russia and thus its sovereignty would be compromised. Ukraine's partnership with the West would not have been possible had Kyiv chosen to retain nuclear arms. After all, "nuclear weapons would likely have become a security liability, not an asset, for Ukraine."[96] However, despite no credible alternative to Ukraine's nuclear disarmament, policymakers in Washington and Kyiv failed to turn the Budapest Memorandum into a more robust U.S.-Ukrainian partnership for defense cooperation in the long run.

Even though the Budapest Memorandum brought Ukraine two decades of peaceful development, the Clinton administration struggled to find the country a place in the Euro-Atlantic security architecture. Given Russia's and Ukraine's turmoil and instability, the Budapest Memorandum reflected the search for practical solutions and achievable outcomes in times of crisis. In June 1994, Talbott said the Clinton administration "deliberately avoided theological debates about how Russia and Ukraine fit into Europe. The important thing is that neither country feels isolated and that we in the West support integrationist pro-democracy and pro-market economy forces throughout Europe."[97] Although the Budapest Memorandum broadened Ukraine's relationship with the United States, the country was still caught in a grey zone between Russia and the West.[98] The Clinton administration and its European allies constantly searched for ways to address Ukraine's security issues. In a January 1994 conversation with Clinton, Helmut Kohl noted that "the situation in Ukraine was precarious. . . . There was an additional risk pertaining to the tendency to put Ukraine's sovereignty into question. . . . One must not just focus on Moscow and forget Ukraine." Clinton agreed. In response, he said that "if there was a backlash in the way the Chancellor had alluded, namely a tendency for Ukraine's return to Russia, then we would be faced with the collapse of the entire theory of the NATO summit. Ukraine was indeed the key to the entire development in Central and Eastern Europe . . . If anything happened in Ukraine, this would increase the pressure for the NATO accession of the Central and Eastern European countries."[99]

A Gradual Approach to NATO Enlargement

Clinton was right. Belarus was already reorienting itself toward Russia politically, economically, and militarily. The danger was that Ukraine could follow, given its political gridlock and the lack of economic reform. The situation in both countries caused anxiety in the other central and eastern European countries. The new democracies in the region wanted to join the West to be safe from Russia. Policymakers in central Europe saw the enlargement of NATO and the EU as anchors to promote the transition to democracy and market economy.[100] In November 1990, for instance, Czechoslovakia's President Havel emphasized that "with the collapse of communism in Czechoslovakia, Poland, Hungary, and other countries, we may be facing a temporary vacuum as all the old links cease to exist. It could be a breeding ground for chaos and instability. Our democracies are just emerging. To fill this vacuum is not just our problem; it is also an obligation of the West."[101] However, like George H. W. Bush, Clinton was utterly careful to crack open NATO's doors. Both presidents prioritized Russia's stabilization. During the 1992 election campaign, Bush avoided discussions over new NATO members and new NATO missions. Given the economic crisis in the United States, it was not promising to talk about potential new defense commitments. Eventually, the debate over NATO enlargement was deferred. It was the Clinton administration's task to find new schemes to open up NATO for new members and missions and support Russia's engagement simultaneously.[102] The challenge was threefold: to open NATO to new members, to reform it so it could take on new missions such as peacekeeping in the wake of new post–Cold War security challenges, and to facilitate the peaceful transformation of Russia and the other post-Soviet states and their participation in the emerging security architecture. The challenge was to square a triangle, not to choose Russia or NATO enlargement.

During the first months of Clinton's tenure, NATO enlargement was not a priority either. It was on the back burner in Washington though others discussed it more openly. In March 1993, German Defense Minister Volker Rühe was the first Western policymaker to advocate it in public in a landmark speech he gave at the International Institute for Strategic Studies in London. The key theme of Rühe's address was that "we must not exclude our neighbors in the East from Euro-Atlantic security structures. Eastern Europe must not become a conceptual no-man's-land . . . and the Atlantic Alliance must not become a closed shop."[103] Rühe's rationale was to give the nations of eastern Europe the same kind of security that France and Germany enjoyed in NATO—equal security was the precondition for the emergence of a genuinely united new Europe, and NATO enlargement was the only credible way to provide security for the newly emerging democracies in the East, Rühe thought. If NATO did not open its doors, the countries in the East would search for bilateral security arrangements with Russia and outside of NATO, Rühe said. Hence, it was time for NATO to act and to project security to the East. This was an urgent task. After the demise of the Soviet Union and the end of the communist regimes, Europe was still without a clearly defined security system.

Rühe's March 1993 address in London was the first step in bringing NATO enlargement to the international affairs agenda. Another step followed in April 1993 when policymakers from the Visegrad countries visited Washington for the opening of the United States Holocaust Memorial Museum. Czech President Vaclav Havel told Clinton that he wanted "association, followed by full membership" in NATO.[104] Polish President Lech Walesa underlined Havel's case, arguing that "after decades of Soviet domination, we are all afraid of Russia. It is important to remember that this is the first time in history that the Soviet army has withdrawn from territory peacefully. If Russia again adopts an aggressive foreign policy, that aggression will be directed toward Ukraine and Poland. The U.S. is needed to prevent this from happening. . . . Poland cannot be left defenseless; we need to have the protection of U.S. muscle."[105] These requests touched Clinton personally and reaffirmed his conviction that NATO had to be at the center of Europe's security system. However, the Clinton administration did not have a policy on NATO's adaption and its potential enlargement. This was apparent at the NATO ministerial meeting in June 1993 when Christopher noticed that "at an appropriate time, we may choose to enlarge NATO membership. But that is not now on the agenda."[106]

Things began to change soon. The domestic debate on NATO's post–Cold War purpose started in August 1993, when Senator Richard Lugar (R-Indiana) made a bold case for expanding NATO's mission and membership.[107] Lugar argued that a transformed and enlarged NATO was the best guarantee to reorder the Euro-Atlantic security structures after the end of the Cold War.[108] NATO's new purpose had to go beyond collective defense—the alliance had to project stability beyond its old border "to enlarge the community of democratic states throughout the Euro-Atlantic area while providing its growing number of members with the military foundation to undertake joint military action in defense of their common territory, values, and interests."[109] Lugar argued that "NATO had to go out of area or it would go out of business. . . . The alliance's new mission must strike a balance between its traditional role of collective defense and a new role of crisis management beyond its borders."[110] It was an urgent plea for the adaption of NATO to the changing geostrategic landscape in Europe after the end of the Cold War. NATO had to stand up and defend the values of civilization in Bosnia. If NATO failed to intervene, it would lose the peace after it prevailed in the Cold War. "How many potential aggressors, within central and eastern Europe and beyond, will now feel that they can defy the international community with impunity—that the West is all bark and not bite?" Lugar asked. "The current crisis may be on Europe's periphery, but they are not peripheral to Europe's security," Lugar said. "This is where Europe's future will be decided and underscores the link between what happens in the East and the future of the West."[111] In summary, as Ivo Daalder put it, NATO had to transform from a "military alliance with a political function to a political alliance with a military foundation."[112]

August 1993 saw another milestone in the emergence of the NATO enlargement debate. Walesa received Yeltsin for a visit to Warsaw and managed to get the Russian side to agree to a statement indicating that Russia would no longer object to Poland's future NATO membership.[113] This was a watershed moment and set NATO enlargement firmly on the agenda of international affairs. It was no longer possible to ignore the issue. NATO had to address enlargement. NATO Secretary General Manfred Wörner was jubilant and noted that "there is currently a historic moment of opportunity regarding NATO's engagement in the East."[114] However, Yeltsin soon retracted his words, arguing that the 1990 settlement on Germany precluded NATO's expansion. On September 15, 1993, he wrote Clinton a letter and justified his position with a reference to the Two Plus Four Treaty on Germany.[115] Yeltsin's argument was nonsense. The Two Plus Four Treaty pertained only to Germany.[116] Russia did not have the right to define the security arrangements of sovereign states in central and eastern Europe. The 1990 arrangements on Germany only precluded NATO force deployments in East Germany—this is the meaning of Secretary James Baker's famous phrase "not one inch to the East."[117] In the mid-1990s, when Russian policymakers started to misinterpret the settlement on Germany in their campaign against NATO enlargement, the State Department pointed out that "in broader terms, we should also remind Moscow that its Two-Plus-Four involvement in internal German affairs (i.e. prohibiting certain force deployments), was unique, arising from the post-war settlement, and did not set any legal or political precedents; Russia does not have a similar right to define or dictate the security arrangements of other sovereign states."[118] The provision did not apply to Poland, the Czech Republic, or elsewhere; nor was Baker contemplating such a step; at the time, those countries were still members of the Warsaw Pact. However, Yeltsin's argument foreshadowed Russia's standard line in the future. Russian officials repeated it endlessly and claimed that NATO had broken a promise not to enlarge. There was no promise. The question of NATO enlargement had not been on the agenda in 1990.[119]

It emerged only in 1993, and the Clinton administration hesitated to embrace it. The debate on NATO's opening began to accelerate in the autumn of 1993 when three political scientists from the RAND Corporation wrote a pathbreaking article on the need for NATO's opening. Ronald Asmus, Richard Kugler, and Stephen Larrabee made a case for "building a new NATO" and an alliance that would "deal with the issues of conflict and instability and would project collective defense, democracy, and security. . . . Such a strategy must be, first and foremost, political and economic. But the West must also establish a stable security framework for these regions," they wrote.[120] "They did not write the article out of the blue but were in communication with Ruehe, Lugar, and individuals in the administration trying to articulate a way to square the triangle of opening NATO, expanding its mission, and engaging Russia at the same time," Daniel Hamilton recalled.[121] Building a new security architecture had to include both the enlargement of NATO and the European Union to bolster the region's political and economic integration, Asmus, Kugler, and Larrabee argued. NATO's opening was envisaged in steps. Defense cooperation and agreements on associate status could precede eventual NATO membership. Moreover, the three RAND analysts proposed a new security partnership between the West, Russia, and Ukraine. To that end, they suggested the establishment of a security charter to spell out the basic principles to structure Russia's relationship with NATO and the European Union. They argued that "such a charter would be designed to reassure Russia that it will be included in efforts to build a new European security order. Extending the alliance eastward should be seen as the West taking a step toward Russia, rather than against it."[122] They argued that NATO's opening would not antagonize Russia as long as it was combined with the emergence of a strategic partnership. NATO's opening and Russia's engagement were compatible, and combining both tracks was necessary.

However, there was no easy way or premade solution to achieve both objectives. NATO's leaders thought hard about ways to integrate the central European countries and engage Russia simultaneously. There was no consensus on how both could be achieved. The debates inside the Clinton administration and the Kohl government signaled the issue's complexities. Kohl and Clinton were more cautious than Rühe. In 1993, Kohl's focus was entirely on Russia's stabilization.[123] Kohl thought NATO enlargement was less pressing. At the same time, he was determined to address the security concerns of the Visegrad states. In September 1993, Kohl told Clinton that "it was absolutely necessary to find a forum for an uncertain transitory time in order to cover the security interests of these countries, especially the Czech Republic, Hungary and Poland. He did not know whether it was feasible at all to contemplate NATO enlargement at the current point in time. He had doubts. But perhaps one could find a temporary solution for an indefinite time in order to satisfy their needs."[124] The Clinton administration did not have a unified position either. Secretary of Defense Aspin and his successor William Perry argued that nuclear arms control and cooperative threat reduction should be the key priority. Although the Pentagon was hesitant to extend NATO's security guarantees eastward, White House and State Department officials envisaged a more assertive approach to NATO enlargement.[125] The group of NATO fast-trackers included Anthony Lake and Undersecretary of State Lynn Davis, who thought along Rühe's lines and argued that "Germany is on the front line of Central European instability and has neither the resources nor the political inclination to handle these problems unilaterally."[126]

In the fall of 1993, General John Shalikashvili, the Joint Chiefs of Staff chairman, devised an idea for establishing Partnership for Peace to reconcile the competing approaches. He envisaged PfP as a program of practical bilateral cooperation between NATO and individual countries, offering a variety of mechanisms to foster partnerships, including military-to-military cooperation, defense policy planning, and joint military exercises. PfP would not extend NATO Article 5 guarantees to new member states instantly. It would put enlargement at the end of a long-term process rather than the beginning. Moreover, it promised to buy additional time to stabilize the NATO-Russia relationship and the search for a new security architecture. Thus, PfP helped NATO square several circles—"to revitalize NATO, to avoid antagonizing Russia by feeding nationalist tendencies, and to calm down growing fears in Central and Eastern Europe."[127] On October 18, 1993, Clinton approved the PfP approach at a meeting of principals.[128] However, interpretations of PfP differed. Before the meeting, Christopher, Aspin, and Lake met for lunch to try to reconcile the differing positions "over whether NATO would commit at the January [1994] NATO Summit to expansion, or simply hold out the vague possibility"—yet to no avail.[129] Although Clinton approved PfP, each side of the debate thought the president had approved their version of it—to defer NATO enlargement as per the Pentagon—and as a next step toward NATO enlargement, as some at the State Department and the National Security Council thought.

Initially, it seemed that Christopher leaned strongly toward the advice of the NATO fast-trackers.[130] In October 1993, his position was given particular attention as he visited Budapest, Moscow, Kyiv, and Brussels. Given Russia's precarious domestic situation, Talbott thought Christopher's trip could be damaging if the secretary made the case for NATO's rapid enlargement. On October 19, Talbott decided to intervene. He wrote Christopher a candid memo arguing against NATO's swift opening. Given Russia's domestic turmoil, Talbott advised a gradual approach to NATO's enlargement. He thought that "an expanded NATO that excludes Russia will not serve to contain Russia's retrograde, expansionist impulses; quite to the contrary, it will further provoke them." Talbott believed a fast-track approach to enlargement would run into powerful opposition both in Moscow and within NATO. He wrote that "it seems to me that just about the worst possible scenario would be one in which we decide perhaps tomorrow on a NATO-plus-V-3 [Visegrad-3] strategy (or again, one that would be universally interpreted as such), then run into a buzz saw with it (or several different buzz saws—i.e. in Moscow, Kyiv, and several NATO capitals) and have to retreat."[131]

Talbott advised Christopher to emphasize PfP and the partnership with Russia as the key elements of NATO's position rather than enlargement. PfP was open to everybody, including Russia and Ukraine. It promised to strengthen NATO and to help avoid antagonizing Russia at the same time. Talbott argued that "my recommended bottom line is this: We should take the one new idea that seems to me almost universally acceptable, the Partnership for Peace, which is truly inclusive, and make that rather than expanded NATO partnership (which is at least implicitly exclusive) the centerpiece of our NATO position. We can hold open the possibility that our peacekeeping partners, in the future, be eligible for membership. But we should avoid criteria and talk of associate status." Talbott emphasized that "we must do everything we can do to encourage reformers in Poland, Hungary and the Czech Republic to make them feel they that they have a place in the West. However, we must not advance that goal at the expense of our support for reform further East, especially in Russia—which, after all the President keeps saying is our no. 1 priority."[132]

Talbott was not against NATO enlargement per se. His appeal was in favor of a slow and incremental approach. He thought the context and the process mattered as much as the substance. If Christopher decided to endorse a fast-track enlargement, Talbott's advice was to accompany it with the offer to establish a security agreement between NATO and Russia to try to "off-set" and "console" Russia, as he put it. Talbott even went one step further and suggested the conclusion of similar security arrangements between NATO and Ukraine, Kazakhstan, and Belarus in this case. They were all on the way to abandoning their nuclear weapons and had to be included in the process of Europe's transformation—especially if NATO went for a fast admission of Poland, Hungary, and the Czech Republic. "We'll surely have to offer something similar to both Ukraine and Kazakhstan since those two will be dickering with us over the terms of giving up their nuclear weapons, and perhaps even to Belarus, since it should not be penalized for having given up its nukes. So, you see, even 'offsets' are a pandora's box," Talbott concluded.[133] The offset question was another reason to avoid NATO's fast-track enlargement, Talbott argued. Talbott's assistant, Eric

Edelman, envisaged NATO enlargement as a process with several stages lasting a decade or even longer. In the autumn of 1993, Edelman argued that high-performing states such as the Visegrad countries could join after seven or ten years as a reward for their reforms. In contrast, others could accede later, including Russia.[134]

Finally, Christopher followed Talbott's advice. When he visited Moscow in October 1993, Christopher presented PfP as the cornerstone of NATO's approach to Europe's transformation. He assured Yeltsin and Kozyrev that, for now, NATO would not take in new members. Rather than enlarging swiftly, NATO would open up gradually. The focus of U.S.-Russia diplomacy should be on PfP. Yeltsin's question was whether "all countries in CEE and the NIS would, therefore, be on an equal footing." Christopher replied, "yes, that is the case, there would not even be associated status." Yeltsin was enthusiastic: "This is a brilliant idea, it is a stroke of genius." Later in the conversation, Christopher noted that NATO enlargement would stay on the agenda: "We will, in due course, be looking at the question of membership as a longer-term eventuality."[135] Yeltsin did not seem to care about this caveat. In contrast, Kozyrev did care. He thought Christopher's performance was "deceptive," although it accurately reflected the U.S. position.[136] Although it was deceptive from Kozyrev's perspective, it reflected the ambivalence in NATO's position at the time given the differing interpretations of PfP, which were revealed at the meeting of NATO defense ministers in Travemünde on Germany's Baltic coast in October 1993. Secretary of Defense Les Aspin was reluctant to mention PfP's connection to NATO enlargement, but Ruhe and Worner were determined to reiterate that PfP would undoubtedly lead to enlargement.[137] Rühe's position was that the forthcoming NATO summit in Brussels in January 1994 had to send a clear message in this regard—yet without mentioning potential new members and without a timetable. Russia would not have a veto in all of this. Although one had to consider Russia's interests, it was wrong to link NATO enlargement to what was happening in Russia.[138] Like Rühe, Henry Kissinger and Zbigniew Brzezinski made the case for NATO's rapid enlargement to hedge against the potential revival of Russia's imperialism. Brzezinski argued that "insurance is needed against the possibility—one might even argue the probability—that the weight of history will not soon permit Russia to stabilize as a democracy." Kissinger agreed.[139] "His skepticism about whether 'the bear can change his spots' leads him to question both our NATO policy and our Ukraine policy," Talbott reported to Christopher after he had spoken with Kissinger in November 1993.[140]

Talbott's Promotion to Deputy Secretary

In the autumn of 1993, Talbott's impact grew amid one of President Clinton's most severe foreign policy crises. The president sought his advice after the disastrous battle of Mogadishu when dead U.S. soldiers were dragged through the streets by enraged Somalis broadcast on U.S. television stations. Clinton knew he needed a new secretary of defense to replace Aspin, who was held responsible.[141] Overall, Clinton was in search of a credible strategy to deal with civil wars, mass murder, and genocide in Bosnia, Somalia, and Haiti, though it was challenging to garner public support for "humanitarian interventions" in "remote places." Beyond resolving the underlying political conflicts in crisis regions, "peacekeeping" needed a sustained military presence and continued engagement with the conflicting parties on site.[142] In a *Foreign Affairs* article, Leslie Gelb wrote that "the main strategic challenge for the United States is to develop plans for multilateral action to stem civil wars without drowning in them."[143] At the outset of his presidency, Clinton was hesitant to use force. He refused to attack Yugoslav troops in Bosnia and withdrew the U.S. military from Somalia in October 1993. Moreover, just a week after the fiasco in Mogadishu, he recalled a U.S. ship that he had dispatched to send two hundred U.S. and Canadian engineers and military police on board to prepare for the return of President Jean-Bertrand Aristide in Haiti when they were met by a mob of people threatening the use of violence at the pier in Port-au-Prince.[144] Given the multitude of failures in the autumn of 1993, Clinton contemplated replacing Christopher and picking retired General Colin Powell, the former chairman of the Joint Chiefs of Staff, as his new secretary of state to establish more of a bipartisan foreign policy.

On the evening of November 1, Clinton called Talbott to float the idea. He wanted to see whether Talbott would discuss the legion of problems with Christopher. The president thought that Powell's appointment promised to give the whole administration more credibility with the military. In public, Clinton's foreign policy team was vulnerable to the charge that it lacked the competence to pull off military operations, especially compared with the Bush administration—"Bush was a decorate[d] ww2 vet, Baker a marine, Scowcroft a general—that more than made up for Cheney being some kind of draft dodger," Talbott noted.[145] Powell could fill the gap on the Clinton team and "had real charisma," Clinton said.[146] His preliminary idea was to bring in Christopher as chief of staff at the White House. At the end of the conversation, Clinton emphasized that he wanted "a clean sweep." It was Talbott's task to think about the process and develop recommendations. The challenge for Talbott was to discuss the multitude of problems with Christopher without telling the latter precisely what the president said. Clinton promised to protect Talbott— "particularly cuz I'm in a helluva tricky position re Chris," Talbott noted in his diaries. Indeed, Talbott was in a tight spot. The following night, he slept "very badly, fretting and rehearsing," as he noted. "One of my biggest concerns is how to square my loyalty/obligation to Bill with that to Chris," Talbott wrote in his diary. "I decide that the only way to do it is somehow to play straight with him; let him know there's a general problem, that the president is unhappy with the foreign policy as a whole and with the team as a whole, but that we've identified Aspin as the most urgent problem, and find a way to deal with that first, and secondarily with the second echelon at state. I can't quite play this out in my head, since it will be devastating to Chris, so I decide to enlist [Christopher's chief of staff] Thomas Donilon."[147]

The next day, November 2, Talbott sat down with Donilon to discuss the puzzle of problems. In his diaries, he noted, "I tell him pretty much everything, although I make clear I'm not going to lay out exactly what the President said about Chris; he gets it; I ask him hypothetically how Chris would feel about going over to the White House."[148] Resigning as secretary of state and working as Clinton's chief of staff was not a good option for Christopher, Donilon thought. Being secretary of state was the only job Christopher ever really wanted. Talbott sensed Clinton needed "a phased way of dealing with the problem—grasp the nettle on Aspin now—or as soon as we can identify the right person to replace him— move on the second echelon at state, and then see what develops with foreign policy in general, with Chris in particular, and with Powell's availability."[149] Talbott wanted to proceed gradually. He thought that sudden changes in the foreign policy team would not make sense. The "trouble with massacre is it looks like panic, like the president blaming everyone but himself."[150]

On the evening of November 3, Clinton called Talbott again to hear his recommendations. Talbott went through the gradual scenario, and Clinton agreed that it was essential to avoid a massacre. The solution was to replace Aspin right away. The option to replace Christopher would remain on the table. "His judgement is good; he's a good lawyer, he's a good advocate in private, but not in public," Clinton commented on Christopher.[151] Finally, at the end of the week, on Friday, November 5, Talbott and Christopher discussed the situation over lunch. Before their meeting, Talbott spoke with Donilon again. Both made sure the conversation with Christopher would go well. Talbott thought that Christopher's position was "vulnerable but not irretrievable. I don't put it quite that bluntly to Donilon, but he figures it out and urges me not to even hint at it being that bad with Chris," Talbott noted. It was important that Christopher could save face. At the same time, it was, of course, also essential for Talbott to have a face-saving atmosphere. In the preparatory meeting with Donilon, Talbott rejected Christopher's idea to assess the latter's situation during the lunch meeting. "I urge Donilon to urge Chris not to do that, since it really puts me—and Chris—on the spot."[152] Instead, Talbott's approach was to get Christopher to work on a new State Department team and to make replacements in the second echelon.

In the end, Talbott's lunch with Christopher went as planned. In his diaries, Talbott noted how Christopher still managed to find a way to discuss his situation. "Please tell me whether you think I would be helping the President if I were to offer to remove myself?" Christopher asked, according to Talbott's notes. "I laugh, say I'd wracked my brain to figure out what incredibly gracious way he would find of putting that question to me, but I hadn't figured out that one," Talbott said. "Then I answer: no. The president is clearly worried about policy as a whole and the team as a whole, but it was clear from our conversation that he's focused on one urgency, which is defense; I say a couple of times that I think Chris' own position will depend in part—indeed in large measure—on what happens in the weeks and months to come, whether the policy and the perception of it get back on track, and whether Chris steps into a leadership position with regard to the team as well as the policy."[153] Finally, Talbott's advice for Christopher was to hire new aides with the ability to do conceptual work and people who would help present foreign policy in public.

The following weekend was full of discussions about the reshuffle of Clinton's foreign policy team. Finally, on Monday, November 8, Deputy

Secretary of State Clifton Wharton resigned. Wharton had been a Foreign Service officer, a former president of Michigan University, president of the sixty-four-campus State University of New York system, and chairman of the Rockefeller Foundation. He had broad administrative and bureaucratic experience but lacked the foreign policy background and conceptual skills needed amid the crises of the autumn of 1993. His position had been weakened by press leaks alleging that both Clinton and Christopher were not happy with Wharton, the highest-ranking African American official in the history of the State Department. Wharton's ouster was widely criticized in the media. He had not been directly involved in policymaking. His portfolio focused on the department's reorganization, the foreign aid budget, and the restructuring of the Agency of International Development.[154] Nevertheless, he had to go because Clinton and Christopher needed someone to help get foreign policy back on track.

Who could be his successor? At the time, it seemed that four candidates were under consideration. Thomas Pickering, the U.S. ambassador to Russia; Michael Armacost, the former undersecretary of state and ambassador to Japan; Rozanne Ridgway, the former assistant secretary of state for European affairs; and Morton Abramowitz, the president of the Carnegie Endowment for International Peace. Talbott's name was publicly mentioned, but his nomination seemed unlikely because he already had a key position and was performing well. Finally, however, Talbott got the job. He was on the search committee to come up with several potential candidates and recalled that "a couple of people said no, a couple of people didn't work out, and I was sort of in, not quite the same way, in the Dick Cheney position. 'Well, why don't you do it, Strobe?' So that's how I got to be deputy secretary."[155] Clinton announced his nomination on December 28, 1993.[156] Talbott's diary entries do not tell the exact story of how his appointment emerged. Clinton and Christopher may have decided that Talbott's appointment was in their best interest. Talbott was the key foreign policy broker in the administration. He was sort of a mouthpiece and a bridge between them. He was the bearer of hope and one of the key figures in the restart of Clinton's diplomacy—and he benefited from his direct access to Clinton. In November 1993, for instance, in the week after Thanksgiving, Clinton and Talbott discussed personnel issues in depth when Talbott and his family spent a weekend at Camp David at Hillary Clinton's invitation.[157]

Talbott's new job brought more responsibility. In addition to Russia policy, he was also in charge of NATO and Bosnia, the two other critical

European security issues. Talbott admitted that it seemed impossible to square all circles. "I'm afraid I agree with you about the impossibility of the job," he wrote in a January 1994 letter to William and Mary Bundy: "I might not feel that way if it weren't for Bosnia, etc., which is the only problem I/we face that strikes me as truly intractable. But I guess I now have no excuse for not facing up to it."[158] In addition, Russia's domestic crisis and Zhirinovsky's landslide victory in the Duma elections turned Talbott's nomination into a contested issue. Conservative commentators criticized Talbott's interpretation of the Cold War and his view that "the doves in the Great Debate of the past 40 years were right all along."[159] The Republicans in Congress saw him as a Russia-firster. Republican senators wanted to make sure Talbott would not be Christopher's potential successor.[160] Eventually, in February 1994, Talbott was confirmed with sixty-six votes in favor and thirty-one against.[161] Among other things, Senator Jesse Helms attacked Talbott for his criticism of Israel's settlement policy at *Time* magazine during Prime Minister Menachim Begin's tenure in the late 1970s and early 1980s.[162] In his diaries, Talbott noted that "for the first time of any length since joining the government, I am plain not having fun in my work. In fact, I'm finding this whole controversy over my anti–Begin stuff to be psychologically wrenching in the extreme. I really do find myself wondering whether it's all worth it. But obviously, I'll hang in there and try to preserve both my dignity and my career."[163]

In his new job as deputy secretary, Talbott searched for ways to reach out to Warren Christopher, who was extremely cautious and almost shy in personal meetings. In January 1994, Talbott started to send Christopher personal notes indeed for the secretary's eyes only. He sent compilations of miscellaneous notes through Christopher's secretary Liz Lineberry. The "Liz channel" facilitated a candid exchange of views without formal meetings and a predetermined agenda.[164] It gave Talbott a chance to communicate with Christopher and to explore new initiatives carefully between the two of them. Talbott wrote that "these notes from me to you will impose on me the discipline of putting my thoughts to paper, and they will give you an additional way to know where my mind is headed. That way, if there's something going on in my head that strikes you as misguided, you'll have a way of blowing the whistle."[165] Talbott also used the Liz channel to keep Christopher informed on crucial meetings taking place in Washington while the secretary was traveling. He applied it when traveling and would use it repeatedly to discuss the whole spectrum of foreign policy issues in extensive compilations. Christopher appreciated the memos. As a case in point, when Talbott sent over a thirty-four-page compilation after the summer break in August 1994, Christopher returned it with plenty of annotations and comments. "This is a brilliant memo, and it provides a wonderful way to exchange views," Christopher wrote in the margins.[166]

Talbott would rework it, incorporate Christopher's thoughts, and then share it with the key people in the State Department's leadership before it was put into the bureaucratic process. This way of working was a win-win: It gave Christopher a way to exercise leadership—in a quiet way—and it provided Talbott the opportunity to inject his ideas into the policymaking process. The private written exchange of thoughts suited Christopher's discretion and unassuming, almost shy, and low-key style. It was important for Talbott to point out that he did not see a need for Christopher to adopt a more self-aggrandizing manner or more aggressive way of operating: "I do *not* think you should spend a lot of time honing your delivery skills. I've seen some examples of politicians who have let others try to remake their public persona, and the result was artificial if not a bit goofy," Talbott wrote. Instead, as he pointed out, "where I do really think we should put more energy is the formulation of integrative concepts for our policies and in the presentation of those concepts in a way that will capture public imagination and solidify public support."[167]

CHAPTER II

Engaging Russia and Enlarging NATO

U.S.-Russian Conflicts Over NATO Enlargement

Talbott's promotion came at a crucial point against the backdrop of NATO's January 1994 summit in Brussels and Clinton's subsequent visit to Moscow. In the context of the summit, Clinton emphasized NATO's decision to enlarge in the future while the who and when and how were still unclear. A couple of days later, in Moscow, Clinton put PfP and NATO's partnership with Russia in the foreground. The challenge was to keep both tracks in sync. The NATO summit established PfP but did not set criteria or a timetable for the accession of new alliance members. Clinton's key message was that the countries of central and eastern Europe would join NATO as essential members of a transformed alliance, but not immediately. First of all, they would become partners in PfP. "While the Partnership is not membership," Clinton noted, "neither is it a permanent holding room. It changes the entire NATO dialogue so that the question is no longer whether NATO will take on new members but when and how."[1] Clinton envisaged PfP as an inclusive and incremental way to enlarge NATO and transform Europe over time. "By pushing NATO expansion this way," Clinton said, "we leave open the best possible future for Europe including a Russia that is democratic and market oriented and committed to respect the territorial integrity of its neighbors."[2] At the same time, NATO remained a collective defense organization to contain

Russia. Christopher and Talbott thought that "one of the best things about PfP was that it could go in either direction: it could lean forward to accept Russia if the 'good bear' emerges, but could also lead to a post–Cold War variant of containment to confront a post–Cold War variant of Russian expansionism."[3]

One of Talbott's tasks was adding meat to the PfP concept. This was challenging given that none of the potential new NATO partners appreciated it. The central Europeans saw PfP as a waiting room and dubbed it a "partnership for procrastination."[4] Polish, Czech, and Hungarian policymakers wanted to join NATO as soon as possible after all Solidarity, Charter 77, and the Hungarian reformers had done to facilitate the downfall of communism and the demise of the Warsaw Pact.[5] Yeltsin's problem was that PfP did not acknowledge what he believed to be Russia's special status as a great power with a vast nuclear arsenal. It did not provide Russia a pivotal role as an arbitrator in the emergence of Europe's post–Cold War order. PfP included Russia but put it in a category with all the smaller countries. Instead, Yeltsin wanted a special NATO-Russia partnership beyond assurances that Russia would be eligible to join the alliance someday. In January 1994, Andrei Kozyrev began to contemplate alternatives. He thought about a "Partnership for a United Europe" that would place NATO under the authority of the Conference on Security and Cooperation in Europe. "Essentially what Kozyrev is trying to do with his plan is dilute the primacy of NATO," Talbott wrote.[6]

In January 1994, Clinton emphasized PfP in his meetings with Yeltsin. However, American and Russian visions for Europe's future were hardly compatible. Clinton and Yeltsin talked past each other regarding NATO enlargement. Clinton planned to melt away Yeltsin's opposition to NATO's opening by emphasizing their joint achievements and the constructive spirit in U.S.-Russia relations. Clinton said that "he was committed to building structures that took account of Russia's legitimate security interests and aspirations. But Yeltsin had to be similarly sensitive to the hopes and fears of the Central Europeans."[7] Yeltsin did not object in principle but stressed that Russia wanted to be part of the process. Yeltsin's message was that all countries of the East had to be integrated into the West in one package. "If, however, you try to dismember us, accepting us and admitting us one by one—that will be no good. I'm against that; I'm absolutely opposed to it. That's why I support the president's initiative on the Partnership for Peace," Yeltsin argued.[8] Yeltsin saw PfP as an alternative to NATO's opening and was only willing to join PfP if it was conceived this way. It was a huge misunderstanding that was not clarified while Clinton was in Moscow. Although PfP's ambivalence was an advantage in bridging competing ideas in the West, its ambiguities were a problem in relations with Russia and prevented a sense of clarity about NATO's forthcoming enlargement. In response to Yeltsin's opposition, Clinton even pointed out that enlargement was still far away. "The President had just given the can another kick," Talbott noted.[9]

It seemed that Yeltsin did not want to be a supplicant, whereas Clinton did not want to tackle the issues that could hurt Yeltsin's feelings. Yeltsin did not want to ask for a fast establishment of a special security arrangement between NATO and Russia. In contrast, Clinton shied away from telling Yeltsin that NATO was about to enlarge whether Russia liked it or not. Thus both failed to clarify the future of the NATO-Russia relationship. They did not discuss how and when NATO would enlarge and who would come in. Neither did they look into the details of a new security partnership between NATO and Russia, its content, and whether Russia would be eligible for NATO membership. Both were uneasy and missed a significant chance to examine the principles and norms governing the new Euro-Atlantic security architecture. Both were hesitant to discuss the conflicting concepts for the post–Cold War order. Yeltsin could not prevent NATO's opening but wanted to have a say in the context in which it would emerge. Russian policymakers were desperate to seek ways to increase Russia's say in the new security system. It seemed that an early U.S. initiative to formalize the strategic partnership could have addressed Russia's desire to gain a broader role in Europe's security affairs. Before the summit, Kozyrev said that the Russian people were nostalgic over the loss of grandeur:

> Suspicions of the U.S. and the West are growing. We need a joint strategy for the future. NATO was a sensitive issue. Russia is grateful for the partnership for peace. Many Russians however will see it only as a half step or a short term way to postpone a decision. On the one hand, Russia as a great country will have trouble seeing itself in the waiting room with all the other supplicants competing for membership. On the other, if the future of Europe is going to be dominated from Washington or Brussels, Kozyrev said that will not be easy for the Russian people to swallow.[10]

In February 1994, in addition to the debate over NATO's opening and its new missions, the war in Bosnia again became a critical issue in U.S.-Russia relations. Frictions over Bosnia had long been in the background and escalated when the Bosnian Serbs fired a mortar shell into the Markale marketplace in Sarajevo, killing sixty-eight people and wounding another two hundred on February 5, 1994.[11] The following day, UN Secretary-General Boutros Ghali asked NATO for airstrikes.[12] In turn, NATO issued the first real ultimatum in its history, requesting the withdrawal of Serbian artillery from around Sarajevo within ten days. Heavy weapons found within a twelve-mile zone around Sarajevo would be destroyed.[13] Although the crisis was resolved without NATO air strikes, it foreshadowed future NATO-Russia tensions in the Balkans. Russian policymakers wanted to avoid an increasing NATO role in the conflict, fearing that the alliance could use its new peacekeeping efforts to exclude Russia as a major player in the region. For NATO, the war in Bosnia was a litmus test of its credibility in the post–Cold War world. Warren Christopher recalled, "as long as Bosnia was unresolved, it was a cloud that hung over our heads. . . . If NATO could not find a solution for Bosnia, then why think about enlarging it? Did NATO have a mission worth enlarging for if it could not solve Bosnia?"[14] Indeed, beyond enlargement of membership, NATO's goal was also the enlargement of its mission in the post–Cold War security environment. NATO's ability to deal with Bosnia and other instabilities was just as crucial as the enlargement of NATO membership. A bigger NATO would be meaningless if it couldn't deal with situations like Bosnia.[15] Hence, in addition to enlargement, NATO's transformation entailed the adaption of its command structures to generate multinational military forces that could be deployed at short notice with appropriate command and control arrangements. In October 1993, the adoption of the Combined Joint Task Forces at the meeting of NATO defense ministers in Travemünde was an essential step in this direction. Its concept foresaw the establishment of NATO contingency capability and a genuine European military capability that was "separable, but not separate" from NATO's existing military structures.[16]

In April 1994, NATO pulled the trigger for the first time in its history, conducting airstrikes against Serbian paramilitary forces overrunning the primarily Muslim town of Gorazde in Bosnia. The military operations were pursued due to UN Security Council action in which Russia had acquiesced. After that, Talbott briefed the North Atlantic Council.

Regarding Russia's role, he observed that "it bothers the Russians profoundly—particularly the 'number-one-Russian'—that Russia is not a member of the instrument that is applying force there—NATO."[17] In 1994, the expansion of NATO's mission bothered Russia perhaps even more than the expansion of NATO membership did. Talbott saw Milosevic's atrocities of war as a direct challenge to Europe's civilization and to NATO's credibility and even existence. The more he worked on Bosnia, the more he saw it as a reason for NATO to adapt and enlarge. This was the essence of a Talbott-Clinton phone conversation on April 24, 1994. "Undivided Europe—that's your vision," Talbott said. "There's no hope for it if we have Rwanda times ten in the middle of Europe. Since January, you've had a concept that drives the policy. Can the Bosnian Serbs be allowed to defy and defeat the greatest power on earth, the U.S., NATO, the Alliance? Run out of Gorazde on a rail? It can't happen."[18]

Talbott believed that NATO had to intervene in Bosnia, and he thought it might be possible to include Russia in a joint peacekeeping mission under PfP after the end of the Bosnian War. However, in 1994, Kozyrev refused to sign the PfP framework agreement because it put Russia in the same category as all other PfP countries. Russia sought special status, and Kozyrev said, "it is one thing if a small poodle tries to walk through these gates [joining PfP] but quite another matter when an elephant like Russia tries to do the same thing."[19] Russia wanted to join PfP on its own terms rather than as a result of persuasion by NATO. In June 1994, Kozyrev refused to sign the official PfP framework agreement, although he came to the North Atlantic Cooperation Council Summit in Brussels. Instead, he insisted on signing only a protocol and a declaration of intent to join PfP at some point in the future.[20] His aim was to achieve what he called PfP plus, a document that went beyond the ordinary PfP framework agreement and would emphasize Russia's status as a nuclear power and UN Security Council member.[21]

The summer of 1994 saw further tensions in U.S.-Russia relations as Yeltsin pursued a revisionist policy toward Georgia. The Russian army intervened in Georgia's domestic affairs when it started to deploy five battalions of peacekeeping troops via airlift in Georgia's breakaway republic of Abkhazia, backing the ethnic cleansing of Georgians.[22] In addition, Yeltsin was reluctant to withdraw forces from Estonia and Latvia until the agreed deadline of August 31. During a press conference at the G-7 summit in Naples in July 1994, he balked when asked whether Russia would withdraw its troops from the Baltics in time. "Nyet" was his answer. Vital unresolved issues pertained to the status and the treatment of Russian ethnic individuals remaining Estonian and Latvian citizens—this was a test case for ethnic Russians in other former Soviet republics. "We are not prepared to accept infringements on the rights of the Russian minorities," Yeltsin said.[23] It was clear that Russia's failure to withdraw its troops by the deadline would inflict severe damage on U.S.-Russian relations and cast a shadow over the September 1994 Clinton-Yeltsin summit in Washington, DC. Talbott discussed the issue with Kozyrev several times and warned that "hardliners in the U.S. are lying in wait for Moscow to miss the August 31 deadline so that they can pronounce the end of Russian reform."[24]

Clinton's diplomacy with Yeltsin and their upcoming September 1994 summit in Washington appeared to be the most promising way to solidify U.S.-Russia relations. Indeed, Clinton used the talks to show his appreciation for the partnership with Yeltsin. During official conversations, they discussed many issues but not NATO enlargement. Clinton followed Mamedov's advice before the summit when he said that the best thing was to "take the high road with Yeltsin and to stay clear of details."[25] Finally, on the last day of their meetings, Clinton and Yeltsin spoke about NATO enlargement in more detail. Clinton promised that U.S. policy would be guided by three premises—no surprise, no rush, and no exclusion. Yeltsin understood: It seemed that he accepted NATO enlargement as a gradual and lengthy process taking into account Russia's interests.

"My objective is to work with you and others to maximize the chances for a truly united, undivided, integrated Europe," Clinton said. "There will be an expansion of NATO, but there's no timetable yet. If we started tomorrow to include the countries that want to come in, it would still take several years until they qualified and others said 'yes.' The issue is about psychological security and a sense of importance to these countries. They're afraid of being left in a gray area or a purgatory. So we're going to move forward on this. But I'd never spring it to you," Clinton argued. Yeltsin thanked Clinton for the clarification saying, "if you're asked about this at the press conference, I'd suggest you just say that while the U.S. is for the expansion of NATO, the process will be gradual and lengthy. If you're asked if you'd exclude Russia from NATO, your answer should be no. That's all."[26]

The summit went smoothly but was another lost opportunity to clarify the details of NATO enlargement and the rationale of the NATO-Russia partnership. Both Clinton and Yeltsin were eager to focus on the commonalities and did not dare to launch a detailed discussion on contentious issues and competing interests. This was not miscommunication but instead a deliberate effort to avoid conflict. Clinton did not bring across the message that NATO enlargement was a top priority on his agenda. It backfired that the conflicting objectives were not addressed: The Clinton administration saw PfP as a waystation in the NATO enlargement process. The Russians envisaged their special relationship with NATO as a way to postpone or avoid enlargement in general. Yeltsin was still against it and not reconciled with it. Rather than debating these essential questions, Clinton and Yeltsin had deliberately avoided them again. Sir Brian Fall, the UK ambassador to Moscow, identified the gap in U.S. and Russian ideas and noted that the problem was that "the Russians thought after the NATO summit [in January 1994] that they had a deal, whereby everyone would stop talking about early NATO enlargement and concentrate on PfP. They also thought Kozyrev had secured a special relationship when he signed PfP in June. Now they find that some Americans are already talking of early work on NATO enlargement and that the special relationship with NATO consists of the right (as Marshal Shaposhnikov put it to me recently) to be informed of NATO's decisions before the Albanians are, but not to be consulted before they are taken."[27]

Meanwhile, in his new job, Talbott had difficulty focusing on managing the U.S.-Russia relationship. He was preoccupied with several urgent assignments and carried responsibility for U.S. policy toward Haiti. In June 1994, he traveled widely in Central and Latin America. He spoke separately with the presidents of Nicaragua, Guatemala, and Costa Rica and the foreign minister of Colombia to gather support for a new UN mission to ensure a peaceful transition to democracy in Haiti.[28] Domestically, Talbott supported Clinton in pursuing a more credible Haiti policy backed up by the threat of using force to impose the international community's will.[29] In the summer of 1994, the crisis in Haiti prevented Talbott from participating in the NATO ministerial meeting and the G7 summit in Naples. In September 1994, he was preoccupied with Haiti when the U.S. military intervened in the UN-authorized Operation Uphold Democracy with about twenty-five thousand military personnel. The local junta broke down, and President Jean-Bertrand Aristide was restored to power.[30] Given the expansion of his portfolio, Talbott did not manage to visit Moscow as frequently as in 1993. Throughout 1994, it seemed that his promotion did not benefit U.S.-Russia relations. Brian Fall, the British ambassador to Moscow, noted that "Talbott, who ought to be a plus, is almost invisible here following his promotion."[31]

Richard Holbrooke and the Push for NATO's Opening

In 1994, Talbott helped bring his longtime friend Richard Holbrooke back to Washington as assistant secretary of state for European affairs. Sensing that his preoccupation with Haiti kept him away from European security issues, Talbott believed that the State Department's European Bureau needed an influential leadership figure not just to push for the enlargement of NATO but also to advance its internal transformation, including the expansion of its missions so it could address new post–Cold War security challenges and end the Bosnian War.[32] During his previous tenure as the U.S. ambassador to Germany, Holbrooke became convinced about the need for NATO's rapid opening, something that he frequently discussed with Volker Rühe in Bonn.[33] Talbott needed Holbrooke in Washington to enforce President Clinton's commitment to enlarge NATO. Ronald Asmus recalled that "Talbott knew that Holbrooke was more forward leaning on NATO enlargement than he was. But he felt that Holbrooke's creativity and forcefulness were essential if the Administration was going to get it done in practice."[34] Talbott began to work on Holbrooke's return in early 1994.[35] Both had telephone conversations daily. "We assume you will be aggressive," Talbott said when he offered Holbrooke the job. "That's why we need you. We'll back you up—and you'll finally be part of our team."[36] Subsequently, Holbrooke wrote,

> Strobe and I agreed that we should try to reach a common position on NATO enlargement before I returned, and that he was perceived as its main opponent. . . . He needed no persuading that the countries of Central Europe needed the reassurance of an American commitment to their security; the issue was whether or not this could be accomplished without wrecking the U.S.-Russia relationship. By the time I returned to Washington Strobe and I had reached a common position: it was possible to bring new members into NATO, slower than the Kissingers and the Brzezinskis wanted but faster than the Pentagon and some others desired.[37]

Over time, Talbott evolved into a more outspoken advocate of NATO enlargement, whatever hesitations he had initially harbored. In an interview, he said that "he had always been in favor of NATO expansion, provided it took place gradually. 'What I was concerned about and am still concerned about now, is not whether NATO should expand, but how this should be done. In particular, how this can be done in a way that serves the larger goal of European integration,'" Talbott said.[38] His promotion to deputy secretary was one factor in the evolution of his thinking. After all, the aphorism "where you stand is where you sit" rings especially true in Washington. Talbott's intellectual broad-mindedness was a decisive factor as well. Ronald Asmus recalled that Talbott

> was not afraid to change his mind if he became convinced of the merits of another position. He intentionally recruited people with different backgrounds into his inner circle of lieutenants and encouraged debate among them, believing that the resulting tensions would produce better policy. After becoming Deputy Secretary, Talbott started contacting proponents of NATO enlargement to hear their views. In his mind, the Administration already had a right Russian strategy. But it did not have a clear European strategy, let alone the right integration of the two. Talbott wanted to find that balance. As Talbott often remarked to his staff, he wanted a policy that was "bilobal"—i.e., one that used the two lobes of the brain to integrate policy toward Europe and Russia into a common and consistent approach.[39]

Indeed, in September 1994, Talbott concluded that "an expanded NATO in an integrated Europe is not a contradiction. But keeping it from becoming one requires conceptual sophistication, deft statesmanship, consistence, patience—and disciplined interagency considerations of tactics and strategy alike."[40] Starting in September 1994, Holbrooke's task was to articulate a clear NATO enlargement rationale when the Clinton administration had not yet developed specific plans on the how and when and why of NATO enlargement except for the president's public statements. Clinton had already emphasized that NATO enlargement should not just be seen as a hedge against the potential revival of Russia's imperialism. It served a broader purpose. In an address before the Polish parliament, Clinton said that "bringing new members into NATO, as I have said many times, is no longer a question of whether, but when and how. And that expansion will not depend upon the appearance of a new threat in Europe. It will be an instrument to advance security and stability for the entire region."[41] In reaffirming the case for NATO enlargement in public, Clinton followed the advice that Lake had provided with Talbott's blessing in a July 1994 memo on NATO enlargement. At the time, Clinton did not feel a need to adopt a formal policy directive on NATO enlargement. As Asmus wrote, Sandy Berger recalled that "there are some decisions [in government] that are top-down and others that are bottom-up. This was a decision that was both. The top-down part came from the President. The fundamental concept of enlargement was something that he believed in. What came from the bottom-up were the how, the when and the what. Perhaps the reason there was not an orderly decision making process in the bureaucracy was that the President had made his decision. The President believed in this—and Tony and I believed in it, too. We did not feel the need to formalize this."[42]

Meanwhile, Secretary of Defense William Perry tried to put off specific steps toward NATO's opening, yet to no avail. In September 1994, Holbrooke won an important bureaucratic battle against Perry in the preparations for a public address that Gore gave at the first New Traditions Conference on September 9, 1994, on the occasion of the departure of the U.S. Berlin Brigade. Holbrooke wrote most of the draft for the speech emphasizing NATO's continued relevance as a hedge against a revisionist Russia and an instrument to deal with immediate security threats of instability such as Bosnia. The fight between Holbrooke and Perry was over a sentence in the speech about NATO taking the next steps toward enlargement. Holbrooke won. In his address, Gore said, "beyond Partnership for Peace and NACC [North Atlantic Cooperation Council], several countries have already expressed a desire to become full members of the alliance. We will begin our discussions on this important question this fall."[43] Rühe, who spoke next in Berlin, reaffirmed Gore's argument and stressed that "Russia cannot be integrated, neither into the European Union nor in NATO. It was wrong to pursue a policy that is determined by the highest possible degree of ambiguity."[44] Rühe criticized PfP's vague distinction between partnership and future NATO membership. He thought it did not make sense to retain the option of Russia's eventual joining NATO. Rühe's concept was to enlarge NATO swiftly and establish a strategic partnership with Russia in parallel.[45]

When Holbrooke was back in Washington, he chose his staff and chaired a newly established interagency working group on European security. At its first meeting on September 22, he picked a fight with officials from the

Pentagon over NATO enlargement. At the time, many administration officials were still reluctant to endorse it even though the president had emphasized NATO's opening as a key foreign policy objective. Holbrooke wanted to establish "a sense of inevitability" about NATO's expansion rather than put Russian concerns in the foreground. His point was that "we should not be deterred by whether a rationale for expansion can be sold to the Russians or others. They won't buy it now under any circumstances, and will try to block or delay."[46] Holbrooke chose to confront those who challenged him. When General Wesley Clark from the Joint Chiefs of Staff objected in the first meeting of the interagency group, Holbrooke emphasized that he had a direct mandate from the president. When Clark continued to raise doubts, Holbrooke accused him of disloyalty to the president. "It sounds like insubordination to me," Holbrooke said. "We need to settle this right now. Either you are on the President's program or you are not."[47] Holbrooke was in control of the subject. James Goldgeier wrote, "he was not reopening a discussion of the issue; rather, he was presenting his counterparts with a fait accompli."[48]

Holbrooke's assertiveness was essential to overcome the bureaucratic obstacles in Washington. Talbott had hired him to balance those officials eager to procrastinate NATO's opening. Talbott himself got a sense of the anti-enlargement mood in an interagency meeting on September 29, 1994, when he noted that Deputy Secretary of Defense John Deutch was

> deadset against, says U.S. military is downright mutinous on the subject, we should use [the] existing NATO and give it more of an economic/commercial thrust. . . . Sandy [Berger] is in favor of moving on NATO before the end of the first term—at least establishing a process for early admission—and Leon [Fuerth] is cautious, feeling that the problem is we've got a defensive alliance "with no enemy de jure"—we've got to keep Russia on our side, follow the Potus line on not excluding Russia and think about a special relationship between Russia and NATO when others come in.[49]

Despite an increasing sense of certainty about NATO enlargement, the Clinton administration was already contemplating concessions in the military field to offset Russia. In a September 1994 meeting with Clinton on the U.S. nuclear posture, Perry and Deutch presented a study arguing that the United States should lead the process of further nuclear reductions while hedging against a potential reversal of Russia going back on the offensive. Talbott noted that "Gore did a fascinating number of the implications of reductions in non-strategic nukes for Nato expansion, saying that if we were to expand NATO and put Euro-based nukes into new Nato member states, like Poland, 'it would drive the Russians up the wall'—and indeed, one reason that they were so neuralgic about Nato expansion itself was because it carried w/ it the prospect of U.S. nukes coming nearer their territory."[50]

At the time, Talbott thought hard about balancing the NATO and Russia tracks of Clinton's diplomacy. His concern was that the NATO enlargement track could outpace Russia's track, and this could trigger the kind of Russian suspicions that the Clinton administration was determined to avoid. Talbott's premise was to get Russia used to NATO enlargement in steps. He brought Holbrooke back to advance NATO enlargement in Washington but pleaded for more patience in how the West would get Moscow accustomed to it. From his conversations with Mamedov, Talbott concluded that "we can, if we handle the issue properly, ultimately get Russia to accept expansion. But the pace and tone and context have to be right. Otherwise, the tide could turn seriously against Yeltsin internally, with serious external ramifications as well."[51] In September 1994, Talbott shared these conclusions in a personal letter to Christopher. In it, Talbott referred to his intervention in October 1993, when he had made the case for caution and patience before Christopher's talks with Yeltsin. He thought that if NATO had adopted the fast-track approach in 1993, obtaining the trilateral deal with Ukraine, Russian cooperation on Bosnia, and Russian troop withdrawals from the Baltics would have been impossible. "I know that we as an Administration—and I personally—are vulnerable to the charge that we're letting Russia have a veto of some kind over NATO enlargement," Talbott noted. "I'm not eager to rekindle that debate. But I'm even less eager to see us slip, willy-nilly, into the opposite problem: an insufficiently well-thought-out NATO policy that jeopardizes the single most important and positive strategic trend in Europe, which is a reformist Russian foreign policy."[52]

Talbott's concern was that the NATO enlargement process could get too much ahead of everything else. He thought it was still too early to announce the formal start of NATO consultations on membership criteria and a timetable for enlargement. His priority was to add more meat to PfP and to fix NATO's internal troubles over its Bosnia policy. Talbott wanted to have a "Russia-friendly" discussion on enlargement.[53] The focus would be on the how of NATO enlargement, not the who and when. The substance and the process were pivotal, especially with regard to PfP. Talbott worried that the fast-track rationale for NATO's opening was conceived too much in terms of a hedging policy against Russia and an insurance policy against the failure of Russia's integration. "We must not think about NATO in a vacuum; we've got to look at it in the context of the other institutions and groupings that are to some extent cooperating, and to some extent vying, with each other for influence over the nature and shape of the new Europe," he argued.[54] Building the Euro-Atlantic security architecture, the Clinton administration was determined to use NATO enlargement to build security across Europe, including Russia. "We want Russia to increasingly see NATO as a partner, not an enemy," Gore said in Berlin. "We want all countries to come to view NATO as an instrument for continued stability and security on the continent, and perhaps also as a resource for dealing with problems outside the traditional framework of European security, such as peace-keeping."[55] The key idea in the new security concept was that NATO's opening, its transformation, and its evolving partnership with Russia would improve the security for all European countries, whether they were new or old NATO countries or non-NATO members. NATO would not set forth specific criteria for membership. A decision on new members would only be taken at the start of a second Clinton tenure. NATO would also abstain from discussing a specific timetable yet. In the autumn of 1994, the Clinton administration would merely start preliminary discussions in NATO capitals and aspiring NATO countries.[56] Clinton argued that "how and when we expand the alliance while (all of us in the West) manage our relations with Russia depends in part on whether we believe we can make the future markedly different from the past. Poland and Hungary and the others want to be in NATO because they believe that the impulse of Russian empire will reassert itself."[57]

The Dual Enlargement of NATO and
the European Union

In addition to NATO, the European Union was, of course, among the key institutions to shape the future of Europe. The emergence of the EU's single market and the EU's enlargement promised to create an undivided Europe.

In 1994, the EU signed accession treaties with Austria, Finland, and Sweden, which all joined in 1995. The EU had an open-door policy and pursued a gradual approach toward potential new member states. In 1993, it adopted a pre-accession strategy to bring the central and eastern European countries closer to the European Union through a structured dialogue and the promise to provide financial and infrastructural help. Each aspiring new member needed a custom-made approach. Indeed, "the old Communist bloc does not lend itself to a universal method and we must propose various solutions," Polish Prime Minister Waldemar Pawlak stressed.[58] The purpose of the EU's enlargement was to project freedom, economic welfare, and security to the East, inspiring democratic change and economic liberalization after the region's countries had suffered from communism for more than forty years. President Clinton thought that it was in the interest of the United States "to have a Community that integrates both economically and politically and also allows us to look more towards the East in avoiding the creation of new dividing lines."[59] The enlargement of NATO and the European Union promised to project military security, economic stability, and America's continued engagement as a European power.[60] The EU's enlargement was in the U.S. interest as it put the newly emerging democracies in the East on the trajectory of Western integration at a time when "the future there is uncertain."[61] The Clinton administration saw the EU as a critical partner in a globalized world. At the July 1994 U.S.-EU summit in Berlin, Clinton had lively discussions with Helmut Kohl and EU President Jacques Delors, stressing that "his full commitment to the EU as not only a fact of life but a good thing. He said that the key goal of our partnership was to see a more integrated and even more independent EU."[62]

The dual enlargement of NATO and the EU introduced a liberal security concept in post–Cold War Europe involving a new system of openness, supranationalism, and transparency in a networked world. In contrast, Russia's world was still the chessboard—and Russia's security policy was still based on the traditional concept of a hostile international environment and the assumption that the country needed a sphere of domination over its neighbors for its security. Russia was reluctant to abandon its great power ambitions for the sake of integration and partnership with the West. Moreover, the Russian side struggled to accurately imagine what Europe's future security structures would look like.[63] The Russian reluctance to deal with NATO and the European Union as institutions was permanent because Yeltsin and his advisers did not sufficiently understand their inner workings. "In part," as Clinton thought, "Yeltsin has a real concern. The Russians don't understand how everything will look 10–15 years from now."[64] Russian policymakers seemed to underestimate the swiftness and irreversibility of the European Union's enlargement process. In contrast, many in the EU underlined the urgency of its opening, given concerns about Russia's potential retrogression. In April 1994, EU Foreign Affairs Commissioner Hans den Broek told Talbott that "the EU is concerned it faces a narrow and possibly closing window of opportunity to integrate Central and Eastern European states before Russia objects."[65]

At the same time, the EU pursued a partnership strategy with Moscow. In June 1994, the EU signed a Partnership and Cooperation Agreement (PCA) with Russia at the European Council meeting in Corfu.[66] Boris Yeltsin participated in the summit with the sixteen leaders of the European Union and promised to do "everything possible to support European integration."[67] Yeltsin's idea for Russia was to participate in the economic sphere of the European Union as an equal partner. He had already emphasized this notion when the president of the European Commission, Jacques Delors, visited Moscow in 1992. "Current developments in Russia will enable integration into the European Community," Yeltsin said. "Russia belongs to Europe and the time has come to have a substantial treaty of entry of Russia into this community."[68] The PCA eventually went into effect in 1997. Under it, the EU and Russia pledged to hold two annual summit meetings. However, Moscow had a hard time dealing with the complex horizontal structures of the EU. The PCA could not bridge the conceptual gaps about the meaning of integration and partnership. The foremost reason was that Russia had a different notion of security, principles, and equality. Sweden's former prime minister Carl Bildt recalled that "when Moscow asks to be treated as 'an equal,' it effectively means that it does not want to join Europe by accepting EU principles of behavior, but that it wants to be an equal partner with whom Europe should negotiate these principles in the first instance. At the time, Russia had not yet clearly spelled this out, but the attitude was ever more present in Russia's vision of the world and began to complicate its attitudes towards Western organisations."[69]

In addition to Russia's evolving partnership with the EU and the modernized U.S-EU relationship, the Conference on Security and Cooperation in Europe was another pillar to stabilize the Euro-Atlantic security architecture. Both the late Soviet Union and the new Russia were champions of the CSCE as an all-European security organization. One of the CSCE's many strengths pertained to the fact that it was the only pan-European organization in which both Russia and the United States were members, along with all members of the EU and other European states. Hence, in parallel to NATO's transformation and its enlargement, Talbott and his colleagues from the State Department's European Bureau were determined to strengthen the CSCE—its norms were critical to Talbott's thinking about the nature of the evolving security architecture and enshrined in the Helsinki Final Act, including the principles on sovereignty, the nonuse of force, the inviolability of frontiers, the territorial integrity of states, the peaceful settlement of disputes, the noninterference in internal affairs, and the respect for human rights and fundamental freedoms such as the freedom of thought, conscience, religion or belief.[70] An additional advantage of the CSCE was the inclusion of Ukraine, the Baltic countries, and the southern tier countries such as Romania and Bulgaria, which would all not make the first round of NATO enlargement. Talbott's idea was "to make the CSCE part of a larger, inclusive, integrative context within which to lay the ground for NATO expansion."[71] In October 1994, Talbott and Mamedov agreed that the CSCE summit in Budapest in December 1994 was the ideal opportunity to launch the CSCE's expanded role. The summit transformed the CSCE into the Organization for Security and Cooperation in Europe (OSCE), including a formal secretariat, a senior council, a parliamentary assembly, a conflict prevention center, and an office for free elections.[72] Indeed, the OSCE played a substantial role in addressing violence and ethnic conflicts in the Balkans and in the former Soviet space, including in Chechnya, Nagorno-Karabakh, and Georgia. Talbott thought, "we've got to find ways to deepen its involvement in those situations and look for opportunities to engage it elsewhere, if possible in the Balkans after the dust of the current fighting settles."[73] At the same time, Talbott took note of Russian efforts to beef up the OSCE at the expense of NATO. "Russia's idea of setting up a 'security council' within CSCE is a transparent attempt to check NATO and block its expansion; everyone sees it as such and isn't buying, even those who have their own reservations about NATO."[74]

The Clinton-Yeltsin Confrontation in December 1994

Even though Clinton shared the notion of having several institutions as pillars of the Euro-Atlantic security architecture, he was hesitant to attend the CSCE summit in Budapest in December 1994. His domestic advisers were against it, arguing that Clinton would have a hard time explaining the merits of his visit domestically, especially given the situation in Congress in the aftermath of the Republican victory in the November 1994 midterm elections. On November 7, 1994, Talbott sent Clinton a note and asked him to go. "Chief," Talbott wrote, "believe me, this is an absolute, total, no-question-about-it-MUST. You gotta go. If you go, you'll do a lot of good, diplomatically and politically; if you don't, it'll cause big problems on both fronts."[75] Moreover, Yeltsin appealed to Clinton. He saw the Budapest CSCE summit as a way to solidify the U.S.-Russia partnership.[76] Neither of them anticipated that the meeting would turn into a confrontation even though its timing was problematic. It was scheduled to take place just three days after NATO's December 1994 ministerial meeting when the alliance announced its plan to spend 1995 doing a study on enlargement focusing on the "how" but not setting a timetable and not identifying potential new members.[77] The Russian side had previously agreed to all of this. Two days before the Budapest summit, Clinton reassured Yeltsin that NATO was not rushing enlargement: "I do not intend to propose a timetable or list for NATO expansion at the NAC [North Atlantic Council]. Instead, I plan to focus attention on what is involved in NATO membership—what are the requirements, and what the rationale is for a new, expanding NATO, which is not directed at any country," Clinton wrote.[78]

However, on December 1, 1994, the Russian news agency ITAR-TASS released misguided reports claiming that NATO's communique entailed new initiatives for NATO's fast enlargement. Yeltsin was furious when he heard the news in Moscow. Kozyrev was already in Brussels to officially sign the NATO-Russia framework agreement on PfP. Yeltsin called him up to inquire what was behind all of this. Kozyrev further stoked Yeltsin's anger when he complained, "I've been invited here for breakfast, but I got served a dinner instead. Maybe it was a fine meal, but it was different from the one I'd been invited for. Now partnership is subsidiary to enlargement."[79] Yeltsin was mad at Clinton. Kozyrev did not approve Russia's individual PfP program with NATO. Russia's accession to PfP was postponed yet again. The misunderstanding in Brussels cast a dark shadow on the Budapest summit.[80] On December 2, Clinton reassured Yeltsin again when he wrote a letter that reaffirmed their understanding on NATO enlargement at the September 1994 Washington summit. Clinton was upset that Yeltsin did not trust him but believed in obscure Russian media reports. "I must tell you frankly how surprised and disappointed I was of Andrei Kozyrev's action in Brussels on December 1," Clinton wrote. "At a meeting arranged at Russia's request to acknowledge your adherence to the partnership for peace and to begin a new stage in Russia's relationship with NATO, Andrei unexpectedly stated Russia's reluctance to take these steps. I would have hoped that such serious reservations could be addressed first in private," Clinton added.[81]

Given the scope of the misunderstandings piling up, it remained to be seen whether the Budapest summit could be used to mend fences. Unfortunately, Budapest was not a suitable format and not the right occasion. Clinton had a flying visit and only stayed for a couple of hours. There was not enough time for both presidents to clarify the situation. Substantially, Yeltsin's concern was not justified. Psychologically, Yeltsin feared that the Clinton administration could lose control over the speed of NATO's opening. In a December 3 letter to Clinton, Yeltsin reiterated, "we need assurances that enlargement, rather than partnership, is not being emphasized now." Yeltsin even referred to "specific obligations" and mutual "security guarantees" that he saw as a precondition for the emergence of a new NATO-Russia relationship.[82] The Budapest summit on December 5 revealed the scope of Yeltsin's anger. It also disclosed the conflicting interests about the future shape of the Euro-Atlantic security system. In Budapest, Clinton stressed that "NATO remains the bedrock of security in Europe, but its role is changing as the Continent changes. . . . No country outside will be allowed to veto expansion."[83] Yeltsin used his address in Budapest to attack Clinton: "Europe," Yeltsin said, "even before it has managed to shrug off the legacy of the Cold War, is at risk of plunging into a cold peace."[84]

Yeltsin's public assault signaled that Clinton's two-track policy was stuck for now. Talbott concluded that "quite simply, this strategy has, at least for the moment, misfired. Or, to put it more bluntly, failed. Worse, it's failed in a way that complicates next steps."[85] Yeltsin felt misled—he had always been thinking that PfP was a substitute for NATO's opening instead of a stepping stone for the enlargement of NATO membership.[86] The challenge for Clinton's foreign policy team was to repair the damage instantly. First, it was essential to figure out the underlying reasons. Second, Yeltsin wanted more precise reassurances and a strategic partnership document with NATO. Talbott's idea was that "we really ought to say that NATO expansion is unlikely before the end of the decade. This has the advantage, as Henry Kissinger might say, of being true."[87] Talbott's second suggestion for NATO was to develop a special relationship and "a special security understanding with Russia that seems the right choice down the road."[88]

After Budapest, Clinton was furious at his foreign policy team. Talbott took a lot of blame. He had been the key advocate arguing in favor of Clinton's participation. The problem was that Talbott was not able to be in Budapest. He was still assigned to work on Haiti in the aftermath of the UN-authorized invasion in September 1994. Hence he felt all the more responsible for the blowup. He thought it could end the U.S.-Russia partnership and perhaps the end of his government career. It remained unclear whether Clinton and Yeltsin could repair the damage. In his diaries, Talbott noted, "I'm probably the No. 1 idiot/villain in the eyes of quite a few people around the White House. I pulled out all the stops to get the Pres to go on this trip, and so for that reason I deserve the blame I'm getting."[89] Talbott's family backed him up. His wife Brooke and his sons Devin and Adrian were the anchors of his life.

In December 1994, when he felt discouraged after Budapest, Talbott wrote Brooke an emotional note: "I've just got to stay strong and philosophical and clear-headed about it all. I'll be able to do that in no small part cuz of you and what's going on between us. It has been one of the great joys of my life, seeing you as happy as you've been in general and as happy as you seem to be with me (in both senses of that prepositional phrase) this past couple of months." The family helped Talbott to see things in perspective. The note to Brooke was a cheerful reminder that he was "not a total goner" as Talbott put it. "I'm in great shape; I'm developing what Adrian would call a 'washboard gut;' I'm learning how to use E-mail and Windows and a mouse on my new computer; Devin and I have entered into the most terrific E-mail correspondence on virtually a daily basis; Devin got an A- on his big paper; the roof is fixed; for the first year in a decade or more, I got the Christmas tree. . . . and I've got you and you've got me and we're happier than we've ever been together. So we can figure something out that makes sense," Talbott wrote.[90]

One lesson from Budapest was that Talbott would not permit other diplomatic tasks to draw him away from the Russia account. He was determined to maintain his stewardship of the U.S.-Russia relationship to put it back on track. His work with Yuri Mamedov was crucial in this endeavor.

In a December 12 letter to Mamedov, Talbott admitted that "the NATO issue is very difficult; it doesn't lend itself to quick fixes. We may have been too clever by half to think we could do it in one fell swoop."[91] Talbott acknowledged that both sides needed more time to resolve the underlying issues.

In a December 11 memo to Christopher, he noted that the problem was "we're saying to the Russians, 'Don't worry—NATO expansion is not in any way directed against you.' But what we're really saying is not in the present declarative—it's in the future conditional: 'You don't need to worry if you stay on a reformist course; if you behave yourselves and continue to evolve in a way that suits our standards and interests, then NATO will not be directed against you. But if you go bad—if you revert to historical type—then you bet your bottom ruble its purpose will be to contain and deter you.'"[92] Talbott thought that this kind of uncertainty was perhaps inevitable as a way to square several circles. "I say that ambiguity is inescapable because the future of Russia truly is . . . uncertain, and our policy must, accordingly, be strategically flexible; we must be able to pivot from integration to containment/deterrence, depending on what sort of Russia we end up having to deal with."[93]

After Budapest, Clinton's foreign policy team searched for ways to revitalize the U.S.-Russia relationship. U.S. diplomacy was based on the assumption that Yeltsin's public "Nyet" to NATO enlargement would not be his final word. The confrontation in Budapest was perhaps not related to questions of substance in the first place. Instead, it was a sign of personal and psychological issues and lousy timing, all of which boiled over. The challenge was finding a formula for a NATO-Russia partnership parallel to NATO enlargement. The most promising way for Clinton was to abstain from public criticism. He did not want to get into a shouting match with Yeltsin. On December 12, Clinton sent Yeltsin a letter to combine criticism with renewed calls for more consultations.[94] Clinton was determined to mend fences instantly. The idea was to use the previously scheduled meeting of the Gore-Chernomyrdin Commission in Moscow.

It took place in mid-December, and Talbott joined Gore's delegation. During the flight to Moscow, Gore and his team thought about ways to elucidate the parallelism between NATO enlargement and the emergence of the NATO-Russia partnership in the forthcoming meetings with Yeltsin and Chernomyrdin. Gore's national security adviser, Leon Fuerth, came up with the metaphor of "a spacecraft docking mechanism—two huge-mass objects, under steady control, moving slowly and carefully before docking," as Talbott recalled.[95] Gore loved it and used it with Yeltsin during their meeting in the latter's room at Krylatskoye Hospital, where Yeltsin was recuperating from minor surgery. Yeltsin loved it as well. "Da, Da . . . making the docking hand motions with his hands. Simultaneous," Yeltsin said.[96] He understood the concept of gradualism. At the same time, he did not believe in the possibility of Russia's potential NATO membership. "I'll take your word for it that it's not probable, but in the process of consultations, we should seek to find the very best relationship between Russia and NATO. Our goal is an undivided Europe and we must reach it," Gore said. "Agreed, but we may not reach our goal," Yeltsin said. "Europe may break down into two blocs. What then will be Russia's relationship with NATO and Russia's relationship with the U.S.?" Gore responded that "our friendship is very important. No matter what happens, we will be interested in our partnership." This was a decisive statement. "That is very important to us. If you mean that, what you have said is very important. . . . Great, I think we can consider this behind us," Yeltsin said.[97]

Meanwhile, Talbott had two crucial meetings with Kozyrev and Yeltsin's national security adviser, Dmitry Ryurikov, to discuss the underlying reasons for Yeltsin's bitterness and betrayal. The main concern in Moscow was perhaps that the U.S.-Russia partnership was subsidiary to NATO enlargement. Ryurikov told Talbott that Yeltsin's "reaction to the NAC communique on NATO expansion was that of a businessman who has just learned that his partner has taken out a new insurance policy in case the venture fails. Yeltsin had taken personal affront at what he perceived as an uncertainty in the West—particularly in the U.S.—about Russia's reliability as a partner. . . . Now, Russia needs 'something constructive,' some way of being included in decision-making on NATO's future, because it is entitled to be included in the designing of Europe's new security architecture," Ryurikov said.[98] Talbott's task was to discuss the details of the envisaged NATO-Russia partnership with Mamedov, including its format as a charter, its consultation mechanisms, and confidence-building measures. During the talks, Talbott strongly rejected Kozyrev's idea of "full Russian 'political membership' in the North Atlantic Council a la the political G-8 [Group of Eight]."[99] In its relationship with Russia, NATO had to draw a line between membership and partnership. As a partner, Russia could not obtain a say in NATO's internal decisions, although this was precisely what Yeltsin and Kozyrev wanted. Moreover, regarding the strategic partnership document, Talbott was wondering about including security guarantees for the countries that would not make the first round of NATO enlargement, such as Ukraine and the Baltics.[100] However, such a scheme was problematic given that NATO's aspiring members in the East could interpret it as a new sort of condominium over their heads at a time when they wanted to join NATO.

The urgency of NATO enlargement loomed even more significant against the backdrop of Russia's war in Chechnya. It started on December 11, 1994, when Russian forces launched a massive ground attack on the Chechen capital, Grozny. From the outset, it was clear that the war was bound to be a setback to Russia's reform. "Yeltsin's decision to invade Chechnya represented not only a setback for democratic consolidation but in several respects resulted from the weakness of democratic institutions and forces in Russia," James Goldgeier and Michael McFaul recalled.[101] The war shocked the Russian public and the rest of the world. Policymakers in central Europe were determined to speed up NATO enlargement as a hedge against a resurgent Russia. Walesa thought that "the West must not permit a veto for Russia. Experience taught him that it did not pay off to 'appease the bear with mildness.' . . . One must not cave in in one's relations with the Russians. Rather, one had to act very decisively as the Russians would otherwise perceive one's position as a sign of weakness and would be demanding ever more. If one did not act now, Russia's opposition would even grow at a later point in time."[102] Talbott also increasingly saw NATO enlargement as an insurance policy, arguing that "our current position is based on the proposition that an expanded NATO will not be directed at Russia. Rather, its purpose will be to ensure stability in Central Europe—a goal that Russia should be able to support. Hmmmm . . . Do we really, or at least entirely, believe this? I don't think so, nor does anyone else. Certainly, the Poles and Czechs don't."[103]

The Budapest confrontation and the start of Russia's war in Chechnya led to a shift in Talbott's thinking on NATO enlargement. He noted that "Chechnya is a dreadful lapse into the habits of the past and, simultaneously, a warning of horrors that await Russia in the future unless reformist, democratic, integrationist instincts prevail in Moscow."[104] In terms of NATO enlargement, Talbott changed gear and began to switch from a patient pattern to a position of more visible and muscular support. Likewise, Clinton started to advocate NATO's opening more forcefully in public. In January 1995, the president gave an address in Cleveland emphasizing that "we want to help countries throughout Central Europe achieve stability, the stability they need to build strong democracies and to foster prosperity. . . . And we have taken the lead in preparing for the gradual, open, and inevitable expansion of NATO."[105] After the Republican landslide victory in the November 1994 midterm elections, it was important for Clinton to emphasize his commitment to voters with East European backgrounds. Hence, given its large local population with Polish origins, he deliberately chose Cleveland as a site. At the same time, Clinton countered Republican demands to end U.S. Russia aid and to impose sanctions after the start of the war in Chechnya.[106] Domestically, Clinton had a hard time. The Democrats lost control of the Senate and the House of Representatives to the Republicans for the first time in forty years. Clinton was confronted with Republican requests for tax cuts, welfare reform, and plans to reduce the size of the government, which were summed up in the proposal for a "Contract with America," mainly sponsored by Newt Gingrich, the Republic majority speaker in the House of Representatives.[107]

All of this dashed Clinton's hopes for reelection in 1996. Talbott's advice was not to bother too much about the election but to focus on the present and the need for America's global leadership in times of uncertainty. "The biggest foreign-policy challenge you've got," Talbott wrote in a note to Clinton, "is to construct a bipartisan foreign policy that will preserve the Western Alliance, preserve the U.S.-Russian partnership, preserve your prerogatives as President, keep alive your vision of the post-Cold War world."[108] Talbott's recommendation boiled down to one piece of advice:

Do not, repeat not, start running now for re-election as President in '96. Instead, BE the President who was elected in '92. Screw '96. You've got two years until then. If it helps, take it as a working premise that you'll be a one-termer. Being President of the United States of America for four years is not chopped liver. . . . You can do much for the country and the world in "only" four years. So do it! Do the most and the best you can. Let '96 take care of itself. I'm sure that this is not only good governance but good politics.[109]

Building NATO's Strategic Partnership with Russia

The year 1995 was a decisive one for Talbott. It was hard to predict whether it was possible to square the triangle, deal with Russia, push NATO to take on crisis management missions, and open the alliance to new members. Moreover, U.S. policy in 1995 geared toward upgrading the U.S.-EU track resulted in adopting the new transatlantic agenda at the EU-U.S. biannual summit in Madrid in December 1995. Clinton also nudged the EU to take steps toward its enlargement, complementing that of NATO. The consensus was that "the stability of Central and Eastern Europe depends on accession to the EU and NATO. . . . But how should we build a European security architecture," Spanish Prime Minister Felipe Gonzalez asked at the EU-U.S. summit.[110] NATO did not have good answers to the questions who will come in and when. Would the Visegrad 4 or the Visegrad 3 come in? What would be NATO's approach toward the countries that would probably not make the first round? To what extent was it possible to build a credible NATO-Russia partnership after the troubles of 1994? The bottom line was that the Clinton administration had to assume more leadership to resolve Europe's post–Cold War security issues. Four years after the end of the Cold War, European security was still a mess.[111] European policymakers knew that they needed U.S. leadership to tackle the multitude of challenges. Like Clinton, Kohl also saw an urgent need to stabilize Europe's crisis spots. "No matter what we do with Moscow," Kohl argued, "if we fail in Ukraine (and the former Yugoslavia) we are lost. . . . The situation in Europe is very vague and ambiguous."[112]

Russia's domestic situation was an enormous challenge. Yeltsin struggled domestically and drove a hard bargain in Russia's relations with the West. The Soviet Union had lost the Cold War, but the new Russia was not willing to play by the rules of the West. Russia did not follow the example of Germany and Japan, both determined to integrate themselves into the liberal order after World War II. Talbott's colleague James Collins noted, "the problem was that the Russian side didn't see it that way at all. They didn't see they lost. They saw that they got a way to get rid of the Soviet Communist system, changed their society, . . . got rid of the empire, but they expected to be a part of the decision-making process about the future."[113] Yeltsin and Kozyrev had unattainable goals. They demanded a say and a veto in NATO's decision-making process and proposed fundamental changes in NATO's core mission and identity as a collective defense organization. When Mamedov presented these ideas in a meeting in January 1995, Talbott cut him off: "Yuri, your boss is on his way to making a huge mistake. You've given us a sneak preview of a disaster movie. We've had some serious indications recently that Kozyrev is living in a dangerous dream world."[114] Russia wanted to become NATO's partner, but it insisted on having the rights of a NATO member. Russia could not prevent NATO enlargement, but Yeltsin and Kozyrev wanted to define the context in which it would happen. Talbott noted, "we're not in the business of having to compensate Russia or buy it off. Russia is not doing us a favor by allowing NATO to expand." He concluded that Russia had de facto accepted NATO enlargement in the following three to five years—but Yeltsin wanted "maximum control over the process and inclusion in the outcome. Ideally, they'd like to be in the front seat of this vehicle as it moves forward, with access to the brakes."[115]

Three weeks later, in mid-January 1995, Kozyrev ignored Talbott's warnings and approached Christopher with maximalist demands. He identified four desiderata that the Russian side wanted to address in a charter on the NATO-Russia partnership. First, the Russians wanted NATO to overcome its traditional Cold War concept of security. Second, Russia wanted to participate in NATO's consultation mechanisms and decision-making process. Third, Russia sought guarantees that there would be no expansion of NATO's military bases or nuclear deployments farther east. Fourth, Kozyrev emphasized that Russia's nervousness over NATO enlargement could be reduced if there were a chance for the Russian military to cooperate with NATO in joint collaborative projects such as sophisticated military technology.[116] A month later, Kozyrev repeated the four points in a meeting with British Foreign Minister Douglas Hurd, whose reaction was that the first one was "straightforward and achievable." The third one "should not be impossible given that there would be many in the West who would want to avoid entering new commitments to set up military bases." The fourth point was also "conceivable." Hurd said that "the most problematic was finding a procedure for consulting Russia in NATO decisions. This could clearly not be an all NATO activity. The areas covered would need to be carefully defined, and processes worked out."[117]

The underlying problem was Yeltsin's notion that the United States and Russia would meet halfway to create a new post–Cold War relationship—this was the notion behind the space docking mechanism metaphor that Fuerth and Gore used in December 1994. In fact, the United States and Russia were not equals and would not meet halfway. The United States had won the Cold War. Russia had lost it. Talbott wanted Russia to abandon its imperial dreams of empire and to instead become a more liberal and globally integrated state. Talbott thought that the space-docking mechanism metaphor was misleading. In March 1995, he came up with a new metaphor to underline the necessity for U.S. leadership and the need for Russia to follow the U.S. role model. "Fact is," Talbott noted, "we and the Soviet Union didn't meet each other halfway, and we and Russia aren't going to do so either. Russia is either coming our way, or it's not, in which case it's going to founder, as the USSR did."[118] At the same time, Talbott acknowledged that Russian leaders still had difficulty coping with the loss of the country's status as a global superpower. "What drives Kozyrev and his boss nuts about NATO expansion is that, even in its most benevolent form (eventual Russian membership), it entails their submitting to U.S. leadership."[119]

In the first half of 1995, after the Budapest confrontation, Talbott fought the notion that the relationship with Russia was exhausted. Clinton was unsure whether he should go to Moscow in May 1995 for meetings with Yeltsin on the margins of the VE (Victory in Europe) Day celebrations to commemorate the fiftieth anniversary of the end of World War II in Europe. It was doubtful whether Yeltsin could remain in power given his drinking habits and failing health. In March 1995, Christopher and Talbott assembled a few colleagues to discuss scenarios for a potential post-Yeltsin Russia. Assuming Yeltsin could stay on for a while, they thought a "constitutional muddle" was the most likely screenplay, including a weakened yet reform-oriented Yeltsin. The second most likely playbook was an "authoritarian shift" based on recentralization and the logic of a new strong center and a strong leader. The third scenario was that Yeltsin would die in office, and Chernomyrdin would succeed him. Yet the extent to which Chernomyrdin was associated with the aims of reform and integration remained to be seen. The fourth and least likely scenario was another coup. The Clinton administration had only a marginal influence on the outcome. The conclusion was that "we're playing for time . . . so that they [the

Russians] can sort this out themselves," National Security Council (NSC) Senior Russia Director Coit Blacker said.[120] Talbott fought hard for Clinton's continued engagement with Russia. In February 1995, he brought Yuri Mamedov to participate in several group meetings with Christopher, Lake, and the Clinton foreign policy team. Talbott let Mamedov make the case for continued U.S. support. "Do you have the right to lose Russian reform?" was Mamedov's fundamental question. "Yeltsins come and go, but if people like Lebed and Zhirinovsky are elected . . . then you will ask yourselves if there isn't more you could have done. The choice in 96 will be between chaos and civil war on the one hand and the continuation of reform."[121] The choice for Clinton was not so much about endorsing Yeltsin in person—it was mainly about America's support for Russia's reform trajectory in general.

Mamedov's most important request was for Clinton to accept Yeltsin's invitation to attend the May 1995 Moscow summit. Yeltsin took it for granted that Clinton would come. Yet, Clinton was undecided and eager to avoid another confrontation. He was under domestic pressure to pursue a more hard-nosed Russian policy given the war in Chechnya, the Republican midterm victory, and rising nationalism in Russia. Talbott thought canceling or threatening Clinton's trip to Moscow was not an option. Clinton had to remain engaged and proactive to maintain leverage. Talbott thought the key to success was to give Clinton the proper framework to deal with Yeltsin, who would not act according to the playbook anyway. Talbott advised Clinton to play the ball into the Russian court. Clinton had done all he could for Russia integration, "but it's up to Russia to walk through the door, to bring the right credential with it, to sit at the table; and the point of Moscow [summit] may have to be that the world sees who's at fault for the opportunity being lost," Talbott said when Clinton called him on April 20, 1995.[122] Clinton agreed. "I'm ready to do that if necessary," he said. Moreover, Clinton said he wanted Talbott at his side in Moscow—even more so as Talbott had not been available during the December 1994 confrontation in Budapest. "I'm devoting 110% of my time to making the meeting a success," Talbott said. "And if I fuck up and it's a bad meeting, you can leave me there, but I'll try to get you there and back without being sorry."[123]

Meanwhile, Yeltsin was determined to set his preconditions for the May 1995 summit. He tried to secure written guarantees on NATO enlargement by exchanging letters with Clinton.[124] His familiar concern was that an expanded NATO must not threaten Russia. Yeltsin still had difficulty acknowledging that an expanded NATO could be an advantage for Russia because it promised to project stability on Russia's Western borders. Neither did he embrace the prospects of joint peace keeping missions under PfP so far. His primary aim was to play for more time. On a positive note, Yeltsin did not repeat the four Russian desiderata of early 1995 in his letters to Clinton. Instead, he asked Clinton for a slower approach to NATO's opening, given his concern that the alliance could take new steps toward enlargement at its May 1995 ministerial meeting. Clinton was not sure whether Yeltsin thought Russia could delay NATO enlargement. It was also unclear whether Yeltsin was willing to join PfP. Clinton had to argue this out in Moscow. Meanwhile, Talbott's talks with Kozyrev signaled that the Moscow summit could go wrong if Yeltsin maintained the notion that PfP was an alternative to NATO enlargement, especially because Kozyrev was still lamenting that "you say that we can enter NATO ourselves someday, but that's not really serious either. If we were to say Russia first, that would be one thing. But we know we're last in line. That's the position we know best and hate most."[125]

Much depended on the results of Kozyrev's visit to Washington and New York in late April 1995. Initially, the omens were not good. While in Washington, Kozyrev refused to join Christopher for a private meeting to see the Republican leadership in Congress. When Christopher insisted, Kozyrev agreed reluctantly and saw the Senate Foreign Relations Committee for a coffee meeting. The whole gathering was awkward. It was a lackluster performance, and "Kozyrev arrived 20 minutes late due to allegedly abnormally bad traffic. Once seated, he assumed an invertebrate posture and spoke inaudibly so that both [Senators] Helms and Pell asked him repeatedly to speak up without much effect."[126] The Senators were appalled and concerned about the future of the U.S. relationship with Russia. Following his arrival in New York on April 24, Kozyrev played hard when Christopher called him to settle Russia's accession to PfP. Talbott was in Washington and heard the news instantly. In his diary, he noted that "the conversation could not be shittier—the ops center watch guy who monitored it told Toria [Nuland] it was the worst he'd ever heard."[127] Talbott was alarmed and went to New York to see Kozyrev. The meeting revealed that Kozyrev was still thinking Russia could delay NATO enlargement. Talbott's message was that "the expansion track would go forward unimpeded—and that it was now largely up to Russia what happened on the other track. He [Kozyrev] seemed to accept the point. While still worried about Russian domestic repercussions of expansion, he seems prepared to try to manage the problem by bringing Russia, belatedly, into the tent of PFP."[128]

Finally, despite the bad omens, the Christopher-Kozyrev meeting on April 26 went well—it even brought a tacit breakthrough: Kozyrev affirmed Yeltsin's readiness to join PfP and sign the accession protocols. NATO would use its forthcoming ministerial meeting in May 1995 to inaugurate the NATO-Russia dialogue and put fresh emphasis on PfP. It seemed that Russia was willing to accept NATO enlargement and the emergence of a strategic partnership with NATO. At the same time, Kozyrev added a note of caution. Opposition from the Russian hard-liners was continuous, fueled by public rhetoric on NATO enlargement. Kozyrev complained that "stones are falling on our heads before anything really happens; nobody has actually entered NATO yet. But there is so much talk around about the expansion of NATO and about the acceleration of that expansion that it is like an echo in a valley in the mountains that causes an avalanche." In turn, Christopher emphasized NATO enlargement as a balanced, gradual, and integrative process preserving the NATO-Russia partnership. Kozyrev was still desperate and complained about his difficult domestic position and his fights with the hawks in Moscow. "I need an ally," he said. "For this package, you have an ally at 1600 Pennsylvania Avenue," was Christopher's response.[129]

Indeed, the next day, April 27, Kozyrev went to see Clinton, who was glad to hear the good news. The Moscow summit was on. Following Kozyrev's visit to the White House, Clinton called Yeltsin to make sure they were on the same page. When Clinton spoke, his staffers realized that the communication link with Yeltsin had just broken down. Yeltsin had hung up. He was drunk and had other people at his office listening in. When the conversation resumed, Yeltsin commented vaguely that "on a preliminary basis I do agree with this, but during our personal meeting you and I can discuss it and seek some clarifications with you."[130] Kozyrev had just made all the right noises, and then Yeltsin came and put everything into question again. Talbott didn't like it, so he jumped into his car and raced to the Russian embassy to clarify things with Kozyrev. The latter shrugged.[131] Yeltsin was hesitant to seal the deal before the summit. Clinton had to argue it out.[132] In early May, the president did comprehensive preparatory work with his foreign policy team. Talbott wrote several scripts for the Moscow summit, entailing a range of scenarios and including a worst-case option. Clinton would be well prepared if Yeltsin rejected Russia's accession to PfP and if he insisted on delaying NATO enlargement. In his diaries, Talbott noted that Clinton said he wanted "to look for 'a middle course' on every possible issue"—says he's prepared to spend the plane ride going over the permutations and combinations of potential deals. "If Yeltsin is determined to look strong at my expense, then I'll have no choice but to say no to him," Clinton thought. "But my experience has been that he always comes wanting to do some sort of initiative or deal that will make us both come out okay, and I think we should be ready for that this time," Clinton added.[133]

Finally, it turned out that the Moscow summit would not be a repetition of the December 1994 Budapest fiasco. The VE Day celebrations were not too heavy on the military aspects. On May 10, 1995, Yeltsin used his first private meeting with Clinton to ask for a pause in NATO enlargement. "I see nothing but humiliation for Russia if you proceed," Yeltsin said. "How do you think it looks to us if one bloc continues to exist while the Warsaw Pact has been abolished?"[134] In response, Clinton went through the timetable of NATO enlargement and assured Yeltsin that it was a deliberate process entailing various stages. The first specific steps on NATO enlargement would only emerge in 1997 after the July 1996 Russian presidential elections. From Yeltsin's vantage point, timing was the decisive issue: He wanted to be safely reelected before NATO would take specific moves on enlargement. For Clinton, it was essential that Russia would join PfP at the May 1995 NATO ministerial meeting in Noordwijk. Clinton summed up their discussion by telling Yeltsin, "I've made it clear to you that I'll do nothing to accelerate NATO [enlargement]. I'm trying to give you now, in this conversation, the reassurance you need. But we need to be careful that neither of us appears to capitulate. For you, that means you're not going to embrace expansion; for me, it means no talk about slowing the process down, putting it on hold, or anything like that."[135]

Eventually, Clinton and Yeltsin had a deal. Russia would join PfP, and Yeltsin reaffirmed his readiness to cooperate with an enlarging NATO to conclude a new strategic partnership. However, Yeltsin did not abandon his opposition to NATO enlargement. Russia's new policy was "agreeing to disagree," as Mamedov put it. "Russia opposes NATO expansion. This is its official position, but Moscow will not make a lot of noise about expansion unless it is provoked by expansionist words or deeds from the

West."[136] Clinton's NATO-Russia policy was back on track. Talbott saw NATO enlargement as a necessity and a hedge against uncertainty, chaos, or a potential revival of authoritarianism in Russia. While in Moscow, Talbott noted, "I say that every day I ask myself if we're right about NATO+, that I think we are, that I believe our own religion, that the reason is uncertainty about what's going to happen in this place—Russia (not the Raddison 8th floor)."[137] At the same time, Clinton and Talbott thought it was important not to overemphasize the urgency of NATO's opening. Instead, for the time being, it was important to focus on PfP and the potential of a joint NATO-Russian peace mission in Bosnia once the war came to an end. In June 1995, at the Halifax G-7 summit, Clinton told Yeltsin, "one way to make people less frightened would be for the U.S. and Russian militaries to cooperate in PfP. I know you have other concerns, but I still feel that U.S.-Russian military cooperation will help people see that there's nothing to be afraid of here. That is what PFP is supposed to do. You can send your soldiers to other places—that will send the right signal. . . . It will help people see what the words like partnership and cooperation actually mean. Our soldiers can do things together. It will send a good signal."[138]

Initially, Yeltsin was very much against NATO's peace-enforcing role. He still saw the United Nations as essential to ending the Bosnia war. Aside from Russia's alignment with Yugoslavia, something more was at stake: Russia felt sidelined in the peace process and could not be an arbiter in the making of the post–Cold War order. The United States and Russia had contradicting interests in the Balkans. Talbott noted that the "U.S. sees Bosnia as way to 'save' NATO, create a vital post–Cold War mission for it. Russia fears Bosnia operation . . . as first step in NATO's dangerous transformation from a 'defensive alliance of limited post-CW importance' to an exclusive (vs. inclusive) European collective security system (w/Russia as Shirley Temple at window)."[139] Russian policymakers felt powerless when NATO pursued airstrikes against the Bosnian Serbs in Operation Deliberate Force in late August and September 1995. It involved four hundred aircraft from fifteen nations flying 3,500 sorties and dropping about one thousand bombs, most of them precision guided. Yeltsin was flatly against NATO's air strikes.[140] On September 9, Russia's ambassador in Brussels, Churkin, was instructed to point out that Russia might provide aid for the Serbs—but he did not go into further detail. This was perhaps less a threat and more a demand for Russia's continued inclusion in the search for peace.[141] The hope was that Russia would continue its cooperation with NATO over Bosnia as long as NATO consulted and integrated the Russians to the maximum extent possible.

In the autumn of 1995, Russian policymakers realized they had to respond to NATO's initiatives to maintain some control in the Balkans. Yeltsin was willing to find a way for Russia's participation in the Implementation Force (IFOR) to monitor a peace settlement in Bosnia and Herzegovina. The challenge was to do it without placing Russian troops under NATO command. Clinton's position was that NATO had to be in the lead. Eventually, the solution was a compromise under which Russian troops would be subordinated to NATO's Supreme Allied Commander Europe (SACEUR), General George Joulwan, and a Russian deputy, General Leontiy Shevtsov. Joulwan wore two hats—one as SACEUR and one as head of the U.S. forces. From a political point of view, it was important for the Russian side to ensure that Joulwan commanded their troops as a U.S. general and not as NATO SACEUR. This face-saving solution enabled Yeltsin to agree that Joulwan and Shevtsov would direct the two thousand Russian IFOR soldiers from NATO's military headquarters in Mons, Belgium.[142] Talbott was involved in the emergence of the framework for the joint peacekeeping operation in Bosnia. In the autumn of 1995, he visited Moscow several times to discuss Russia's inclusion in IFOR. Talbott was determined to frame Russia's participation not as a problem but as an opportunity to be seized. This way, Bosnia could strengthen the U.S.-Russia partnership.[143] Finally, the solution was found at the October 1995 meeting between Clinton and Yeltsin. Clinton appealed to Yeltsin at the outset: Their joint task was to prove the doubters wrong. The U.S.-Russia relationship was not exhausted. It was a personal appeal to grasp the nettle—and it worked.[144] Clinton said, "one thing . . . we should continue to do is prove the newspaper pundits wrong. They want to write about a big blowup. Let's disappoint them. We've accomplished a lot together. . . . And on Bosnia, we've worked together to achieve a peace that cannot come about unless the U.S. and Russia work together."[145]

In November 1995, the Dayton peace talks ended the Bosnian War. The NATO-led IFOR was in charge of implementing the military aspects of the agreement and took over the forces under the auspices of the United Nations. Clinton secured congressional support for deploying twenty thousand American troops as part of IFOR. NATO needed America's leadership and its military involvement. "The Alliance can no more ignore the conflagration in the Balkans than an architect can ignore a fire raging in one wing of a building on which he is working," Talbott said at the time.[146] Daniel Hamilton of the State Department's Policy Planning staff, who worked with both Talbott and Holbrooke, put it in more immediate and personal terms: "You can't build a new European home that is safe and secure if a fire is raging in the basement."[147] The Dayton peace agreement was a keystone in the evolving Euro-Atlantic security architecture. Promoting stability and democracy in crisis regions necessitated America's military involvement. In a meeting with congressional leaders in November 1995, Clinton laid out his "overall approach to the post–Cold War world saying that we should do what we can to 'give em a chance,' whether it's democratization in Haiti or peace in Bosnia; 'no guarantees,' we're like 'a mother bird pushing the little ones out of the nest.' Long after I'm gone from here, we'll know whether this approach made sense or not and whether it worked."[148]

Another important aspect of NATO's IFOR mission pertained to NATO enlargement and the inclusion of aspiring countries already acting like NATO members before even joining the alliance. Hungary, Poland, the Czech Republic, and other aspirants sent military forces and joined the peace implementation process in Bosnia and Herzegovina. Four years before Hungary joined NATO, Hungary's airbase in Taszár became the site of the IFOR base, "a breakthrough in the cooperation between NATO and aspiring non-member nations," as former Hungarian NATO Ambassador András Simonyi recalled.[149] In Bosnia and Herzegovina, NATO, the EU, and OSCE worked in mutually reinforcing ways—a visible expression of the Clinton administration's broader architectural design for Europe's security.[150] Moreover, the European Union was determined to play a stronger foreign policy role when it nominated former Swedish Prime Minister Carl Bildt as its mediator and special enjoy. Following the conclusion of the Dayton Accords, Bildt served as the first high representative for Bosnia and Herzegovina with responsibility for the implementation of Dayton's civilian aspects.[151] The OSCE also had an important role to play. It was in charge of monitoring elections and supervising democratization initiatives and confidence- and security-building arms control measures in the region.[152]

CHAPTER III

Building a New Security Architecture

NATO Enlargement as a Mutual-Gains Approach

The end of the Bosnia War was a decisive moment in the emergence of the new Euro-Atlantic security architecture. NATO's leadership in the Balkans signaled that the United States remained a European power. In a landmark 1995 *Foreign Affairs* article, Richard Holbrooke wrote that "the United States must lead in the creation of a security architecture that includes and thereby stabilizes all of Europe—the West, the former Soviet satellites of central Europe, and, most critically, Russia and the former republics of the Soviet Union. . . . Those with the ability to preserve peace have the responsibility to build lasting structures."[1] The rise of new structures still needed more time, though. Daniel Hamilton pointed out that the "Cold War architecture was static; it reflected the nature of the East-West stalemate. The new architecture, in contrast, had to be dynamic; it needed to address the open nature of the new Europe."[2] Hence NATO had to be dynamic and open as well. To establish a lasting peace, extending security guarantees to aspiring new alliance members was not enough. The key U.S. message to the nations in the East was that "stability did not come solely from external guarantees; it must be built from within."[3] The central and eastern European countries had to internalize the need to stay on the trajectory of reform and openness. They had to respect a free press, human rights, and fundamental freedoms to build democracies and stable societies. In February 1995, William Perry emphasized these principles in an address at the Wehrkunde Conference in Munich. He set forth what became known as the Perry Principles, the criteria by which NATO would judge the eligibility of new members: They had to make commitments to democracy and markets, to the sovereignty of others, to NATO's consensus decision-making, to developing interoperability in military doctrine and equipment, and to the defense of the other allies.[4]

The Clinton administration's overall objective was to "extend the Europe of institutions to the Europe of the map," as Richard Holbrooke put it.[5] Integration was the fundamental premise of building security across Europe. Working on the new security architecture necessitated a variety of diplomacies in several regions and across a multitude of issue areas. In 1995, after the end of the Bosnian War, Talbott turned to the age-old European trouble spots that still threatened to undermine the peace. He helped establish new institutions and partnerships to stabilize Ukraine, the Baltics, the Caucasus, and the southern tier of NATO. The construction job was not done yet. The whole project of building a new Europe was still in an early phase. In May 1995, Holbrooke listed the desiderata in a landmark speech before the North Atlantic Assembly in Budapest: "Even as democracy and free markets sweep the continent, armed conflict and political instability are more pervasive and severe than at any time during the past half-century," he said:

> They are concentrated in Southeastern Europe, extending to the region beyond our NATO allies, Greece and Turkey. Ottomans and Habsburgs, czars and commissars have left behind them un-resolved legacies that continue to roil the entire area. Some, such as Bosnia, Croatia, Moldova, Nagorno-Karabakh, and Chechnya, have already exploded. . . . A typical 80-year old resident of Galicia, for example, has lived under Austrian, Polish, German, Soviet, and now, Ukrainian rule without ever leaving home. She has seen the two worst wars in history and the Cold War begin in her neighborhood. Walking down the streets of her hometown of L'viv or Lvov, or Lwow, or Lemberg, she can see the past everywhere: in the marble steps of the Habsburgs, in the German names engraved on public fixtures, in the baroque church of the old Polish commonwealth, in the cracked windows of the synagogue or the courtyard of the Armenian church,

and in buildings dedicated to Hungarian merchants or adorned with Yiddish or Cyrillic inscriptions.[6]

The mission was to make sure that the children and grandchildren of the eighty-year-old from Lviv would live peacefully and in security in Ukraine. In addition to Holbrooke, his deputy and later successor John Kornblum played a vital role in conceptualizing the new Euro-Atlantic security architecture. In early 1995, Kornblum argued that

> since 1991, '92, with the end of the communist regimes in Central Europe and the collapse of the Soviet Union, Europe has been without a clearly defined security architecture. It has been in a period of considerable transition, and this has led both to conflicts—many of which were papered over under the old security architecture—and to a good deal of uncertainty among peoples, both East and West, as to what, in fact the future security relationships in Europe are to be. . . . Building a security architecture in Europe is essential to building democracy, building stable societies, and ultimately building a stable and just peace across the continent. . . . I want to stress that the approach of the United States is not to define NATO as the only aspect of the security architecture. It's an important one, a very important one, but it's not the only one. And we would never argue that you can have any kind of stable peace in Europe if you just base it on NATO.[7]

Moreover, regional security in the Black Sea area and the Caucasus were crucial issues that the Clinton administration addressed throughout the 1990s. The southeastern borderlands of NATO were an arch of crisis. Talbott knew that the unresolved regional conflicts in Moldova, Georgia, and Nagorno-Karabakh could lead to proxy wars and renewed confrontation with Russia. The Clinton administration wanted to change Russia's attitude toward its neighbors. Clinton told Georgian President Edvard Shevardnadze, "Russia cannot continue to see the future of Europe through the lenses of the past. The Russians cannot continue to believe that that they can enhance their image by dominating their neighbors like Napoleon and Hitler. Russia has such great assets—its people, talents, scientific base. It can be a great country. It must give up its pretension of empire and embrace the future."[8] The U.S. strategy involved Russia's settling regional conflicts through international institutions such as the OSCE. In Moldova's case, for instance, Talbott pushed for the withdrawal of the remaining former Soviet soldiers in discussions with Russian interlocutors, and supported the OSCE Mission to Moldova in its efforts to facilitate a lasting political settlement of the Transdniestrian conflict. Moreover, he encouraged the continuation of economic reforms in meetings with Moldova's first postcommunist president, Mircea Snegur, who oversaw the country's breakaway from the Soviet Union and its transition to independence.[9] The OSCE played a vital role in the search for a settlement of the long-standing conflict over Nagorno-Karabakh to clarify the status of the enclave, controlled by ethnic Armenians but situated within Azerbaijan. Talbott traveled to the region frequently to spur a solution within the OSCE Minsk Group, created in 1992 as an ongoing forum for negotiations to find a peaceful settlement.[10] The Clinton administration was willing to be an honest broker to find a statute of autonomy for Nagorno-Karabakh and protect Azerbaijan's territorial integrity.[11]

Moreover, Talbott worked bilaterally with Turkey and Israel to stabilize the former Soviet space.[12] He saw the reformist Turkey of the 1990s as the critical partner to project security beyond NATO's borders, including in the Middle East, the Black Sea Region, the Caucasus, and the former Soviet republics in the Caspian Sea region.[13] President Clinton advocated Turkey's accession to the European Union for several reasons. An enlarged European Union, including Turkey, promised to extend the space of freedom, prosperity, and peace beyond the traditional and narrow old Western Europe. A European Union, including Turkey, could expand the scope of its role as mediator and stabilizer in potential conflicts within the Muslim world. An enlarged EU, including Turkey, could also address security issues in the Middle East that the United States could not resolve on its own. Time and again, Talbott said that "Turkey has been a part of the European system since the 16th century."[14] In 1995, the conclusion of the partial customs agreement signaled progress in Turkey's rapprochement with the EU, and the Clinton administration worked closely with Turkish Prime Ministers Tansu Ciller and Mesut Yilmaz to spur Turkey's EU accession talks.

In April 1995, in the speech "U.S.-Turkish Leadership in the Post–Cold War World" at Bilkent University in Ankara, Talbott reiterated that "Turkey's efforts to define statehood and civil society in the post-imperial phase of its own history offer valuable lessons to other countries and particularly to those who are just now emerging from the wreckage of Soviet-style Communism, and who, therefore, now have another chance at building civil societies of their own."[15] With regard to the former Soviet space, policymakers in Ankara had a tremendous interest in opening up the traditional trade routes between the Central Asian countries and the West that promised to turn Turkey into the key marketplace of a new Silk Road that was to be created on Western terms. In March 1996, for instance, Turkey's President Süleyman Demirel told Talbott that "Turkey wants peace between Azerbaijan and Armenia. This is important not only to bolster the independence of these countries, but also to open land routes for the Central Asians to export their goods to the West and to have the West's ideals important to Central Asia."[16] Moreover, Talbott worked on resolving the long-standing tensions between Turkey and Greece in the Aegean area. The aim was for Greece to lift its veto regarding Turkey's rapprochement with the European Union.[17]

Meanwhile, Talbott went public to explain the rationale for NATO's enlargement and the transformation of its post–Cold War mission. In the summer of 1995, he wrote an important article in the *New York Review of Books* titled "Why NATO Should Grow." In it, he made a powerful argument for NATO's opening as the most promising way to build lasting peace in post–Cold War Europe. He also emphasized the need to expand NATO's mission and its new roles in peacekeeping and crisis prevention as part of NATO's post–Cold War adaption. After the Gulf War and the Bosnian War, the alliance needed to develop the political mechanisms and military capabilities to deal with violent conflicts before they would explode and turn unmanageable. Although collective defense remained NATO's critical mission, its new post–Cold War purpose was also to project stability out-of-area. "An expanded NATO is likely to extend the area in which conflicts like the one in the Balkans simply do not happen," Talbott argued.[18] He quoted Polish Defense Minister Janusz Onyszkiewicz, who recalled that "the fact is that our countries have elements like those that destroyed former Yugoslavia. We have to show our peoples that the Western way is best economically and in terms of security. NATO can help on both counts."[19] Talbott also wrote that NATO's expansion could be a hedge if Russia turned to its imperial past. "If, however, reform in Russia falters, NATO will be there to provide for the allies' collective defense." Fear about a return of Russian expansionism should not be the only reason for NATO's opening, though. "It would be far better to encourage the Central Europeans, the Russians, and the peoples of the other former Soviet states all to see NATO's enlargement as a process that can help to promote better domestic and international behavior, even as it may serve as a hedge against the worst. It should be seen as a process that benefits for everyone and is not directed against any particular state."[20]

Again, the key idea of the new security concept was that NATO's opening, its transformation, and its evolving partnership with Russia would improve the security for all European countries, whether they were new or old NATO countries or non-NATO members. NATO's enlargement and its transformation were conceived as a mutual-gains approach. In September 1995, NATO's official enlargement study emphasized that the purpose of enlargement was to "provide increased stability and security for all in the Euro-Atlantic area, without recreating dividing lines."[21] NATO's opening was not directed at Russia. Talbott thought it was essential to maintain the option of Russia's eventual accession to NATO if it fulfilled the criteria and was willing to integrate and subordinate its military into a unified command structure.[22] However, for Russia to join in the foreseeable future was not a realistic prospect. Russia did not embrace NATO's goals, nor was it willing to earn NATO membership by fulfilling essential criteria such as civilian control of the military. Talbott reiterated that it could not join because it was entitled to do so as a superpower and for geopolitical reasons. For the time being, it was essential to establish a strategic partnership between NATO and Russia without weakening NATO's cohesion and its collective defense.[23] Hence, in terms of NATO's emerging partnership with Russia, the Clinton administration defined five guiding principles to protect NATO's interests—no veto, no second-class membership, no subordination of NATO to other bodies, no dilution of or interference in the NATO command structure and no appearance of condominium or Yalta.[24] Talbott believed that a new NATO-Russia relationship could emerge from "a package of understandings that will enable Russia to adjust cooperatively to NATO enlargement. . . . We are not going to solve this problem unless we think outside of the box, and unless we're willing to question some of the orthodoxy," Talbott noted.[25] First, the Clinton administration's policy was that Russia must not be excluded a priori from NATO membership. Second, NATO was ready to establish a permanent NATO-Russian consultation mechanism. Third, NATO was willing to forgo the deployment of nuclear weapons on the territories of its new Eastern member states to accommodate Russian concerns. Fourth, NATO had to continue the process of its adaptation—its post–Cold War strategy was not directed against Russia.[26]

Yeltsin's Weakness and Russia's Old Thinking

However, Russia did not perceive NATO enlargement as a win-win situation. In January 1996, Andrei Kozyrev's dismissal and Yevgeny Primakov's appointment as Russia's new foreign minister signaled an increasing re-sovietization of Russia's foreign policy after the Communist Party victory in the December 1995 Duma elections. Primakov was a former KGB official. After the failed August 1991 coup, he served as deputy KGB chairman and director of foreign intelligence. He maintained the old KGB structures under the Russian Foreign Intelligence Service roof in the new Russia. His image as a hard-liner promised to help Yeltsin win the 1996 presidential election. Primakov was a product of Soviet training and assumed that the new Russia was in an existential conflict with the West. He was determined to constrain NATO's enlargement to reestablish Russian primacy in its near abroad.[27] Talbott sensed that it would be challenging to continue cooperation with Primakov, whose definition of the term *partnership* differed from the U.S. concept. Talbott noted that "for him, the underlying dynamic of relations between states was competitive, and the bigger the states, the more competitive. The principal requirement for peace and stability was a balance of power. . . . It meant the power of the states as manifest in military, political, and economic leverage over others."[28] Primakov still fought NATO enlargement. He wanted Russia to get a say in the overall context in which it evolved. He aimed to limit the military dimension of enlargement to pull NATO's military teeth as a collective defense organization. Primakov fought NATO's open-door approach and attempted to project red lines to prevent NATO accession to Ukraine and the Baltics. All of this was not acceptable to the alliance. After all, the rationale for enlargement was to give the states of the East a chance to become members of the liberal institutions that helped the Western part of Europe to prosper during the Cold War, whereas the East suffered from Soviet domination.[29]

Again, Talbott was challenged with the task of squaring circles. How could Clinton pursue a NATO-Russia partnership while maintaining

NATO's interests and its military posture? In mid–July 1996, Talbott finalized the Clinton administration's framework concept on NATO's opening, its transformation, and its evolving partnership with Russia. He wanted to get Primakov's reaction on all issue areas, including nuclear weapons and military infrastructure in NATO's new member states, new structures, old or existing institutions, the question of a formal treaty, Russia as a potential NATO applicant, NATO's adaptation, others such as the Baltics and Ukraine, and cooperative and consultative steps outside NATO.[30] From Russia's perspective, the first two issue areas were crucial. Primakov wanted a formal treaty entailing a ban on nuclear weapons and military infrastructure on the territories of NATO's new member states. The U.S. position was clear. A permanent, formal ban was not an option. There could only be one class of NATO membership. "We're not going to discriminate against new members or undermine the fundamentals of the Alliance," Talbott said. Primakov was in a combative mood. "Enough of this fantasy or game about only one class of membership. You know perfectly well there are several classes. Norway has no troops or nuclear weapons; there are no troops in the eastern part of Germany; America is in first class along with Britain and France; there can be at least three classes in this airplane," Primakov argued.[31] Another contentious point pertained to the eligibility of Ukraine and the Baltics for NATO membership. Primakov was determined to draw red lines and said, "this is a special and emotional problem. In reality, it is not acceptable to us that NATO is open to everyone." Talbott countered this right away. "If by 'red line' you mean that you're not prepared to accept the Baltic states' and Ukraine's eligibility for NATO membership in the future, then we've got a collision of red lines, yours and ours. We'll be at an impasse if not in a train wreck. In other words, one of our red lines is now and will continue to be that no country is going to be ruled out of eligibility, certainly not by some other country."[32]

Talbott was increasingly concerned about the hardening of attitudes in Moscow. Yeltsin was in a reelection campaign and unsure whether he could prevail in the race with his communist contender, Gennady Zyuganov. Talbott thought it would be counterproductive for Clinton to support Yeltsin too visibly. In times of crisis, the communists and nationalists in Russia would portray Clinton's endorsement as interference in Russian domestic affairs. Talbott thought that Clinton and Gore were too much out there backing Yeltsin at a time when his political and medical prospects were not good at all. Talbott assumed that the U.S. approach should not be about

Yeltsin's reelection but about the fate of Russia's democracy over the long term. The Bill-and-Boris relationship could backfire if a Yeltsin election defeat were seen as Clinton's loss. As a case in point, after Clinton's phone conversation with Yeltsin on February 21, 1996, rumors spread that Clinton had allegedly said, "I love that guy" after they rang off. Talbott noted, "if it gets out, this will be the '96 equivalent of Carter's giving Brezhnev a big kiss in Vienna."[33] Talbott's advice was that Clinton "should help Yeltsin without embracing him, that we've got to steer a course using the limited influence we have to help him get re-elected but not engagement or outright endorsement which could be counterproductive for Yeltsin and for Potus if Zyuganov wins—don't want a Yeltsin defeat to be a Clinton defeat."[34]

In the spring of 1996, Yeltsin was battered domestically. In April 1996, given his precarious position, Yeltsin wanted Talbott to come to Moscow to prepare for Clinton's forthcoming visit. The normal diplomatic procedure would have been an invitation from Primakov to Christopher. Yet Yeltsin sensed that Talbott was the best communication channel with Clinton.[35] Yeltsin wanted to have a candid conversation. In the April 12 meeting with Talbott, Yeltsin spoke freely, improvised expansively, and launched into a one-hour monologue on Russia's status as a great power. This was a weakened Yeltsin who yearned for support and recognition. Yeltsin beamed that Russia was on the rise again. "I don't like it when the U.S. flaunts its superiority," he said. "Russia's difficulties are only temporary, and not only because we have nuclear weapons, but also because of our economy, our culture, our spiritual strength—all of that amounts to a legitimate, undeniable basis for equal treatment."[36] When Talbott entered Yeltsin's office, he noticed it had been richly redecorated with statues of Peter the Great, Catherine the Great, and Alexander II. Talbott recalled that "this pantheon of predecessors not only served as a reminder of the scope and complexity of Russia's past but also as a hint of the wide range of options for its future: there was Peter the Original Westernizer, Alexander the Liberator of the Serfs (and the Seller of Alaska to the U.S.) and Catherine the Conqueror of the Near Abroad."[37]

Yeltsin was searching for ways to combine several options. He saw Russia as a superpower and wanted "equality" with the United States and a combination of global economic integration and dominance in the former Soviet space. In a Freudian slip, Yeltsin referred to the newly independent countries as "our republics." Yeltsin's position was clear: This was Russia's space. He wanted the United States to stay out of Russia's sphere. From Yeltsin's vantage point, U.S. relations with the newly independent states amounted to espionage and foreign interference:

> We know both sides are continuing espionage against each other. . . . But we know you are also going around to all our neighbors trying to talk them out of integration with Russia. You're conducting political agitation, telling them not to cozy up to Russia. You're telling them we have bad intentions, that we're still the evil empire. This is what they—the leaders of our republics (he corrects himself) I mean the leaders of these sovereign states—tell us about you . . . You're trying to pull them into your sphere of influence. . . . We don't try to counteract your influence with Mexico or with Canada or with the EU. . . . So why do you conduct these operations all around us to create a belt around Russia? Besides, it won't work. We're drawing closer all the time. We will integrate faster than you could agitate against it.[38]

At the end of his conversation with Talbott, Yeltsin was pushing for full Russian membership in the G-7, something that Clinton was willing to discuss only after the Russian elections as he was determined to avoid the risk of having a communist President Zyuganov as a participant.[39] Moreover, the G-7 countries' finance ministries opposed Russia's inclusion because its economy was too small. They won the day, so a compromise emerged to split the political and economic elements of Russia's accession to the G-7—the solution was to have a political G-8 but an economic G-7. "There are certain economic decisions we may have to take that they can't be part of yet," Clinton thought.[40] Yeltsin was impatient and saw the Clinton administration's hesitancy as an insult. "This formulation 'G-7 plus one' is insulting," Yeltsin said. "Why is Clinton so scared of admitting Russia to the 'Eight?' . . . We don't need to rehearse any more. We're ready for the real thing."[41]

Later, in April 1996, Clinton went to Moscow to counter the anti-Western feelings and resentment that Primakov was stirring up as Yeltsin's critical foreign policy spokesperson. Clinton's April 1996 visit was crucial in yet another respect: It was the first time Clinton and Talbott were confronted with Vladimir Putin—without even knowing it. What happened? On April 19, Clinton was in St. Petersburg. He had an emotional visit to the Piskaryevskoye Memorial Cemetery, where he paid tribute to the more than five hundred thousand Russian soldiers and civilians who died during the nine-hundred-day Nazi siege of the city then called Leningrad during World War II. After he visited the cemetery, Clinton toured the famous Hermitage Museum. He visited the Cathedral of Our Lady of Kazan, which had been used as the Museum of Atheism and Religion during communist rule. It was a fantastic and emotional program.

However, Clinton did not have a chance to interact with the people of St. Petersburg.[42] In his diaries, Talbott noted that Clinton was "very pissed off . . . aboard the plane as we left St. Petersburg." In front of his advisers and staffers, Clinton said, "that was a good stop, a good visit, but I gotta tell you, I'm really upset about something, and that is that I didn't see jack shit in terms of real people; they keep me in a goddamn caccoon [*sic*]."[43] Indeed, Clinton did not have any real contact with people. After the visit, Talbott learned that Vladimir Putin had been behind this. At the time, Putin was deputy mayor in St. Petersburg. He worked for the reform-oriented Mayor Anatoly Sobchak, who greeted Clinton warmly, picked him up at the airport, and shepherded him through St. Petersburg. However, Putin had his agenda and managed to keep Clinton from mingling with the people on-site. In an interview with PBS in 2017, Talbott reminisced that this was the first time he heard Putin's name. Talbott recalled the visit in great detail and said, "there was a meal in a dungeon-like restaurant, with no windows and that kind of a thing. He was basically kept away from the people."[44] The following day, April 20, Clinton was still upset when heading toward his meetings with Yeltsin in Moscow. Clinton was venting his anger during the car ride from the hotel to the meeting site. "I could tell looking out the window that there was a lot of alienation, a lot of anti-American feeling there. A lot of those people were giving me the finger. I might as well have been a visiting king or something. It's what they used to get from their czars and their communist big shots. I really hate not being able to get out and move around."[45]

Meanwhile, the first round of the Russian presidential elections was approaching on June 16, 1996. By mid-May, Yeltsin was still behind Zyuganov in the polls. The good news was that he was catching up. The danger was that Yeltsin could be tempted to cancel or postpone the election to stay in power. Talbott did not think the Clinton administration could tolerate Yeltsin taking extraconstitutional measures to keep Zyuganov out of office. On June 5, 1996, when this option was discussed among Clinton's key Russia advisers, Talbott strongly criticized it. "We would have to take a very tough line, no business as usual; we'd have to put Yeltsin in the same category as a Soviet leader under those circumstances since he would have trammeled democracy which was core to reform."[46] Eventually, the results of the first round were encouraging. Yeltsin won but did not break the 50 percent barrier. Finally, Clinton and Talbott were relieved about Yeltsin's victory in the second round in July 1996. However, it was unclear to which extent a frail Yeltsin would be able actually to govern in a second term.

Russia's partnership with the West could be the target of increasing domestic opposition. Yeltsin was not at all in an enthusiastic state of mind when Clinton called to congratulate him. He had to take a few weeks off after the inauguration on August 9. He seemed tired and depressed. The campaign had taken its toll. He was perhaps more exhausted than ever before.[47] From Talbott's perspective, Yeltsin was the key in terms of continuity. He thought that "Yeltsin's re-election was a very big deal, comparable in importance to the end of the USSR in '91," he argued in a personal note to Clinton on July 9, 1996. Moreover, he used the letter to review Clinton's previous four years on his side briefly:

> Chief, just a short note, out of channels, to tell you how immensely proud I am to have had a chance to work with you on Russia over the last three-plus years. . . . While it was essentially the Russians' doing—and Yeltsin's—we played our part, and you played yours in a way that will earn you a special place in the history of the end of the Cold War. . . . Anyway, Chief, while you've let me branch out a bit, you originally brought me into your Administration to help you work this whole cluster of problems and opportunities, and, boy, has it been great.[48]

Initial Struggles over the NATO-Russia Charter

The initial debates over the NATO-Russia charter signaled that U.S.-Russia relations would turn rougher and more contested in a second Clinton term. Talbott thought that Russia's search for identity and purpose would concern the United States for a long time. In a May 1996 speech at Amherst, Talbott argued that "in its new, post-Soviet phase, Russia will

Figure 3.1 Talbott's grandfather, Nelson "Bud" Talbott, was captain of the Yale University football team (1913–15). Courtesy of Strobe Talbott.

Figure 3.2 Three generations of Talbotts—with his father, Nelson Talbott Jr., and his grandfather, Nelson Talbott. Courtesy of Strobe Talbott.

Figure 3.3 Strobe as a toddler with his mother, Josephine Talbott. Courtesy of Strobe Talbott.

Figure 3.4 Strobe and Brooke on their wedding day with Talbott's parents and his siblings Marjo, Page, and Kirk. Courtesy of Strobe Talbott.

post a major challenge to U.S. foreign policy for at least another half-century. It's going to take at least that long for the Russian people to work their way through the fundamental questions they face over what kind of nation they want to be now that they've decided, to their immense credit, that they do not want to be a tyranny, isolated and backward, at odds with much of the rest of the world."[49] Talbott anticipated that Russia's internal struggles and the revival of imperialist elements in its foreign policy would complicate its relationship with the West for decades.[50] Moreover, Talbott knew that the diplomacy on the NATO-Russia charter was another litmus test about Russia's willingness to cooperate. Pitfalls were numerous. In terms of substance, Primakov maintained the three conditions that would

Figure 3.5 Strobe Talbott and his housemates Bill Clinton and Frank Aller during their Rhodes scholarship at Oxford. Courtesy of Strobe Talbott.

Figure 3.6 Strobe, Brooke, Devin, Adrian. Courtesy of Strobe Talbott.

Figure 3.7 At *Time* magazine. Courtesy of Strobe Talbott.

Figure 3.8 Talbott and his extended family on a joint vacation, Galapagos Islands, 1998. Courtesy of Strobe Talbott.

Figure 3.9 Strobe Talbott and Barbara Ascher at their wedding in New York City, 2015. Courtesy of Strobe Talbott.

make NATO enlargement acceptable to Russia: a binding prohibition of nuclear weapons deployments on the territory of new NATO member states, a requirement for co-decision-making between Russia and NATO on European security issues, and a codification of these provisions in a legally binding treaty. NATO could not accept any of these and was willing to enlarge without the conclusion of a NATO-Russia charter. Russia's main aims were twofold—namely, to forestall a substantial expansion of NATO's military structure in the East and to keep Ukraine from eligibility for NATO membership. Privately, Mamedov even went so far as to argue that Russia could redeploy nuclear weapons in Belarus if Ukraine became a NATO member. "We would see Ukraine in NATO as a grave threat and something which is vital to our national security. . . . I understand that 'theoretically' no one is banned. Our position: Ukraine in NATO is a great threat to our national interests. On others, like Belarus, we just haven't thought about it. Mostly what could happen would be reactions to NATO expansion as we change our own nuclear posture, perhaps returning nukes to Byelorussia."[51]

Given the clashing positions, it seemed almost impossible to achieve a NATO-Russia charter. Russia applied the traditional Soviet approach to raising maximalist demands at the start of a negotiation. In August 1996, Talbott warned Mamedov, "if we don't get NATO-Russia right, there will be a distinct 'chill' in the bilateral relationship over the next years, and perhaps longer."[52] The situation improved in September 1996 when Mamedov gave Talbott a three-part paper emphasizing that NATO and Russia were no longer enemies but partners. Part 2 of the paper pertained to decision-making processes and included the idea of a consultative mechanism that would not give Russia a veto but a voice. "This is not meant to gain a Russian veto over decisions the NAC may take. Russia is not a member. But NATO itself should want to have Russian views before it decides. It's what we do now ad hoc, but this would be an established mechanism," Mamedov said. Part 3 of the paper dealt with specific measures of military restraint, confidence building, and transparency. Talbott's reaction was positive: "In general, what you have said about the charter seems to be in the same universe as our own thinking."[53]

Meanwhile, the Clinton administration was determined to move forward with NATO enlargement in Clinton's second term. In October 1996, Clinton used a key foreign policy speech in Hamtramck, Michigan, to sketch the next steps in NATO's opening. The first of NATO's partners should become "full-fledged members of NATO" by NATO's fiftieth anniversary summit in April 1999. "NATO must . . . take in new members, including those from among its former adversaries," Clinton said. "It must reach out to all the new democracies in Central Europe, the Baltics, and the New Independent States of the former Soviet Union."[54] Moreover, Clinton announced that NATO would name the first group of new members in 1997. The president's remarks conveyed his concept of the broader Euro-Atlantic security architecture that Warren Christopher laid out in a speech in Stuttgart in September 1996 when he proposed a specific timetable for NATO enlargement, a formal NATO-Russia charter, the addition of a political dimension to PfP, an adaption of the existing Conventional Forces in Europe (CFE) Treaty provisions, an enhanced Ukraine-NATO partnership and a free and open transatlantic marketplace. Daniel Hamilton recalled that Christopher's address in Stuttgart was envisaged "to reinforce the architectural design and chart a roadmap for advancing each element for Clinton's second term. . . . The Stuttgart speech updated and expanded upon the architectural framework first introduced by Richard Holbrooke in his *Foreign Affairs* article almost two years earlier."[55]

In Stuttgart, Christopher sketched out a vision for a New Atlantic Community. "This community," he said, "will build on the institutions our predecessors created, but it will transcend the artificial boundaries of Cold War Europe. It will give North America a deeper partnership with a broader, more integrated Europe on this continent and around the world."[56] Although NATO and the European Union were the key pillars, the vision included Russia as a full partner. "In this Community," Christopher said, "NATO will remain the central pillar of our security engagement. It will be a new NATO, adapted to meet emerging challenges, with the full participation of all current Allies and several new members from the east. NATO's Partnership for Peace and the OSCE will give us the tools to prevent conflict and assure freedom for all of our citizens. In our vision for this new Atlantic Community, a democratic Russia will be our full partner."[57]

However, the Russian side, especially the Russian military, used the negotiations to adapt the CFE Treaty to avoid further NATO enlargement rounds. The treaty was concluded in 1990 to create a new military balance between NATO and the Warsaw Pact. It established comprehensive and legally binding limits on key categories of conventional military equipment in Europe and destroyed excess weaponry, especially in Russia.[58]

Russian policymakers wanted to keep the old CFE limits negotiated before the Warsaw Pact's collapse when NATO was still an alliance of sixteen. The Russian aim was to constrain the military dimension of NATO enlargement and avoid equipment deployment in NATO's new member states. Talbott recalled that "in practice, the Russian proposal would have the effect of limiting enlargement to one wave, since a second wave, to say nothing of a third, could cause NATO's head to bang up against the 1991 ceiling."[59] NATO's objective was CFE adaption and establishing sixteen national ceilings that could be reviewed and adapted in the future. As a concession, the Clinton administration was ready to provide legally binding constraints that would make it impossible for NATO to amass forces in central Europe. This was not enough for the Russian side, though.

Primakov and new Russian Defense Minister Igor Rodionov were determined to ban NATO from deploying Western troops and equipment in its new member states—and they wanted to obtain legally binding agreements demanding parliamentary ratification in all NATO states. Even Mamedov suggested backward-looking schemes such as establishing three zones under a new CFE Treaty—the former USSR, Warsaw Pact countries, and NATO. This was, of course, a blatant attempt to discriminate against NATO's aspiring new members. Talbott was upset.

> I gotta tell ya, Yuri, if it weren't so serious, I'd laugh at this one. This is my personal candidate for an Academy Award (or maybe I should say, Grammy) for Killer Proposal of the Year. . . . It's as though some genius in your system had been assigned the task of designing a proposal guaranteed not only to stymie the negotiations forever—but to piss off absolutely everyone, and frighten a whole lot of folks I would have thought you were trying to reassure. The proposal is grotesquely backward looking: it's based on the idea of perpetuating past categories and divisions. What we need to do is exactly the opposite—look ahead and address existing and prospective concerns.[60]

All of this indicated that Russia was trying to slow down, torpedo, or prevent NATO enlargement in the years to come. Especially Primakov rejected the open and liberal security concept that Christopher presented in his address in Stuttgart. He still thought in spheres of influence and fought the interconnected and open Europe and the involvement of NATO as the crucial pillar. Time and again, he was hinting that the Russian side might be better off without the conclusion of a NATO-Russia charter. He might wait until after NATO enlargement and conclude arrangements with individual NATO allies instead. Talbott wrote, "it was gruesomely clear that Primakov will not give up in his efforts to slow down or, if he can, stop enlargement, or, failing that, to impose on its military dimension constraints that would violate several of our red lines . . . Primakov will lie, cheat, weasel, double-deal right down to the end."[61] The good thing was that Primakov did not shut down the Talbott-Mamedov channel. This was a real possibility. Talbott himself proposed to close it twice. In September 1996, Primakov was willing to retain it, and Talbott thought, "there's now just enough gas in this vehicle to get us down the road six or seven weeks. That gives us enough time to have several more exchanges of non-papers. It also gets us past our elections."[62] Talbott anticipated further trouble down the road. The schedule for NATO enlargement would be contested. Russia would pressure France and Germany against a firm decision on enlargement in 1997. Talbott was cautious and held his cards close to his vest in his contacts with the Russian negotiators. In September 1996, he did not share the latest U.S. draft of the NATO-Russia charter with Mamedov—Primakov might use it to undermine NATO solidarity.[63]

Bilateral U.S.-Russia meetings grew contentious. In September 1996, the Christopher-Primakov discussions at the UN General Assembly produced new tensions. Primakov rejected the evolution of parallel tracks on the NATO-Russia charter and NATO enlargement. He also came down hard against the Clinton administration's scheme for the transformation of Euro-Atlantic security architecture, which Talbott illustrated when he took a piece of paper and drew four lines symbolizing NATO enlargement, NATO's internal transformation, NATO-Russia, and the CFE Treaty moving forward in parallel. He drew another line symbolizing Russia's intention to stop or slow down enlargement. Talbott then turned to Primakov and said, "We have a four-letter word for what this would amount to—veto." Primakov lost his temper: "You want to expand NATO and tell us that nothing we do or think or say will have any effect on your plans. Yet, you also accuse me of wanting to veto it. Are you playing us for fools?" Eventually, Primakov consented to further discussions on the NATO-Russia charter: "Okay, let's go back to square one: You can't let go of NATO expansion and we can't agree to support it in advance and then applaud it when it happens. That's not a veto. We realize we have no veto power. . . .

But that does not mean we have to agree to a scheme that merely provides cover for NATO to expand."[64]

Yeltsin's reelection and Primakov's approach signaled that Russia might return to an increasing sovietization of its foreign policy. The risk of regression was still considerable, given the daily economic hardship of ordinary Russians and the country's painful economic transition. The war in Chechnya and Zyuganov's strong results in the 1996 presidential election were proof enough. Talbott anticipated that Russia's turmoil would directly affect the sovereignty and territorial integrity of Ukraine, the Baltics, and the rest of the newly independent states. Their fate largely depended on the future of Russia's reform trajectory. Talbott did not take it for granted that Russia would accept the sovereignty of its neighbors over the long term. He anticipated that Russian policymakers might be tempted to revive Russia's imperial nostalgia and the desire to restore its great-power status at the expense of its neighbors. He noted that "a major problem facing all the NIS and the Baltics . . . is uncertainty over the post-Soviet definition of statehood. Borders, citizenship, the prerogatives and limitations of central government, 'commonwealth'—these are all the objects of doubt and dispute within the NIS; they are subject to the competing forces of secessionism, chauvinism and irredentism on the one hand and, on the other, multiethnic democracy, civil society and integration."[65]

NATO Enlargement and the Have Nots: Ukraine and the Baltics

Hence, in addition to enlargement, Talbott was determined to improve the security of those who would not make NATO's first enlargement round, including Ukraine and the Baltics. They wanted to join NATO and the EU to be safe from Russia's neo-imperial ambitions. Their fate was a significant question of European security. Many in the West were reluctant "to extend the Europe of the institutions to the Europe of the map," as Richard Holbrooke put it in his May 1995 address in Budapest. Many thought doing one NATO enlargement round, including Poland, the Czech Republic, and Hungary, was enough. Talbott thought bigger and strategically and believed that the Baltics and Ukraine had a right to join NATO in the future, especially because they were increasingly vulnerable to Russia's political and economic pressure. Russian opposition to their NATO membership increased the urgency for new Western partnerships with the Baltics and Ukraine. Talbott was determined to build new regional security frameworks that would include Russia as well. As Ronald Asmus and Stephen Larrabee put it in a 1996 *Foreign Affairs* article—"The way to accommodate Russia is not for NATO to undercut its principles and offer to compromise on who is in and who is not. Instead, NATO must go the extra mile and offer Russia its own, more attractive relationship with the alliance."[66]

The same was true about the evolving relationship between NATO and Ukraine at a time when the country's sovereignty was contested.[67] The peaceful disintegration of the Soviet Union overshadowed the fact that Russia was never really willing to accept Ukraine's independence. The essential question pertained to Russia's borders. Where did Russia end? Where did Ukraine's territory begin? Russian leaders began to question Ukraine's sovereignty over Crimea and Sevastopol as the host location of Russia's Black Sea Fleet. In 1997, Richard Pipes warned that "a modified Brezhnev Doctrine was still in force. . . . Russia's claim to be a world power has traditionally rested on military prowess, and the temptation is to resort to this expedient once again."[68] Russia used the newly established Commonwealth of Independent States to exercise influence and control over the countries in its near abroad. The new Russia was not content with the Soviet Union's disintegration. "In the former Soviet space Russia is not a status quo power but a revisionist one. The argument in Russia is how to revise the post-1991 status quo, not whether to revise it," wrote James Sherr in a foresighted 1997 paper.[69]

Ukraine was a potential theater for a renewed cold war between Russia and the West. In the early 1990s, Western policymakers were not enthusiastic about the breakup of the Soviet Union and preferred stability over change in the former Soviet space. Ukraine was mainly seen as a nuclear proliferation problem that was resolved after the conclusion of the 1994 trilateral agreements and the country's accession to the Non-Proliferation Treaty. After that, Western attention was mainly focused on Russia and the Visegrad 3, which were supposed to enter NATO in the first enlargement round. Ukraine was somewhere in between, and the country struggled to find a place in the Euro-Atlantic security architecture and establish closer relations with NATO and the European Union without annoying Russia. In October 1994, Ukrainian Deputy Foreign Minister Boris Tarasyuk approached Talbott with an inquiry about Ukraine's future place in the new order. "Would Ukraine be consigned to a no-man's land or a gray zone of insecurity?" Tarasyuk asked.[70] Talbott did not have a ready response but emphasized that the Clinton administration would respond to Ukraine's pledge for security.

In October 1993, when NATO enlargement emerged on the agenda, Talbott had already considered establishing a special relationship with Ukraine to provide security assurances in return for Ukraine's nuclear disarmament.[71] Ukrainian Foreign Minister Udovenko pushed the idea in September 1995, arguing that Ukraine should be eligible for a special relationship with NATO when he said that "it is unilaterally surrendering nuclear weapons, it meets several requirements for NATO membership, and in the absence of close ties to NATO would be pushed into the Russian sphere of influence."[72] However, even Russia's reformers were uneasy about Ukraine's sovereignty. The liberal Andrei Kozyrev thought that, in a sociocultural sense, "we can't deal with Ukraine as a totally independent state." In an April 1995 meeting with Christopher, Kozyrev referred to Ukraine, Belarus, Uzbekistan, and Kazakhstan, saying "these aren't 'real' independent states at all." "As examples," Talbott noted, "he refers to Karimov having kids in Moscow, coming there frequently; Nazarbayev having family and friends there; Zlenko, the f.m. of Ukraine coming to Moscow frequently to see family—and how it would be a 'casus belli' if Kozyrev had to receive him according to ministerial protocol every time Zlenko came; how there are family, economic and other ties interknitting all the former republics."[73] The recurring argument was that Russia could not let its neighbors go and establish closer relations with the West. Even Yeltsin and Kozyrev used the Commonwealth of Independent States as a fortress and a way to keep the thumb on them.[74]

Ukraine was in a sandwich between Russia and the West, and the only feasible way to increase its elbow room was a gradual approach. Ukraine used PfP and its peacekeeping activities in Bosnia to gain time to expand its relations with NATO. Meanwhile, the country retained its nonaligned status for years to come so as not to provoke Russian pressure—Foreign Minister Udovenko argued that "a request by Ukraine to join NATO would not be in the interest of Ukraine, Russia, or the U.S."[75] However, in private, many among the younger and pro-Western-oriented Ukrainian diplomats confessed their ambitions for Ukraine to join NATO. In March 1995, for instance, Tarasyuk said, "no matter what we say publicly, I can tell you that we absolutely want to join NATO."[76] It took some more time until the Ukrainian Foreign Ministry officially argued in favor of NATO membership at a point in time when NATO began to formulate the timetable for enlargement in 1996. Knowing that the first round of NATO's opening would merely include the Visegrad countries, Ukrainian policymakers felt pressure to shift gears and establish closer ties with the alliance. In September 1996, Ukraine and the United States signed a strategic partnership document and established the Gore-Kuchma Commission to solidify the bilateral relationship. In a letter to Christopher, Udovenko summed up Ukraine's desire to join the expanded institutions of the West: "Ukraine, as a great European state and integral part of European civilization, has clearly and unambiguously favored full integration into European organizations. This is our strategic goal and one of our foreign policy priorities."[77]

At the same time, the Ukrainians were afraid that the military dimension of NATO enlargement and the potential deployment of NATO nuclear weapons in the East could lead to increasing pressure from Moscow. Thus, in the autumn of 1996, Ukraine suggested the establishment of a nuclear-weapons-free zone in central and eastern Europe. Talbott learned about the idea in October 1996 in discussions with Kuchma's national security adviser, Volodimir Horbulin. However, NATO could not accept the initiative and was still sorting out its position on the nondeployment of nuclear weapons in new member countries. Thus Horbulyn raised the issue of NATO security guarantees to Ukraine in combination with the conclusion of a NATO-Ukraine charter. Talbott endorsed both ideas to bolster Ukraine's security and sovereignty without antagonizing Russia. In the conversation with Horbulyn, Talbott said, "NATO must have a steadily strengthening relationship with Ukraine as it expands. The relationship must include the possibility that Ukraine might at some future date decide to join NATO. That decision is for Ukraine to make. In the meantime, the Deputy Secretary cited two things NATO will not do: 1) put pressure on Ukraine to apply for membership in NATO, and 2) accept anyone else's attempt to exclude Ukraine from eligibility for membership in NATO."[78] Finally, in 1996, Ukraine was on a trajectory of establishing formal relations with NATO.

Meanwhile, Baltic security was another critical issue in the Euro-Atlantic security architecture. Like Ukraine, the Baltic states were in a security vacuum and had no prospects to join NATO in the first enlargement round. Much as in the case of Ukraine, the independence of Estonia, Latvia, and

Lithuania had always been contested. In January 1991, Gorbachev resorted to military force in Vilnius to suppress the Lithuanian independence movement—the Soviet army killed fourteen people and injured another 140 civilians. After that, the Soviet leadership resorted to sanctions and an economic blockade to avert Lithuania's independence. After the dissolution of the Soviet Union in December 1991, all three Baltic countries were in a constant struggle to assert their newly gained sovereignty. Russia only began to pull out its troops from the Baltics under significant pressure from the Clinton administration—the withdrawals started in Lithuania in August 1993. They were completed by August 31, 1994, when the last Russian troops left Estonia.[79] In the early 1990s, the military's ongoing presence gave Russia powerful leverage in the conflict about the demarcation of its frontiers with Estonia, for instance. In a July 1994 meeting with Talbott, Estonian Foreign Minister Luik said he was concerned that "Russia would use 'physical power' to demarcate the disputed Russian-Estonian border."[80] Given Russia's pressure, policymakers in the region wanted the fastest kind of NATO membership to protect their recently gained sovereignty. When Talbott visited Tallinn in May 1993, Estonian President Lennart Meri "asked wryly if Talbott had come to town to sign Estonia's accession to NATO . . . Russia is still trying to divide Europe and he wondered where the frontiers of the West are."[81] Meri's life symbolized the destiny of the Baltics in the twentieth century. After the Soviet invasion of Estonia in 1940, the Meris had been deported to Siberia along with thousands of other Baltic families. Meri and his family survived and returned to Estonia, and Meri was one of the key figures in the Singing Revolution in the late 1980s.

Moreover, the Baltic countries were determined to become members of the European Union when Western attention was mostly on the Visegrad states.[82] Hence, in terms of economic competitiveness, the Baltics felt compelled to outdo Poland and the rest of the eastern EU candidates standing in line for EU membership. In a 1992 conversation with Delors, Meri argued that "nowhere in the former Soviet Union was there such stability—no clashes, no bloodshed, no refugees. The Russian propaganda campaign was directed particularly against Estonia precisely because that country had been the most successful."[83] Moreover, regional security organizations such as the Council of the Baltic Sea States and the Nordic Council promised to enhance Baltic security in multilateral institutions and cooperation with Russia.[84] At the same time, all three Baltic countries were determined to obtain the kind of hard security guarantees that only NATO could provide. In December 1993, the presidents of Estonia, Latvia, and Lithuania issued a joint statement declaring that only NATO membership would guarantee Baltic security.[85] In 1994, in the spirit of the PfP program with NATO, the three countries established the trinational Baltic Batallion as a peacekeeping force, signaling their ambition to become an exporter of security and a contributor to international stability.[86] In 1994, under the PfP roof, the Baltic armies were able to establish contacts with NATO's military and to operate day by day alongside the nations they aspired to join in NATO. The first Baltic infantry platoons were deployed in Croatia under the UN Protective Force starting in 1994.[87]

In the summer of 1995, Talbott turned to Baltic security at a time when he had a clearer sense of the emerging Euro-Atlantic security architecture. In July 1995, he spoke with Baltic Embassy representatives in Washington. The purpose was to provide reassurance. There were no secret U.S.-Russian deals over the heads of the Baltics at a time when the three countries feared being left out.[88] Over the long term, Talbott's aim for the Baltic region was the emergence of a postnational system of politics. The goal was to overcome historical conflicts over identities and national rivalries.[89] Talbott's idea was that transnational cooperation between the Baltics and Russia would mitigate the urgency of Baltic NATO membership. In a September 1995 conversation with Estonian Prime Minister Vahi, Talbott "noted U.S. concerns that the evolution of NATO not be perceived as a new form of containment against Russia. Estonia could help us promulgating this false perception by developing institutions other than NATO so that NATO evolution is seen as part of a larger context. Thus, we applaud Estonia's participation in such activities as the Baltic Batallion, PfP, and exercises."[90] Talbott argued that the three countries would be excellent candidates for NATO membership over the long term because their reforms focused on regional and cross-border cooperation, economic development, law enforcement, the construction of civil society, and, of course, strengthening their military under civilian control. Nevertheless, despite these assurances, Baltic policymakers still saw the question of NATO membership as the essential anchor for the long-term success of reforms. In March 1996, Estonian Foreign Minister Slim Kallas told Talbott that "Estonia's main goal is to create a peaceful environment for small states in Europe, a goal made ever more urgent by Russia's increasingly aggressive rhetoric. Estonia is the bellwether in the eyes of some NIS states, e.g., Ukraine, which is watching to see whether Estonia turns back from its reform course under Russian pressure."[91]

Indeed, the Clinton administration was determined to anchor the Baltics in the West. In 1996, Talbott worked on new schemes and played a key role in the evolution of the Baltic Action Plan (BAP), sketching out a clear and transparent way to address Baltic security needs short of NATO membership. The concept was to facilitate "the integration of the Baltics into the West by fostering the development of institutional links, regional cooperation, peaceful relations with neighbors; and a deepening bilateral relationship with the U.S."[92] The idea for the BAP rationale came as much from the White House and Talbott. In the winter of 1996, the White House tasked Daniel Hamilton of the State Department's policy planning staff and Carole van Voorst of the State's Office of Nordic and Baltic Affairs to work on the BAP concept.[93] Based on a three-track approach, the BAP focused on helping the Baltic states prepare for integration into multilateral and regional institutions, encouraging improved relations between Russia and the Baltic states, and strengthening the U.S.-Baltic bilateral relationship.[94] In a nutshell, the BAP was a waystation to NATO membership. NATO's doors would remain open. In June 1996, Bill Clinton told the Baltic presidents that "the Baltic states are a great success story of the post-communist world. We seek the integration of the Baltics states with the West, that's what we want. . . . The first new members to join the alliance shall not be the last. The Baltic states should be included in the new security order emerging in Europe."[95] Baltic reactions were muted.[96] Although it was clear that the Baltics would not join NATO in the first post–Cold War enlargement tranche, Baltic policymakers were annoyed when Secretary of Defense Perry said this publicly in October 1996 arguing, "they are not ready, not yet."[97] On the positive side, the message was not no, but not yet. Moreover, Ronald Asmus and Robert Nurick from the RAND Corporation helped bring Baltic NATO membership to the agenda when they wrote an important article in a 1996 *Survival* issue.[98]

Talbott's schemes for Baltic security were new, entailing a modern concept of regional security in Europe. At the outset of Clinton's second term, Talbott and his colleagues developed the Hanseatic strategy idea to create a postnational northern European community of nations providing security by interlocking international and transnational institutions.[99] The strategy adopted the vision of the medieval Hanseatic security structure—between the thirteenth and fifteenth centuries, nation states and identities mattered relatively little. Hanseatic settlements encompassed about two hundred entities across eight modern-day states from Estonia to Germany and the Netherlands. The Hanseatic League was "a concert of city-state precursors of nation states that felt secure enough in their identities and in their neighborhood to make a virtue of their diversity and derive benefit from their interactions with one another," Talbott said.[100] He pointed out that the goal was to encourage Russia, over time, "to view this region not as a fortified frontier but as a gateway; not as a buffer against invaders who no longer exist, but as a trading route and a common ground for commerce and economic development—in a word, that Russia will come to view the Baltics Hanseatically."[101]

After the July 1997 NATO summit and building on the Hanseatic strategy, the Clinton administration launched the Northern Europe Initiative (NEI) prompted by Madeleine Albright, who kept pushing the issue of Baltic NATO membership as the litmus test regarding the overall strategy of integration.[102] The NEI aimed to create a zone of security, stability, and prosperity on the shores of the Baltic Sea, to include the Baltics, Scandinavia, and Russia.[103] To prepare the Baltics for NATO membership, the Clinton administration promised to provide security assistance, business and trade promotion, private-public partnership networks, and support for continuing market reforms over the long term. Albright and Talbott designated Ronald Asmus to devise the NEI after Asmus had joined the Clinton administration as deputy assistant secretary for European affairs. Their joint work on the NEI led to the establishment of a U.S.-Baltic Commission and the adoption of the U.S.-Baltic Charter, by Clinton and the Baltic presidents in January 1998. In his meeting with them, Clinton said, "the Charter of Partnership is an historic document and a demonstration of our commitment to advancing your countries' integration into Western institutions through concrete initiatives. . . . We welcome your aspirations to join the Alliance and are committed to keeping NATO's doors open. The first round of enlargement will not be the last."[104] Indeed, the charter was vital to boost Baltic prospects for EU membership, given the EU's December 1997 decision to include the Baltic states among the candidates for EU expansion and to start accession negotiations with Estonia when Latvia and Lithuania felt "left standing at the altar by the EC."[105]

Talbott's Role in Clinton's Second Term

In 1996, it was not preordained that Talbott would remain on Clinton's foreign policy team in the second term. Talbott ruled himself out for the position as secretary of state, given that the Republican majority in the Senate would refuse his confirmation. He also rejected the idea of accepting the position of U.S. ambassador to Moscow when Christopher pitched him in the summer of 1996. There were two reasons. Talbott's teenage sons were thriving in Washington, and, if he stayed on, Talbott wanted to be at the center of decision-making. "I'm spoiled," he noted, "I now know how much difference there is between being an ambassador, even on a par with the best in the biz, Tom Pickering, and being a policymaker. Once you've done one, it's very hard to contemplate the other with satisfaction or enthusiasm."[106] Talbott was unsure whether staying on in a new foreign policy team made sense. He thought Christopher's successor would want to pick a new deputy secretary. He was also reluctant to compete with his friend Sandy Berger for the position of national security adviser. At the same time, Talbott was motivated to continue. He had accomplished so much; Clinton trusted his advice, and business with Russia was not finished. "It has been truly the most exciting and gratifying professional experience of my life to have a whack at shaping the world," Talbott wrote in a letter to his father, Nelson. "I'll feel the loss of that exciting very, very deeply. Even in anticipation, there's a kind of postpartem depression. I'd be leaving undone, or at least unfinished, the Russia project. I'm convinced I could keep the thing on track if I stayed in—and I'm doubtful that the new team will handle it in quite the same way. That's a very, very big deal."[107]

In the end, Talbott would not decide alone. He would discuss everything with Brooke. The bottom-line guiding principle was that he and Brooke would jointly undertake the next steps in their careers as colleagues. Initially, Brooke's advice was that he should leave. In November 1996, Talbott wrote his father that "she and I talked on the phone the day before yesterday, and she was leaning very far toward my getting out. At the end of the day, as with other decisions, I think I trust her more than I trust myself. The last four years have been the best of our marriage, and that's saying a lot. I credit both of us for that. I've made a real attempt to keep the family at the center, and she's transcended her own frustrations and disappointments in a whole new way, making the best of her opportunity to get the most out of gov't, doing a uniquely good job at the fellows and now having fun as well as doing well at interior."[108]

In early November 1996, Strobe and Brooke used a car ride along the Connecticut River to discuss various scenarios. Talbott thought Clinton would not ask him to be national security adviser. If he did, Talbott felt the only circumstances he could imagine doing it would be if Brooke could stay at the White House, if Berger could be a counselor at the State Department, and Talbott himself was genuinely comfortable with the secretary of state.[109] Another scenario was that Talbott could become national security adviser while Berger would serve as Clinton's new chief of staff. This scenario seemed a possibility given that Clinton's initial candidate for the chief of staff position, Erskine Bowles, was hesitant to accept the offer. However, when Bowles finally confirmed, this scenario evaporated.[110] Finally, on November 7, Talbott had a chance to discuss the future foreign policy team with Clinton. In his diaries, he noted, "I sit across from Potus, other side of the desk. He says, 'fire away.' I ask if he wants to give me any 'parameters.' 'No, just pretend that I don't have any thoughts and no one has given me any advice. Blank slate.' "[111] Talbott did not talk about his position. His primary aim was to endorse Richard Holbrooke as the new secretary of state.

> I take a deep breath (literally), short prologue, "my concern here is what will give you the most successful possible second term in foreign policy." Then do my number on RCH. My point is that Holbrooke, warts and all, stands the best chance of giving you the imagination and boldness and results you want. . . . This is about performance; this is about the ability to deliver. This is about having as much success as possible on the tough issues that will be coming at you. Pound for pound, ounce for ounce, Dick is the most talented, energetic, experienced, able, articulate, broad-gauge foreign-policy operative of our generation, maybe of our time. Also a royal pain in the ass. Lots of enemies, lots of detractors . . . But worth maintaining because of the unique value. He'd bring home the bacon, over and over.[112]

Talbott thought Holbrooke's talents made him the ideal candidate. He had unique effectiveness, experience, and tremendous energy. Holbrooke's temper and style, however, often caused resentment and resistance. Holbrooke was bold, aggressive, and exhausting. He was impatient with forms, bureaucracies, and processes. Clinton and Talbott knew all of this. In response to Talbott's spiel on Holbrooke, Clinton said, "he likes him, admires him, was intrigued by the idea. Worries about his always wanting to steal the limelight. Campaigned so hard for the Nobel prize that that's probably one reason he didn't get it. I want to ask you a very unfair question: if I picked him, would you stay, at least for a while, and handle him, hold his hand? Keep him under control?" Talbott replied, "you said for a while, maybe six months or so. I've got to talk to Brooke more about the lay of the land once I see what it's going to look like. She and I are a package, as you know." Clinton signaled understanding. "Yeah, and you're the better for it. I say that being part of a package myself. . . . I sense you really want out of here, don't you?" Clinton noted. "Not necessarily. It's complicated," Talbott said. "I want you to have a good second term in foreign policy. Whether it makes sense for me to be part of it is tricky. We can have that conversation whenever you want."[113]

During the meeting, Clinton did not mention bringing Talbott to the White House as his national security adviser. From Clinton's vantage point, Talbott was more valuable at the State Department and would even remain valuable if he left government. In November 1996, Secretary of Labor Robert Reich shared an interesting observation with Talbott. Reich had been in Talbott's and Clinton's Rhodes scholars cohort at Oxford and confided to Talbott that "someone very close to Potus had just told him earlier in the day, 'if you leave the gov't, your I.Q. in the president's estimation will go up 10 points.' In other words, Potus' desire to have your advice is inversely proportional to proximity."[114]

In the aftermath of the November 1996 election, it seemed that Talbott's staying in government depended on Holbrooke's nomination for the position of secretary of state. Talbott kept pushing for Holbrooke, although he knew that Clinton, Gore, and Berger were not enthusiastic. In a November 11 letter to Clinton, Talbott reaffirmed his willingness to stay on longer and potentially until the end of Clinton's second term to handle Holbrooke and to be his deputy. "I'm prepared to and I'm prepared to make an escape-clause-free commitment: I'll stay until one of three things happens: 1) you fire Dick; 2) you fire me; 3) I jump out of a window on the 7th floor of the State Department or otherwise go to that Great Deputies Committee in the Sky," Talbott wrote.[115] Meanwhile, Holbrooke's job interviews did not go well. His meeting with Gore was like an oral exam. Gore was "stern grim," Holbrooke felt he "could never break the ice, felt he flunked his oral." When Gore asked about Holbrooke's faults, the latter replied, "you know them," later interrupting Gore, "oh yes another of my faults is that I interrupt people."[116] At least that one got a laugh, Holbrooke said in a long meeting at Talbott's place on November 14.

On November 16, Talbott had another long session with Holbrooke to prepare for the interview with Clinton. Would Holbrooke be able to adapt if he got the job? Talbott wrote that "self-control is maybe the essence of what you're worried about. Can this force-of-nature/brilliant/maddening Hurricane Holbrooke control himself, whether in a 5-minute encounter you arrange with POTUS or in a PC or a Cabinet meeting or in a back-grounder with the press? Or will the self-promotional instinct get the better of him, and of us? That's what this comes down to."[117] Talbott was aware that Holbrooke's interview with Clinton was not promising either. The president liked and appreciated Holbrooke but was doubtful whether he was "sufficiently self-aware" to handle the job including the relationship to Clinton himself.[118] Finally, Clinton chose Madeleine Albright as the new secretary of state. Talbott called her on the morning of December 4, 1996, when the story of her nomination broke overnight. He congratulated and said Albright could pick anyone she wanted as deputy secretary. The following day, Albright asked Talbott to stay on as her deputy. She wanted him to work on the transition immediately. Talbott spoke with Brooke, agreed, and wrote his first eyes-only memorandum to Albright the same day.[119]

Albright was the first woman to serve as U.S. secretary of state. Her father, Josef Korbel, had been a diplomat. He escaped communist Czecho-slovakia with his family and went to the United States in 1948. A year later, he accepted a position teaching international relations at the University of Denver, where he later helped found the graduate school of international studies. Albright studied political science and earned a batchelor's from Wellesley College and master's and doctorate degrees from Columbia University. She went into politics in the Carter administration when her mentor, Zbigniew Brzezinski, brought her onto the National Security Council staff.[120] During Clinton's first term, she had been a powerful advocate of a robust U.S. foreign policy as the U.S. ambassador to the United Nations. Albright saw the United States as the "indispensable nation" and the beacon of freedom. She had been a critical proponent of NATO enlargement and felt the case for it in her bones, given her personal experience of authoritarianism. She recalled she was "determined to show the American flag wherever we had interests at stake . . . and had goals in mind on every continent."[121] Like Talbott, she spoke fluent Russian. In terms of style, she was different from her predecessor Warren Christopher. She had a reputation as Madam Steel whereas Christopher was a soft-spoken gentleman. In terms of substance, Albright hit the ground running. She had been involved in all key foreign policy issues in Clinton's first term. At the start of the second term, the single most significant foreign policy challenge was the six-month drill to conclude the NATO-Russia charter to be signed sometime before the NATO summit in Madrid in July 1997.

CHAPTER IV

The NATO-Russia Founding Act and Its Aftermath

Strobe Talbott and the Negotiation Process

At the start of Clinton's second term, the negotiations on the NATO-Russia charter were still preliminary and needed more time. While Yeltsin was still recuperating from quintuple bypass surgery, NATO was searching for a position. Clinton was careful and did not want to create the impression of pushing NATO enlargement at the expense of a debilitated Yeltsin. In January 1997, Clinton told Kohl that "it is important that all of us be supportive of him during his surgery and that we do not create an impression of taking advantage of him during his recovery. He has been a vital supportive ally."[1] Moreover, NATO still sought ways to make it easier for Russia to accept NATO enlargement—especially in terms of its military consequences. At the December 1996 NATO ministerial meeting, the alliance reaffirmed that its nuclear umbrella would be extended to new member states but that enlargement would "not require a change in NATO's current nuclear posture and, therefore, NATO countries have no intention, no plan, and no reason to deploy nuclear weapons on the territory of new member states."[2] In December 1996, Gore communicated NATO's concessions in a key meeting with Chernomyrdin at the OSCE summit in Lisbon.[3] On December 4, Talbott repeated the signal in a meeting with Primakov: "I hope you understand the importance of what the Vice President said to the Prime Minister about nuclear weapons and the alliance," Talbott noted. Primakov understated the relevance of Gore's statement: "Yes, we understood, but there wasn't anything really new there. We've heard it before. What we really need to do is tackle the infrastructure problem," Primakov said. Talbott then shifted gears: "There you go again, Yevgeny! That's a perfect example of what I was talking about earlier. Why can't you take 'yes' for an answer? Go back and take a look at the record of the Gore–Chernomyrdin conversation. Read the memcon carefully. Then imagine it as an official statement by NATO at some point in the future. You should declare victory rather than grumping about how what the best we can do isn't good enough."[4]

Another challenge pertained to Russia's hesitance to accept NATO Secretary General Javier Solana as the official NATO negotiator. Rather than dealing with NATO as an institution, the Russians preferred to talk with the leaders of NATO's key nations. However, the Clinton administration rejected Russia's idea of negotiations among the Big Five—the United States, Great Britain, France, Germany, and Russia. NATO had to decide as an alliance of sixteen member states. Talbott wanted Primakov to have constructive negotiations with Solana. "It's very important for you to have a decent relationship with Solana. He's not just a functionary; he's not 'staff.' He's a key participant in the deliberations that will lead to the ultimate NATO position on these issues. You have tended to dismiss him as merely an American hired hand," Talbott noted.[5] Primakov followed Talbott's advice. On December 11, he displayed a constructive attitude during his visit to NATO headquarters to launch the negotiations on the NATO-Russia charter. "The Russian presence at today's meeting," he pointed out, "indicated Moscow's view that NATO was important."[6] It seemed that the Russian side would finally be reconciled with NATO enlargement. At the same time, Russian policymakers continued to raise unacceptable demands. In December 1996, for instance, Chernomyrdin argued that "Russia was not clear about the path of cooperation, unless the functional core of NATO was changed. . . . If Russia had to face a unified Europe alone, she would need full nuclear protection, and nuclear reductions would no longer be appropriate. Russia could not be bought off by a charter— that would not convince the Russian people that NATO enlargement was not dangerous."[7] In addition, Yeltsin's frail health was a factor of uncertainty in the equation. Clinton was determined to go for a NATO-Russia charter as long as Yeltsin was in charge. In January 1997, Clinton's first step was to send Talbott to Europe for talks with Kohl and Chirac to figure out the best way forward. At this point, Talbott was acting secretary because Albright was not yet confirmed.

Talbott was not sure whether the Clinton administration could elaborate on a joint strategy with France and Germany. Chirac believed that NATO should delay or even suspend enlargement if Russia objected.[8] He feared that enlargement would destroy the chance of a cooperative relationship with Russia for years to come. He hoped Clinton would relent on the timetable and the substance of NATO's opening. Chirac assumed that Russia was not ripe for Clinton's scheme. "The Russian side is all screwed up. It will take 100 years—or if you're an optimist, 50 years—for the Russians to be completely confident in themselves and in the vision that you and President Clinton have for an undivided Europe."[9] The problem for Clinton was that Chirac would give Russia a veto over NATO enlargement. When Talbott arrived in Bonn, he was relieved when Kohl renounced Chirac's position. Kohl advocated NATO enlargement and emphasized that a united Germany could not remain Europe's eastern border state forever. Germany was perhaps the largest beneficiary of NATO's opening. Its strategic position would change in fundamental ways. Enlargement promised to keep the United States engaged as a European power while giving the Federal Republic stability on its eastern borders and reinsurance against a volatile Russia. Kohl also saw NATO's opening as a moral issue. The fall of the Berlin Wall began with Solidarnosc in Poland and Charter 77 in Prague. The dissident movements in central and eastern Europe had paved the way for the peaceful end of the Cold War. Kohl argued that "we can't tell the Poles and the Czechs that they are not welcome after what they did to survive communism. Europeans cannot build a common market without also defending each other as well. That means that entry into the EU is not a substitute for membership in NATO."[10] Talbott was relieved and noted that "Kohl's clarity and steadfastness was the best imaginable antidote to Chirac's talk of 'finesse.'"[11]

On January 16, Talbott briefed Clinton and Gore on the results of his visits to Paris and Bonn. The best way to proceed for Clinton was to speak with Yeltsin bilaterally on the NATO-Russia charter. Meanwhile, it was important for Solana to start official negotiations with Primakov. The bottom line was that Russia would not get a say in NATO decision-making, and there would be no dual-key. On January 20, 1997, Solana carried these ideas forward in a meeting with Primakov, who was less forthcoming this time and argued that "it needed to be recognized from the outset that our effort to enhance NATO-Russia relations would not lead Russia to withdraw its opposition to enlargement. That opposition would remain, but both sides wanted as few dividing lines as possible."[12] Solana gave a one-hour presentation reviewing the progress made so far. His initial focus was establishing a consultative mechanism and creating Russian military liaison missions at NATO. As always, the question of NATO's military infrastructure was central to Primakov's presentation. Solana referred to NATO's assurances in the December 1996 communique, whereas Primakov insisted on legally binding documents. Finally, Solana and Primakov released a joint communique on their consultations. It emphasized the constructive spirit and their plans for further talks according to a jointly set schedule.[13]

Next, Talbott was due to visit Moscow on January 22. Primakov used the meeting for another long presentation on the difficulties in the negotiations. Talbott did not respond to every point. Instead, he emphasized the importance of constructive talks. He felt that "we collectively and you and I personally are working to solve this problem; we're not fighting the problem."[14] The crunch was Primakov's request for a legally binding charter stipulating co-decision-making between NATO and Russia. Talbott once more rejected this. It seemed that Primakov was stalling and waiting for Yeltsin's recovery. Solana's and Talbott's January 1997 visits to Moscow revealed that NATO and Russia were only in the foothills of their work on the charter. The objective was to finalize it by May, before the convocation of the July 1997 NATO Madrid summit and the decision about the candidates for the first enlargement round. This was ambitious but not unrealistic. In a briefing before the North Atlantic Council, Talbott made a case for specific results—but also noted that NATO could do without a NATO-Russia charter. Talbott pointed out that "we cannot predefine completion of the charter as 'success,' because that would mean that absence of the charter is 'failure.' Rather, we must think in terms of constructing the mosaic from its individual, worthwhile parts."[15]

Meanwhile, given the anti-NATO mood in Moscow, NATO leaders discussed the need for gestures of goodwill toward Russia to strengthen Yeltsin's domestic position. Vice President Gore in particular was determined to do something for the Russian side and present some political gifts when Chernomyrdin visited Washington in February 1997. Talbott noted that "he's leaning hard toward being able to do something for his buddy Cherno [and] presses hard on why we can't do legally binding (I give him the basic lowest-common-denominator spiel)."[16] Moreover, Gore wanted

Clinton to go to Moscow for the next summit with Yeltsin rather than convening it in a neutral place. Talbott pushed back again and argued that the summit venue could be decided later. Clinton wanted to bring at least one concession in his next meeting with Yeltsin and suggested repeating the three no's on nuclear weapons in the NATO-Russia charter.[17] In early 1997, Clinton and Gore were again inclined to be a tad more conciliatory and ready to lean toward potential concessions. This pertained to Clinton's willingness to give Russia full membership in the G-7. "If we're asking them to eat NATO expansion, it's crazy to be dicking around on . . . who goes to a meeting . . . We're asking them to eat NATO expansion with a smile, and we're nitpicking over delicacies over who sits where," Clinton said.[18]

In February 1997, Talbott went to Moscow again to prepare for Albright's initial visit to Moscow. He used his trip to explain the U.S. position in meetings with Yeltsin and Primakov and reported that "my two days of talks in Moscow convinced me that the Russians are making a real effort to get past the polemics and teeth-gnashing over NATO enlargement. They are finally concentrating instead on preparing for the best possible Helsinki Summit."[19] The Russian side seemed to be getting serious in developing a NATO-Russia charter. The way forward was to use the Solana-Primakov channel as the official negotiation forum and the U.S.-Russian talks for the heavy lifting. Solana was okay with the division of labor. Talbott noted that "he is content to let us do the heavy lifting, both conceptually and with the Russians, while concentrating his own efforts on helping us to cope with the sensitivities of the other Allies, especially the French, who are likely to resist in principle an American lead on the charter."[20] Albright's visit to Moscow went well. Her talks with Yeltsin and Primakov were not about negotiations but to lay out the U.S. position. Albright radiated firmness and a readiness for dialogue. Yeltsin clarified Russia's position: Previously, his approach had been that NATO's door had to be open for Russia, at least in theory. Now he emphasized that Russia was not ready for NATO membership. The Russian people were not prepared for it, he argued. "We cannot accept that. We have to say that Russia is not joining NATO and will not join. The Russian people are concerned about NATO and will not permit this. You have your politics on this; so do we. Finding a balanced document—or an agreement Talent—will be difficult, but let us find it."[21]

On February 23, 1997, Primakov came to Brussels for further negotiations with Solana. He brought several Russian papers on the substance of the NATO-Russia charter. His central theme was the non-advancement of NATO's military infrastructure in the territories of NATO's new members. The challenge for NATO was to reassure Russia while avoiding second-class membership for newly acceding allies. Primakov told Solana, "we won't be satisfied if Poland says today that it doesn't want foreign troops; this should be in our document; words are not enough for us." Solana emphasized the minimum required infrastructure needs of NATO's new member states. "As for military infrastructure, we will have to have some. . . . We don't need great stockpiles and you should be aware that any possible upgrading of infrastructure after 1999 will be a gradual process."[22] Both sides were struggling to find an adequate formula. Talbott noted that "we could still have what I call a 'Charter Lite' and what Solana calls a 'Decaf Charter': lots of good stuff on doctrine and political context and military cooperation and a joint consultative mechanism, but no calories (or caffeine) in the area that Primakov says really matters—tanks and APCs and artillery."[23] Talbott and Solana were determined to retain NATO's flexibility as a collective defense organization. NATO had to maintain the ability to adapt and switch to a containment-oriented policy if Russia went back to its imperial past. It was important to avoid a Russian veto through the NATO-Russia charter. British Defense Secretary Michael Portillo noted, "the three nos did not commit NATO for all time; we could change our intentions if circumstances made that necessary." Solana agreed: "It would be stupid if the Charter was too prescriptive."[24] Having a fourth no on the expansion of NATO's military infrastructure was impossible.

On March 5, 1997, Talbott and Solana discussed avoiding a fourth no. During their meeting, NSC Director Alexander Vershbow scribbled a sentence trying to summarize the essence of NATO's thinking. It read, "in the current and foreseeable security environment, the collective defense of the Alliance and the participation of all its members in the Alliance's military activities will be based on interoperability and capability for reinforcement rather than on the permanent stationing of substantial, large combat units where they are not currently deployed."[25] The formulation became notorious as "the sentence from hell."[26] Indeed, for the time being, NATO refrained from deploying permanent foreign combat forces in its new member states. The assumption was that enlargement did not necessitate a military policy as long as Russia showed restraint.[27] However, policymakers in Warsaw, Prague, and Budapest saw this as a fourth no and a sign that NATO only enlarged half-heartedly. Although NATO preserved the right to deploy troops and equipment on the territory of the new member states, it abandoned this right for the foreseeable future. NATO could not easily change its policy because no consensus had been established about what would constitute a Russian breach of the partnership. This became clear after Russia's 2014 invasion of Crimea and the start of Russia's war in Donbas, where two "statelets" were declared in Donetsk and Luhansk. Even after these actions, in 2016, NATO explained that its enhanced forward presence in NATO allies in the Baltics and Poland consisted of rotating rather than permanent deployments. Only after Russia's full-scale invasion of Ukraine in 2022 did NATO shift its position.[28]

In 1997, Talbott and his advisers knew that NATO had to avoid the conclusion of an agreement with Russia at any price. Deputy Undersecretary of Defense Jan Lodal noted that "unless we resolve some of our substantive disagreements in the security area, our relationship with Russia will continue to be strained, and the Charter and Council could prove to be a hollow victory."[29] Talbott was especially critical of the fact that the Russian side used the term *infrastructure* in trying to extract NATO's military teeth. "I wish that word had never been invented. Its constant use in this discussion has caused no end of difficulties. Part of the problem is that it is too-vague; another problem is that when it turns precise, it refers to things that must be in Central Europe and anywhere else in the Alliance," he argued.[30] On March 6, 1997, Talbott introduced the sentence from hell in his meeting with Primakov. He did not go into the details of the language. Instead, the purpose was to float the general idea of NATO's renunciation of permanent troop deployments to address Russian concerns. "I think that this could be useful," was Primakov's answer. "What are the criteria for such words?" he wondered. "There must be a formula that says that there cannot be any stationing of forces on a permanent basis," he insisted. Talbott countered, "you've got to accept the premise that these countries are coming into the Alliance as genuine, equal members, including in the military dimension. If you keep trying to block or deny that, we're not going to get anywhere."[31] There was still no consensus. Solana's next visit to Moscow confirmed this. Infrastructure was still the main sticking point. On March 14, 1997, NATO made a vital gesture when the alliance formally adopted the language of the sentence from hell in its official position.[32]

Before NATO officially adopted it, there was considerable discussion in Washington. On March 10, Talbott introduced the "magical sentence" to National Security Advisor Sandy Berger, who was unaware of it.

Talbott recalled that Berger's "initial reaction was between skeptical and negative. His concern is that it crosses the red line of no 2nd-class. . . . He's quite worried about how it will play on the Hill and with the CEEs."[33] The following day, Berger convened a principal's meeting to discuss the sentence and its impact. Meanwhile, Talbott and his assistant, John Bass, began to search for NATO precedents with regard to the substance of the sentence. "In other words, what do we say about reliance on interoperability and interoperability and capacity for reinforcement, and about limited need for combat troops in large units?"[34] The Clinton administration wanted to ensure that the sentence did not violate its five red lines on enlargement—no delay, no veto, no exclusion, no second-class membership, and no subordination. Talbott was utterly aware that the whole NATO-Russia negotiating process was an ambivalent issue for the central and eastern European countries. He noted that "on the one hand, the CEEs want a NATO-Russia deal, since the absence of one will make for a less predictable, potentially more threatening Russia; on the other, having so often been the losers in a zero-sum game with Russia in the past, they fear that anything 'good' for Russia in such a deal will be 'bad' for them."[35]

Meanwhile, NATO-Russia relations became a contested domestic issue in the United States. George Kennan's opposition to NATO enlargement triggered enormous public debate. In a February 1997 op-ed in the *New York Times*, Kennan called NATO's opening the "most fateful error of American policy in the entire post–Cold War era."[36] Throughout his lifetime, Kennan had criticized NATO, opposing Italy's entry in 1949 and West Germany's accession in the mid-1950s, arguing in favor of German neutrality in the early Cold War.[37] Given his long-standing distrust of the alliance, his opposition to NATO's post–Cold War enlargement was unsurprising. Nevertheless, Talbott continued to engage with Kennan and visited him several times at his Princeton home. In response to Kennan's February 1997 *New York Times* op-ed, Talbott wrote Kennan a letter explaining the Clinton administration's rationale. "A decision not to enlarge NATO," Talbott wrote, "would send to the Central Europeans that their future does not lie with the West; it would imply that they are, as the President has sometimes put it, consigned to a 'security limbo.' It would underscore the old divisions of the Cold War at a time when Western policy is committed to overcoming those divisions. The resulting sense of isolation and vulnerability would be both discouraging and potentially destabilizing."[38] Brzezinski and Kissinger raised criticism from the opposite side and argued that the Clinton administration was too lenient in its relations with Russia. Kissinger thought NATO was on a trajectory of giving Russia a veto in terms of NATO's internal decision-making process.[39]

Talbott was determined to refute Kissinger's criticism by emphasizing the specifics of the negotiations, arguing that "NATO remains NATO—the NAC remains NAC; Russia will be neither de facto nor otherwise. The fact that we are willing to carry out institutionalized 16+1 consultation activities with Russia does not undermine, dilute, or corrupt the integrity of NATO's processes, rights, etc."[40] Despite these clarifications, it was clear that the Clinton administration had to do a better job of explaining its policy at home. Albright was increasingly nervous about public unease. She was especially sensitive about the long-term implications of the NATO-Russia charter and asked Talbott "whether the Charter would put the NATO-Russia relationship on automatic pilot, committing us to arrangements with the Russians that would run their course and provide benefits to the Russians irrespective of Russian behavior." Absolutely not, was Talbott's short answer. NATO could put on the break at any point in time—and NATO was free to stop the endeavor in case of Russian misbehavior in the future. "Think of it as a pay-as-you-go plan—with the Russians under a reciprocal obligation to 'pay' in the coinage of good behavior—as opposed to one that requires a big down-payment on our part. There are no fixed deadlines by which we commit ourselves to begin the activities that are of interest and benefit to the Russians."[41]

In mid-March 1997, shortly before the Clinton-Yeltsin summit in Helsinki, agreement on the substance of the NATO-Russia charter had still not been reached. On March 15, Primakov came to Washington for another round of talks. Time was running out. It was perhaps the last chance to reach consensus. The aim was to produce a bilateral U.S.-Russia statement on European security that would lay the groundwork for the forthcoming Clinton-Yeltsin summit in Helsinki later in March. So far, the two sides had made considerable progress on the first four parts of the draft charter—the preamble, the principles, and the consultation mechanisms in the NATO-Russia Council, including the areas for joint NATO-Russia projects. The contentious issue was section 5 and the military ramifications of NATO enlargement. At the outset of the talks in Washington, Primakov reiterated that he found NATO's statement on infrastructure "totally unacceptable."[42] He insisted on a permanent and legally binding ban on NATO deployments and infrastructure beyond NATO's old borders. This provoked a firm answer from Albright: NATO's policies were not to be negotiated with non-NATO countries, especially Russia. "Look Yevgeny," Albright said, "neither the President nor I are going to negotiate over the heads of the Central Europeans about their security arrangements. That's been done in the past and it is not going to happen again, not on my watch." Primakov continued to push the Russian position, but Albright cut him off: "We've said 'no' to all of this stuff before, and if you've come here simply to hear me say 'no' again, I'm happy to do so." Primakov was upset. "Madeleine," he said, "why aren't you willing to meet us halfway." Albright also countered this one. "Halfway? Halfway," she said, "you keep going back to square one." Primakov was desperate and concluded, "I don't really think we can have an agreement." This statement did not bother Albright. "Well," she responded, "so be it."[43] The Clinton administration did not need a NATO-Russia charter and could move on with NATO enlargement.

Following the confrontation at the outset, Talbott invited Mamedov for a private conversation at his house to review the contentious issues. The following day, March 16, Talbott and Berger told Mamedov that the Russian draft was inadequate. The Russian side had to stop its war of words and its efforts to secure further concessions. That evening, Albright and Primakov had a private dinner at Talbott's house. It was the turning point. Both were able to make their points in a relaxed atmosphere. They discussed the joint statement all evening and eventually agreed on a common line.[44] This eased the way for Clinton's meeting with Primakov the following day, March 17. Clinton stressed the need for the Russian side to tone down its public rhetoric against NATO enlargement—"if President Yeltsin's public statements are negative, I fear he will undermine belief in Russia that the NATO agreement means anything, and thus undermine his position. Here, it will create the impression of second-class new members. This rhetoric could undermine both your and our interests. It is advantageous to both of us to reduce the rhetoric so at Helsinki we can say we made a good deal."[45] Clinton's meeting with Primakov went well. However, on the way to the airport, Primakov raised the issue of potential NATO membership for the Baltic states. He told Talbott that Yeltsin would use the Helsinki summit to suggest an agreement to exclude the Baltics from NATO.[46] This was entirely unacceptable. NATO would maintain its open door. Talbott tried to talk Primakov out of the idea. "If Yeltsin persisted," Talbott warned, "it had the potential of blowing up the summit."[47] Meanwhile, Clinton thought it was essential to offer Yeltsin another sweetener to keep him engaged—Clinton planned to use their forthcoming Helsinki meeting to propose Russia's permanent accession to the G-7. "As we push Ol' Boris to do the right but hard thing on NATO, I want him to feel the warm, beckoning glow of doors that are opening to other institutions where he's welcome. Got it, people?" Clinton said.[48]

The start of Clinton's and Yeltsin's talks in Helsinki on March 21 was promising. Their first session was devoted to the sustainability of the U.S.-Russia partnership. Clinton emphasized that "together we've made a great deal of progress, first of all, in dealing with the consequences of the Cold War. Now both of us are in our second terms and need to decide what to do together. I believe our lasting legacy must be a partnership and framework of peace and security that our successors will embrace and that others might not otherwise embrace." Yeltsin agreed: "Neither of us will have a third term. We want to move into 21st century with stability and tranquility." Thereafter, Clinton and Yeltsin discussed their competing positions on NATO enlargement. Yeltsin was still not reconciled with it and stressed that "our position has not changed. It remains a mistake for NATO to move eastward. But I need to take steps to alleviate the negative consequences of this for Russia. I am prepared to enter into an agreement with NATO not because I want to but because it is a forced step. There is no other solution for today."[49]

Clinton anticipated such a statement and was relaxed about it. The problem was that Yeltsin raised his opposition to NATO membership for the Baltic states—and he tried to frame the issue as a new condition for his consent to the NATO-Russia charter. Yeltsin asked Clinton for a promise that NATO would not allow former Soviet republics to join the alliance. Clinton rejected this straight away and said that "if we were to agree that no members of the former Soviet Union could enter NATO, it would be a bad thing for our attempt to build a new NATO, but it would also be a bad thing for your attempt to build a new Russia." First of all, Clinton pointed out, "there are no secrets in this world. . . . Second, it would create exactly the fear among the Baltics and others that you're trying to allay and that you're denying is justified. A third point: the deal you're suggesting would totally undermine the Partnership for Peace. It would terrify the smaller countries that are now working well with you and us in Bosnia and elsewhere." Finally, Clinton said, "I can't make the specific commitments you are asking for. It would violate the whole spirit of NATO."[50]

Yeltsin then turned to his fallback position and asked that the first round of NATO enlargement not include any former Soviet republics. Clinton rejected this as well. There would not be any deals over the heads of the central and eastern European countries. Yeltsin gave up, but he was not convinced. He was still concerned about the domestic repercussions in Russia. When they were alone, Clinton asked Yeltsin, "Boris, do you really think I would allow NATO to attack Russia from bases in Poland?" Yeltsin shrugged. "No," he replied, "I don't, but a lot of older people who live in the Western part of Russia and listen to Zyuganov do."[51] In turn, Clinton emphasized his commitment that there would be no nuclear expansion of NATO, and this concession would be codified in the NATO-Russia charter. Yeltsin was not convinced. He struggled to conceive the NATO-Russia partnership as a win-win issue. First and foremost, he saw it as a way to avoid further rounds of NATO enlargement. Yeltsin's aim was to make NATO enlargement so painful for the United States that future administrations would not be willing to repeat the experience. Talbott's executive assistant Eric Edelman observed that "the Russians are pursuing a 'root canal strategy,' which means that they're trying to make NATO+ so painful that we'll never go to that particular dentist again."[52]

When Talbott briefed the North Atlantic Council on the Helsinki summit, he said that "it had been hard going but constructive. It was possible that we had crossed the threshold. But there was still much to do and much that could go wrong."[53] Yeltsin's frail health was an uncertainty in the equation. It was unclear whether he would still be alive until the conclusion of the NATO-Russia charter. He was recovering from quintuple bypass surgery and was in bad shape and still drinking too much, polishing off several glasses of wine and champagne during the official state dinner with Clinton and Finnish President Ahtisaari in Helsinki. Talbott watched Yeltsin during the talks and social events and noted that "Yeltsin's complexion is what astonishes me. It's cadaverous. It's either too much makeup or not enough. . . . He also seems tired and stiff. I'm watching carefully as the dinner goes on, I hope not too obviously (seated to my right is the 'left alliance' minister of culture, a psychiatrist who clearly hates NATO enlargement)."[54]

By mid-April 1997, it seemed that the Helsinki consensus was already unraveling. The Russian side began to reopen debates on the core military issues and demanded more concessions on infrastructure and stationed forces. Yeltsin and Primakov launched a diplomatic gambit to build up pressure. On the one hand, they were stalling. On the other, Yeltsin raised public expectations by proposing Paris as the venue for the NATO-Russia summit and the conclusion of the NATO-Russia charter on May 27, 1997.[55] The Clinton administration was determined to stick to its five red lines and highlighted them repeatedly in the clearest and firmest terms. Talbott emphasized steadiness—there would be no movement on the NATO side. He still believed in the conclusion of a NATO-Russia charter in May 1997 as Russia's negotiating position would worsen after NATO's July 1997 Madrid summit and the nomination of the first new NATO member states. Yet Talbott doubted whether anything meaningful could be agreed upon given that Primakov's diplomacy was "anti-enlargement by other means."[56]

In late April and early May 1997, Talbott and Albright undertook a final effort to achieve agreement. On Monday, April 28, Talbott went to Brussels for a working dinner with Solana. On Tuesday, April 29, he reviewed the negotiating strategy in a meeting of the North Atlantic Council. In the afternoon, he arrived in Moscow for a one-on-one working dinner with Mamedov. On Wednesday, April 30, he had a full day of negotiations with Primakov. On Thursday, May 1, Albright arrived in Moscow for her meeting with Primakov. The week ended with a final Albright-Primakov session on Friday, May 2, and a further NAC briefing in Brussels. Before the trip, Talbott sent Albright a memo detailing "a menu of scenarios" for the forthcoming visits referred to as the Good, the Bad, and the Ugly. The good scenario meant consensus and a mandate for Solana to hammer out the final agreement with the Russian side. The bad scenario meant no consensus, no NATO-Russia charter, no Paris summit. The ugly scenario was that the Russian side would stall hoping to get additional concessions at the Clinton-Yeltsin level during the Paris summit. The ugliest scenario was that "the Russians show a temper tantrum and accuse us of bad-faith follow-up on Helsinki, of insufficient flexibility and unwillingness to meet them halfway. This would be part of a strategy of shaking up the Allies and inducing them to put pressure on us for concessions on stationed forces, nuclear infrastructure etc."[57]

Talbott's initial talks with Primakov did not go well. Was the Clinton administration in for the ugly scenario? Primakov repeated his hard-line position on infrastructure. He proposed that NATO would not be permitted to exceed limits under the CFE Treaty. The purpose was to establish a single limit for NATO in the CFE talks—and this sufficiency rule would prevent a second or even third round of NATO enlargement as NATO would soon exceed the 1991 ceilings. Moreover, Primakov demanded a limit of just one brigade of NATO stationed forces in each new member state and an overall cap of 1.5 percent of NATO's total entitlements stationed in all new member states combined. "We estimate that this could limit the Alliance to two brigades for a small group of new allies," Talbott noted.[58] This proposal was simply unacceptable. NATO had already made an enormous concession when it agreed to renounce permanent foreign troop deployments in the East. It could not go further and needed flexibility for temporary deployments comparable to what Russia had on its flanks.[59]

Eventually, in the evening, Talbott's mood improved considerably. Mamedov said the Russian side might be willing to go along with NATO proposals as a fallback option. Talbott noted that Mamedov's "motive in doing this is probably that he doesn't want me to lose heart; he doesn't want us to throw up our hands and walk away from the whole thing."[60] Afterward, Talbott sent Albright a new telegram saying they could obtain a better result than he had previously indicated.[61] The next day, May 1, Primakov was willing to resolve the contested issues.[62] Yeltsin underlined his constructive spirit in a prescheduled fifteen-minute telephone conversation with Albright. "We all want progress, Kohl, Chirac, myself, President Clinton and yourself—and if Solana is for it too, then we can do it," Yeltsin said.[63] Finally, Albright and Primakov agreed on a final text on May 2, 1997.[64] Thereafter, Albright went to the Carnegie Moscow Center for a discussion with prominent Russian defense experts. She framed the NATO-Russia charter as a win-win, but the debate revealed that the Russian defense establishment was still unconvinced. Albright's theme was that "Russia should abandon its outdated us-versus-you thinking. . . . She emphasized that the U.S. and NATO view Russia as a great power, not a defeated one; she urged the Russians not to engage in self-isolation."[65]

The results of Talbott's and Albright's visit to Moscow enabled Solana to iron out the final language of the NATO-Russia charter in meetings with Primakov. Their next round of talks was scheduled for May 6 in Luxembourg. It went well. They had four and a half hours of intense discussion and made progress but could not resolve every point. On the positive side, they found a consensus to incorporate the NATO text into the CFE language in the draft of the NATO-Russia charter. However, they disagreed on infrastructure and the military implications of NATO enlargement. Talbott noted that "if NATO elects to forego permanent stationing, it needs to have the capability to move troops, and to support them when they arrive, in the event they're needed."[66] Solana resisted Primakov's salami tactics of using a series of many small actions on each chapter to produce the final text. "I again made the point to him that nothing could be regarded as agreed until every part the document was agreed," Solana said.[67] Another meeting was scheduled in Moscow on May 13. Primakov did not appreciate that he had to discuss the final deal with Solana. He called Talbott from the Luxembourg airport and complained that "Solana was not a negotiator, and was not ready to conclude an agreement. Solana only wanted to learn the Russian view so as to deliver it to NATO members. Therefore, it was necessary to end the discussion of those items on which the parties agreed and focus on those aspects where views differed," Primakov said. Talbott replied, "Solana negotiated on behalf of NATO."[68] These were Talbott's final words. Eventually, the Russian side approved the text of the NATO-Russia charter in a final Primakov-Solana meeting on May 13.

On May 14, Clinton praised the Founding Act in an exchange with reporters. He knew it was essential to explain it in public. Clinton said, "it is possible to enlarge NATO, to maintain its effectiveness as the most successful defense alliance in history, to strengthen our partnership with Russia, and to do all this in a way that advances our common objectives of freedom and human rights and peace and prosperity."[69] The same day, Talbott briefed the central European ambassadors in Washington, DC. He clarified Yeltsin's previous and misleading television remarks on the NATO-Russia Founding Act. "Yeltsin asserted the consultative mechanism will give Russia a veto over NATO action. The veto will be only over [NATO-Russia] Joint Council action, not the NAC, and they are two different entities," Talbott reiterated.[70] Meanwhile, Solana returned to Brussels to present the agreed text to the NATO permanent representatives. The text remained confidential as long as it was under consideration in the North Atlantic Council. After the NAC's approval, it was ready to be signed at the NATO-Russia Summit in Paris on May 27, 1997. The ceremony in Paris was moving. History was in the making. Everybody was laying it on thickly. Kohl saw the Founding Act as the cornerstone in the emergence of a new Europe whole and free. "We sense a new something of that wind of change sweeping across Europe since the dramatic developments of the years 1989/1990 and which indeed brought us to Paris once before, for the signing of the Charter for a New Europe in November 1990," Kohl said. "Just ten years ago who would have dared predict that the countries of the Atlantic Alliance would enter into a close and forward-looking partnership with Russia?"[71] Yeltsin beamed and loved the moment. He put his script away, improvised, and announced that he had signed a decree that would detarget and remove the nuclear warheads of missiles directed at NATO member states. Yeltsin's impromptu reference caused astonishment. Nobody was exactly sure what he meant.[72]

The Western public saw the conclusion of the NATO-Russia Founding Act as a signal of Russia's consent to NATO enlargement. However, Yeltsin used his address at the Paris summit to underline Russia's continued opposition to NATO's opening. "Russia still views negatively the expansion plans of NATO," he said. In addition, he highlighted the difficulties in the search for a new security system. "The fate of this continent, Europe, is far from easy. It is very easy to account of all the wars and skirmishes it has undergone. And each century brought with it new tests and new challenges, new wars to the soil of this continent. Several attempts to stem this tragic chain of events have been made, but now our efforts can and should bear fruit."[73] Yeltsin's remarks revealed that the NATO-Russia Founding Act was a "conditional peace" and a modus vivendi document.[74] NATO and Russia settled for an "interim arrangement," something between collective defense and collective security—a system in which confrontation and war between NATO and Russia could not be excluded.[75] In 1997, no one knew whether it would lead to a stable peace in Europe or to the return of tensions and new confrontations. It was not certain whether Russia would turn into a consolidated democracy at all. NATO and Russia could not agree on the Euro-Atlantic order's norms, rules, and structures. The competing aims remained in place. NATO sought Russia's approval to enlarge, whereas Russia tried to use the Founding Act to slow down enlargement and make its military dimension as meaningless as possible. The Russian side tried to use the newly established consultation mechanisms to secure a say in NATO's decision-making process to weaken NATO's core as a collective defense organization. NATO-Russia relations were still ambivalent. In Paris, Yeltsin informed Clinton that he could not attend NATO's Madrid summit in July 1997. Yeltsin worried that his attendance would be interpreted as a personal endorsement of NATO enlargement. He referred to the counsel of his advisers and said that "our people believe NATO is something evil and that, if Yeltsin went to Madrid, it would be seen as blessing NATO enlargement. Here we have a strong Founding Act. But it is still a dilemma for me."[76]

At the Madrid summit, NATO had to decide which new members it would invite. The issue was at the center of discussion when NATO's foreign ministers met at the coastal town of Sintra in Portugal on May 29, 1997. The U.S. idea was to invite three new NATO members in the first enlargement round, namely, the Visegrad three—Poland, the Czech Republic, and Hungary. The preference for a small group was based on the assumption that NATO was more likely to remain united and also more likely to be able to grow in the future. The Clinton administration combined a "small but beautiful" first NATO enlargement round with "a robust open door."[77] The first round would not be the last, and NATO would build on the Partnership for Peace for those left out in the first tranche. The U.S. approach was opposed by Chirac, who was determined to include Romania and Slovenia in the first round. The French rationale pertained to geographical balance and matching Poland's accession in the north with Romania in the south—and Chirac gained support from several other countries in the south, among them Portugal, Spain, Italy, Greece, and Turkey.

Chirac's key argument for Romania's NATO membership pertained to the country's post–Cold War fragility.[78] Romania had only begun to make more progress in its transition to democracy and market reforms under the newly elected government of President Emil Constantinescu. It was not certain how permanent these changes were. Hence, Chirac saw NATO membership as a way to keep Romania on its reform trajectory. He argued that "Romania would not be able to become a member of the EU rapidly. . . . So they only had one ambition, universally supported by their people: to get into NATO. If they were not accepted, they would turn away from democracy, and it would be our fault, because we had not held out the hand of friendship."[79] Clinton disagreed. He flipped Chirac's argument. The very fragility of Romania's democracy was the reason why it should not be allowed in at this stage—"the prospect of their joining in the future would keep them up to the mark," Clinton thought.[80]

NATO was in full debate. The Madrid summit turned into a battle. No consensus was reached between those who supported the U.S. view and those who favored the French approach. All eyes turned to Germany. Kohl backed Clinton but hesitated to oppose Chirac in public. Another question was whether NATO should set a date for a second enlargement round and commit to bringing Romania and Slovenia in then. The Clinton administration was firmly against such ideas: This would undermine the integrity of the 1997 decision on enlargement. NATO had to make a political decision on each country's application based on its merits and readiness to join the alliance. Each aspirant had to meet all the political, economic, and military accession criteria. Clinton said, "we ought to say that these three are the most-ready, but that we have an interest in building NATO's southern flank, and that we'll review it in 1999. Then we can send a clear signal to the individual countries that if they can keep their democracies going and stay on the path of reform, they will be excellent candidates."[81] On the flight to the July 1997 Madrid summit, Talbott argued for "taking a tough line against any mention of Romania and Slovenia, on the grounds that it will greatly complicate the Baltic strategy, that it will piss off the Turks and Greeks, since they'd like mention of Bulgaria too, that it will put us on slippery slope of showing that we can be pressured and rolled."[82]

Clinton did not want a fight at the Madrid summit. He wished to be generous and thought Chirac could blow up the summit if he did not get his way. Talbott worried that Clinton left to his own devices at the summit might go along with Chirac and the European leaders. In his diaries, Talbott noted that Sandy Berger's most significant concern for the summit was Clinton himself. "He doesn't have his heart in the argument against mention of Romania and Slovenia; he wants to do something generous for Chirac; he doesn't want a fight w/Chirac; he thinks our theology is bullshit."[83] The challenge for NATO was to achieve a balanced outcome in Madrid. During the summit discussions, Chirac continued to fight for a commitment that Romania and Slovenia would get in at the next NATO summit in 1999. The heads of state were not able to find a solution. Thus the issue was transferred to the foreign ministers, who produced a text that was again discussed by the delegations. The compromise was to review enlargement at the NATO 1999 summit. Moreover, the communiqué recognized the progress of Romania and Slovenia and used more general language on the headway the Baltic states had achieved.[84] In Madrid, NATO invited Poland, the Czech Republic, and Hungary, and the alliance reached out to those who wanted to join in the future. Clinton was determined to keep NATO's door open. In a private conversation, he told Talbott that he was "hoping for the best and creating the conditions for the best, but also being prepared for the possibility of history reasserting itself!!!! . . . We're walking on a tightrope . . . I'm getting flak from people who are arguing on behalf of Romania and Bulgaria but who would abandon the Baltics in a heartbeat, which I think would be unconscionable."[85]

NATO's July 1997 Summit and Its Aftermath

Although the Madrid summit is mostly known for its decisions on NATO enlargement, it also established the Euro-Atlantic Partnership Council (EAPC) to build a broader security architecture beyond NATO's opening. The new council worked alongside PfP and promoted closer contacts and cooperation between NATO and its partner countries in eastern Europe and Eurasia.[86] The EAPC succeeded the North Atlantic Cooperation Council and allowed NATO to undertake specific partnership activities, joint military missions, and exercises with all former Soviet republics and Warsaw Pact states. On July 9, 1997, NATO assembled the forty-three leaders of the EAPC countries on the second day of the Madrid summit. When Clinton addressed the EAPC summit, he told the representatives of the smaller nations that previously "the big powers have had the habit of talking about you without you. We're getting away from that way of doing the world's business, and it's about time."[87] Talbott sat in the audience, watched the scenery, and caught the mood in his diaries. "I look around the room and find myself looking at the Albanian, Armenian, and Azerbaijani (Aliyev) across the way; the Uzbek is next to Potus (alphabet!), and some 40 other countries," Talbott noted. "I find myself thinking about all those pictures I've seen of great int'l conferences in the 19th and 20th centuries. . . . There's something different here . . . In those past ones, whether Congress of Vienna or Versailles, the two that come to mind, the Great Powers are meeting to recarve up the map, deciding the fate of the little guys; here the big and the little guys are together. . . . I think of the Polish phrase that we've all learned [not about us without us] and how that has become the motto of the whole exercise and how this EAPC if it works, could be the vindication of that."[88]

Like the OSCE, the EAPC reflected the assumption that Russia and its neighbors could be part of a joint institution that could discuss security issues on an equal footing without Russia flexing its muscle. In many ways, the EAPC was based on the premise that Russia would accept its neighbors' sovereignty and statehood in the future. However, as policymakers were not certain about Russia's trajectory, NATO membership remained the critical foreign policy objective of the countries that did not make the first NATO enlargement round. At the time, the theory was that Romania, Bulgaria, and Slovenia could be part of the second round, whereas the Baltics could join NATO in a third tranche.[89] But what was Ukraine's role and place in all of this? After all, Ukraine was the linchpin of Europe's security and the theater of potential future conflicts between NATO and Russia. The signing of the NATO-Ukraine charter on the second day of the Madrid summit reflected the assumption that Ukraine could not be left out at a time when NATO enlarged and established a new relationship with Russia.[90]

The charter was much less than Ukraine had envisaged. It did not entail the robust security assurances that President Kuchma wanted. It did not give Ukraine a long-term perspective on NATO membership either. It left the country in limbo between Russia and the West at a time when its reform process was not consolidated. Kuchma admitted Ukraine's precarious domestic situation when he spoke with Clinton in Madrid. "The emphasis in Ukraine today is not to enhance security vaguely but to guarantee no return to communism. Such a danger does exist today," he said.[91] Ukraine still struggled to maintain its sovereignty given the perils of disintegration and a split between Western-oriented Ukrainians in the west and ethnic Russians in the east. The considerable risk remained that Ukraine could turn into "some sort of Belarus-style province integrated with Russia," Talbott noted.[92] Kuchma was disappointed that NATO missed a chance to bolster Ukraine's security more decisively. In May 1997, when he visited Washington, he made a bold case for more powerful language in the document to assert Ukraine's sovereignty vis-à-vis Russia. "I am deeply confident that Russia will never agree to an independent Ukraine in its mentality and thinking," Kuchma said. "We are dealing with the Russia of

Boris Nikolayevich today, but there may be someone else with a completely different policy in the future," he added.[93] Kuchma did not like the text of the NATO-Ukraine charter either and thought it was "strictly declarative" and "a watered-down version of the NATO-Russia document."[94]

In their conversation with Kuchma, Clinton and Gore understood his position. "If I was a neighbor and heard that Ukraine must be subject to Russian hegemony, I would probably react the same way as you," Gore said.[95] His point was that the picture looked different from Washington's perspective, especially after the conclusion of the Russo-Ukrainian Treaty of Friendship and the Black Sea Fleet agreement in May 1997. It foresaw Russian leases of the Sevastopol ports for the deployments of its Black Sea Fleet. Russia implicitly recognized Ukraine's sovereignty over the city by agreeing to a lease.[96] However, Kuchma's concern was that Russian policymakers could reclaim Crimea and Sevastopol as Russian territory at some point in the future after Yeltsin's tenure. Hence, he wanted more robust Western commitments to protect Ukraine's security. This was not in sight, though. It seemed impossible for Ukraine to join NATO even in the long run. After all, NATO had made major military concessions to Russia when it declared it would not station permanent foreign forces in its new member states. Defending Ukraine against a potential Russian attack would be impossible without such forces. In fact, "NATO could not readily carry out Article 5 guarantees to Ukraine against a major military threat without building a large military infrastructure in Eastern Europe."[97]

In the late 1990s, Ukraine was not ready for NATO membership either. The country was in deep crisis, and the West could still lose it. At the time, it seemed that a coalition of communists and agrarian parties could win the parliamentary elections in March 1998. In this case, Ukraine could turn into another "Belarus-type" scenario.[98] When Talbott visited Kyiv a couple of weeks before the March 1998 election, his interlocutors expressed frustration about the lack of more comprehensive Western financial aid packages. Ukraine's soon-to-be Foreign Minister Boris Tarasyuk complained that "some Western contacts had compared the possible leftist victory in the Rada to similar events in Poland, Bulgaria and Romania. He warned that Ukraine was unlike those countries in that Ukraine's existence as a sovereign state was at stake."[99] The underlying problem was that Western financial institutions had lost confidence in Ukraine because of its inability to live up to its reform promises. Eventually, the March 1998 parliament elections brought a positive outcome because the Communist Party did not assume power. However, the downside was that the elections perpetuated the rule of an informal alliance of four oligarchic factions supporting Kuchma.[100]

Given its internal situation, Ukraine did not stand much of a chance of getting closer to NATO or EU membership. The country's economic transition was much slower than expected. No domestic consensus had been reached about Ukraine's identity and whether the country should see its future in the West or in a closer association with Russia. Another burden was that even the liberal Yeltsin was waging a "continued trade war" that included severe restrictions on Ukrainian exports.[101] From a Western vantage point, Ukraine was still difficult to do business with. The country remained dependent on economic assistance from the United States and international financial institutions. The Clinton administration was determined to support Ukraine over the long term. Talbott told Ukrainian Ambassador Shcherbak that Ukraine's membership in NATO was not just a theoretical option but "a guiding principle which we have restated over and over. It is an 'article of faith' for the U.S. NATO's door will remain open in the future to a democratic, reformist Ukraine."[102] In April 1998, Talbott reiterated this point in an address at the workshop on Ukraine-NATO relations sponsored by the Harvard University Project on Ukrainian Security and the Stanford-Harvard Preventive Defense Project. He concluded that "an independent, unitary, secure, democratic, prosperous, self-confident, integrated Ukraine is a keystone in the architecture of this new Europe. . . . The keystone keeps in place the arch in architecture; if the keystone crumbles, the structure collapses. We cannot let that happen—for Ukraine's sake or for our own."[103]

Compared with Ukraine, the Visegrad 3 were in a different position. Poland, the Czech Republic, and Hungary would soon join NATO. Following the July 1997 Madrid summit, Clinton went on a tour of emotional visits to Warsaw, Bucharest, and Copenhagen. Polish policymakers greeted Clinton with gratitude and appreciation. Poland was a critical new NATO member in terms of its strategic importance, its size, and its geography. Poland's security has been threatened by hostility from Russia and Germany throughout its history. After the end of the Cold War, Poland sought security in NATO against Russian domination and German resurgence. NATO membership promised to prevent a repetition of history.[104]

During his July 1997 visit, Clinton reminded Polish President Aleksandr Kwasniewski about Poland's responsibilities as a future NATO member, pointing out that "Poland can have a positive impact among the countries that were not invited to NATO but want to join in the future. We hope you will share your experience with others and be a good example to them. Poland, Hungary, and the Czech Republic will be in a unique position to point out to countries not invited the real benefits of reforms and the opportunities available through the Partnership for Peace, the Euro-Atlantic Partnership Council, and other forms of cooperation with the international community."[105] While in Warsaw, Clinton enlisted former President Lech Walesa to secure bipartisan support in the congressional NATO enlargement ratification debate in the United States. Given his popularity in America, Walesa was essential to this endeavor.[106]

Clinton's next visit was to Bucharest on July 11. Unlike Poland, Romania was not slated to join NATO in 1999. Its reform process was considerably slower, and its eligibility for NATO membership only improved after the victory of the liberal Emil Constantinescu in the 1996 presidential election.[107] The purpose of Clinton's visit to Bucharest was to keep Romania engaged. He wanted a firsthand impression of the situation in the country. Still, he was unsure what to expect given NATO's decision to not include Romania in the 1999 NATO enlargement tranche. If Clinton had any concerns, they proved unwarranted. He was greeted by more than a hundred thousand people when he addressed the crowds at University Square in downtown Bucharest. During his private meeting with Constantinescu, Clinton emphasized his gratefulness for Romania's patience and the overwhelming welcome. He asked for understanding that "the U.S. and U.K. position on Romania's and Bulgaria's membership in NATO now was not a negative one for your countries, but we believe that a smaller number of new members from among those most financially capable of sustaining the costs is best."[108] Talbott formulated Romania's emerging relationship with NATO in positive terms and told Prime Minister Victor Ciorbea that "in our public dialogue, the most important thing was to avoid the word 'no' and to find ways to embrace the word 'yes.' . . . Our common task over the next years was to make that outcome as natural, non-controversial and inevitable as possible."[109] First of all, Romania established a strategic partnership with the United States. This was an important sign. In an earlier meeting with Talbott, Constantinescu recalled that Romania could have quickly taken Yugoslavia's road. "After 1989," he said, "Romania had all the elements for becoming another Yugoslavia: a concentrated Hungarian minority in Transylvania; nostalgia for territories lost to Ukraine and Bulgaria; and an initial assumption that Moldova would reunite with Romania."[110] So, the good news was that Romania did not relapse into the past, though the speed of its reforms was somewhat slower than elsewhere.

Meanwhile, NATO-Russian relations were in crisis even though the two sides no longer considered each other adversaries. The NATO-Russia Founding Act established the Permanent Joint Council as a new consultation mechanism.[111] The first PJC meeting at the ministerial level was promising. It took place on September 26 at the margins of the UN General Assembly in New York. It produced a detailed work program through the end of 1997, including Russia's participation in PfP and expanding cooperation in the military and defense realm.[112] The consensus in NATO was to integrate Russia in joint peacekeeping operations in the Balkans and NATO's humanitarian relief work. Russian policymakers seemed to have exaggerated expectations regarding the PJC's scope, however. Primakov had difficulty acknowledging that the PJC would not give Russia a lever for co-decision-making or a veto regarding NATO's internal consultations. Moreover, Primakov tried to use the PJC talks to continue the battle over the terms of the Founding Act and NATO's military infrastructure in its new member states—a spiel that Albright rejected at the PJC ministerial meeting in December 1997.[113] The competing aims remained in place. The NATO-Russia Founding Act and the convocation of PJC meetings could do little to narrow the gap in conceptions.

The Founding Act failed to bring stability. In 1997, Talbott was hopeful when he wrote Mamedov that "we should move quickly to put the protracted debate over NATO enlargement and European security behind us. We need to ensure that the NATO-Russia Founding Act becomes a mechanism for transforming both the Continent and Russia's role in it."[114] However, in the next three years, various shocks and setbacks led to a downward spiral in U.S.-Russia relations. Russia's financial collapse in 1998 destroyed the country's reform project. The Kosovo War of 1999 led to a nationalist groundswell in Russia. Finally, starting in 1999, the second Chechen War catapulted Vladimir Putin into the president's office. The trifecta of crisis forever changed the struggle for Russia's future. The downward spiral started in 1997 when Russia began to withdraw from its 1995 agreement banning arms trade with Iran.

CHAPTER V

Russia's Financial Crisis and the End of Reform

Talbott, Albright, and the Search for the
Right Russia Policy

Talbott approached the next phase in U.S.-Russia relations with "strategic optimism."[1] In September 1997, he used an address at Stanford University to take stock, reviewing the achievements of Clinton's Russia policy in the first term and assessing the challenges in the years to come. Talbott saw Russia "at a turning point" and believed the country had to clarify what kind of a state it wanted to be. "It's a matter," he said, "of how Russia will define statehood itself. Will it be in terms of Russia's specialness and separateness? Or will it be in terms of those heritages and interests it has in common with the rest of the world, particularly with Europe and the West?" Talbott thought that Russia had not figured this out. "We are helping make it happen. We are doing what we can to ensure that the international community is as open as possible to Russia."[2] Talbott hoped Russia would unlearn aggression and imperialism through diplomacy and contacts with the West. Given Russia's slow pace of adaptation, Talbott argued for "strategic patience."[3] The prospects for Russia's integration seemed good. In June 1997, at the G-7 summit in Denver, Russia was formally invited to join the political part of the G-7; the financial and economic part remained confined to the traditional G-7. Russia's international status was elevated. Russia's inauguration to the Group of Eight in Denver and the conclusion of the NATO-Russia Founding Act opened up new prospects for a closer relationship between Russia and the West.

At the same time, Talbott identified Russia's policy in the Middle East as a problem on the horizon. Evidence was abundant that Russian entities were helping Iran acquire ballistic missile technology despite Russia's 1995 pledge to end its arms deliveries to Iran.[4] Given Russia's role as Iran's key arms provider, Madeleine Albright grew increasingly skeptical about the trajectory of U.S.-Russia relations.[5] She doubted whether Yeltsin and Primakov played it straight—hence she thought about a more assertive U.S. Russia policy. In December 1997, on Talbott's instigation, she convened a meeting with her senior Russia advisers to discuss her discontent. "Deep, deep lingering in my soul I'm ambivalent about Russia," she said as the meeting started. "Our responsibility is not to let our view of reality be cleared [clouded] by what we want to have happen; we've got to be driven by what we think actually will happen," she continued. She appreciated the good chemistry between Clinton and Yeltsin, Gore and Chernomyrdin, and even herself and Primakov, but she was "putting . . . her weight on the side of skepticism. I'm not sure that Yeltsin is truly connected to anyone," she noted. Her primary concern was whether Yeltsin was still in charge and whether he cared at all. Albright thought that the Clinton administration was too compliant toward Primakov's assertive policy in the Middle East. She assumed that Primakov was "trying to screw us; he's riding high and trying to take over the Middle East. . . . We've got to keep open the possibility that they're lying through their teeth, that they have every intention of regaining the near abroad, that we're being naïve." Talbott did not share Albright's assumptions. He thought that Russia was not the sponsor of a terror regime, but that it was still behaving like a normal state. He believed Russia was playing by "normal rules as a state (Iran is exception, but that's not really the state/ gov't)."[6]

As a Czech émigré, Albright had a different perspective: Her formative Russia experiences were the communist takeover of Czechoslovakia in 1948 and the violent oppression of the Prague Spring in 1968. After World War II, Albright's father, Joseph Korbel, returned to Prague to help build a democratic government with the previously exiled President Edvard Benes. The 1948 communist coup in Prague forced Korbel to emigrate to the United States.[7] In the 1970s, Albright wrote her doctoral dissertation on the role of the Czechoslovak press in 1968 during the Prague Spring.[8] Given her biography, Albright was especially sensitive about the dangers of

Russian retrogression. In the December 1997 meeting on Russia, Albright praised Zbigniew Brzezinski's 1997 book *The Grand Chessboard*, in which Brezinski made the case for American preeminence in Eurasia at Russia's expense.[9] Regarding Brzezinski, Albright said, "he's so he's so much smarter than the rest of us." Talbott disagreed. "I say I'm not sure that's true, his smarts are a matter of being able to systematize, of putting different events and trends and facts into a conceptual framework which he then explains brilliantly—but that it often doesn't fit reality or policy very well. I point out that the essence of his book is to make the case for the dismemberment of Russia—that way lies disaster," Talbott said.[10]

In his diaries, Talbott captured Albright's reaction, noting that "she sees the emphasis on genuine independence for the non-Russian nis [newly independent states]; I say look at how he talks about 'loose federation' of Russia—that can only be understood, certainly in Moscow, as more of Chechnya, Tatarstan, and eventual breakup; she agrees, says that 'worst thing about the time we live in is the emergence of all these too-small ethnically based countries . . . having big countries come apart like matryoshka dolls.'" In response, Talbott said, "well, Zbig's book will be read only one way in Russia: Russia is the ultimate matryoshka doll, and Zbig wants to take it apart, piece by piece." During the conversation, Albright turned to Talbott, saying, "I know you have the President's ear on this." Talbott replied, "actually the President has my ear, and hers; it's his policy we're talking about." Albright's response was, "I agree with everything you're saying, but there's still a small soft voice whispering in my ear that says we're being played for a sucker."[11]

Given Russian missile sales to Iran, Albright was skeptical about the usefulness of another Clinton-Yeltsin summit in 1998. Moreover, she doubted the adequacy of the U.S.-Russian talks on Iran.[12] In January 1998, she decided to deprioritize Russia in U.S. foreign policy. On her behalf, State Department Policy Planning Director Greg Craig suggested "the relegation of Russia policy to . . . the second tier" of U.S. diplomacy. This ran counter to the way Talbott envisaged America's Russia statecraft. Talbott rebutted Craig's argument: "In a way, I wish I could subscribe to that idea, since it would imply that Russia's progress to date is irreversible," Talbott wrote in a memo to Craig, but "I don't think we're anywhere near that point."[13] Talbott rejected the terms of the debate. He argued that Russia was not lost but was undergoing a difficult phase in its foreign policy—and Russia's domestic transition was far from complete. The country needed continued U.S. support. Russia had just become a partner of NATO and a member of the G-8, he reasoned, and, for better or worse, had to be included in the search for stability in the Middle East and the Gulf. Craig's line of thought signaled the start of a broader policy debate on Russia in the context of the 1998 financial crisis when Congress made the case for a return to a more containment-oriented policy or even for disengagement.[14] Albright's experience as an NSC staffer in the Jimmy Carter administration was another important factor that contributed to her advocacy for a tougher line. In January 1998, Albright told Talbott that she was "determined not to let the President seem 'naïve, Carteresque.'"[15] In the late 1970s, given the U.S.-Soviet tensions, she witnessed how a frequently indecisive and weak President Carter failed as a Wilsonian idealist. Moreover, she had seen the feuds over U.S. foreign policy between a hawkish Brzezinski and a hesitant Secretary of State Cyrus Vance.

Finally, in terms of U.S. Russia policy, Albright and Talbott had many things in common as well, despite their different backgrounds. Both were astute and tireless policymakers with in-depth knowledge of central and eastern Europe and Russia. Both spoke several Slavic languages. Of course, Albright spoke Russian with a Czech accent, and Talbott's Czech had a Russian accent. This was evident in January 1998 when Talbott messed around reading the front page of a Vaclav Havel letter that Albright had just received. Albright was puzzled and said, "you know, Strobe, your Czech has a classic Russian accent." After a little pause, she laughed, "of course, my Russian has a classic Czech accent, so I guess that says it all about the two of us, right?" Still, both found ways to deal with their dissimilarities. In January 1998, Talbott noted he was grateful for "the degree of license and support I've had, esp. given the difference in our 'software'—on her part, cuz of biography and background."[16]

Russian Missiles Sales to Iran

By late 1997, Russian missile technology sales to Iran turned into a pivotal issue in the U.S.-Russia relationship. It was evident that Russia reneged on its 1995 pledge to stop the transfer of sensitive technologies, although Yeltsin vigorously denied this vis-à-vis Clinton. On October 30, 1997, Clinton called Yeltsin to underline the gravity of the issue. Yeltsin turned cranky and denied the issue when Clinton pressed him directly. "Iran is not getting any missiles from us. There's no way they can get it," he said.[17] Clinton knew the facts and sent out Gore and Talbott to discuss the magnitude of the problem with Chernomyrdin and Mamedov. In Moscow, Talbott's message was that "we need demonstrable, verifiable actions in the next few weeks. When Iran gets a ballistic missile capability, the question will be asked to what extent did Russia help make this possible? Greater transparency is the key. We do not want this issue to stop our promising relationship."[18] Moreover, Congress demanded U.S. sanctions against Russia. Talbott agreed on the importance of keeping sanctions on the table to obtain a negotiated solution.[19] He wanted to get the Russians to issue "catchall" legislation to close the loopholes in Russia's nonproliferation laws.[20] In March 1998, the Clinton administration pulled out another carrot for Russia to deliver on its promises to tighten its nonproliferation export controls: Gore took Chernomyrdin to Silicon Valley and argued that Russia could secure billions of dollars in trade with U.S. high-tech companies. Chernomyrdin promised to work things out in Moscow.[21] However, he did not get a chance to fulfill his promises. On March 23, 1998, he was dismissed as prime minister. Yeltsin appointed the thirty-five-year-old Sergey Kiriyenko as his successor.

Although Kiriyenko had the credentials of a reformer, Chernomyrdin's dismissal was considered a severe loss. He knew how to get things done, and it was not clear whether a Kiriyenko-Gore commission could be equally efficient. Talbott was surprised when he heard about Kiriyenko's appointment. Russia was like "a roller coaster," he noted. In response to Chernomyrdin's dismissal, Talbott proposed launching new initiatives and sending a "steady stream of visitors" to overcome the fatigue in the U.S.-Russia partnership. "Let's do it again," Talbott argued.[22] On April 20, 1998, Talbott visited Moscow for his first talks with Kiriyenko.[23] He tried to avert U.S. sanctions at a point when most observers expected them against the backdrop of a severe incident: In late March 1998, Azerbaijanian authorities intercepted a shipment of twenty-two tons of a particular sort of Russian steel for the production of rocket fuel tanks that several Russian shell corporations were trying to smuggle to Iran.[24] Clinton was incensed. On April 6, 1998, he called Yeltsin with an urgent request to do something about the situation. "The interception of specialty steel destined for Iran is potentially a disastrous setback for our relationship," he said.[25] Talbott wrote Mamedov that "we're at another of those absolutely critical moments that have punctuated U.S.-Russian relations over the past five years. Either we reverse the vicious cycle in the coming days, or we may not be able to control the fallout."[26] The struggle over Russia's missile assistance to Iran caused a spiral of mutual suspicion. Talbott observed that the atmosphere of his meetings in Moscow was entirely different from 1997. "Just to drive the point home: I doubt we could get a NATO-Russia Founding Act today," he noted.[27]

In April 1998, Talbott's objective in Moscow was to establish the framework for the resolution of the Iran missile issue before the forthcoming Clinton-Yeltsin meeting at the Birmingham G-8 summit in May 1998. Yeltsin's chief of staff, Valentin Yumashev, reaffirmed that the Russian side would stand by Yeltsin's assurances. "Yeltsin is determined that Iran will not get weapons of mass destruction," he said.[28] While in Moscow, Talbott also spoke with Yeltsin's new national security adviser, Andrey Kokoshin, who was in charge of the Iran issue. Talbott used the meeting to emphasize the gravity of the problem. "From our side," he said, "the problem remains that it is only with high-level intervention that we get action and movement on issues like this. . . . We have got four weeks to get this situation under control. . . . We can have a bad spiral downward unless we act."[29] Kokoshin understood. He was determined to work on a solution and tighten the whole system of Russian export controls. The plan was to open up a new channel between Berger and Kokoshin.

U.S.-Russia relations were at a critical juncture. Clinton wanted to use the Birmingham G-8 meeting with Yeltsin for a restart. Further delays and unpleasant surprises had to be avoided. Among the G-8, the Clinton team wanted to establish a hotline for rapidly exchanging information on nonproliferation issues. Another objective was to produce a joint statement to fight missile proliferation. In early May 1998, Talbott sensed that the whole endeavor could fail. "Can't stop train wreck with what we've got. Need a breakthrough, quantum leap. Time is very, very short. Every day counts," he noted.[30] Berger and Kokoshin were scheduled to meet in Moscow on May 7. The Russian side had to implement a catchall policy on missile proliferation at once. The Clinton administration had been deferring a decision on sanctions for several months despite heavy legal and political pressures from the Republican majority in Congress.[31] The U.S. Senate would soon consider a sanctions bill with eighty-two cosponsors. Berger alerted Kokoshin, saying, "If we cannot break the back of the Iran proliferation problems, Birmingham could be about the past. It could be a discussion of sanctions leading to mutual recriminations. We do not want that."[32]

Indeed, Berger's May 7 meeting with Kokoshin proved that the latter had the authority to act. Talbott recalled that "it seemed at the time to be one of the most productive Russian-American encounters in five years. Kokoshin agreed to all the measures Sandy laid out."[33] Indeed, Kokoshin could bring many Russian authorities in line, including the military-industrial complex and the intelligence services. Kokoshin was pragmatic and solution oriented and did not shy away from conflicts with hard-liners. He endorsed the U.S. draft for a G-8 statement on missile proliferation. "He had no problem with the U.S. draft and would fax it to Mamedov in London. He wanted Yeltsin to approve it and present it to Primakov as a fait accompli," Talbott noted.[34] While in Moscow, Talbott had productive meetings with Kiriyenko and Yumashev. His message was clear: "President Clinton gives no issue greater importance than developments in Russia and our bilateral relations."[35] Talbott hoped that close contacts with Kiriyenko would help sustain Russia's reform path—and Clinton was determined to signal his endorsement by visiting Moscow in the autumn of 1998.[36]

The Talbott-Berger talks in Moscow had an immediate effect. The Russian government began a campaign against companies doing business with Iran—and several Iranian "businessmen" were expelled from Russia. Moreover, Yeltsin emphasized his determination to tighten export controls in a public speech at the Russian Foreign Ministry. Clinton praised these deeds in a telephone conversation with Yeltsin on May 12. "I hope we can work this out in Birmingham," he said. Yeltsin responded, "Yes, it's a very good thing, and I agree. I accept it fully."[37] Clinton was proud of his foreign policy team. Talbott and Berger had achieved a real breakthrough. They were a good team and trusted each other. Talbott praised Berger as a "totally honest broker, highest intellectual standards, astute mind, completely trusted by all members of the team, conscientious and hardworking beyond belief, runs terrific meeting, preserves quality control, genuinely coordinates, immensely effective in dealing with foreign counterparts as I'd seen in Moscow with Kokoshin."[38]

Clinton approached the Birmingham G-8 summit with optimism and praised Yeltsin, who appreciated Clinton's patience and the mutual efforts to resolve the Iran problem quietly and cooperatively. "You know, Bill," Yeltsin said, "people keep saying that we're losing confidence in each other, that our partnership is running aground. Let's make sure they know we're doing fine. With the policy you've pursued toward Russia these past five years, you can't lose, and in the time remaining to you in office you can score more points."[39] Meanwhile, however, congressional pressure for sanctions was overwhelming. The Senate passed a sanctions bill with a vote of 90–4.[40] Clinton vetoed it but was forced to issue several less severe sanctions. Finally, the Russian government implemented its enhanced export control regulations and began investigating suspicious companies' activities. In parallel, the Clinton administration imposed what it called trade restrictions—a euphemism to avoid the term *sanctions*. Talbott recalled that "we preserved the appearance of cooperative rather than punitive action, and the Senate was sufficiently mollified to hold off a vote on overriding the veto."[41] However, it was already too late. In July 1998, Iran tested its first medium-range Shahab 3 missile, which had been developed with Russian aid, according to CIA estimates.[42]

Russia's 1998 Financial Crisis and the End of Stability

At the outset of Yeltsin's second term, Russia was seemingly on the path of economic stabilization and had its first modest growth in a decade. Russia got into the eurobond market and raised $2 billion, and Clinton envisaged Russia's World Trade Organization accession as the next step.[43] Russia's relationship with the International Monetary Fund (IMF) also worked reasonably well. The country had become a member in 1992 when its inflation was 2,500 percent. By 1996, Russia's inflation was under control, and the Russian economy began to grow.[44] In 1997, Yeltsin and his advisers worked on a bold land reform, a tax reform, and the deregulation of the electricity sector and the railway system. Yeltsin was proud to tell British Prime Minister Tony Blair that "the GDP was now beginning to rise, and there had even been deflation in the last two months. Wages were going up while prices were not."[45]

The potential for foreign investments was enormous. Russia had vast natural resources, a sound education system, and talented young managers. Western policymakers embraced Yeltsin's young reformers, Anatoly Chubais and Boris Nemtsov, who had both been appointed deputy prime ministers. In November 1997, when Blair visited Moscow, he spoke with both and announced Britain's intention to provide an additional £500 million export credit to establish more substantial investments. When Blair inquired whether foreign investments were welcome, Chubais's reply was straightforward: "It needed to quadruple to make a real difference. Privatization was the obvious route for this." Despite their optimism and can-do attitude, Chubais and Nemtsov did not ignore the fundamental political and economic problems beneath the surface. "There was no real middle class in Russia, and this encouraged aggressive and extreme political parties," Nemtsov said. "Democratic capitalism was needed to encourage the creation of small companies and a new middle class. But until the latter existed, there was no base of support for democratic capitalism. This was the vicious circle Russia faced," Nemtsov pointed out.[46] The underlying question was whether markets in Russia were actually working and whether the ruble's exchange rate could be kept stable over the long term. Politically, as Grigory Yavlinsky put it, "the vital question for Russia is whether it will become a quasi-democratic oligarchy with corporatist, criminal characteristics or take the more difficult, painful road to becoming a normal, Western-style democracy with a market economy."[47]

Russia's economic problems grew more severe in 1997 when Asia's financial meltdown led to a fall in oil prices and decreased Russian export revenues. The sharp loss of reserves threatened the ruble's stability and caused an acute need to raise funds to cover the budget expenses. In December 1997, Yeltsin approached the IMF again for financial assistance.[48] In November 1997, Chubais had been dismissed as finance minister due to his involvement in a privatization scandal. His influence was waning but he retained his position as deputy prime minister.[49] Yeltsin and his team were still reasonably confident that the reform process was on track. The Clinton administration shared this assessment. When Talbott saw Yeltsin's chief of staff, Valentin Yumashev, in October 1997, he stressed that "President Clinton believes that the fundamentals of the U.S.-Russian relationship are still sound and promising."[50] However, Russia's Achilles' heel was its continued dependency on oil export revenues. Following the 1997 Asian financial shock and the severe decrease in global demand for crude oil and nonferrous metals, Russia's foreign exchange reserves began to melt away. Russia was increasingly integrated into the worldwide market but tried to maintain a soft budget and subsidies feeding higher fiscal deficits.[51] Moscow had financed its budget with international credits, which were beginning to dry up.[52]

By mid-May 1998, the situation was already bleak. Asia's financial crisis deeply affected Russia, causing soaring interest rates and plunging oil prices. Russia's growth perspectives started to vanish. Banks began selling off their dollars, though Russia's authorities managed to raise another $3.8 billion from eurobonds issued in June 1998.[53] On May 28, 1998, Yeltsin called Clinton with an urgent plea to help stabilize the situation: "We need your support," Yeltsin said. "People in the world must know that you support us and that you are sure that Russia will handle the situation, that everything will be in order. Well, the situation is difficult. Did you get me, Bill?"[54] Clinton got Yeltsin's message and pushed for a massive IMF bailout. On July 13, the IMF and the World Bank helped Russia with an emergency package of $22.6 billion. The injection of new liquidity was supposed to buy time for further Russian reforms and efforts to swap out short-term ruble treasury bills into long-term eurobonds. The Russian government tried to keep the ruble exchange rate within a narrow band to stabilize the currency. In July 1998, Yeltsin emphasized the situation's urgency in another telephone conversation with Clinton: "If we do not get a decision soon, by the end of next week, it would mean the end of reform and basically the end of Russia. The consequences would be catastrophic and drastic, not only for Russia but for the global financial system as well."[55]

The reformist rescue plans faced domestic opposition, though. The left-wing parties in the Russian Duma refused to adopt most of the Kiriyenko government's ideas. Hence the government was forced to rely on presidential decrees. On July 29, Yeltsin interrupted his vacation in the Valdai Hills region and flew to Moscow, prompting fears of a cabinet reshuffle. Still, he only replaced Federal Security Service Chief Nikolay Kovalyov with Vladimir Putin, the previous deputy chief of the presidential staff. The inability of the Russian government to implement a coherent set of economic reforms led to a severe erosion in investor confidence. Investors fled the market and sold rubles and assets. The Central Bank was forced to spend its foreign reserves to defend Russia's currency, which further eroded investor confidence, undermining the ruble. Until August 1998, the Central Bank expended approximately $27 billion of its U.S. dollar reserves to maintain the floating peg.[56] Could Russia be rescued? The U.S. Treasury Department and Clinton's finance advisers were skeptical, given Russia's track record of mismanagement and doubts about the competency of Yeltsin's team. Clinton's finance people were unwilling to provide Russia with additional aid packages. Secretary of Treasury Robert Rubin argued that July's first IMF assistance tranche would also be the last. Rubin thought that "by the time that you got to 1996 and 1997 and 1998 there was a general feeling that an awful lot that needed to occur in Russia for Russia to be successful economically simply wasn't happening."[57] The Treasury Department and the IMF increasingly saw Russia as a lost place—their patience ran out. In contrast, Clinton, Berger, and Talbott tried to do more to help Russia. "If the island is going to sink, I want to talk about how to live under water," Berger said.[58] "The real problem is," Clinton argued, "that the Russians are taking their own money out of the country. All the money the IMF put into Russia in the first installment is gone now. Somehow, we have to get some clarity in there as quickly as possible—that they will stay with the reform program—and get the money flowing in instead of flowing out."[59]

As the crisis grew even more severe, Yeltsin fired Kiriyenko on August 23, 1998. He planned to appoint Chernomyrdin as prime minister again to establish a government of reformers and business leaders.[60] Yeltsin needed Chernomyrdin as a problem fixer but not as a potential candidate for his succession as president—and it seemed Yeltsin wanted Chernomyrdin to avoid Primakov's promotion to prime minister.[61] The Russian Duma had one week to confirm or reject Chernomyrdin's nomination. Meanwhile, Russia's political turmoil jeopardized Clinton's forthcoming visit in just a week, in early September. In these circumstances, Talbott went to Moscow again to assess the situation. When Talbott heard the news of Kiriyenko's dismissal, he got on the phone with James Collins, the U.S. ambassador in Moscow. Talbott assessed that "the situation is critical but not hopeless; they're shaking the dice in a very Russian wacko way; it's at least possible we could have Kiriyenkoism under Chernomyrdin. The previous situation was not tenable. Key will be who sticks around—Fyodorov, Chubais, Gaidar behind the scenes." Collins agreed: There was "lots of uncertainty, but no indication they're going to turn it over to the crazies and/or the communists. Is it going to be Kiriyenko in Chernomyrdin's suit, or will it go back to compromise/lowest-common-denominator, delaying nasty decisions."[62]

The Clinton-Yeltsin Summit in September 1998

Given the scope of Russia's turmoil, Clinton was not certain whether it would make sense for him to visit Moscow at all. His domestic advisers were against it, fearing that Yeltsin might be forced to resign on the eve of Clinton's visit. Another concern pertained to Clinton's weakened domestic situation against the backdrop of the Lewinsky scandal. On August 17, 1998, Clinton had confessed his affair with Monica Lewinsky. He faced impeachment.[63] Clinton's troubles began to impair his ability to conduct foreign policy. Another danger was that Clinton's Moscow visit could be seen as a way to escape domestic pressure. Moreover, the U.S. public grew increasingly critical of U.S. Russia's policy. American aid to Russia was increasingly seen as a waste of resources. Domestic critics viewed Clinton's visit as the epitome of a flawed U.S. Russia policy. Russia analyst Thomas Graham wrote that "the financial collapse of last August shattered all illusions about Russia's trajectory. It marked the failure of the Western policy of the past seven years, the end of the grand liberal project of rapidly transforming Russia into a normal market economy and democratic polity."[64] Talbott saw things differently: In a memo to Albright and Berger, he pointed out that "for reasons of enlightened self-interest, we are as committed as ever to supporting Russian reform and transformation. That is not to say we're committing to 'saving' or 'rescuing' Russia. Only Russia can save itself from the darker forces of its past and its immediate crisis. There's no silver bullet. But the Russians can, if they choose, help us help them."[65]

Yeltsin saw Clinton's visit as a litmus test, fearing that his friend Bill would abandon Russia at this crucial time. Primakov and Mamedov told Talbott that they viewed the summit as the last chance to preserve "continuous engagement."[66] When Talbott went to Moscow on August 26, his task was to figure out the chances for a successful Clinton visit the following week. He wanted to get a sense of whether Yeltsin would still be president then— and he was determined to figure out whether Clinton could still trust Yeltsin or whether the Russian side was trying to exploit the visit for its purposes. On August 25, Clinton called Yeltsin and announced Talbott's visit. "Strobe is coming to Moscow this week, and I hope you can find time to meet with him. He will have my latest thinking about our upcoming meeting."[67] Talbott wanted to use his "scouting expedition" to get a complete picture and to discuss the state of affairs with a broad spectrum of people in Moscow.[68] Collins communicated this approach to Mamedov: "We don't have a one-person or two-person-oriented Russia policy; we're going to continue to deal with anyone and everyone who we feel is an important part of the equation. I am not a wholly owned subsidiary of Primakov, Mamedov Inc. I'm going to see Andrei, Boris, Chubais, everywhere."[69]

For starters, Talbott had a formal and businesslike meeting with Primakov to convey that Clinton's visit was still in limbo. Next, Talbott used a private meeting with Mamedov to bring up an unusual proposal. In confidence, Talbott brought up the idea of deferring NATO's first enlargement round against the backdrop of Russia's crisis. "I'm personally committed to recommending to the president that we not take in new members in '99 (or probably 2000), but that it's not a gov't position or a NATO position and that he's got to protect me," Talbott said.[70] Talbott suggested that Clinton might discuss this privately in a September meeting with Primakov at the UN General Assembly. Three weeks later, in mid-September, Mamedov was no longer interested when Talbott raised a potential postponement of the first enlargement round. One of the reasons was the change from Primakov to Ivanov in the Foreign Ministry. In his diary, Talbott noted that Mamedov said "he's not sure it will make that much difference any more, with ISI [Igor Sergeyevich Ivanov] in charge—he's the kind [of a guy] who would say, 'they didn't say "never" and they're still talking about the Balts, so that's unacceptable!' "[71] Finally, Talbott did not pursue the matter further. NATO's timetable on enlargement stood firm. It would have been almost impossible for him to try to change NATO's position on enlargement.

On August 26, while in Moscow, Talbott's most important discussions were with Kokoshin, who tried to convince Talbott that Yeltsin would survive the crisis—and that a summit meeting with Clinton would help and energize him. Talbott doubted the feasibility of a summit. The meeting with Kokoshin remained inconclusive. It did not result in a decision favoring or against a Clinton visit. Finally, Talbott and Kokoshin agreed to meet again the next day.[72] Late that night, Talbott spoke with Albright and Berger on the phone. Both authorized Talbott to press for more robust and specific assurances regarding the reform process and Yeltsin's future—and they gave Talbott a mandate to raise the prospect that Clinton might finally not come. The following day, Berger called Talbott again, saying he had just spoken with Clinton, who was "much more strongly inclined not to come, that he thinks Yeltsin has been handling decisions 'like a fool'. . . . POTUS is considerably more negative than earlier in the day."[73] This was the pretext for Talbott's meeting with Kokoshin on August 27. At the outset, Kokoshin reported about a meeting between Yeltsin and Chernomyrdin the previous night: "There will be no retirement or resignation. Everything is okay. Your President will have a good summit." Talbott was not convinced. "That's not good enough, Andrei. It is likely now that I will recommend to my President that he decide not to come. . . . We do not want our

President to be a walk-on player or a stage prop in the drama of Russian politics, especially without knowing the play, the plot or the ending." The lack of predictability was perhaps the main reason for skepticism. Clinton could not be sure that Yeltsin would not pull another surprise. "I must tell you that I personally have the mounting concern that your side is not coming clean with us, at least not entirely, and that seems to include President Yeltsin himself, whom our President has stuck by through thick and thin for nearly six years," Talbott said.[74]

As a case in point, Talbott referred to March 1998 meetings between Clinton, Gore, and Chernomyrdin and the latter's surprise ouster a few days later. This awful surprise had stuck with the president. Clinton was not sure whether he could trust Yeltsin this time. Kokoshin tried his best to reassure Talbott. Nobody on the Russian side was attempting to abuse Clinton. Canceling the visit would further contribute to Russia's downward spiral. Talbott was not convinced. "Andrei, after hearing all this, I must tell you I rate fairly low—let's say 10–20%—the chances that we will feel it proper to proceed with the visit."[75] Kokoshin did not give up. He urged Talbott to see Primakov and Yeltsin instantly. Primakov conveyed the same message: Yeltsin would certainly not resign—and canceling the visit would be a severe setback for the bilateral relationship. Again, Talbott demanded more transparency and openness about Yeltsin's plans. Who would be the new prime minister? Would Primakov stay on as foreign minister? Was Yeltsin determined to continue the reform agenda?

Talbott wanted to get personal assurances from Yeltsin. Primakov left the room to take a phone call from Yeltsin, who was willing to see Talbott instantly at his Kremlin office. The meeting was contentious. At the outset, Talbott referred to Clinton's concerns about the situation in Russia. He then touched on rumors about Yeltsin's impending resignation in the Russian and American press. Yeltsin turned animated and forceful. Leaning forward and pounding the tabletop with his fist, Yeltsin said, "Look, Mr. Talbott, first of all, I'm absolutely healthy—especially now. Just look at me. Shake my hand again. My grip is firm in more ways than one. . . . I swear . . . to you, both as a person and as a President, that, without any doubt or condition, I will persevere and stay in office not just for now but all the way until the next elections. I will continue to work."[76]

The next day, August 28, Talbott called Clinton and the foreign policy leadership team on a secure conference call.[77] It seemed that Yeltsin's assurances helped change the mood in Washington despite Russia's gloomy economic situation. Berger asked Talbott whether the president should go. "You should still come, Mr. President," Talbott said. "Okay, I'm more than willing to do it. So it's decided," Clinton said after Talbott's presentation. At the same time, Clinton remained cautious. He would not bring fresh IMF money. Albright's concern was that Yeltsin might install communists in decisive positions. Gore strongly encouraged Clinton to go. "The risk of a Russian implosion is great and it's increasing. 'Who lost Russia?' is out there. And cancellation of this trip could be seen as the last straw," Gore argued.[78] On August 28, Clinton announced that he would go to Moscow as planned. "I should go to Russia," Clinton said. "And we should tell them that if they'll be strong and do the disciplined, hard things they have to do to reform their country, their economy, and get through this dark night that we'll stick with them."[79] Talbott went back to Washington for a brief return over the weekend. Three days later, on August 31, 1998, he was on the plane with Clinton heading to Moscow again.

Over the weekend, Talbott reflected on Russia's crisis. He asked his friend Gregory "Grisha" Freidin for an estimate of the situation. Freidin was a professor of Slavic languages and literature at Stanford University and a former dissident Talbott had first met in Moscow in the late 1960s. From Freidin's vantage point, "the question was never whether he [Yeltsin] will resign or not, but whether he concedes that he is a lame duck or not. This, I believe, was the depth of it, not resignation. That much he has conceded," Freidin wrote.[80] Indeed, Yeltsin faced a dilemma. He wanted to remain in office but lacked the power to back up Kiriyenko. Thus Yeltsin launched "a soft coup" by appointing Chernomyrdin as the new prime minister. Clinton thought Chernomyrdin was perhaps the best choice, provided he would continue the reform agenda. "While we know that he will have to make some accommodations, he will have to be very careful to stay with reforms and not tilt too far toward the communists," Clinton said.[81]

On August 31, 1998, Clinton and Talbott discussed Russia's future on the flight to Moscow. They debated several bad scenarios, including a complete financial meltdown, a red or brown takeover, an illegal Yeltsin presidential election win, and a bad compromise leading to a reversal of reforms. Clinton's briefing books were also quite reserved about the prospects of a successful summit, given that Russia was "at a moment of testing and uncertainty not unlike August 1991 or October 1993."[82] At the same time, Clinton and Talbott also considered an optimistic scenario in which Yeltsin would combine fast economic reform with political adjustments and a strong government. Clinton was skeptical, though. "Conventional wisdom about him is right. He's a sick, weak, erratic, jerk," Clinton argued. In response, Talbott said that although "the conventional wisdom is the truth, it's not the whole truth. He's also stubborn, resilient, defiant, tough—and not a quitter. He thrives on adversity and comes alive in the face of a crisis." Clinton interjected, "The thing about Yeltsin is that he's not a Russian bureaucrat. He's an Irish poet. He sees politics as a novel he's writing or a symphony he's composing. I've got to convince him that for two years he's got to come to work every day and be a bureaucrat and make the government work."[83]

Clinton thought there was a one in five chance to avoid the bad scenarios if he could show the Russians a way forward and provide more financial help faster. After unification, Clinton said, "West Germany put $100 billion into East Germany, which has a population of only 18 million, for ten years, for God's sake. What the IMF and the banks have done for Russia is chickenshit when you look at the size of the problem and the size of the stakes." The problem's size necessitated a new Marshall Plan, provided Russia was ready to adopt the IMF precepts. "The IMF tranche is a 40-watt lightbulb in a damned big darkness. To do what we want, they're going to have to be eatin' a very big cow turd for the next 3 or 4 years," Clinton argued.[84] He could not say all of this in public. The IMF and Clinton's finance people insisted on conditionality. They wanted to see Russian deeds first—and the new government under Chernomyrdin would not likely pursue a bold and liberal reform program. Second, Congress was not willing to support a new Marshall Plan–size support package for Russia at a point when everybody was withdrawing money from the country.

On the plane to Moscow, Talbott sat next to Deputy Secretary of Treasury Larry Summers, who had been a protagonist in providing economic advice to the Russian government—both in his capacity as the U.S. Treasury Department and the Harvard Institute for International Development.[85] The institute had played a controversial role in the emergence of radical economic reform plans and the promotion of shock therapy to eliminate price controls and subsidies in post–Cold War Russia. Summers wanted to impose strict conditionality on Russia concerning its fiscal policy.[86] He thought Western financial support packages had failed because Russian policymakers had not implemented budgetary austerity measures.[87]

On the flight to Moscow, Summers gave Clinton a gloomy brief, assuming that "we've reached more than just a setback but an end of reform, that in a real sense it's all over, at least for the foreseeable future." Summers then turned to Talbott, assuming the latter must be in despair given Russia's gloomy situation. "All of us have a lot invested in this country and this policy, but it must be especially hard on you, Strobe," Summers said. "Larry," Talbott replied, "the difference between us—and it doesn't keep us from working well together—is that you think it's over and I think it's just moving into a new stage."[88]

On his arrival, Clinton had a chance to discuss the situation with Chernomyrdin in the limousine ride from the airport to downtown Moscow. Talbott accompanied them and witnessed how Clinton emphasized the necessity of further economic reforms as Chernomyrdin asked for more patience from the IMF.[89] Clinton's meeting with Yeltsin started on a sobering note. On Clinton's inquiry, Yeltsin confessed that he was unsure whether he could get Chernomyrdin confirmed. The Duma had rejected his appointment in the first vote, and Yeltsin was submitting his nomination the second time. A third rejection would imply the dissolution of the parliament and new elections—something Yeltsin could not afford against the backdrop of broad protest against his policy. Yeltsin admitted that he had two alternative candidates for the position of prime minister in case Chernomyrdin's confirmation failed. At this point, he did not want to disclose their names. Clinton did not inquire either. Although Yeltsin was a weakened president, he was still determined to fight the communists and revive the spirit of 1991, when he climbed up onto the tank to avert the coup.[90]

During a break in the meeting with Yeltsin, Berger intercepted Clinton and Talbott. Kokoshin had just confessed that Lebed and Luzhkov were the two alternate candidates for prime minister. Clinton thought about the best approach to react to the news. After the break, he put more pressure on Yeltsin. After the talks on the first day, Talbott thought about the script for the second day. He saw Clinton again, and they spent some time reflecting on the right strategy. Finally, they agreed to boil it down to a straightforward message for Yeltsin: "Stand on principle; protect your legacy."[91] At the outset of the second day, Berger summarized the rationale in the car ride with Clinton and Talbott: "You came into office standing on a tank—serve out your term standing on principles."[92] At the outset of the second day, Clinton told Yeltsin that the bold decision was not about the choice of the new prime minister. It was about the Russian presidency and Yeltsin's legacy. Clinton expressed his support for continued reform but stayed away from endorsing or repudiating Yeltsin's candidates for the position of prime minister. When Yeltsin referred to his plan to crush the Communist Party and go on the attack, Clinton expressed his concern that such a struggle could further worsen Russia's domestic crisis. Talbott noted that "Clinton headed home unsure about what Yeltsin would do—and suspecting that Yeltsin had still not made up his own mind."[93]

The convocation of the summit was an attempt to preserve some normalcy and continuity in the U.S.-Russia relationship. However, Russia's financial collapse forever changed Clinton's Russia policy. It was no longer a shining example of his liberal foreign policy agenda. James Goldgeier and Michael McFaul pointed out that "the dual blow of the August 1998 financial crisis in Russia and the Lewinsky scandal at home permanently altered the way in which Clinton engaged on Russia issues for the rest of his second term."[94] Handling Russia turned into a permanent crisis operation. Talbott worked hard to prevent Russia from being relegated to the second tier of Clinton's foreign policy priorities. He worked feverishly to counter the widespread perception of Russia as a lost place.

Various theories were offered for Russia's failure. Some Russian experts, such as George Kennan, argued that the Clinton administration should not have pursued an idealistic policy, envisaging itself as the lighthouse and teacher of Russia trying to export free markets.[95] Conservative critics saw U.S. financial aid as a waste of resources and a way for Russia to build up its military capabilities. Clinton was under pressure to abandon Russia. That was out of the question. However, given increasing public criticism, it was essential to highlight the limits of America's ability to help Russia. The leadership in Moscow had ownership of the country's reform process—this was Albright's key theme in an address before the U.S.-Russian Business Council in Chicago shortly after the crash. Albright pointed out that "we cannot say that Russia has lost its way when in fact it has just begun its journey. Nor can we say that Russia is ours to lose. We can help Russia make tough choices, but in the end Russia most choose what kind of country it was going to be. They have to heal themselves."[96]

Could Russia heal itself? It was clear that there would be no return to the liberal economic reforms of the early 1990s. It was predictable that the new Russian government would run a soft budget with high inflation and more spending in social safety. How should the Clinton administration react? In a staff meeting on September 8, Talbott framed the choice in terms of "continued engagement and constructive disengagement."[97] The latter was not an option. Yet, it was clear that cooperation would be increasingly complex with the new prime minister, Yevgeny Primakov. Talbott learned about Primakov's nomination when he called the State Department operations center at 6 a.m. on September 10, inquiring whether there was anything new from Moscow overnight. "Holy shit," Talbott thought—another surprise.[98] During the talks at the Moscow summit, Primakov pretended that he was uninterested in the job. He was finally elected after the Duma had rejected Chernomyrdin's nomination. Primakov was willing to work with the Communists in the Duma. His election was a personal defeat for Yeltsin, who sounded "exhausted and depressed" when he shared the news in a telephone conversation with Clinton.[99] Yeltsin admitted that he "wanted very much for Chernomyrdin to get this post, but it was not to be."[100]

The End of Russia's Reform Project

Primakov was not an economist. He was an antimonetarist and blamed the West for Russia's problems. He was an antireformer and, in many ways, a relic of the Soviet Union. That's just why the Communists in the Duma favored his appointment. As foreign minister, he had perceived foreign policy as a zero-sum game. He resented America's preeminence and saw liberal globalization concepts as a direct threat. Primakov had been part of the problem regarding the resolution of Russian missile assistance to Iran. How could he be part of the solution as prime minister? Clinton's foreign policy team was concerned about the future of U.S. relations with Russia. Larry Summers predicted that "he'll be Chernomyrdin minus the good relationship with Al Gore. He's just another unreconstructed Soviet. He won't even talk the talk, much less walk the walk of reform."[101] Talbott shared this concern and decided to send Primakov a note of warning via Mamedov: "If he tries to do with economic policy what he's trying to do with foreign policy—i.e., force the world to integrate on Russia's terms rather than help Russia integrate, . . . it will mean that he'll try to [pursue] an economic policy that does not take into account international economic realities, isolate Russia from int'l markets, destroy investor confidence, run down infrastructure; this is a time when he needs to use his f.p. experience to put Russia into the world rather than opting out."[102]

Primakov would be a problematic partner. He was willing to compromise with the Communists. His political instincts were rooted in old Soviet thinking. He was not receptive to liberal economics and saw globalization as a problem for Russia rather than a solution. He did not sufficiently understand the relevance of foreign investments and currency stability and saw austerity measures as threatening Russia's unity. In a nutshell, he had a different understanding of the term *reform*. This was evident in a telephone conversation with Albright when he was confirmed as prime minister on September 11, 1998. "I will continue the course of reform, but I've got to correct the mistakes of the past," Primakov argued. "We have to have a normal, calm transition to the market. Of course, we need loans and credits, but we can't take instructions from other countries. Strengthening the role of the state doesn't mean de-privatization. We're going to do what Roosevelt did—not savage capitalism, but moving to the market in a way that protects the society." Albright confronted Primakov right away and cautioned him not to try to apply the recipes of the past to overcome Russia's current crisis. "We try hard not to interfere in your domestic politics, but you have a tax system that doesn't work, a bank system that is insolvent— you've got to have foreign investments. You've got to have help from other industrialized countries. The world is not the way it was during Roosevelt. . . . No matter how strong Russia is and will become, it can't do it by itself."[103]

Despite concerns about Primakov, the Clinton foreign policy team did not see his election as a reason to turn away from Russia. There was too much at stake. Clinton resented Newt Gingrich's proposition that the United States should lean back and do nothing and let Primakov and the Communists prove they could not resolve the crisis with their old recipes. Talbott noted that Gingrich's advice was "to let the communists run the place into the ground for a couple of years—'don't take ownership of this problem.'"[104] Talbott also rejected the Treasury Department's approach, which was passive, to stay away from Russia's mess for some time. This was not the time to abandon Russia. The country was not a lost cause, Talbott thought. "Whatever uncertainties hover over Russia's future, Russia is, today, a far more promising country than it was a decade ago," he argued. "Many of its political leaders, with the support of many of its citizens, are still trying to define— redefine—Russian statehood in a way that will make them, or at least their children, full participants, contributors and beneficiaries of the community of democratic nations of which the rest of us are a part."[105]

In mid–September 1998, Talbott fought for continued engagement with Russia at a G-8 meeting on Russia's crisis in London. He emphasized the need for urgent reforms against hyperinflation and more defaults in the private banking sector.[106] Deputy Finance Minister Mikhail Kasyanov and Mamedov were receptive, although the new Primakov government was focused on keeping the banks and big industries in business and meeting payrolls. Moreover, the meeting in London provided Talbott and Mamedov a chance to discuss the changes in the Russian Foreign Ministry and the implications of Igor Ivanov's appointment as Russia's new foreign minister. Unlike Primakov, Ivanov did not have political aspirations to rise even higher. Ivanov had never expected to get the top job at the Foreign Ministry. He had been Kozyrev's and Primakov's deputy and was a known quantity. Still, he had largely been kept away from the America account in the ministry. Instead, he focused on the Balkans and the Middle East. Ivanov's appointment made Mamedov's position a little more vulnerable, Talbott thought. The good news was that the Talbott-Mamedov channel would stay in place. The bad news was that Sandy Berger lost his effective counterpart, Andrei Kokoshin, who was replaced by General Nikolai Bordyuzha, an old KGB-nik, as head of the National Security Council.

From London, Talbott went directly to Brussels for a presentation before the North Atlantic Council to assess Russia's situation. On the upside, Russia was still playing by its constitutional rules in a situation of upheaval, Talbott said. He went through several scenarios regarding Russia's future and said that, for the time being, "Russia will proceed at two steps forward, one and three quarters backward, muddling through. Such prospects mean that it will be harder, more uncertain to see how we can advance our agendas with Moscow."[107] Russia was weakened and would not accept Western policy prescriptions under the new Primakov government. Whether Russia was still interested in the strategic partnership with the West was questionable. Moreover, Talbott used his presentation before the NAC to share his assessments of Primakov and Ivanov. Solana knew Primakov well and had negotiated the NATO-Russia Founding Act with him. When Talbott spoke with Solana in September 1998, the latter recalled a January 1997 conversation with Primakov when both had a long walk in the snowy Russian woods. Back then, Primakov laid out his vision for the emergence of a new Russia in the tradition of Roosevelt, following the example of the Scandinavian countries and trying to find a balance between a market economy and social safety. "I want this country not to be rich and getting richer, not to be corrupt," Primakov told Solana. "I can't stand all this corruption with all these people suffering. America had its Rockefellers in the 19th century who built railroads from Boston to San Francisco. But these bastards of ours like Berezovsky aren't Rockefellers—they put their money abroad and go to London."[108]

In November 1998, Talbott shared his assessment of Russia's crisis when he gave another speech at Stanford University. In it, he argued for "strategic patience in a time of troubles" assuming that Russia might take the wrong path if left to its own devices. Talbott admitted that post–Cold War Russia was still searching for its identity amid the crisis. Both the nationalists and communists tried to weaponize Russia's history in an attempt to revive the past. The seventy-four years of Russia's Soviet experience had alienated the country from the rest of Europe—thus it would take generations to shake off Russia's Soviet past, Talbott said. The 1998 financial crisis impaired Talbott's optimism about Russia's future. Compared with his September 1997 speech at Stanford, his remarks in 1998 were more cautious and even alarming. Talbott warned that "it is too early to proclaim Russian democratization irreversible. The longer the economic meltdown continues and the more serious it becomes, the harder it will be for Russia to sustain and consolidate the various institutions and habits of what might be called political normalcy: constitutionalism, give-and-take compromises, constituency politics, coalition building, all of which need for their sustenance an atmosphere of pluralism, vigorous public debate and open media. . . . But just because Russia has been relatively restrained to date does not mean it will be so forever," Talbott said.[109]

Although Talbott emphasized the need for "strategic patience," the Republicans in Congress thought that the Clinton administration should no longer give Russia the benefit of the doubt. Primakov's delaying reforms fueled the perception of Russia as a lost cause. It seemed that most financial analysts had written off Russia. Two-thirds of Russian banks and the entire private sector had collapsed. Russia's connections with the international economy had fallen except in exports and commodities. The Primakov government struggled to assemble a coherent tax and bank reform. How much patience could the Clinton administration afford? Talbott was wondering whether one could let the Russian side have "some socialism as part of their plan" in the sense of an increase in tariffs and capital controls. In other words, "How many steps backward are we prepared to see them take now, with our support, however qualified," Talbott asked

Summers.[110] On the one hand, a second tranche of IMF assistance was out of the question—Russia's beggar diplomacy would not work. On the other, the Clinton team had to show some flexibility to avoid further turmoil and chaos in Russia. "It's pretty clear we can't get an ideal reform program under present circumstances and under present management on their end," Talbott noted.[111]

In December 1998, Talbott, Summers, and Fuerth bundled their energies and competencies and visited Moscow to evaluate Russia's development. The Treasury Department's position was clear. Treasury Secretary Robert Rubin said that "if I were the IMF, I wouldn't give them any money because the IMF is not a welfare fund. Therefore, we should think of welfare payments in the form of debt rescheduling and perhaps from the World Bank, although there's a terrible Russian corruption problem there, not the IMF itself. We should get the G–7 to coalesce around big welfare payments."[112] At the start of his visit, Talbott discussed Russia's situation and future with Media Most Vice Chairman Igor Malashenko, the liberal cofounder and president of NTV, an independent television channel founded by a group of leading journalists. Malashenko had been a leading force in Yeltsin's 1996 campaign for reelection. In December 1998, Malashenko made dark predictions about the fate of Russia's democracy. He was concerned about the former KGB people in Primakov's team and specifically identified Federal Security Service (FSB) Chief Vladimir Putin as a potential wrecker of Russia's democracy. Malashenko said that "the fate of FSB Director Putin, a Chubais protege, would be a litmus test of intentions on safeguarding civil liberties." Finally, Malashenko thought that neither chaos not the continuation of the reform path were likely alternatives for the future. His concern was the emergence of another scenario: "isolation and a xenophobic regime, which had scant regard for human rights and freedom of the press—albeit a milder version than in the Soviet era."[113]

For the time being, Talbott had to cope with Primakov's old team, a weakened Yeltsin, and a battered Clinton who still faced impeachment over the Lewinsky scandal. In December 1998, the House of Representatives impeached Clinton and charged him with "high crimes and misdemeanors" for lying under oath and obstructing justice to cover up his affair with Monica Lewinsky.[114] Clinton and his legal team fought against an impending trial in the Senate. Talbott's hope was that Clinton would not resign. The president was still his friend, and Talbott was determined to stay on. "In a funny way," Talbott noted in his diary," I've reached a kind of personal peace on this. I'm more than satisfied with my own six years. If I conclude that I'm personally too much of a target of partisanship, I'll quit, with my head held high, though I'd rather not do so until I finish up—or at least further advance—three pieces of business: getting US-Russian relations through their current crisis; moving the ball further on India–Pakistan; and ensuring a successful NATO Summit in April (with a NATO-Russia component)."[115] At the time, Talbott did not anticipate the 1999 Kosovo War. Russia nearly crossed swords with the United States over Kosovo and then invaded Chechnya. Yeltsin resigned on December 31, 1999, and appointed Putin as acting president.

CHAPTER VI

The Kosovo War as a Game Changer

The Kosovo conflict had been simmering for a long time. In the last years of the Cold War, Yugoslavia's leader, Slobodan Milosevic, began to use ethnic tensions between Serbs and Kosovo Albanians as a way to extend his influence in Yugoslavia's Communist Party. In 1989, he started to revoke Kosovo's autonomy. In the first half of the 1990s, Milosevic's belligerence contributed to the disintegration of former Yugoslavia. However, he managed to stay in power after the 1995 Dayton Peace Accords. In 1998, Milosevic began to turn his military against Kosovo, committing renewed war crimes and ethnic cleansing. In response, the Kosovo Liberation Army (KLA) attacked Yugoslav authorities in Kosovo. By February 1998, the region was on the edge of civil war.[1] The Clinton administration was determined to prevent renewed war in the Balkans and imposed new sanctions that would lead to Yugoslavia's international isolation if violence in Kosovo mounted.[2]

Despite these warnings, Yugoslav forces killed twenty-four people in the Kosovar villages of Qirez and Likosane on February 28, 1998. Within days, Madeleine Albright traveled to Europe for consultations. In mid-March 1998, Talbott went on a long trip touring the Balkans to avert the start of a new war in the region. He pursued a two-track approach to address the Kosovo crisis—a diplomatic track to defuse tensions and a military track to help stabilize Kosovo's neighborhood. NATO applied a carrot-and-stick strategy toward Milosevic. This approach was backed up by the threat of freezing assets and a potential ban on investments in Yugoslavia.[3] However, Milosevic did not meet NATO's benchmarks and deadlines. He knew that the alliance did not consider airstrikes an option and thought he could play the Contact Group members against each other. In 1994, the Contact Group had been established to mediate between the conflict parties in response to the war in Bosnia. It consisted of the United States, United Kingdom, France, Germany, Italy, and Russia but failed to stop the war in Bosnia.[4]

In 1998, events in Kosovo revealed that ultimata from the Contact Group could not deter Milosevic. In early March 1998, the Yugoslav army killed sixty Kosovar Albanians in a large-scale offensive in the Drenica Valley. Talbott recalled that "the Contact Group had a long, unfortunate history of conditional threats which are not followed through. Milosevic has demonstrated that he responds only to pressure, and we must find new ways to turn up the heat in Belgrade if we are to effect significant change in Kosovo."[5] In April 1998, Talbott regretted the lack of severe military pressure. He missed "the 'big stick' that the international community had when NATO pursued air strikes against the Bosnian Serbs in the summer of 1995. We hit Milosevic over the head with it then, but we do not have the same stick today, even though we still have a threat of spillover to the periphery of Kosovo," Talbott said in a briefing before the North Atlantic Council on April 22, 1998.[6] In the spring of 1998, the European allies objected to the use of force given their concern over the security of their troops in neighboring Bosnia and Herzegovina. For now, NATO's preferred approach was stabilizing neighboring Albania and Macedonia.[7]

Russia's inclusion in the search for a solution was another challenge. In September 1998, the Russian attitude hardened when NATO issued its activation warning and intensified preparations for military operations such as a phased air campaign. NATO policymakers tried to convince Yeltsin to put more pressure on Milosevic. Clinton hoped that Russia would not block NATO on Kosovo. However, whether Russia would refrain from vetoing a resolution on Kosovo in the UN was questionable. Clinton and Ivanov discussed Russia's position during their meeting on September 24, 1998, and Ivanov toyed with the idea that Russia might retaliate if NATO resorted to force against Milosevic. Ivanov was under personal instructions from Yeltsin and stressed that "Russia would 'not countenance' air strikes / a phrase that in diplomacy goes beyond disapproval and carries with it at least the option of reprisal," Talbott recalled.[8] Ivanov argued that "Kosovo has great proximity to us. . . . By the domino theory, we know that military force will lead to escalation in the Balkans. Two times the Balkans have been the source of two world wars in this century. We know how explosive it can be."[9]

Clinton assumed that Ivanov spoke more for Primakov than for Yeltsin. This was not true. On October 5, 1998, Yeltsin followed up, called Clinton, and launched into a fierce monologue arguing that "he was alarmed about aggressive talk of late about inevitable, irreversible use of force by NATO in Yugoslavia. My position is that the situation cannot be resolved by use of force, and it is absolutely clear that a military gamble might have very grave consequences for the world at large and the Balkans in particular, and this must not be allowed to happen. We are very firm on that," Yeltsin concluded.[10] Clinton tried to respond several times, but Yeltsin continued to rant and interrupt. Neither did he wait for translations. Eventually, Yeltsin just hung up. He had never done that before. The conflict in Kosovo threatened to undermine the Bill and Boris relationship.[11]

Clinton was determined to go the extra mile to bring Russia back on board. In October 1998, he sent Holbrooke back to Belgrade and Pristina to negotiate the establishment of a UN verification system to monitor Milosevic's compliance.[12] Milosevic consented to the withdrawal of Yugoslav troops from Kosovo and agreed to the presence of two thousand unarmed UN observers to verify compliance. The Holbrooke agreement bought time and promised to help fifty thousand displaced people through the winter. However, it was a temporary and fragile truce that did not address the underlying conflict. Its major flaw was the absence of enforcement. Eventually, the agreement did not hold beyond the winter and failed to deter Milosevic from further atrocities.[13] Meanwhile, Russia's attitude had slightly changed. When Holbrooke signaled NATO's readiness for airstrikes, Russia no longer demanded a UN resolution. In a crucial Contact Group meeting in London, Ivanov said that "Russia would never support NATO action in the Security Council. But, in a subtle hint of Russia's changing posture, he made unmistakably clear that Russia would not insist on the matter coming to the council and indicated he was ready to support Dick's [Richard Holbrooke's] ultimatum to Milosevic, which, Ivanov understood, would be backed by the NATO threat."[14]

NATO, Russia, and the Road to the Kosovo War

On January 15, 1999, Yugoslav paramilitary troops and armed forces executed forty-five people in the Kosovar village of Racak. Monitors of the Kosovo Verification Mission entered the town within twenty-four hours of the killing. Racak was a turning point. NATO needed a new approach, but the allies hesitated to use military force.[15] Eventually, the Clinton administration's plan for a response was to combine the threat of air strikes with a high-profile peace conference under the auspices of the Contact Group—this finally became the Rambouillet conference in February 1999. The core question at Rambouillet pertained to the incompatible Yugoslav and Kosovar approaches to Kosovo's status. Whereas the representative from Kosovo wanted outright independence, Yugoslavia insisted that Kosovo was a domestic affair. To bridge the gap, the Rambouillet conference attempted to establish Kosovo's autonomy for an interim period without touching on the issue of its status. However, both sides refused to enter an agreement that would force them to abandon their maximalist positions. The Kosovo Albanians conditioned their consent to the acceptance of their request for a referendum on Kosovo's independence after three years. The Yugoslav side gambled and put its money on the assumption that NATO would avoid using force.

As Milosevic refused to negotiate seriously, his military continued atrocities in Kosovo. In March 1999, NATO's military authorities got ready for airstrikes. On March 22, 1999, Clinton sent Holbrooke to Belgrade with an ultimatum. NATO would begin airstrikes if Milosevic did not agree to the immediate cessation of military operations in Kosovo. Holbrooke reported that Milosevic "took the position that he would never accept a 'foreign occupation' of his soil. He invoked memories of two legendary occupations of Serbia—by the Ottomans and by the Nazis."[16] The request did not work. Milosevic did not change his position. "You are a great and powerful nation. We are small. If you want to bomb us, go ahead," Milosevic said.[17] He rejected a cease-fire. He would not sign the Rambouillet texts. There would be no settlement. NATO airstrikes were imminent.[18]

Russian policymakers placed great emphasis on being informed in advance. On March 18, 1999, Gore cautioned Primakov that Milosevic's hardened position would soon force NATO to start airstrikes. "I have to tell you frankly that Belgrade's intransigence and aggression will leave us no choice but to act." Primakov still shied away from making a public statement condemning Yugoslav atrocities. "We can't say directly that Yugoslavia is itself to be blamed because the problem has many deviations."[19] Russia expected that NATO's bombing campaign would start after Primakov's long-scheduled visit to the United States on March 23 and 24, 1999. But NATO could not further delay airstrikes. Primakov was in mid-air on March 23 when Gore informed him about the swift start of NATO's military operations. "Milosevic had 'blood dripping from his hands'—he was using every passing day to kill innocent men, women and children," Gore said. Talbott recalled that "Primakov retorted that it was NATO that would have blood on its hands, and the impact on U.S.-Russian relations would be devastating."[20] Primakov had his plane turn around. He did not want to be in Washington when NATO started airstrikes.

Yeltsin was furious when Clinton called him the same day. Clinton argued that Milosevic must not be allowed to come between the United States and Russia. "Basically, it will be your decision if you decide to let this bully destroy the relationship we worked hard for six and a half years to build up," Clinton argued. "I have always been there for you, working hard with my people to support Russia economically. I came there last Fall. I was there in 1996 when a lot of people said I shouldn't go. You may decide to let this get in the way of our relationship, but I'm not going to because I do not think he is that important. I won't sit still while Europe is pleading with me to help them avoid another Bosnia," Clinton emphasized.[21] Yeltsin's primary concern was that NATO's airstrikes would trigger the rise of nationalism and revisionism in Russia. In his memoirs, Yeltsin recalled that "the crisis in Russia would not only be a government crisis but a crisis of faith in the leaders. . . . Did the NATO leaders not understand? Wasn't it obvious that each missile strike against Yugoslavia was an indirect strike against Russia?"[22] Yeltsin blamed NATO's airstrikes for the nationalist groundswell in Russia. "Our people will certainly from now on have a bad attitude with regard to America and with NATO. I remember how difficult it was for me to try and turn the heads of our people, the heads of the politicians towards the West, towards the United States, but I succeeded in doing that, and now to lose all that."[23] Clinton did not have a chance to respond—Yeltsin just hung up. "Something pretty basic is broken and it'll take a lot of fixing," Clinton thought.[24] In his memoirs, Yeltsin recalled the conversation in detail: "I didn't have any complaints against Bill Clinton,

I even heard some sympathy in his voice. But as President of the United States, he was letting me know in no uncertain terms that negotiations with Milosevic were pointless. This was a mistake, a very big mistake," Yeltsin concluded.[25]

In response to the start of NATO's military operations, the Russians withdrew their military representative from NATO headquarters, reduced their liaison staff at SHAPE, announced the suspension of all PfP and NATO-Russia activities, and immediately canceled several working level meetings of the Permanent Joint Council. Meanwhile, the Russian negotiators at the CFE talks in Vienna remained engaged and were determined to reach substantial progress on the adaption of the CFE Treaty. So far, the Russian side was not willing to burn the bridge of U.S.-Russian and NATO-Russian relations. Yeltsin was still determined to keep open the possibility of getting back to something like a normal relationship if NATO stopped bombing.

NATO did not expect a long war and failed to prepare for an extended air war campaign. It began Operation Allied Force with just 350 planes in range of Yugoslavia—only one-third the number ultimately necessary to win the war. NATO feared that a more vigorous air campaign could undermine support from the European allies. The alliance did not have a robust and forceful strategy to win the war—"NATO had no plan b."[26] It could have lost the Kosovo War. Milosevic was determined to hunker down, tolerate the bombing, drive wedges in NATO, and wait for Russia to put pressure on the alliance. One week before the start of NATO's air campaign, U.S. Secretary of Defense William Cohen pointed out that "NATO has to be prepared for the possibility that Milosevic will not be persuaded by Phase I of the air campaign and will decide simply to hunker down. . . . The allies need to be aware of these dangers and we need to get an understanding with them that they'll be with us and prepared to respond vigorously if he reacts in those ways."[27] Several European allies were against the bombing campaign. Mainly, the Italian government was concerned about a new wave of refugees and boat people in the Adriatic searching for shelter in Italy.[28] Greek policymakers struggled to balance their NATO requirements with domestic opposition to NATO air strikes. The Simitis government in Athens was concerned about the Kosovo conflict's fallout regarding changes in regional borders. Eventually, Greece went along and did not risk standing alone against the will of the other NATO allies.

The principal targets of NATO's airstrikes included Yugoslav air defenses, command and control centers, military infrastructure, and transportation routes. NATO soon expanded its set of targets considerably. In late March, NATO aircraft began to attack Yugoslav radio and television transmitters as well as Milosevic's residence in Belgrade. Initially, NATO's bombing campaign strengthened Milosevic's internal position. He further escalated atrocities in Kosovo, leading to a major flow of refugees and frictions within NATO.[29] Moreover, the NATO military campaign caused various challenges in the Balkans region. The situation in the frontline states was especially precarious.[30] The destruction of Yugoslavia's infrastructure immediately affected Romania's and Bulgaria's fragile economies—the transportation routes via the Danube and Yugoslav motorways were blocked.[31] Romanian President Emil Constantinescu called Clinton with an urgent appeal for security guarantees.[32] Indeed, NATO provided guarantees to the non-NATO states surrounding Yugoslavia, including Albania, the former Yugoslav Republic of Macedonia, Bulgaria, and Romania.[33]

Moreover, starting in late March 1999, the Clinton administration and the European Union worked on a long-term Stability Pact for the entire southeast European region. The rationale was that the entire area had to be part of U.S. efforts to project stability across Europe. The day after NATO began bombing, Daniel Hamilton of the State Department's Policy Planning Staff wrote Secretary Albright a memo arguing that "we would win the war . . . but victory would be hollow unless we and our European allies were prepared to offer Southeastern Europeans the same bargain we had offered those in Central and Northern Europe—to stand with them on reforms and to keep the doors to our institutions open, if they created the conditions to make it possible someday to walk through those doors."[34] The initiative for the Stability Pact emerged from U.S. talks with German Foreign Minister Joschka Fischer under Germany's EU presidency at the time. Based on consultations with the United States, Fischer first broached the idea on April 1 in a troika meeting with neighboring states affected by the crisis. The United States was fully invested but wanted the EU to lead because the key was for the EU to commit to eventual enlargement for these states as well—which it had not yet done.[35] Negotiations were held at the Hotel Petersberg near Bonn in May, and scores of countries were present, including Russia.[36] Bill Clinton set out the logic of the Stability Pact in an April 15 speech in San Francisco when he said that "we should try to do for Southeastern Europe what we helped to do for Western Europe after World War II and Central Europe after the Cold War; to help its people build a region of multiethnic democracies, a community that upholds common standards of human rights, a community in which borders are open to people and trade, where nations cooperate to make war unthinkable."[37] Finally, in late July and early August 1999, the Sarajevo summit launched the Stability Pact. Clinton and Albright participated in the gathering to underline the U.S. commitment to stabilizing southeastern Europe. Bodo Hombach, the special coordinator of the Stability Pact, told Albright that "one of his most important jobs is to keep Russia engaged in the Stability Pact (through the G-8) while assuaging the concerns that regional states have with Russia's involvement."[38]

Russia had indeed been an equal partner in the negotiations on the Stability Pact. The Clinton administration worked hard to reengage the Russian side. On April 3, Clinton wrote Yeltsin a letter highlighting their joint achievements in times of crisis.[39] Yeltsin tried to make a serious effort to revive the Kosovo negotiating process. He suggested the convocation of a G-8 ministerial meeting on the conflict. Albright was in daily contact with Ivanov. Both called for a withdrawal of Yugoslav forces from Kosovo.[40] The sticking point was Russia's continued opposition to an international security presence in the region. Another problem was that Western public opinion increasingly doubted the feasibility of NATO's air campaign— Milosevic's forces killed Albanians faster than NATO managed to destroy Yugoslavia's military targets. Some policymakers in Washington began to see Kosovo as a new Vietnam War. Holbrooke highlighted the parallels, such as the call for bombing pauses and the danger of deploying ground troops.[41] In fact, differences were numerous. Talbott emphasized that Kosovo was not Vietnam. The Kosovo War and its Russia dimension were "about Europe and civilization—we want Russia in Europe, but we want it into a new Europe, which is civilized, not an old one, that is barbarized; and we shouldn't want a Russia into Europe that sides with Milosevic," Talbott noted in a conversation with Solana.[42]

On April 7, 1999, while in Brussels, Talbott undertook another effort to include Russia in the search for a Kosovo settlement. He assured Russian Deputy Foreign Minister Avdeyev that NATO wanted to maintain the territorial integrity of Yugoslavia. NATO was not preparing for a ground war in Kosovo, but it insisted on an international security presence after the end of the conflict. Moreover, Talbott envisaged far-reaching autonomy for Kosovo. "We're thinking about a solution that recognizes

Belgrade's formal control but acknowledges that Belgrade has lost its authority to govern Kosovo," he pointed out. The NATO formula for a peace
settlement entailed crucial preconditions, including the removal of Yugoslav forces from Kosovo, the return of refugees, the disarmament of the
Kosovo Liberation Army, and a long-term deployment of international
peacekeepers. Talbott hoped that Albright and Ivanov would be able to
work out language on these principles in the Contact Group. Avdeyev
turned this down: "I can't imagine a Yugoslavia with its center in Belgrade
and autonomous centers in Kosovo and Montenegro, and the implementation structures you've chosen."[43]

The conversation then turned to the U.S.-Russia partnership and potential
ways to salvage it. Avdeyev complained that "there's already been damage. . . .
Strobe, certain stereotypes were starting to break down. We had started to
value our relationship with you and this concept of partnership. This was
one of the major results of President Yeltsin's two terms. The destiny of
Russia will be defined by the succession of President Yeltsin. Isn't that
important to you? Or is Milosevic more important than that?" Avdeyev
asked. "I don't accept that either-or choice," Talbott replied. "I understand
the tension between these two objectives—maintaining our partnership
and finding a solution to the Kosovo crisis. But I don't accept that they're
irreconcilable."[44] This was Talbott's central theme in a Contact Group
meeting of the political directors in Brussels on April 7. The mood was
tense and emotional. The Russian representative, Ambassador Boris Mayorskiy, argued that Russia could not join NATO in its demands toward
Milosevic. Mayorskiy refused to condemn Yugoslav atrocities in Kosovo
and demanded a pause in NATO's bombing in response to Milosevic's hollow cease-fire proposals. It seemed there was no common basis to move
forward. In response, Talbott said that "NATO was the only the instrument for exerting force. The victory we sought was the victory of the basic
values that Milosevic was trampling upon in the most abominable way."[45]

Five days later, on April 12, Albright and Ivanov met in Oslo to discuss
Kosovo. They agreed on the need for a formula to end the violence, the
withdrawal of the Yugoslav army, and the return of all refugees and displaced persons. However, no consensus had been reached over NATO's
requirement for an international security force. Albright reported that the
Russian side "did not say they were against such a force, but rather stressed
the need to work and bring Belgrade along on this issue. In the meantime,
they would only support an undefined 'international presence' to provide

security and confidence. That is not enough," Albright concluded. She wrote that "it is unclear how the Russians see the next step unfolding. . . . Our feeling is that the Russians have put themselves back more in the mainstream, but they also see what our disagreements are. We can't paper over major differences."[46] Russia was still not on board regarding the need for an international security force. For now, the convocation of a G-8 foreign ministers meeting on Kosovo did not make sense. Mamedov told Talbott that Russia was no longer interested in such a gathering.[47]

Hence, the Clinton administration had to search for new ways to get Russia on board. At the time, it was unlikely to find a sensible solution with Primakov or Ivanov, who lacked Yeltsin's trust. It seemed that Yeltsin sensed this as well. On April 14, 1999, he appointed Chernomyrdin as his personal Kosovo envoy as opposed to the Russian government under Primakov and Ivanov. Talbott recalled that "the move caught us completely by surprise, but once he'd made it, it seemed entirely explicable. Yeltsin wanted to stop the war and get Russia as much credit as possible. He had never been enthusiastic about Primakov as his prime or foreign minister. Now he was taking the Kosovo account away from Primakov, turning it over to someone he was confident could get the job done."[48] Chernomyrdin had a proven ability to work with the Clinton administration. Moreover, as Talbott recalled, he "could also talk tough with Milosevic. Serbia was dependent on Russia as a source of energy, and Chernomyrdin, as the former head of Gazprom, the state-owned oil company, had connections that would be useful in applying pressure on Belgrade."[49]

Would Chernomyrdin's appointment be the key to a solution and a revival of creative diplomacy? On April 19, 1999, Clinton and Yeltsin discussed their difficulties in a lengthy telephone conversation. This time, Yeltsin did not hang up—he pursued a balanced criticism of NATO's bombing campaign and went to great lengths to talk about the domestic pressure he faced from the Communists in the Duma. His key theme was that Clinton and the NATO allies had "miscalculated the consequences of the situation itself. Milosevic will never capitulate. Instead of resolving the humanitarian problem, what has been achieved is a giant humanitarian catastrophe, and significant damage has occurred to U.S.-Russian relations."[50] At the same time, Yeltsin reiterated his determination not to get involved in the conflict and not to assist Yugoslavia.

Meanwhile, the Clinton administration was confronted with the specter of deploying ground troops in Kosovo. NATO did not have a plan B if its air campaign failed. Given the widespread but misleading Vietnam War analogy, several of Clinton's key advisers were hesitant to even start planning the use of ground troops. In a small group meeting with the State Department's leadership, Berger argued that "ground troops will lead to a disaster for POTUS, for the administration, for NATO." His concern was that "our grandchildren will still be fighting in Kosovo." Talbott emphasized the need to consider the ground troops option. To win, NATO had to use every necessary method. Talbott said that letting the KLA continue the fight against the Serbs was not an option. "The KLA 'home alone, without adult supervision'—a recipe for simmering, spreading war, freaks out the neighboring states. We've got to be prepared to go in ourselves under that circumstance."[51]

Ending the War, Saving the U.S-Russia Relationship

While NATO's bombing campaign continued, it was not clear who would negotiate a settlement with Milosevic. Under what kind of conditions was he willing to give in? Would he be able to remain in power after a peace

Figure 6.1 Talbott and Clinton jogging at the Presidio Military Base in San Francisco, California, July 1993. Clinton Presidential Library.

Figure 6.2 Clinton meeting President Shushkevich of Belarus in the Oval Office. Seated on the couch: Deputy Secretary of State Clifton Wharton, National Security Advisor Tony Lake and Strobe Talbott, July 1993. Clinton Presidential Library.

Figure 6.3 Clinton and Gore participating in a briefing on Russia in the Roosevelt Room with Warren Christopher, Tony Lake, Toby Gati, Strobe Talbott, Nick Burns, and Nancy Soderberg, among others, March 1993. Clinton Presidential Library.

Figure 6.4 Taking notes at the Oval Office. President Clinton and Deputy National Security Adviser Samuel Berger are in the background. Clinton Presidential Library.

Figure 6.5 Clinton meeting Secretary of State Warren Christopher and Ambassador to the United Nations Madeleine Albright, April 1993. Clinton Presidential Library.

Figure 6.6 Assistant Secretary of State Richard Holbrooke and Carl Bildt, the European Union's Special Envoy to the Former Yugoslavia, October 1995. Clinton Presidential Library.

Figure 6.7 NATO-Ukraine meeting at the NATO Summit, Washington, DC, April 24, 1999. *Left to right*: Ambassador Sergio Balanzino (Deputy Secretary General), Boris Tarasyuk (Minister of Foreign Affairs, Ukraine), President Leonid Kuchma (Ukraine), NATO Secretary General Javier Solana. NATO Multimedia, https://www.nato.int/multi/photos/1999/m990603a.htm.

Figure 6.8 Strobe Talbott arriving at NATO to present a peace proposal concerning Kosovo, June 3, 1999. *Left to right*: Ms. Elizabeth Pryor (Public Affairs Advisor, U.S. Mission to NATO); Talbott; Ambassador Alexander Vershbow (U.S. Permanent Representative to NATO). NATO Multimedia, https://www.nato.int/multi/photos /1999/m990603a.htm.

agreement? What were the prospects of regime change in Belgrade? "Our real goal, whether stated or not," Holbrooke thought, "must be a change in the leadership of Yugoslavia. Should we negotiate with Milosevic at all? . . . Dayton may have been a deal with the devil, but it ended a war on acceptable terms. . . . But after Kosovo, he is not the same person he was after Dayton. Whatever the details of an agreement, his sole goals will be to retain power, retain Kosovo and avoid punishment for his own deeds. Can we allow that after Kosovo? Can Milosevic, the most disruptive person in Europe in half a century, become the co-guarantor of Kosovo's future?"[52] However, because a ground war was not an option, the most feasible approach were still negotiations with Russia's assistance. As Sandy Berger

Figure 6.9 President Clinton and President Putin signing the Joint Statement on Strategic Stability Cooperation Initiative between the United States and the Russian Federation at the Waldorf-Astoria Hotel in New York, September 6, 2000. Clinton Presidential Library.

put it, "If we're not prepared to negotiate and deal with him, we should take 200,000 troops to Belgrade and crush his ass. But I don't know how this works. In other words, we've got to be prepared to deal with him."[53]

NATO maintained its coercive diplomacy. Bombing and negotiations were intertwined. On April 25, 1999, Clinton and Yeltsin discussed Gore's and Chernomyrdin's involvement in a new negotiation process. Clinton's formula for a solution in Kosovo was Yugoslav forces out, NATO in, refugees back. NATO would only pause its bombing campaign if all refugees could return, if there were agreement on an international security force, and if the Yugoslav army began its complete withdrawal. The international Kosovo security force should be designed like the Bosnian peace force—under NATO's auspices and with Russia's involvement. "If I could design it the best way I could, I would have it look like the work we are doing in Bosnia. . . . I don't think the refugees will go home unless there is a NATO and an American presence," Clinton said. Initially, Yeltsin demanded a bombing pause as soon as Gore and Chernomyrdin met. When Clinton demurred, Yeltsin became enraged: "Don't push Russia into this war. You know what Russia is. You know how it is equipped, but don't push Russia into this."[54] Eventually, Talbott noted, "Clinton agreed to reopen the Gore-Chernomyrdin channel as long as Yeltsin understood at the outset that NATO would have to be in command of the peacekeeping operation that followed a settlement."[55]

The next day, April 26, Gore and Chernomyrdin spent over an hour on the phone to discuss their forthcoming meeting. Rather than reconstituting the entire commission, they scheduled a one-on-one discussion in Washington the following week.[56] Gore's position was not easy. He was determined to be helpful on Kosovo but had to be careful about his involvement due to his presidential campaign. At this point, Gore could not go to Moscow for a high-profile visit. It was not clear whether the scheme with Chernomyrdin would work at all. Instead, on April 27, Talbott went to Moscow to figure it out. The purpose of his trip was to explore two things, as he told Clinton and Berger. "1) whether we can get the Russians to bring their bottom line into line with ours, in which case maybe we can bring them out of isolation and get them to join the int'l pressure on Milo, perhaps in a USNCR; 2) whether there's any chance they can deliver Milosevic. Both are up in the air, both very hard, the second maybe utterly impossible. Only if we can do at least the first would I recommend that the Vice President get anywhere near this," Talbott argued. "I agree with that," Clinton said.[57]

In Moscow, Talbott had extensive meetings with Chernomyrdin, Ivanov, and Primakov. All of them still expressed strong opposition to NATO's airstrikes and believed that Milosevic would not give in. The Russian leadership was hesitant to come around and support NATO. Chernomyrdin, for instance, was still opposed to withdrawing Yugoslav forces from Kosovo. He thought this would imply that Kosovo was no longer a part of the Federal Republic of Yugoslavia. Such a solution would create a potentially dangerous precedent for Chechnya and the disintegration of Russia. "Russia was concerned about the 'many Kosovos' in the FSU and even inside Russia," Chernomyrdin said.[58] On the positive side, he was willing to be helpful and broker a deal with Milosevic. He acknowledged Russia's critical role as a mediator and interlocutor with Milosevic.[59]

"Victor Stepanovich," Talbott said, "let me be honest. We're beyond compromising with Belgrade. We did give-and-take diplomacy for 14 months, and he not only didn't give [in]—he used the diplomacy as a cover for killing people and shelling villages and driving people out of their homes. We'll have an open, back-and-forth conversation with you so that you'll understand where we can be flexible and where we can't. But when it comes to Belgrade, we're going to have to be very, very firm. . . . Let me make clear that one reason we want very much for you to succeed in your diplomacy on the terms we've discussed is that we would welcome not only an end to the conflict but a leading role for Russia in the design and implementation of a peace."[60]

Working with Chernomyrdin was Talbott's best bet. The lack of constructive Russian interlocutors was a severe problem. The unique military-to-military contacts between Perry and Grachev were gone. The constructive spirit of the NATO-Russia Founding Act no longer existed. This time, NATO and Secretary General Solana could not go and talk to the Russian side. The solution for Kosovo had to be found in bilateral U.S.-Russia diplomacy. On May 3, Chernomyrdin came to Washington for discussions with Gore. The objective was to get Milosevic's consent to NATO's conditions to end the bombing—but the meeting failed to bring tangible progress. Gore and Chernomyrdin merely reviewed their positions. "Gore wasn't going to let himself be drawn into give-and-take and Chernomyrdin . . . was sensitive to the constraints of Gore," Talbott recalled.[61]

First, Gore emphasized that the bombing would stop as soon as Milosevic agreed to a roadmap envisaging withdrawal—and Milosevic would be required to make a downpayment in terms of troop withdrawals because he had violated many past agreements. Gore then explained the term in detail. "In the U.S. if a family wants to buy a house, they sign a contract and agree to payments. But they start with a big payment—the downpayment—and are obligated to continue," Gore said.[62] The aim was zero Yugoslav forces in Kosovo. In response, Chernomyrdin agreed to the necessity of an international military force to end bloodshed—but he disagreed who would provide it. Fuerth noted that Chernomyrdin showed "explicit agreement . . . to NATO presence in force. . . . He . . . is receptive to [an] IFOR-type arrangement."[63] Moreover, Chernomyrdin promised to put real pressure on Milosevic to accept NATO's conditions. Milosevic had perhaps "3–4 months and Yugoslavia will be flattened like a disk. . . . You know he's a sick person, and his nation doesn't know what's happening," Chernomyrdin noted.[64] He loathed Milosevic as much as his American interlocutors did.

However, Milosevic was unwilling to negotiate with a U.S.-Russia consortium. This would smack of a fait accompli to him. He did not want to surrender to NATO or to Russia, only to the United Nations. Hence there was a need to find an international negotiator to accept the sword from Milosevic. Kofi Annan was not an option. He had lost the Clinton administration's trust. "Kofi Annan is untrustworthy. I say this in confidence. We cannot rely on him. The feeling is so strong we are not willing to have him in charge of the negotiations," Gore emphasized.[65] On May 4, Albright, Talbott, and their colleagues assembled at Gore's office for an hour. During the meeting, Albright had the idea to ask Finnish President Marti Ahtisaari to be Mr. X. It was an excellent proposal. Ahtisaari was neutral and tough and had both a UN and Balkans background. Chernomyrdin was enthusiastic. "Cherno goes for Ahtisaari big time, and we undertake to work it with Ahtisaari and the Germans (as presidency of the EU)," Talbott noted in his diaries.[66] Ahtisaari would be a co-negotiator. He was not associated with NATO but fully backed allied conditions and had excellent relations with Yeltsin. Turning to Chernomyrdin, Talbott said, "You're the one to use the hammer on Milosevic, and Ahtisaari is the one to receive the sword from him."[67]

Talbott worked feverishly to coordinate the start of his mission with Chernomyrdin and Ahtisaari. He made sure Annan would give the Troika UN blessing and Annan's own Balkans negotiator, Carl Bildt, would not interfere in the negotiations. The United Nations would be in charge of peace implementation later on, but Annan agreed to stay away from brokering the peace itself. The game plan was for Ahtisaari and Chernomyrdin to negotiate with Milosevic in Belgrade. As incoming EU president, Ahtisaari was supposed to wear the hats of both the EU and the UN.[68] It was agreed that "at the appropriate moment, Ahtisaari would accompany Chernomyrdin on the 'climactic and breakthrough visit' to Belgrade. . . . This would be the ceremonial closer. Ahtisaari was not prepared to engage in shuttle diplomacy over a period of weeks or months," Talbott told Chernomyrdin.[69] The idea behind the anvil and hammer operation was that "Chernomyrdin would be the hammer and pound away on Milosevic, and President Ahtisaari would be the anvil against who [sic] the pounding would take place, so that Milosevic would know what he had to do to get the bombing stopped."[70]

The first trilateral meeting between Talbott, Chernomyrdin, and Ahtisaari took place in Helsinki on May 13, 1999. Beforehand, Talbott spent a day in Moscow for preparatory talks. The Russian idea was still a bombing pause followed by a negotiation with Milosevic. Russia's biggest problem was NATO's request for a total withdrawal of Yugoslav forces. The

Russian assumption was that Milosevic would not surrender and NATO would be forced to start a ground war—which would lead to an escalation of the domestic situation in Russia. Yeltsin was mad at the West for lecturing him about what was needed to stop NATO's bombing. Chernomyrdin maintained his bottom lines and argued that some Yugoslav forces should remain in Kosovo as part of an international security force. Talbott insisted that bombing could only stop when Milosevic agreed to all NATO conditions. Ahtisaari emphasized that the whole package required a complete withdrawal of the Yugoslav forces, including a precise and rapid timetable. After the trilateral meeting in Helsinki, Ahtisaari felt there was enough progress with Chernomyrdin to have another meeting the following week but not enough to justify his going to Belgrade.[71] He therefore worked closely with Talbott and the U.S. ambassador in Helsinki, Eric Edelman. At one point in the negotiations, for instance, Ahtisaari called up Edelman at two o'clock in the morning with a request to discuss a transcript of his latest conversation with Milosevic—and Edelman was supposed to transmit it to Washington in the wee hours.[72]

On May 14, on the way back to Washington, Talbott assembled his team and asked them to think about circumstances under which the Clinton administration could consider a pause in bombing for forty-eight hours while Chernomyrdin and Ahtisaari negotiated in Belgrade. The next day, May 15, he approached Albright and Berger with the idea of a bombing stop "in exchange for a guaranteed, unconditional, up-front Russian commitment to go along with a Chapter VII resolution supporting our efforts in Kosovo, including the resumption of bombing immediately after Ahtisaari and Chernomyrdin get what we unilaterally regard as a no from Milosevic."[73] Albright did not endorse the idea—she did not even want to present it to Clinton as a State Department proposal.[74] The Pentagon and Secretary Cohen rejected it as well. Finally, Talbott went around Albright and Cohen and approached the president, asking for permission to go forward in his next meetings with Chernomyrdin and Ahtisaari. Talbott's rationale was guided by the assumption that a forty-eight-hour bombing stop would ease the management of the allies and relations with Russia at a crucial time. "I'm thinking about the full calendar. I'm thinking about October, when we may well still be at this war," Talbott said in his final spiel with Clinton. "Our chances of having the Allies with us would be better if we'd gotten our own hands on an acceptable pause. And I'm thinking about the [G-8] Cologne Summit a month from now, which, if we don't have this thing with the Russians resolved, could be the end of the G-8—it could make the Budapest Summit in 94 look like a love fest. But all I'm asking for right now is an okay to go ahead with step one. I'll await your answer overnight and proceed accordingly."[75] However, Clinton did not approve Talbott's proposal. The bombing continued when Chernomyrdin went to Belgrade. Ahtisaari did not go because Chernomyrdin was not willing to endorse the creation of a NATO-led implementation force—at least not yet.[76]

The next trilateral meeting was on May 21 in Moscow. Talbott, Chernomyrdin, and Ahtisaari agreed that they had made enough progress to have another meeting in Moscow the following week, which was supposed to lead to a joint Chernomyrdin-Ahtisaari trip to Belgrade. On May 21, Ahtisaari and Talbott managed to bring Chernomyrdin to agree to virtually all of NATO's key points, including the total withdrawal of Yugoslav forces and the imperative to have NATO at the core of an implementation force. This time, Chernomyrdin was ready to put the principles on paper.[77] The key questions were these: Was Milosevic finally willing to make peace on NATO's terms? Was Russia willing to endorse troops under a unified command with NATO at the core? Was there a possibility to repeat the 1995 example of the Bosnia implementation force? The issue was that the 1999 bombings of Yugoslavia hurt NATO-Russia relations much more severely than those of 1995—and Yeltsin no longer had the political ability to bring Russia's military in line. Talbott was determined to find a solution that would end the war and keep the U.S.-Russia partnership alive.

On the way home, Talbott and his team ruminated where all of this was leading. Would the hammer and anvil rationale with Chernomyrdin and Ahtisaari really work? Talbott thought that the Clinton administration should give it another week or so. He could not pursue trilateral Kosovo diplomacy forever. He was the guy out on the limb—and he had to be careful not to overdo it. It could not be "Madeleine's war" and "Strobe's peace." The trick of Talbott's Kosovo statecraft was the combination of dialogue and bombing. The Clinton administration's diplomacy was in support of force. While NATO continued its bombing campaign, Ahtisaari and Chernomyrdin spoke with Milosevic. During all of this, Albright had a hard time endorsing Talbott's diplomacy and his leadership role when she could not progress on Kosovo in her bilateral talks with Ivanov. It seemed that she did not want Chernomyrdin and Ahtisaari to go to

Belgrade for fear that she could not control the process. At the end of the day, Albright acknowledged she and Talbott were together in this. "I nominate you to be the final person to bring this together and then wheel me in at the end," she told Talbott in a May 23 conversation.[78]

Clinton and Albright gave Talbott the mandate for the next Moscow trilateral with Chernomyrdin and Ahtisaari. In Moscow, Talbott informed Ivanov that Justice Louise Arbour, the prosecutor of the International Tribunal, was going to announce indictments against the Yugoslav leadership the following day. The Clinton administration had always thought that Milosevic would be indicted for the atrocities that the regime in Belgrade had committed on a massive scale. Chernomyrdin did not like the news of the announcement. He saw it as a further escalation of the situation. His argument was that it would be a very bad day for him and Ahtisaari to go under these circumstances. The Russian side was exasperated. Chernomyrdin's message was that NATO's bombing and his shuttle diplomacy with Milosevic were humiliating to the Russian public. Talbott did not back away an inch. He did not pull the plug. Diplomacy had to remain alive. There was no excuse for Chernomyrdin not to go. Chernomyrdin had to go and tell Milosevic. That's what he did on his fourth trip to Belgrade on May 28.[79] Looking back on his visit to Belgrade, Chernomyrdin said that "the West counted that they could persuade Milosevic to give up. But Milosevic didn't. He would never do that. That's why I brought him around giving an explanation, adducing the facts, why and what has happened, what will happen if he continues persistence and what will be left from Yugoslavia. Can you imagine how uneasy was the discussion for 8, 9 hours? He would jump up, tear the papers, thrust them, go out and come back again. It was hard."[80]

The following week, Talbott, Chernomyrdin, and Ahtisaari had their final meeting starting on June 1 in a German government guesthouse on the Petersberg—a mountain overlooking the Rhine River close to Bonn. It was a most dramatic discussion that started at 3 p.m. and lasted until 4 a.m. and into the next day until 1:30 p.m. The purpose was to elaborate on a joint statement that Chernomyrdin and Ahtisaari would deliver during their forthcoming visit to Belgrade. At the start, it looked as if the trilateral format was dead. At the outset, Chernomyrdin went back to Russia's initial position—pause and talk. Talbott and his colleagues tried for several hours to achieve common ground on the statement—nothing seemed to be working. Meanwhile, in the evening, German Chancellor Gerhard

Schröder arrived by helicopter assuming that he could celebrate success and participate in a joint press conference. He did not listen when the three negotiators politely asked him to leave them alone. Thus Talbott, Ahtisaari, and Chernomyrdin had to sit through a stilted dinner that cost them valuable time and energy. In the early hours of June 2, Chernomyrdin made threats to give up. "This is your war, it's not our war, and it's going to end in disaster for everyone, including you," he said.[81] Chernomyrdin was under tremendous pressure from the Russian military. General Ivashov, the Russian military representative, fought tooth and nail to avoid Russian participation in the Kosovo Force (KFOR) under NATO command. During a late-night break, Talbott overheard Chernomyrdin screaming at Ivashov: "I'm not anybody's puppet. You assholes can do this thing without me."[82] After this incident, Talbott decided to suggest an adjournment so that Chernomyrdin could call Yeltsin to overrule the military.

The breakthrough came on the morning of June 2 when Chernomyrdin accepted the necessity for total Yugoslav withdrawals from Kosovo. After consultations with Washington, Talbott decided to relegate the problem of KFOR's command structure to a footnote in the joint statement. The issue could be fixed for the time being. The main thing was to get the joint statement accepted.[83] In the afternoon of June 2, Chernomyrdin and Ahtisaari went straight to Belgrade for the final round of talks with Milosevic. Would he accept NATO's demands? The next day, June 3, at about 12 noon, Chernomyrdin called Talbott from Belgrade, reporting that Milosevic had accepted the entire proposal. In his diaries, Talbott recalled that "he was calling from Slobo's office—I could hear the distinctive voice of Milosevic in the background." Chernomyrdin said, " 'Strobe, pozdravlyayu tebya. On prinyal resheniye. U menya dlya tebya predlozheniye [He made a decision and has an offer for you].' My heart sank: I feared a pause was coming. Nothing of the kind. He was asking for our military—i.e., NATO—to meet the Yugoslav military to begin making preparations for implementation and suspension. I said "v principe da,' once we'd seen 'with our own eyes' and been satisfied with the decision. He said he understood, but urged me to get arrangements under way."[84] What happened in Belgrade? On the first evening, June 2, Ahtisaari read the joint document aloud to Milosevic and a group of Yugoslav leaders. Chernomyrdin fully endorsed the terms and did not even give them a hint of an easy way out. This time, Milosevic did not put up a fight. He was interested to get the deal done as quickly as possible.[85]

Talbott was still at the Petersberg in Bonn and heading to the airport for the flight to Helsinki when he got the news. He had a short conversation and picture taken with a Kosovar waiter who worked at the Petersberg and was close to tears when he heard the news.[86] On the way to the airport, Talbott called Albright to give her a report. She was in a great hurry and wanted to be the first State Department person to convey the news to Clinton. Next, Talbott called Berger's office at the White House and was patched directly to the Oval Office. Talbott wanted to have a chance to give Clinton a report. "My spiel was warp-speed," Talbott recalled. His recommendation for Clinton was to test Milosevic right away. Would he begin to withdraw his forces from Kosovo? Or would he cheat and retreat and try to go for a better deal? Talbott's advice for Clinton was to make sure that General Robert Foglesong, the State Department's military adviser, would go down to the border of Kosovo to find out. "Meanwhile, we need to be exceedingly careful in public neither to embrace or vouch for what's happened nor to pour cold water on it. We've got to keep very cool, very skeptical: on the military track it's business as usual, but on the diplomatic track we're moving ahead with all prudent haste."[87] Clinton interjected several times and agreed with Talbott's ideas. Thereafter, Albright called Talbott and demanded improved coordination. She was upset and criticized Talbott for calling Clinton directly.[88]

After the breakthrough in Belgrade, Talbott changed his travel plans and first went to Brussels instead of Helsinki. On arrival, NATO Ambassador Sandy Vershbow met him at the entrance of NATO's headquarters. "Well, Strobe, is this too good to be true or too true to be good?" Vershbow asked.[89] Talbott had an emotional moment and almost lost it when Solana came out of his office and embraced and congratulated him. NATO had a special meeting of the North Atlantic Council to discuss the deal, and Talbott used a press conference to urge caution. When he was asked whether the deal would work, he provided a careful response. "During the course of the day, we had some sense from our Finnish and Russian colleagues about what has transpired in Belgrade, and the next stage of this very important process is to confirm, to clarify, and to verify, and that is one of the several issues that I will be discussing with the Secretary General and the NAC," Talbott said.[90] On the evening of June 3, 1999, Talbott flew to Helsinki to meet Ahtisaari the next day.

On June 4, Ahtisaari provided a detailed report of the decisive meetings with Milosevic on June 2 and 3. At the outset of the final talks in

Belgrade, he read the joint statement in full and handed Milosevic the paper. The Yugoslavs read it right away and queried about NATO's leadership role in the Kosovo peace force. "Chernomyrdin never disagreed with me. None of us had any complaints," Ahtisaari said. "I had to do all the explaining. Milosevic asked me if they could improve the text. I said it was a totally useless exercise. Neither I nor Chernomyrdin had any authority to do that. I said this is the best deal you are going to get from the international community, it's only going to get worse."[91] Talbott and Ahtisaari then discussed the next steps in the process. The following day, June 5, an officer of the Yugoslav army was supposed to meet British General Mike Jackson, the head of NATO's Rapid Reaction Force, to sign a document on the retreat of all Yugoslav military forces from Kosovo. The talks would begin at a roadside café called Europa 94, close to the Yugoslav border inside Macedonia. "If the word 'all' is missing . . . the bombing will continue," Talbott noted.[92] During the next few days, nobody was certain whether the deal would stick.

On June 7, Russia's UN Ambassador Sergey Lavrov began to complain over the details of the UN resolution that was needed to authorize the start of the international civil and military presence in Kosovo.[93] The danger was real that Lavrov's rhetoric could make Milosevic think he might be able to get a better deal. He could be tempted to get a bombing pause in exchange for only partial withdrawals. Moreover, Ivanov tried to backtrack, arguing in favor of UN control over the international security presence in Kosovo.[94] On June 7, Clinton called Yeltsin to say that Milosevic had still not delivered. "We have to make sure nothing happens to make Milosevic think he can stall; we can't let him stall or backslide. If he had done what he told Chernomyrdin Friday, there would be no bombs falling today," Clinton said.[95] The next day, June 8, Yeltsin called Clinton with a plea to find a UN resolution. This had not been the deal. "No, Boris," Clinton said. "Ahtisaari and Chernomyrdin made an agreement with Milosevic that Milosevic would begin to withdraw, and when he began, we would end the bombing." Yeltsin continued and insisted on the link between a UN resolution and the end of NATO's bombing. Clinton stayed calm and reassured Yeltsin, "Boris, don't worry, this is going to work out the way you and I agreed."[96]

On June 10, Yugoslav forces finally started to withdraw from Kosovo, and NATO stopped bombing. Eventually, the United Nations adopted Resolution 1244 on June 19, 1999. It authorized the establishment of an international civil and military presence in the Federal Republic of Yugoslavia and established a United Nations Interim Administration Mission in Kosovo.[97] Clinton and Yeltsin were elated and glad that the Kosovo War did not destroy the U.S.-Russia partnership. "You know, it would have been a real tragedy for us if our ways had gone in different directions," Yeltsin said, "because we have been working for many years. But I am very glad about the fact that we will be able to continue working together and cooperating. That is just great."[98] There were still plenty of unresolved questions, though. It was unclear which forces were to enter Kosovo as part of the international security presence and when. NATO and Russia had to address the issue instantly to avoid renewed violence and unrest.

Broken Promises. Talbott's First Meetings
with Putin in June 1999

On June 9, Talbott was on a plane to Moscow again when the deal on the start of Yugoslav withdrawals was concluded. It was his eighth trip to Europe in ten weeks. The visit to Moscow started with a relaxed meeting and a press conference with Chernomyrdin on June 10, followed by a meeting with the new prime minister, Sergey Stepashin, in the late afternoon. Meanwhile, Yeltsin had fired Primakov. Again, Talbott emphasized the importance of immediate implementation under NATO auspices. The commander of the implementation force had to be a NATO officer, and he should receive instructions from the North Atlantic Council.[99]At the same time, there was room for flexibility in terms of Russia's participation. The legal aspects were complex. From NATO's vantage point, the essential document was the Military-Technical Agreement signed between General Jackson and the Federal Republic of Yugoslavia—the other key document was the joint Ahtisaari-Chernomyrdin paper. However, the Russian side wanted to respect only a UN Security Council resolution. During the meeting with Stepashin, Talbott was informed that the Security Council resolution had actually just passed. Everything seemed to be in order—but the mechanism of Russia's participation in KFOR was still not resolved. General Ivashov threatened that Russian troops might invade Kosovo on their own. "If NATO goes ahead and deploys, we will deploy by ourselves," Ivashov said.[100] This was alarming news. Talbott hoped that the military-to-military talks with the Russian side would produce a solution for Russia's participation in KFOR. General Foglesong was supposed to discuss this with Ivashov on June 11 after his return from Kosovo and his meetings with Yugoslavia's military leadership.

However, June 11 turned out to be different: Russia invaded Kosovo. That day, Talbott first spoke with Ivanov telling him he was aware that about two hundred Russian troops from Bosnia had been alerted for a potential unilateral move to Kosovo. Ivanov did not respond. Next, Talbott went to the Kremlin to speak with Vladimir Putin, the new secretary of the Russian Security Council. Talbott wanted some sort of clarification on Russia's internal struggles and their implications for the joint NATO-Russian peacekeeping engagement in Kosovo. Moreover, Talbott planned to open a direct channel between Putin and Berger to work on a variety of issues, notably nonproliferation. Putin thanked Talbott profusely and pointed out that Kokoshin had already acquainted him with Berger. Talbott recalled the encounter in detail.

> Meeting Putin for the first time, I was struck by his ability to convey self-control and confidence in a low-key, soft-spoken manner. He was physically the smallest of the men at the top—short, lean and fit while all the others were taller and most of them were hefty and overfed. Putin radiated executive competence and an ability to get things done without fuss or friction . . . Putin was just about the coolest Russian I've ever seen. With me as with others, he wanted his visitor to know that he'd done his homework for the meeting by reading the dossier prepared by the intelligence services. He made several references to the details of my interest in Russia over the years, mention, for example, the poets I'd studied at Yale or Oxford, Fyodor Tyutchev and Vladimir Mayakowsky.[101]

During the meeting, Talbott was informed that the military talks on a joint peacekeeping mission had just failed. He wanted Putin's assessment of the situation. Was there a danger of a direct military confrontation in Kosovo? Putin was puzzled and denied any change in the Russian attitude. When Talbott referred to Ivashov's threats the previous day, Putin responded, "Who, by the way, is this Ivashov?"[102] Talbott recalled that "he adopted the bedside manner of an experienced physician with a hypochondriac for a patient. Nothing on the Russian side had changed, he said soothingly."[103]

Talbott left Moscow with an uneasy feeling. Half an hour after departing, he received a call from Berger and General Joseph Ralston, the vice chairman of the Joint Chiefs of Staff—the Russian IFOR contingent in Bosnia had just started moving toward Kosovo through Yugoslavia. It seemed that the Russian military took this step without consulting Yeltsin or the Foreign Ministry.[104] Talbott had his plane turn around. On returning, he went to the U.S. embassy in Moscow to wait for Ivanov. Meanwhile, CNN was covering Russia's provocative move from Bosnia to Kosovo with lots of Russian soldiers in tanks flashing the Serb three-finger victory salute. During the remainder of June 11, Talbott and Ivanov searched for a joint formula so that NATO and Russian soldiers could enter Kosovo together. This was both a political and a military problem. Ivanov understood the imperative of a unified command under NATO's leadership—and he did not demand a separate Russian sector in Kosovo either. The fundamental problem was that the Russian side wanted a long-term Russian presence and some zone of responsibility in Kosovo, whereas the primary U.S. objective was to deploy troops ASAP to stabilize the region.

Talbott had Foglesong explain the Clinton administration's ideas on NATO-Russia cooperation in Kosovo. The plan was for NATO and Russian troops to enter Kosovo jointly and have a presence together while working out a long-term solution. Foglesong suggested that the NATO-Russia Permanent Joint Council should be the principal venue for consultations—KFOR should include a Russian deputy commander to whom Russian forces could report. Ivanov replied that he lacked the authority to make a decision on the Russian side. His suggestion was that Talbott and Foglesong take the proposal to Russian Defense Minister Igor Sergeyev. It was on the evening of June 11 that Talbott and Foglesong sat down with Sergeyev and Ivanov. The meeting was tense. It started at 8.30 p.m. and ended at 5.15 a.m. Sergeyev was furious. At the outset, he interrupted Ivanov several times and posed inquisitory questions. Talbott let Foglesong explain the process of the envisaged joint NATO-Russia deployments. Sergeyev objected to the core idea of unity of command. He did not want to have Russian forces directly under NATO command. His position was that each country needed its own sector.

Near midnight, Sergeyev and Ivanov went to the Kremlin to see Yeltsin. The Russian position hardened. Yeltsin wanted to have his own Russian sector, and he was concerned about the movement of NATO forces toward the Kosovo border. Meanwhile, Ivanov tried to reassure Talbott that Russia would not introduce forces into Kosovo. Talbott was not convinced. He anticipated that Russian forces would enter Kosovo unilaterally in a matter of hours. At 12:20 a.m., the Russians called for a break and huddled in Sergeyev's office. As time passed, it was clear that the discussion would not produce agreement. The Russian military played a blame game, arguing that NATO troops had already moved into Kosovo—not true. At 2 a.m. on June 12, Talbott learned via CNN that Russian forces had just passed Belgrade on their move to Kosovo. At 4 a.m., CNN reported the arrival of Russian troops at Pristina Airport. Ivanov and Sergeyev were in an awkward position.[105]

At 5:30 a.m., Ivanov informed Talbott in a bizarre conversation. "He struck the pose of a junior military officer reporting to his superior," Talbott recalled. "He snapped to attention, threw his shoulders back and said: 'Mr. Secretary'—a form of address he had never used with me before—'I regret to inform you that a column of Russian soldiers had accidentally crossed the border into Kosovo, and orders have been issued for them to be out within two hours. The minister of defense and I regret this development.'"[106] Talbott insisted on a public statement from Ivanov to this effect—and it was agreed that Ivanov would do it instantly via CNN. Meanwhile, the Russian military leadership had disappeared and did not reappear to say good-bye. Sergeyev had been kept in the dark by his generals. Furious and screaming, he did not manage to regain his composure to make any farewells. On June 12, Talbott heard from Mamedov that Ivanov offered to resign—but it was rejected.[107] The same morning, June 12, NATO troops went into Kosovo and found two hundred Russian troops who refused to relinquish the Pristina airfield. Why did the Russian side pull this dangerous surprise move at a time when the fighting was over? It was a kind of delayed reaction growing out of anger and humiliation of watching NATO bomb Yugoslavia for seventy-nine days. Yeltsin explained in his memoirs and noted that Russia had "to make a crowning gesture, even if it had no military significance. It was not a question of specific diplomatic victories or defeats; it was a question of whether we had won the main point. Russia had not permitted itself to be defeated in the moral sense. . . . This last gesture was a sign of our moral victory in the face of the enormous NATO military," Yeltsin concluded.[108]

In the afternoon of June 12, Talbott went to the Kremlin for another meeting with Putin. He requested the encounter to confront Putin with Russia's broken promises. Talbott wanted assurances that no additional

Russian troops would be deployed and that the current Russian contingent at Pristina Airport would be redeployed to another part of Kosovo. Talbott emphasized that there would be an interim agreement along the lines of the Bosnia IFOR command arrangements—Russian troops would not be directly under NATO command; they would be under the command of officers in their national capacity, and Russia would maintain ultimate command and control of its forces. Meanwhile, both sides should work on a long-term arrangement on the unity of command in KFOR. Talbott then elaborated on NATO's red lines. Russia could not have its own sector with a Russian commander. Second, as a NATO-led force, KFOR had to remain under the political guidance of the North Atlantic Council.

Putin's spiel was to play things down. "It was as though nothing alarming or surprising had occurred in the twenty-four hours since I'd previously seen him," Talbott recalled. "He set about explaining—slowly, calmly, in a calm voice that was sometimes barely audible—why what he'd promised wouldn't happen had now happened. It was all politics, he said. . . . There were hawks and doves in both Russia and the U.S., he said, and, Russian hawks were behind the preemptive spring to Pristina airport. . . . The damage that Russian hawks had inflicted overnight on U.S.-Russian relations was nothing compared to the injury that NATO had caused to President Yeltsin's prestige with its air war against Serbia."[109] Putin claimed he was in favor of a compromise solution that Sergeyev had rejected the night before. Eventually, Talbott and Putin agreed that the defense ministers would work out the modus operandi of Russia's participation in KFOR. Sergeyev and Cohen were supposed to resolve the problem prior to the G-8 meeting in Cologne, which was only a week away.

Meanwhile, the Russian invasion of Kosovo caused dissent among NATO's key military commanders. How should the alliance react? What could NATO do in light of Russia's move? On June 11, British General Mike Jackson, the KFOR commander, decided not to follow the instructions of NATO SACEUR General Wesley Clark, who wanted Jackson to secure Pristina Airport before the arrival of the Russian contingent. Jackson did not like the idea of sending troops because the Yugoslav army had not yet withdrawn their forces from Kosovo. In his memoirs, Jackson wrote that "by going into Kosovo ahead of time, we would be breaching our newly signed agreement with the Serbs, providing them with a pretext not to withdraw and perhaps to fight."[110] At the time, the Yugoslav army still had more than three hundred tanks in Kosovo alone, whereas NATO's fifteen thousand KFOR troops had just forty. The next day, June 12, Clark overplayed his hand when he claimed he had the authority to give Jackson an order to secure Pristina Airport. During a video conference call, Jackson held his position: "Sir, I'm not going to start World War Three for you," Jackson said.[111] Two months later, it was announced that Clark would be replaced as SACEUR earlier than expected. The Clinton administration and the U.S. military leadership did not back Clark's position.

More diplomacy was needed to resolve the standoff with the Russian contingent at Pristina Airport. On June 12, Gore called Stepashin and proposed the immediate start of talks between Russian and American generals in Macedonia to find a way for the joint deployment of forces in Kosovo.[112] Meanwhile, Talbott had already left Moscow and was on his way home. He could not make another U-turn and go back to Moscow. It had been agreed that Cohen and Sergeyev would find a solution—and Yeltsin had to bring his military into line to resolve the Pristina Airport showdown. On June 13, Clinton called Yeltsin to this effect. The crisis had to be resolved before the Cologne G-8 meeting, which was just six days away. Yeltsin seemed totally out of it and did not understand the situation. It was a bizarre telephone conversation. Yeltsin was unable to engage in real business. He lacked substantive talking points; his remarks did not make sense. He kept saying that he and Clinton should meet in an isolated place to fix the problem—"either on a boat or some submarine or some island so not a single person will disturb us, so you will not be agitated by anyone, and I will not be agitated by anyone or any person," he said.[113] Yeltsin suggested taking a break and having a phone conversation the following day. Meanwhile, Clinton's foreign policy team made sure that Ivanov, Putin, and Stepashin were involved as well—Albright reached out to Ivanov, Berger called Putin, and Gore spoke with Stepashin again.[114] Talbott thought that de-escalation was the best approach to resolve the crisis. "Let's deal with them by surrounding them, checking them, countering them with subtlety, and not confronting them in ways that cause their insecurities and resentments to explode."[115]

On June 14, Clinton called Yeltsin again to find a mechanism under which NATO and Russia could work together in Kosovo. Yeltsin confirmed that the Russian contingent would be under Bosnia IFOR rules and guaranteed that there would be no Russian reinforcement without an agreement. In addition, he emphasized that the Russian commanders at the airport would work out arrangements on-site—he kept saying that he would issue orders instantly. Moreover, he agreed to the convocation of the Cohen-Sergeyev meeting in Helsinki starting on June 16.[116] Talbott did not participate in these gatherings. He had a quiet weekend at home for the first time in months. Albright and Ivanov were in Helsinki, and Cohen and Sergeyev led the negotiations. When Albright called Talbott during the talks, his advice was clear: "Don't leave Helsinki without a deal; Cohen and Sergeyev will never get across the finish line unless you and ISI [Igor Sergeyevich Ivanov] are there to drag them across."[117] Eventually, the Cohen-Sergeyev agreement of June 18 stipulated a unified KFOR command but gave the Russian government complete political and military control over its KFOR contingent. It was agreed that there would be a Russian military representative at NATO headquarters in Brussels and a Russian liaison officer at NATO's southern European headquarters in Naples. The agreement provided Russia with a contingent of 3,600 troops, of which 750 were to be based at the Pristina airfield and the remaining 2,850 were to be deployed in the U.S., German, and French sectors.[118]

Talbott was glad about the last-minute agreement. When Yeltsin arrived for the summit in Cologne on June 20, everyone on the U.S. delegation held their breath, hoping that he would officially endorse the agreement. In his diary, Talbott noted that "BNY arrives, itself a big event. We're all holding our breath. The arrival goes ok. Unsteady coming down the stairs, then makes a beeline to the press (uh-oh!), but no disaster: is he satisfied with Helsinki? DA! Whew!"[119] In Cologne, Clinton applauded Russia's important role in the diplomacy to end the Kosovo War. Yeltsin was pleased and eager to prove he was still in charge despite many domestic troubles. Clinton praised Yeltsin profusely. "We have many things to discuss. Thank you for not giving up on the relationship and making sure we passed this very tough test," Clinton said. Yeltsin replied that "our cooperation came to the brink of collapse with Kosovo. If we had not kept in touch and dealt honestly and openly with each other, it would have gone over the brink. We held that process back."[120] Yeltsin's spiel was that the United States and Russia had to retain their partnership. He did the same riff in his meetings with European policymakers—but "with the edge that only that way can we control and offset these crazy Americans," as Schröder's foreign policy adviser Michael Steiner told Talbott.[121] The meeting in Cologne went well. Yet it also indicated Yeltsin's loss of power. His conversation with Clinton ended when Russian staffers pressed for an abrupt end. Their excuse was that Yeltsin's plane was close to losing its time slot to depart for Moscow.

Talbott and Mamedov used the Cologne summit to strategize over the revival of NATO-Russia relations. Their discussion revealed a clash of interests. The Kosovo War signaled NATO's primacy and America's determination to be a genuinely European power. It revealed Russia's impotence and its role as a bystander as far as the use of force was concerned. It seemed that Russia's helplessness did not lead to resignation. Instead, Russia's spectator role spurred a new determination to regain control over Europe's security affairs and challenge NATO's dominance. Yeltsin wanted the United States to stay out of Europe. He thought Europe was Russia's turf. This was the idea behind Mamedov's repeated calls for strengthening pan-European security structures such as the OSCE. The NATO-Russia Founding Act, it seemed, was just a provisional bandage to cover the clashing American and Russian interests. From Russia's vantage point, NATO was still just a four-letter word.

Mamedov even wanted to delete the word NATO from Russia's dialogue with the West. He lamented that the "principal practical problem is there's no mechanism for genuine joint consultation. We want to erase the word NATO and talk instead about transatlantic structures." Talbott stopped Mamedov. Russia must not try to overachieve its foreign policy objectives. "Don't overplay your hand the way you did with the invasion of Kosovo." Mamedov shot back, "Are you calling Kosovo an independent country? Thought it was part of FRY [Former Republic of Yugoslavia]." Talbott responded that he was "talking about NATO redlines from 97 and how treacherous it would be to try to reopen those issues."[122] After dinner, Talbott and Mamedov had another interesting conversation in the car that took them back to the hotel. It was creepy for Talbott to find out that even Mamedov thought that Russia's invasion of Kosovo was necessary for domestic purposes. "In the car, riding just the two of us back to the hotel, he tries to make the case that we've gotten through a bad patch because of two Russian moves—Chernomyrdin's diplomacy and the Russian rush to Pristina. As best I can make it out, his argument is that the former lanced the boil of the bombing and the latter lanced the boil of Russian domestic resentment over always getting screwed."[123]

Mamedov's remarks reflected Russia's deep domestic crisis. Yeltsin's time was over. He struggled to find a successor. Could the recently appointed Prime Minister Sergey Stepashin set up new structures as he promised during a visit to Washington on July 26, 1999?[124] Stepashin, the former minister of the interior, was more pragmatic than Primakov. He had more economic competence as well. In July 1999, Talbott found Stepashin a competent interlocutor who was on top of his brief and able to discuss a multitude of issues in U.S.-Russia relations with Clinton and Gore. "I sure hope Yeltsin keeps that guy," said Clinton after Stepashin's visit. "He's good. Anyway, Ol' Boris can't be changing his government every twenty minutes."[125] However, it remained doubtful whether Stepashin would be able to remain in power and even run for the presidency. In early August, Talbott received information that Yeltsin would fire Stepashin soon. Apparently, he was not close enough to the Yeltsin family. On August 7, Talbott heard that Putin was perhaps the most likely candidate to replace Stepashin as prime minister. Israeli President Ehud Barak gave Clinton a report on his recent visit to Moscow and said Stepashin would be replaced within a few days. "The name that was mentioned to me as a replacement was a guy whose name is Putin," Barak said.[126]

Indeed, on August 9, 1999, Yeltsin announced Putin's nomination as prime minister and his personal pick for the presidency. Yeltsin read through a prepared statement: "Next year, for the first time in the country's history, the first president of Russia will hand over power to a newly elected president. . . . I have decided to name a man who, in my opinion, is able to consolidate society. Relying on the broadest of political forces, he will ensure the continuation of reforms in Russia."[127] Talbott was not enthusiastic about Putin. Their June 11 encounter was still on his mind. "I was still waiting for the public statement Putin had promised me in June repudiating General Ivashov's threat that the Russian military would try to beat NATO to the punch in Kosovo," Talbott recalled.[128] On August 12, 1999, Berger spoke with Putin to congratulate him on the appointment. Putin expressed gratitude for their previous work on Kosovo and promised continuity. "There will be no sharp changes to the cabinet. This pertains to foreign policy and domestic economic policy," Putin said.[129] However, Talbott was skeptical about Putin's willingness to deliver on these promises.

CHAPTER VII

Putin and the Crisis of U.S.–Russia Relations

The War in Chechnya and Putin's Rise to the Presidency

Putin's appointment came as a surprise. He was not well known in Russia but had become an essential figure in Yeltsin's management system over time. Putin had been KGB all his life. In the second half of the 1980s, he had been a counterintelligence officer in the East German town of Dresden, where he witnessed the collapse of communism. Although he recalled the years in East Germany as a dull time in his life, he actually helped support anti-Western terrorist groups in West Germany.[1] After the fall of the Berlin Wall, Putin went back to his hometown of St. Petersburg. In May 1990, the liberal St. Petersburg Mayor Anatoly Sobchak hired him as an international affairs adviser. In June 1991, Putin was appointed head of the Committee for External Relations of the Mayor's Office. His responsibilities included international relations and foreign investments. Putin used his position to accumulate revenues from the sales of raw materials such as rare earth metals and oil products. In 1992, the St. Petersburg City Council investigated Putin and concluded that he sold metals valued at $93 million in exchange for foreign food aid.[2] Finally, Sobchak stopped the inquiry to protect Putin. In March 1994, Putin was appointed first deputy chairman of the government of St. Petersburg.

In 1996, when Sobchak lost his bid for reelection in St. Petersburg, Putin resigned from his positions in the city administration, moved to Moscow, and was appointed deputy chief of the presidential property management department, which was headed by Pavel Borodin. In March 1997, Putin was promoted to deputy chief of the presidential staff. In July 1998, Yeltsin appointed Putin director of the Federal Security Service. U.S. Ambassador James Collins spoke with Putin several times and recalled that he made a significant impression. "He never used any notes when you talked to him," Collins recalled. "He knew his brief. He was well-structured in the way he understood issues or the way issues were discussed. . . . He was confident. He felt he could deal with the issues that were being brought to him or when he was being approached by the American ambassador to talk about something. It was, in that sense, an interesting man to work with."[3]

In March 1999, Putin was appointed secretary of the Security Council. He retained the position as director of the FSB and became one of the most influential figures in Yeltsin's entourage. He was a capable technocrat and managed Russia's consolidation after the 1998 financial crisis. Putin had no reformist credentials of his own but had been close enough to Sobchak to qualify as a proponent of reform. He was part of Yeltsin's team but not too close to Yeltsin himself. This was an advantage because Yeltsin always tended to destroy those around him who acted too independently. This was one of the factors for the dismissal of Primakov as prime minister in May 1999.[4] Putin was a compromise candidate acceptable to competing fractions in the Kremlin and Russia's business elite, including Yeltsin's daughter Tatyana Yumasheva and businessman Boris Berezovsky. Putin suited the needs of the moment. His agenda was focused on the resurrection of Russia's power. Last but not least, Putin could protect the Yeltsin family from potential investigation and prosecution. On December 31, hours after Putin was appointed acting president, he signed a decree providing Yeltsin and his family with financial benefits, including a pension, and granting Yeltsin immunity.[5]

Who was Putin? Talbott recalled that

> most of us in the American government and our allied friends were skeptical about what Putin really was. One of the lines was, "He is what he was." What he was, of course, was not just a KGB officer of middle rank, lieutenant colonel, but a good deal of his KGB work was in counterespionage, which is different from espionage. Spies go out and look for real facts. Counterspies are a little different. They regard it almost as a professional need to be paranoid. They're not

going to get in trouble if they have suspicions about somebody that turn out to be wrong, but if they have suspicions about somebody that turn out to be right, they're doing their job. So there was that.[6]

Putin's rise and the longevity of his reign were, of course, not predictable. Back in 1999, the political scene in Moscow was volatile. It was unclear whether Putin would be able to remain in office long enough to race for Yeltsin's succession. British diplomats noted that "the new Prime Minister, Putin, remains an unknown quantity and may well go the way of Stepashin if he falls out of favor with the Kremlin."[7]

Clinton's first personal meeting with Putin was on September 12, 1999, in Auckland, New Zealand, where both attended the annual summit of the Asia-Pacific Economic Cooperation forum. Before the meeting, Yeltsin praised Putin in a telephone conversation with Clinton: "I found out he is a solid man who is kept well abreast of various subjects under his purview. At the same time, he is thorough and strong, very sociable. And he can easily have good relations and contact with people who are his partners."[8] Putin was different from Yeltsin. He was a cold fish, "businesslike," and factual. There was no small talk, no jokes, and little spontaneity. Clinton did not call him "Vladimir." Nevertheless, Clinton told Putin he was confident about the future of the U.S.-Russia relationship. His message was that "I am counting on Yeltsin and you."[9] Clinton's main aim was to continue the U.S.-Russia partnership with Putin. In his memoirs, Clinton noted that "Putin presented a stark contrast to Yeltsin. Yeltsin was large and stocky; Putin was compact and extremely fit from years of martial arts practice. Yeltsin was voluble; the former KGB agent was measured and precise. I came away from the meeting believing Yeltsin had picked a successor who had the skills and the capacity for hard work necessary to manage Russia's turbulent political and economic life better than Yeltsin now could, given his health problems. Putin also had the toughness to defend Russia's interests and protect Yeltsin's legacy."[10]

However, the war in Chechnya soon revealed the limits of cooperation. In August 1999, Putin's appointment coincided with escalating tensions in the Caucasus. Chechen forces crossed the border with Dagestan under the leadership of militant leader Shamil Basayev to establish an Islamic republic. Weeks later, in September, Basayev's incursion in Dagestan was followed by a series of bombings in Russia against apartment buildings in Volgodansk, Buynaksk, and Moscow, killing several hundred civilians. The bombings provided the pretext for the second Chechen War and catapulted the unknown Putin into the presidency. The Russian military launched a massive bombing campaign against Chechnya, followed by a ground invasion in early October 1999. Several thousand civilians died. Two hundred thousand refugees left Chechnya.[11] Most fled to the neighboring Russian republic of Ingushetsia. Russia's public opinion backed Putin's massive military counteroffensive as a holy fight against terrorism and a way to restore national pride. In October 1999, Russian troops moved close to Grozny and bombarded the city, killing dozens of people when they fired Scud missiles on a maternity hospital and a market. Talbott recalled that "the war in the North Caucasus burst back into flame, this time with a difference that made it as much a political winner for Putin as it had been a loser for Yeltsin."[12] Putin capitalized on the war. It propelled him into a position to win the March 2000 presidential elections. His approval skyrocketed from 31 percent in August 1999 to 84 percent in January 2000.[13]

In February 2000, Russian troops captured Grozny after their attacks had razed much of the city. In March 2000, Putin celebrated victory when he arrived on an SU-27 fighter jet in Grozny. In September 1999, when he ordered Russia's massive air campaign in the North Caucasus, he said that he would target terrorists relentlessly. "We will pursue them everywhere. . . . We'll catch them in the toilet. We'll wipe them out in the outhouse."[14] Putin's raw language and macho appearance conveyed a new sense of determination and brutality. Putin portrayed himself as a guy who could get things done and knew how to use force effectively. In September 1999, Foreign Minister Igor Ivanov was already in his camp. Ivanov told Albright that "there will be no more revolutionary changes; the changes that have already taken place have demolished all institutions, and what is needed is someone who can do the detail work of establishing new procedures for getting things done. Putin is that kind of guy, and will be able to count on the support of youth, and of 'reformers.'"[15] Moreover, Putin had the trust of the Yeltsin family. Yeltsin's son-in-law, Valentin Yumashev, was particularly important in the transfer of power.[16] Yumashev had drawn Putin into Yeltsin's inner circle and was "very, very high on Putin" claiming that "Putin had shown himself to be a well-organized, a decisive leader in his previous positions and had a special talent for acquiring the trust of his interlocutors whether they be generals, governors or the strange folks who lead the special services."[17]

The U.S. response to the Chechen War was to emphasize Russia's territorial integrity but also Russia's obligation to protect civilian life and to permit an observer mission under the auspices of the OSCE in Chechnya. Clinton did not endorse economic sanctions to punish Russia at this point. He assumed that sanctions could not change Russian attitudes and would jeopardize the country's economic recovery and its domestic stabilization after the 1998 financial crisis. Talbott thought that it had been a mistake to shy away from a harsher U.S. response during the first Chechen War, when Clinton had more leverage in his Russia diplomacy.[18] "I regret it [the U.S. response to the first war] not only for humanitarian reasons, but I think that if we had been able to shake Yeltsin and use the Clinton-Yeltsin [relationship] in the way that we did successfully on other issues maybe he wouldn't have been susceptible to Stepashin or Kulikov, who got him to do it again in 1999. And Putin, of course, big time," Talbott said.[19] Privately, Talbott thought the war was "as close to a true, fatal disaster as anything we've experienced in 7 years, our Russian friends are blowing their brains out."[20]

In November 1999, Clinton used the OSCE summit in Istanbul to criticize Yeltsin personally before the assembled presidents and heads of state. Clinton emphasized that Russia's bombardment of Grozny was shameful in terms of Yeltsin's legacy as president. "The strength Russia rightly is striving to build, therefore, could be eroded by an endless cycle of violence. The global integration Russia has rightly sought to advance, with our strong support, will be hindered," Clinton said.[21] The private Clinton-Yeltsin meeting turned into a confrontation. Yeltsin was in a belligerent mood and blamed the United States for Russia's problems in Chechnya. "Well, Bill, what about those camps here in Turkey that are preparing troops to go into Chechnya? Aren't you in-charge of those? I have the details . . . and want to show you where the mercenaries are being trained and then being sent into Chechnya. They are armed to the teeth. . . . Bill, this is your fault," Yeltsin said.[22] He continued his sermon and emphasized that America had no business in Europe at all. "Just give Europe to Russia. The U.S. is not in Europe. Europe should be the business of Europeans. . . . I will take Europe and provide them security," Yeltsin said. Clinton laughed this off: "I don't think the Europeans would like this very much."[23] Yeltsin's remarks were annoying. He did not joke. This was vintage Soviet rhetoric. Talbott thought that a fitting newspaper headline would be "Yeltsin threatens war against Europe."[24]

Apart from the Clinton-Yeltsin confrontation, the Istanbul summit was a landmark event. It brought the conclusion of the adapted CFE treaty and the adapted Vienna document on confidence- and security-building measures, including a real expansion and deepening of commitments by all OSCE states about arms control information exchanges, visits, inspections, and other transparency measures to which Russia signed.[25] Although Talbott emphasized the value of confidence-building measures, the Russian attitude was considerably cooler. Mamedov confirmed Russia's interest in concluding a legally binding agreement on conventional force levels, yet cautioned that "if an agreement was not possible by Istanbul, it would not be the end of the world."[26]

Meanwhile, Chechnya was a running sore in U.S.-Russia relations. Putin brushed off appeals to search for a political solution and a negotiated end to the war. Clinton was frustrated and told Blair that "as long as those in power were gaining popularity due to the Chechnya campaign, nothing would turn it around. He had not spoken to Putin recently because he did not know what to say to him. Anything he asked was likely to be rejected."[27] Putin was determined to continue Russia's military assault without consideration for a political solution. This was evident when he met Clinton for the second time in Oslo on November 19, 1999: "On Chechnya, the question is how we crush this base of terrorism and take minimal losses," Putin said. "Well, what will be done will be done. We have a solid military strategy. We will attack areas with terrorists. But how can we negotiate with terrorists. The Russian people would never accept this. We need to find those we can deal with," Putin pointed out.[28] This was vintage Putin. He displayed vigor and determination as soon as critical subjects were raised. He drew red lines when his interests in the Caucasus and Russia's near aboard were entangled. "I'll say that for that guy. . . . He's tough, and he's strong, and he's got a lot of energy and determination," Clinton thought.[29]

Another U.S. concern pertained to the potential spillover into neighboring Georgia, where Chechen civilians and guerilla forces had fled. Georgian President Edvard Shevardnadze was incensed when Russian forces crossed the border several times to conduct military operations on Georgian territory. Putin thought about a permanent deployment of Russian troops in Georgia. The Georgian side refused to permit it. Shevardnadze complained that "they want to hold leverage over Georgia. They do not want to let Georgia look to Europe and the West and the United States.

This is all very naïve, very short-term thinking on their part."[30] In the autumn of 1999, Talbott made two trips to the Caucasus to prevent a potential Russian incursion into Georgia. Talbott asked Shevardnadze to reinforce Georgia's border with Chechnya so as not to give the Russian side an excuse for an invasion. In Moscow, Talbott's main point was that Russia had to respect the sovereignty of its neighbors in the Caucasus, especially Georgia. Talbott said, "it has always been a cornerstone of US policy to support the sovereignty and independence of all the NIS—and thus to oppose any policy or action that had the look or consequence of intimidating the smaller states. Russia's approach to the South Caucasus states during this crisis seemed dangerously close to that line."[31]

Meanwhile, Putin benefited and portrayed himself as the lean KGB guy and the kind of law-and-order man allegedly uninterested in making money. He claimed that one of his key aims was to fight institutionalized corruption deeply ingrained in the Russian system—especially in the Yeltsin years.[32] In September 1999, Swiss prosecutors looked into the activities of the Lugano-based company Metabex, which secured a lucrative contract to renovate the Kremlin. The Swiss authorities froze fifty-nine bank accounts and investigated whether the company had deposited more than $1 million in one Swiss account controlled by Kremlin property manager and Putin mentor Pavel Borodin, who was alleged to have provided the money through credit cards to Yeltsin and his daughter Tatyana Dyachenko.[33] The Metabex scandal revealed that the Clinton administration had failed to insist on introducing effective money-laundering legislation in Russia. As the scandal unfolded, "it became clear that the I.M.F.'s conditions for macro-economic reforms were not working, it also became clear that efforts by the Clinton Administration to introduce small-scale changes were not working, either."[34] Requests increased that Clinton should distance himself from Yeltsin more visibly.

In the autumn of 1999, Republican commentators portrayed Russia as a lost place and a thoroughly criminal state in which it was impossible to do clean business. Criticism increased that, under the Clinton administration's watch, Russia's reformers had failed to fight corruption and been part of a corrupt system themselves. Some U.S. observers had written Russia off and began to contemplate a world without it.[35] Clinton himself was attacked for having misplaced America's ability to shape events in Russia. In the autumn of 1999, the *New York Times* and the *Washington Post* fueled a "Who lost Russia" debate and criticized Clinton's policy as too idealistic and romanticized. The thrust of the pieces was that Clinton should have stayed away from endorsing economic shock therapy and envisaging the United States as a lighthouse and a shining example for Russia. In an essay for the *New York Times Magazine*, John Lloyd wrote, "the case that we lost Russia begins with America's insistence on exporting the free market. . . . The claim that we have lost Russia, in short, is a proxy for Clintonite failure to reshape Russia as an idealized America."[36] One reproach was that Clinton should have been tougher and insisted on more conditionality. Another was that Clinton should not have supported privatization at all.

Talbott argued that a more distanced attitude toward Russia did not make sense—especially at a time when the partnership with Russia was more vulnerable than ever. Russian reform was not eternally stuck against economic setbacks and the financial crisis. Moreover, Talbott thought that Clinton's Russia policy, first and foremost, served the interests of the United States—Russia was no longer a threat. It was increasingly integrated into the mainstream of international affairs. Another way to gain the upper hand in the public debate was to emphasize the long list of accomplishments in Clinton's Russia policy. In the past, the Clinton team had perhaps not sufficiently reiterated the scope of its achievements in managing the press, the deputy head of the State Department's S/NIS Office, Toria Nuland, argued. Nuland recounted that "the biggest mistake we may have made in '93, '94, '95 and perhaps even in the Kosovo deal was not being more Holbrookian in our press management, a la, 'it's hard, it's really hard, it's not gonna happen, we could well fail, the world could end as we know it. . . . but wow, hey, we got a little something.'" Moreover, her advice for Talbott was to highlight the rationale of Clinton's Russia policy again: The bumper sticker should be "it's about supporting a democracy, stupid," she argued.[37]

Putin's Departure from the Yeltsin Legacy

Putin entered the presidency at a crucial point. NATO enlargement and the Kosovo War triggered new competition over the shape of the Euro-Atlantic security system. America's primacy and Russia's inferiority did not allow for a partnership among equals. Russia's expectations about the partnership were disappointed. Both Yeltsin and Putin increasingly saw America's influence in Europe as a threat. Yeltsin, especially, had often felt betrayed by his expectation of being an influential world leader. Russia's second Chechen War and Putin's appointment deepened the rift and jeopardized the policy of mutual integration and accommodation. The survival of the partnership was in danger. Talbott thought about several future scenarios for the start of the new millennium and pointed out that the partnership could well crash if the war in Chechnya worsened and perhaps even moved to Georgia, which would bring severe U.S. sanctions against Russia. In the bleakest scenario, Russia could then move out of the Permanent Joint Council and KFOR in Kosovo and could increase missile assistance for Iran. Such a script was not out the question.

Arms control was another contentious issue area. The Russians rejected the Clinton administration's plans for the establishment of a national missile defense (NMD) system designed to defend all fifty U.S. states against a small-scale missile attack from so-called rogue states such as North Korea, Iran, and Iraq.[38] Russian policymakers saw NMD as a revival of President Reagan's Star Wars ideas and a way to abrogate the 1972 Anti-Ballistic Missile (ABM) Treaty and its limits on missile defense.[39] Yeltsin and the Russian military feared a race in defense weapons that could result in the loss of Russia's status as a military superpower. They thought that America's new defense technology could deprive Russia of its strategic deterrent and make it vulnerable to Western pressure. Mamedov spoke frankly about Russia's grievances when he told Talbott that "after Kosovo, our military doesn't want any serious discussion with you on these issues. They're convinced that anything, repeat anything you do that is a national defense is intended to push Russia out of its own deterrence; you've got Kosovo, plus uncertainty about the political future, plus the political aspirations and influence of the military . . . plus overall military conservatism—and all of that means no one is prepared for any change in the ABM Treaty."[40] Moreover, Mamedov predicted that the Clinton administration would fail to buy Russia's consent through deep cuts in offensive weapons. Russia would maintain its deterrent of 1,500 strategic warheads and was not ready to reciprocate U.S. reductions. The conclusion was clear: "We violate the ABM Treaty, and they violate START," Talbott wrote.[41]

Each of these contentious issues had the potential to derail the U.S.-Russian partnership in its own right. Taken together, they could amount to a downward spiral and a series of setbacks, which could feed back into negative trends. The situation could become progressively worse and destroy the legacy of Clinton's Russia policy. How could Clinton manage the conflicts with a fresh Russian leadership under Putin in the last year of his presidency? Putin symbolized the revival of Russia's imperial ambitions, the resurrection of the Soviet Union, and the rebirth of Russia's search for a mission and a new place in the world. Doubt about his true intentions was considerable. Policymakers from the Baltics had an urgent sense for the revival of Russia's imperialism. The most poignant assessment of Putin came from Estonian President Lennart Meri. He compared Putin with Hitler. In January 2000, Talbott noted that Meri initially set Putin side by side with Siegfried, the dragon slayer from the Nibelungen saga. When Talbott reacted with puzzlement, Meri asked, "Would it be clearer if I said 'Hitler?'" "Yep, that helps," Talbott responded.[42]

Talbott was more optimistic and assumed that Putin could not go back to a cold war. Russia's economic self-isolation was not an option. The country's integration into the world economy was essential for its economic growth and exports of raw materials. This gave the United States leverage to set the rules for Russia's relations with the West, Talbott thought. The notion was that Putin would play by the rules to obtain foreign assistance. Still, Talbott was concerned about the internal configuration of forces in Russia—the decline of Russian liberals, the opportunism of Russian technocrats, and the ability of Putin's *siloviki* to control the country for a long time to come. Meanwhile, Clinton could no longer build on personal diplomacy with Yeltsin. In the previous seven years, the United States and Russia had always managed to get the relationship back on track after phases of crisis. Clinton had relied on his good personal chemistry with Yeltsin to resolve problems and to drive the whole agenda of U.S.-Russian relations. No initiative and no mechanism had been more important than the Bill-and-Boris channel. "But that was partly because of Yeltsin. Now it's not so clear," Talbott told Mamedov.[43] Clinton could not continue the give-and-take pattern with Putin, who remained an enigma, a dubious figure, and a Jekyll and Hyde character.

The war in Chechnya played to Putin's advantage. By late 1999, he was the most popular Russian leader. The Putin-backed Unity bloc won the Duma elections on December 19, 1999, and defeated Primakov's and Luzhkov's Fatherland-All bloc. The result was a clear move toward nationalism in Russia. The economic collapse of 1998 had led to an unprecedented rise of chauvinism—and Putin was a new Zhirinovsky in disguise. The Clinton administration was concerned about the swing from pro-Western reformers to bureaucrats from the security services like Putin. On December 22, 1999, Talbott met Putin for the third time in person. It was the first meeting after their two June 1999 encounters on Kosovo when Talbott had his plane turn around after he had learned Russian troops were on the way to Pristina Airport. This time, the meeting was about Chechnya and Georgia and Shevardnadze's refusal to allow for the deployment of Russian troops on Georgia's side of the Chechen border. Putin's handling of Georgia would be a litmus test regarding his definition of Russia's statehood and his willingness to respect the sovereignty of Russia's neighbors. Putin put on an assertive performance and spoke with pride about the successes of the Russian military in Chechnya. He was even more determined when Talbott mentioned Shevardnadze's concern about a potential Russian intervention in Georgia. At the same time, Putin seemed to know his limits. He noted that Russia would respect Georgia's sovereignty when Talbott issued a clear warning. "Any Russian intervention in Georgia against the wishes of the Georgian authorities would significantly worsen the already strained relationship between Russia and the rest of the world."[44]

Eventually, Talbott briefed Putin on the discussions with Mamedov and the Russian military on strategic arms control and missile defense. Talbott sensed that Putin would not beg for an agreement and could wait until after the U.S. presidential election. Another stunning aspect was that Putin carefully avoided any kind of reference to Yeltsin. He merely spoke about his own meetings with Clinton and his plans for the future. Talbott recalled, "he was acting as though his assumption of the presidency was not only assured but imminent."[45] Imminent it was indeed. On December 31, 1999, Yeltsin pulled a surprise and announced Putin's appointment as acting president starting the next day, January 1, 2000. Yeltsin resigned and declared that the June 2000 election would take place in March. The presidency would give Putin additional credentials. Yeltsin manipulated the electoral calendar to make sure Putin would win. This was vintage Yeltsin. Yeltsin, the democrat, acknowledged his responsibility to step down due to his frail health. Yeltsin, the autocrat, was determined to choose his successor. His message for Clinton was that "Putin is a strong man who is worthy of being president."[46]

The same day, December 31, Clinton called Yeltsin to say good-bye. "I'm sad, but I am very proud of you," Clinton said. "You have guided your country through a historic time and you are leaving a legacy that will leave Russians better off for years to come." Yeltsin had a heavy heart when he said farewell to Clinton: "You should believe me, it was done for Russia, for the sake of Russia, for its future." Clinton understood: "I promise to be a good partner with Putin," he said at the end of the conversation.[47] In his memoirs, Clinton recalled that "Boris also knew that giving the Russian people the chance to see Putin perform would increase the chances that he would win the next election. It was both a wise and a shrewd move, but I was going to miss Yeltsin. For all his physical problems and occasional unpredictability, he had been a courageous and visionary leader. We trusted each other and accomplished a lot together."[48] The next day, New Year's Day, Clinton called Putin to offer his congratulations. Both acknowledged their differences in terms of Chechnya. "There are certain issues on which we do not agree; however, I believe that on the core themes, we always will be together," Putin said.[49]

Domestically, Putin's election campaign benefited from Yeltsin's endorsement and the backing from the Yeltsin family and key oligarchs such as Boris Berezovsky. In addition, Putin profited from his collusion with the Communist Party over the war in Chechnya. Yeltsin had always battled the Communists, but Putin was shrewd and unprincipled and worked with them to secure his victory in the March 2000 election.[50] Putin's unscrupulous maneuvering spread mistrust among the reform-oriented liberals. Yavlinsky was troubled by Putin's brutality and concerned that "Russia was very unstable politically, the Caucasus episode showed it is easy to create hysteria and manipulate the population. . . . Putin claimed to be fighting a war against terror, but it turned out to be nothing of that sort. He said he was center-right, but then made an alliance with the Communists. He said he favored liberal economics, but could we believe him?"[51]

Initially, Putin held his cards close to his chest. He needed time to develop his agenda and did not participate in the World Economic Summit in Davos in late January 2000. Instead, he participated in a summit meeting of the Commonwealth of Independent States and was elected chairman of the Council of Heads of States.[52] Putin used the context of the summit to establish a new union between Russia and Belarus. On January 26, 2000, he spoke with Belarussian dictator Alexandr Lukashenko. Both ratified a new union treaty, mainly to create a single economic space and joint standards in financial legislation.[53] Russia's neighbors watched all of this with mistrust. They saw the treaty as a sign of Putin's plans to revive the Soviet Union. In a meeting with Clinton, Kazakhstan President Nursultan Nazarbaev ridiculed the new union as the "work of those who want only the resurrection of the Soviet Union."[54] The Belarussian opposition was appalled by the loss of the country's independence. In February 2000,

Talbott obtained a firsthand impression of their concerns during a meeting with former Belarussian President Stanislav Shushkevich, who saw the union treaty with Russia as the end of the Belarusian state against the will of the Belarussian people signed by President Lukashenko, whose term in office had already expired in July 1999 and who was no longer the legal president of Belarus. Shushkevich argued that the treaty should therefore not be recognized. Talbott pointed out that "what has happened in Belarus is a breakdown, betrayal, and abuse of the democratic process."[55]

The Clinton administration did not have much leverage to condemn the Union Treaty. Formally, it did not threaten Belarusian sovereignty. At the same time, everything about the treaty depended on Russia's interpretation. It was clear that Putin, during his first months in office, backed up an illegal president of Belarus, Lukashenko, who had turned to Russia as a protector of his kleptocratic regime. Putin used the treaty as a starting point to rebuild Russia's old empire. In his book *First Person*, published in 2000, he lamented the demise of the Soviet Union and the Soviet retreat from East Germany: "I only regretted that the Soviet Union had lost its position in Europe, although intellectually I understood that a position based on walls and dividers cannot last. But I wanted something different to rise in its place. And nothing different was proposed. That's what hurt."[56] Putin was determined to return to the past. He was at odds and in conflict with the West from the beginning. In January 2000, William Safire detailed the dangers of Putinism in a *New York Times* op-ed when he wrote that "in eight weeks, riding a wave of war hysteria, this K.G.B. apparatchik is likely to be elected president—to take his patient, Russia, to the cooler of repression and autocratic rule."[57]

Clinton had a good sense of potential conflicts with Putin's Russia when he contrasted Yeltsin's trust in democracy with the comeback of imperialism under Putin. In a January 2000 telephone conversation with German Chancellor Schröder, Clinton emphasized that "one thing I wanted to say is that Yeltsin, for all his problems, was a true believer in democracy and he also wanted to have Russia's greatness in the future be more related to economic achievements and international cooperative leadership, not a sort of century version of imperialism."[58] Schröder himself emphasized the need to balance partnership and criticism in the relationship with Putin. It was telling that Schröder envisaged a "special German role" in the EU's relations with Russia. In contrast to Schröder, Clinton anticipated problems with a revisionist Russia under Putin. Clinton pointed out that "until Russia's economy improves significantly and the pressure in Chechnya is off and until the raw feelings they have about our actions in the Balkans and NATO expansion have time to heal, we will still have the risk that Russia will do things they shouldn't do in Georgia and Moldova and putting pressure on Kazakhstan and other states that were part of the Soviet Union. So this has to be managed with real sensitivity to get them through this transition period."[59]

Clinton felt that Putin's mélange of objectives betrayed the traditional distinction between reformers and nonreformers. Leon Fuerth thought that "reformer/non-reformer labels had outlived their usefulness in analysis of Russian politicians. . . . Putin's principal objective was the resurrection of Russian power. If we were looking for a historic model, Peter the Great was as good as anyone."[60] Putin planned to combine an open economic system with an authoritarian regime at home—much like Deng Xiaoping, who used to say that he did not care whether a cat was black or white as long as it caught mice. Most Western policymakers thought that the best approach was to embrace Putin and court him to integrate Russia. Blair said that "to describe him as a Russian de Gaulle would be misleading, but he had a similar mindset. It was right to put pressure on him on a number of issues, including internally—the media etc. . . . But he thought it was better to allow Putin a position on the top table and encourage Putin to reach for Western attitudes as well as the Western economic model. . . . It was important to promote the St. Petersburg aspect of Putin's thinking."[61]

Talbott thought that Putin would test the limits of what the West would tolerate. He was especially concerned about the revival of nationalism in Russia. In February 2000, Talbott was appalled when Sergei Ivanov, the head of the Russian Security Council, argued that the West could be glad to work with nationalist Russian *siloviki*—only they could prevent the rise of ultranationalist chauvinists like Zhirinovsky. Ivanov said that "NATO was still viewed with mistrust, and thus the West needs to work harder to show it doesn't threaten Russia. This will help keep 'normal, healthy Russian patriotism' from changing into unhealthy chauvinism, which is what we fear."[62] Ivanov's stunning statement indicated that Yeltsin's legacy was in danger already. The Clinton administration had to be cautious to not endorse Putin too much.

Albright argued that "we have to be careful not to be Putin's validators, unlike Yeltsin, who had his own established credentials. We can't fall into our usual habit of being the Russian leader's friend in court."[63] Clinton's foreign policy team contemplated a shutdown of Talbott's Russia channels until after the Russian presidential election on March 26, 2000. Talbott was against such a delay strategy and "staying with the gameplan until we get past the Russian election since there's a chance—not great, but not worth wasting—that we can get what we're after, and that would be good."[64] At the same time, he emphasized the need not to return to a business-as-usual approach with Putin, given Russia's war crimes in Chechnya. Talbott told Sergei Ivanov that "we're heading into a whole new patch of controversy and we, the U.S., are going to be accused of seamlessly going from Yeltsin-centric to Putin-centric policy, lawyering for the war criminals."[65]

Putin soon began to test the West. In February 2000, he hosted a multitude of high-level Western visitors in Moscow as his military committed war crimes on a large scale in Chechnya. In his meeting with British Foreign Minister Robin Cook, Putin asserted that the British government allowed groups in the United Kingdom to raise funds for Chechen "terrorists." It seemed that Putin believed in the existence of an Islamic conspiracy against Europe—he downplayed the Russian kidnapping of critical war reporter Andrei Babitsky, who had managed to enter the besieged city of Grozny and reported about Russian atrocities against the civilian population in the Chechen capital. Babitsky was tortured and detained in a "filtration camp" in Chernokozovo in Chechnya, where Chechen men and women suspected of rebel connections were taken for interrogation. He was finally released to Moscow after six weeks of uncertainty.[66] Putin's callous treatment of Babitsky revealed the logic of his KGB thinking. The life and the individual fate of a Russian citizen counted for nothing. On Cook's inquiry, Putin said, "he was sure Babitsky was alive, had not been tortured, and was with people he regarded as friends. The GOR [government of Russia] knew approximately where he was and would act so he stays alive. But, Putin said, Babitsky was in trouble with Russian law and would be questioned when he returned for violations of it."[67]

In addition, Putin used the war in Chechnya to undercut the freedom of press. He only favored transparency and media coverage if journalists followed the Kremlin rules.[68] Talbott raised the Babitsky case with Sergei Ivanov and issued a clear warning. International attention would not wane. The Russians had to expect a war crimes tribunal. Ivanov rejected Talbott's complaints as interference in Russia's internal affairs and argued that the law should be in the hands of the Russian rulers. They would define what was right or wrong and who was a terrorist. "After eight years of lawlessness, it was unrealistic to expect a return to order and quiet in Chechnya in a few months," Ivanov said. "Russian forces were uncovering the true extent of foreign terrorist participation in the conflict. If the ringleaders were allowed to escape, the cycle would repeat itself."[69]

Moreover, Putin's stance on Georgia revealed his willingness to challenge Western resolve. He still toyed with the idea of invading Georgia to fight Chechen terrorists despite the assurances he had given to Talbott in December 1999. In February 2000, in a conversation with Albright, Putin said that "Georgia's territorial integrity had already been violated, with some 1500–2000 armed Chechens in the country. . . . Putin observed Shevardnadze had lost control of Abkhazia, Ajaria, and Ossetia and only controlled Tbilisi and its environs."[70] When Albright pressed for a diplomatic solution and a ceasefire, Putin criticized the plea to stop the fighting and to give foreign journalists access to the area. He perceived criticism as a personal affront and was suspicious that the West wanted to see a weak Russia in the Caucasus.

Meanwhile, Talbott feared that the multitude of Western visitors to Moscow conveyed the impression that everyone took Putin's election for granted. Talbott was surprised about Blair's private visit to St. Petersburg on March 10, 2000—at a highly sensitive point two weeks before the Russian presidential elections. Blair and his wife, Cherie, spent the day with Putin and his wife, Lyudmila. They visited the Tsarist summer palace Petrodvorets (Petergof) as well as the Hermitage Museum. They spent the evening at the opera and attended the premiere of Sergei Prokofiev's *War and Peace* at the Mariinsky Theatre.[71] The Blair visit created the impression that "all roads lead to Putin these days," Talbott noted in a conversation with Christopher Meyer, the British ambassador in Washington, DC. Talbott thought that "it was a huge question as to what Putin would reveal after the election. The pragmatic case suggested he would need to integrate Russia with the West, but many indicators that the U.S. has seen so far suggest things could go in a different direction. Talbott's feeling was that these were still 'panning out' in Putin's own mind."[72]

Russia's relations with NATO were another crucial issue during Putin's time as acting president. On February 16, 2000, Putin spoke with NATO Secretary General George Robertson and agreed to revive the Permanent Joint NATO-Russia Council, which Yeltsin had abandoned after the start of the Kosovo War the previous year. Putin also inquired about Russia's potential NATO membership. "When are you going to invite us to

NATO?" he asked, according to Robertson. When Robertson replied that "we don't invite people to join NATO, they apply to join NATO," Putin said, "well, we're not standing in line with a lot of countries that don't matter."[73] This was the traditional Russian rationale. Russia was too large and too mighty to join NATO. On a positive note, Robertson's visit to Moscow culminated in a joint statement in which both sides pledged to renew their relationship.[74]

However, the announcement did not bring tangible process. NATO hoped that the joint peace mission in Kosovo could catalyze further NATO-Russia cooperation—but it was questionable whether Putin would be willing to keep Russian and NATO forces working together in KFOR. Russia was a bystander in the disintegration of Yugoslavia. Milosevic's reign would soon end, and Kosovo was on a trajectory of independence over the long term. Russia threatened to pull out of KFOR because it didn't "want to stand by and bless the de facto dismemberment of Kosovo, especially given its implications for Chechnya," as Sergei Ivanov pointed out.[75] In addition, it was challenging to have productive NATO-Russia consultations. The Russian side did not want to expand the scope of cooperation with NATO in the PJC. Russia did not want the PJC to become the "UNSC [UN Security Council] of Europe, and it did not expect to move to joint decision-making or actions in the near term."[76]

In March 2000, Russia's relationship with NATO was a crucial theme in a televised interview that Putin did with BBC journalist David Frost. Putin landed a media scoop when he suggested that Russia would consider joining NATO. "Why not?" Putin replied when Frost inquired about Russian membership. "I do not rule out such a possibility—but I repeat—if and when Russia's views are considered as those of an equal partner. I want to stress this again and again," Putin said.[77] At the time, the public celebrated the statement as a symbol of Putin's willingness to join the West.[78] However, from Putin's vantage point, equal partnership meant that Russia would not accept NATO's principles. Instead, Russia wanted a veto in terms of NATO's actions. Second, Putin did not appreciate NATO as a collective defense organization. He assumed that NATO undermined the United Nations as the main guarantor of international security. He said that "the main problem here lies in attempts to discard previously agreed common instruments—mainly in resolving issues of international security."[79] Talbott was right when he wrote that "Putin wants Russia to be in a NATO when it is no longer a military alliance."[80]

The Moscow Summit in June 2000

On March 26, 2000, Putin won the presidential election. His victory was a foregone conclusion and much expected. Putin was the candidate of the party of power and received 52.5 percent of the vote in the first round—above the absolute majority he needed to avoid a runoff election. Gennady Zyuganov from the Communist Party came in second and received 29.5 percent of the vote; Yavlinsky obtained a mere 5.9 percent.[81] More than two-thirds of the eligible voters participated, and the elections went according to the constitution. This was no small achievement, given that it was the first transition of presidential power in post–Cold War Russia. However, as Michael McFaul pointed out, the election "did not occur on a level playing field. Vladimir Putin enjoyed tremendous resource advantages that tainted the process. Although weak in some arenas, the Russian state still enjoys too much power regarding the electoral process, while societal organizations—political parties, civic organizations, trade unions, and independent business groups—remain too weak to shape the outcomes of elections."[82]

Putin's election did not mean that democracy would ultimately prevail in Russia. "It's clear that having an orderly democratic election peaceful transfer of power did not clear all the old habits," Senator Mitchell McConnell (R-Kentucky) said when Strobe Talbott testified on Russia before the Senate Foreign Relations Committee in April 2000. "Yes sir, that's clear," Talbott responded, "I think that was even clear before last August" when Yeltsin announced Putin as his successor, Talbott said.[83] The future of Russia's democracy was still uncertain. In May 2000, five days after his inauguration, Putin pursued an assault against the free press in Russia. He had the federal Russian police storm the headquarters of Russia's prime independent broadcaster NTV and its parent company Media-Most. The raid was a case of political pressure against the company of its chairman, Vladimir Gusinsky, whose liberal television, radio, newspaper, and magazine groups had often criticized Putin when he had been prime minister and acting president. In June 2000, Gusinsky was arrested for misappropriation of funds. One month later, he sold his NTV shares to Gazprom Media and immediately left Russia.[84]

After the election, Clinton called Putin to schedule a visit to Moscow. Clinton congratulated him and said he wanted to meet Putin as soon as possible. Putin was delighted: "I noted what you've said about my modest personality . . . that I'm someone you can work with. This was not unnoticed in Russia or around the world."[85] Putin was formal throughout the conversation, referred to the solid track record of U.S.-Russia cooperation, and pledged to develop it further with Clinton. National missile defense was at the core of their conversation.[86] Clinton wanted to continue preparations for the introduction of NMD without violating the ABM Treaty. Putin was concerned about introducing a sophisticated global U.S. system of radars that could give the United States an edge and an opportunity to intimidate Russia. Talbott recalled that "throughout the fall of 1999, the Russian military was more assertive and confident in stonewalling us on NMD than it had been over NATO enlargement and Balkan peacekeeping."[87] Would Clinton and Putin be able to find a deal on a moratorium? Or would Putin wait and see and take a chance at Clinton's successor? In the spring of 2000, Clinton had not taken a decision. He had to discuss missile defense with Putin first, but it was important for him not to be too eager to reach a compromise. Clinton told Talbott, "I can't go in there and take a dive or box myself in for what I decide later. I've got to go in there and give this thing the best shot on the merits and then do the right thing when the times comes."[88]

Talbott was against NMD and thought its deployment might be deferred for technical reasons. The first NMD tests did not work at all. In January 2000, during the integrated flight test, the interceptor failed to "kill" the attacking missile. The dummy warhead escaped, reentered the atmosphere, and splashed into the Pacific Ocean.[89] The second test in July 2000 also failed. The system's kill vehicle did not separate from its booster. Hence the vehicle collided with the incoming mock target warhead.[90] The two failed attempts revealed a necessity for more testing. NMD was still in a preliminary stage. "I do not in my heart of hearts feel committed to NMD in its current architecture," Talbott noted. "Yes, I'm impressed . . . by all the stuff we see about the threat; but I'm also impressed by all the stuff I read about the defects of NMD, both in its own right for its stated purpose and against the panoply of other threats that it can't deal with."[91] The political implications of NMD were at least equally important: Talbott envisaged a negotiated solution with the Russian side. In his diaries, he noted that "Russia has now, on three occasions, had to eat shit from us and not even had sugar coating: NATO enlargement, the new NATO strategic doctrine, and Kosovo. They're not going to do it again. This time, there must be a compromise—the outcome can't be our going in position."[92] At the same time, it was important to not be too accommodating. Clinton kept his options open and wanted to hear Putin's thoughts at their summit in Moscow in early June.

Talbott did the preparatory work and the briefings for the meeting. He feared Clinton could be too affectionate with Putin. Clinton himself was also uneasy about the meetings—Talbott heard him say several times that he had not yet "broken the code on this new guy."[93] Clinton had to be distanced and formal, which was not his favorite role. First of all, he would not call Putin Vladimir. Clinton's reserve toward Putin should be noticeable—and he had to watch his guard. Talbott's strategy was to frighten Clinton a bit during the preparatory work. He told Berger,

> we need to scare POTUS. I'm worried that Putin will eat him for lunch . . . that it will be like JFK and Khrushchev in Vienna, only without the excuse on our side; POTUS thinks he's in a groove, that he knows how to talk to Russians after 7+ years with Yeltsin . . . that he knows Putin already; he doesn't; this guy is a black belt in toughness, co-option, manipulation . . . you put his mastery of co-option together with POTUS's penchant for saying 'I 'gree with that,' and it will be like Gorgeous George in his waning days getting into the ring with Bruce Lee.[94]

Clinton had to show reserve. This was the essence of Talbott's briefing on Air Force One when Clinton was going to Moscow on June 2, 2000. Unlike Yeltsin, Putin did not have democratic credentials on his own. During the flight to Moscow, Talbott emphasized Putin's dangerous side. "Some of my oldest friends there are saying that for the first time in a dozen or 15 years, there's a real sense of fear in the air," Talbott said. "And that smell emanates from the Kremlin, from Putin himself. . . . He'll try to talk to you pol-to-pol about how you've dealt with hostile, obnoxious parliamentarians and governors, and so has he. But the difference is that you didn't put your opponents in jail; you've had problems with the press, and so has he, but the difference is that you didn't send special forces with masks on to raid media offices. . . . Putin does respect you; but he does regard you as an adversary too."[95]

At the same time, Clinton should express his willingness to work with Putin. After the Moscow summit, there were still three meetings built around international institutions in which the United States and Russia had leadership roles, including the G–8, the United Nations, and Asia–Pacific Economic Cooperation. The purpose was to make the most of it. Clinton told Putin that "despite the elections, I think we can get a lot accomplished. I will do my best to find a way forward."[96] At the same time, Clinton had his press people temper the expectations for the summit. A breakthrough on NMD was unlikely. Clinton sensed that Putin would be waiting for his successor and would put U.S.-Russian relations on hold.

On June 3, 2000, the Moscow summit began with a private dinner in Putin's quarters at the Kremlin. It was all amicable and cheerful, and neither Clinton nor Putin spoke about missile defense. Eventually, Clinton raised it when Talbott gave him a note to bring it up. Clinton said he would retain the deployment option and take a decision before the end of his administration. He wanted to persuade Putin to agree to a revised ABM Treaty that would allow for deployment in the future.[97] Putin's position remained unchanged. He argued that NMD would undermine the ABM Treaty and threaten Russia's strategic deterrent. Putin tried to talk Clinton out of NMD. It was impossible to reconcile the contrasting positions at the summit. Apart from missile defense, the meetings went smoothly. Putin went out of his way to reach out to Clinton. They toured the private presidential quarters at the Kremlin and listened to jazz music until midnight the day before Clinton left Moscow. To charm Clinton, Putin invited veteran Russian jazz composer Oleg Lundstrem and jazz saxophonist Igor Butman. Clinton loved it, snapped with his fingers, and tapped his feet to the rhythm. Putin wanted to do it likewise but missed the beat. Moreover, it was apparent that Putin wished to avoid press photos of Clinton and himself, feeling ashamed of his diminutive height.[98]

After the talks with Putin, Talbott accompanied Clinton to see Yeltsin at his dacha on the Western outskirts of Moscow, where Yeltsin lived in retirement. On Clinton's arrival, Clinton and Yeltsin hugged each other for a full minute. Yeltsin led Clinton and his team through the foyer into the living room, where Naina Yeltsina served a rich, multilayered cake she had been baking the previous night. Clinton expected a relaxed conversation, but Yeltsin wanted to discuss politics, especially NMD, which he strongly resented. Talbott recalled that "Clinton took the browbeating patiently, even good-naturedly. He had seen Yeltsin in all his roles—snarling bear and papa bear, bully and sentimentalist, spoiler and dealmaker. He knew that a session with Yeltsin almost always involved some roughing up before the two of them could get down to real business."[99] Yeltsin then reminisced how he managed to bring the nameless Putin to the presidency. He marveled about Putin's strength, youth, and capability to run the country and preserve his legacy. He thought Putin was the right guy to succeed him. When Yeltsin ended, Clinton kindly took control and explained why he was uncertain about Putin's intentions. "Boris," Clinton said, "you've got democracy in your heart. You've got the trust of the people in your bones. You've got the fire in your belly of a real democrat and a real reformer. I'm not sure Putin has that. Maybe he does. I don't know. You'll have to keep an eye on him and use your influence to make sure that he stays on the right path. Putin needs you. Whether he knows it or not, he really needs you, Boris," Clinton said.[100] Talbott noted that "Yeltsin is holding him by the hand, looking intently into his eyes . . . and totally lapping it up; it's a very moving scene."[101]

After the Moscow summit, Clinton went to Ukraine for talks with President Kuchma, who complained that "Russia tries to pressure us into a free trade zone with the CIS [Commonwealth of Independent States], but doesn't treat us fairly."[102] Indeed, Russia exerted enormous economic pressure on Ukraine. Among the former Soviet countries, Ukraine was the only state charged a value-added tax on all its products in its trade with Russia. Moreover, Russia forced Ukraine to pay higher energy prices than European customers. Russia also undercut Ukrainian efforts to obtain increasing amounts of oil and gas from the countries in the Caspian region. The aim was to perpetuate Ukraine's dependency on Russian supplies. Kuchma's concern was that this increasingly put Ukraine in Russia's stranglehold. "Putin's Russia would be very different from Yeltsin's," Kuchma thought. "Step by step, the new President would show Ukraine how to work with Russia. Ukraine, along with Azerbaijan and Georgia, suffered the most following Yeltsin's departure."[103]

Clinton and Kuchma discussed Russia's future at length. Clinton emphasized his efforts to help set Russia on the trajectory of a modern and enlightened state throughout his presidency. "The big question is how Russia will measure its greatness," Clinton said.

I urged the Russian leadership to measure their country's greatness by the quality of life of the Russian people and by the quality of Russia's relationships with its neighbors. . . . I want them to imagine a future that is different from the past. It's better for Russia to help

Ukraine get rich. And it is in Ukraine's interest to have good relations with Russia. . . . I say Russia should be friends with the United States and with Ukraine. Russia needs to understand that it benefits if Ukraine is successful, and therefore, it should encourage Ukraine's success. This is the kind of language we should use with them. No one denies their right to greatness. The question is whether they'll have 21th century greatness or 19th century coercion. Nineteenth century coercion doesn't generate as much money or prestige as 21th century greatness. There's a lot going on there right now. I'm trying to influence them in a positive way.[104]

The Decline of the U.S.-Russia Relationship

Chechnya and the debates over missile defense symbolized the decline of the U.S.-Russia relationship during Clinton's last year in office. Moreover, Chechnya was a divisive issue within the West. Clinton was fairly isolated when he criticized Russia's conduct in the war. The West generally accepted Moscow's right to defend its territorial integrity.[105] This was apparent during the discussions at the G-8 meeting in Okinawa in July 2000. In his diaries, Talbott recalled Mamedov's reaction when he announced that it was "Chechnya time" at the summit in Okinawa. "He looked deeply pained and rushed off to give Igor a heads-up. I watched them huddling; Igor looked daggers at me, then sent Mamedov back to tell me that we were 'on the brink of a disaster.' I told Yuri that he should appreciate that we weren't pulling any surprises on them, and that it was up to Igor how to deal with the warning I'd given him; my recommendation was a mature, sober, candid discussion."[106] However, America's allies were not willing to pursue a critical assessment of Russia's role in Chechnya. Only the Americans were ready to confront Ivanov in the foreign ministers meeting.

French Foreign Minister Védrine spoke first and "adopted a nearly apologetic, squirming tone that would characterize all of the Euro interventions on the subject. He emphasized that no one in the G8 had the right to question Russian sovereignty or territorial integrity," Talbott recalled. Talbott had anticipated this and asked Cook, Fischer, and Dini to preempt Védrine as a lead-off batter, but they all declined because they did not want to be aggressive about Chechnya. Talbott noted that

the whole thing was beginning to shape up as the march of the Seven
Dwarfs. Not wanting to play Dopey, I did my own spiel, drawing
from points that we'd worked out overnight with Washington. I
didn't want to appear to be breaking ranks with the Euros, since that
would turn the thing into a 7-vs-1 of the wrong kind, so I started on
a positive note: the G8 both symbolizes and operationalizes the single most important geopolitical change of our era, which is Russia's
integration and participation in the community of democracies, and
its co-leadership as a member of the Eight.[107]

Talbott's only forceful supporter was Lloyd Axworthy, the Canadian foreign minister, who intervened with the argument that the G-8 countries
had a special responsibility to advance humanitarian standards and to establish "a culture of prevention and peacebuilding."[108] In a conversation with
EU Commissioner for External Relations Christopher Patten, Talbott
expressed his regret that Axworthy was his only ally. Talbott noted that
"Patten reluctantly concurred, noting that the EU member states were
eager to get 'back to business as usual.' The earlier tough EU line on Chechnya may have been more an anomaly than the norm."[109]

The transatlantic dissent at the G-8 summit had conceptual reasons. Talbott did not share the French rationale for a modernization partnership with
Putin's Russia. He did not believe that it should be the Western aim to
pursue a state-centric policy toward Putin's regime because it would only
strengthen Putin's ability for control and authoritarian rule. Talbott pushed
back when Védrine argued that the liberal Western economic policy had
contributed to the demise of the Russian state and had led to chaos. Védrine
said that his concern was "that by emphasizing 'deregulation' as a priority,
the West has contributed to dismantling repressive controls without anything to replace them—and crime and chaos followed. The West must
acknowledge that Russia also needs a functioning state." Talbott did not
buy the concept and said that "Putin's ability to differentiate between strong
leadership and repression had yet to be fully tested." When Védrine continued to make the case for his strong state rationale, Talbott argued that
"democratic values must not be overlooked in the effort to build an effective modern state: some items in President Putin's speech to the Duma . . .
sounded like a social contract requesting latitude for a little repression now

to be paid back with democracy and civil society later—and gave reason for caution."[110]

Indeed, in July 2000, Putin used his first address to the state of the Union to reiterate the need for a powerful, effective state as the guarantor of Russians' democratic and economic freedoms. In terms of substance, Putin argued in favor of free markets as a remedy to overcome Russia's economic illness. He condemned excessive state interference in the economy and called for "less administration, more free enterprise, more freedom to produce, to trade, and to invest." The crucial point was, as Talbott indicated, the relationship between the state's power and its citizens' freedom—and Putin emphasized that control was his priority. He said that "the debate about the ratio between force and freedom is as old as the world itself. It continues to cause speculation on the themes of dictatorship and authoritarianism. But our position is very clear: only a strong, or effective if someone dislikes the word 'strong,' an effective state and a democratic state is capable of protecting civil, political, and economic freedoms, capable of creating conditions for people to lead happy lives and for our country to flourish."[111]

Chechnya and the freedom of the Russian press were yardsticks to measure Putin's promises. Clinton used his two last meetings with Putin to discuss the state of personal liberties and human rights in Russia. The subsequent encounter was in September 2000 at the UN General Assembly in New York. Before it, Talbott noted that

> by the time he arrives in New York, Putin may have gained control over Russia's main broadcast media outlets via a "forced buyout" of Gusinsky's NTV and a friendlier (but still ominous) takeover of Berezovskiy's shares in the other major networks. Taken together with the renaissance of the security services as the enforcers of Putin's drive for an "effective state," these developments are leading many in Russia and the West to conclude that Putin will—incrementally but inevitably—undermine the major democratic and civil achievements of the Yeltsin years. In New York (and probably again in Brunei in November) the President should not miss the opportunity as the "elder statesman" to impress upon Putin the importance of living up to his own pronouncements that "without a truly free media, Russian democracy will not survive" and "a truly strong power needs strong competition."[112]

Meanwhile, Clinton decided to put off work on the construction of NMD. In a speech at Georgetown University on September 1, 2000, he said he did not believe the technology was ready for an effective national defense system.[113] Clinton's approach was to intensify the strategic defense consultations with Russia parallel to negotiations on deeper arms reductions in START III.[114] Shortly before Clinton's announcement, Talbott called Mamedov to notify the Russian side that deferral did not mean cancellation—a related message was that the Russians should abstain from public triumphalism, which could hurt Gore in the presidential campaign and further strain U.S.-Russian relations. Talbott noted that Mamedov said "all the right things; he's gratified, 'you won't be sorry,' promises to treat it with discretion. My sense he's going straight to Putin with it. He calls back ½ hour later to say that Putin has said all the right things too."[115] NMD no longer strained U.S.-Russian relations during the remainder of Clinton's tenure. Clinton and Putin did not discuss it at their September 6 meeting in New York.

The atmosphere in the meeting was tense. Putin was not willing to have a substantive discussion on contentious issues such as Chechnya, Georgia, Yugoslavia, and the transfer of Russian missile technology to Iran. He took the position of Milosevic's lawyer and was unwilling to look into Yugoslavia, where a democratic revolution had just started and would finally culminate in Milosevic's ousting. Clinton's concern was that Milosevic could steal the elections in Yugoslavia. Putin did not comment in detail and countered Clinton's remarks with a complaint over the elections in Kosovo, where about 100,000 to 150,000 Serbs were not willing to vote as they fled the region. Putin complained that "we weren't consulted in the decision to bomb Yugoslavia and to set in motion the process of taking Kosovo out of Serbia. That's not fair. And it's not fair to the 150,000 Serbs that the fate of Kosovo will be decided without them."[116] Ivanov suggested that democratic forces in Yugoslavia could be strengthened if the United States and NATO brought the country out of its isolation. Talbott countered that this remained out of the question as long as Milosevic threatened an invasion of Montenegro.[117]

It seemed that Putin wanted to have a quid pro quo, seeking Western silence over Chechnya in return for Russia's willingness to work with the G-8 on Yugoslavia. The New York meeting revealed the multitude of U.S.-Russian conflicts. Talbott noted that the Russians "draw invidious and mischievous comparisons if you're so hot to have us get rid of Milosevic, why don't you help us get rid of Shevardnadze? If you want us to control proliferation of nukes to Iran and Iraq, why don't you control Israel's nukes?" The New York discussions confirmed Talbott's estimate of Putin as a problematic leader and a dubious statesman. In his diaries, Talbott noted that "after this latest exposure to Putin, I'm ratcheting downward my assessment of his smarts and his skill. I'm finding him more formulaic and gimmicky, 'tricky Vlad,' and that's even before getting to the substance of his policy, and foreign policy."[118]

The last months of Clinton's tenure validated Talbott's assessment. In August 2000, the accident of the Russian nuclear submarine APL *Kursk* disclosed the mistrust of Russian authorities toward the West.[119] Putin and the Russian Navy rebuffed offers for assistance from the United States, Norway, Britain, France, Germany, and Israel. Russia tried to save face and refused to acknowledge the need for help. Moreover, Putin and his military were concerned about potentially sharing military information about the new Russian Oscar-class submarines. Putin and his advisers handled the accident and the loss of 118 Navy members in the Soviet tradition. The incident was only disclosed after a two-day delay—and the initial explanation was that it involved "only minor technical difficulties." To make things worse, Russian officials came up with claims that the *Kursk* sank after a collision with a foreign submarine. The Pentagon denied Russia's allegations.[120] The *Kursk* tragedy was one of Putin's first lies and revealed the problems that beset the mentality in Russia's military.

Another burden for the bilateral relationship pertained to the case of Edmund Pope, an American businessman and retired intelligence officer who had been convicted on charges of espionage in Moscow in April 2000 and sentenced to twenty years in prison. The Russian authorities claimed that Pope had illegally acquired technological knowledge about new Russian Navy torpedos. Pope maintained his innocence and argued that the technology was no longer secret because it had already been sold abroad. The Pope case was a political issue. It was the first time an American was convicted of espionage in Russia in forty years. Pope suffered from bone cancer and could die in Russian detention if he were denied appropriate medical treatment. Clinton raised Pope's case with Putin when they met in New York in September 2000. "I'd be personally grateful if you'd look into this on humanitarian grounds," Clinton said. Putin did not show movement. "I'll be absolutely candid with you," he said. "I've got the information from my people. He's absolutely healthy. There's no problem there.

There's a different problem. As I told you, I will take a decision here. But I need to wait until the formalities are finished. If I take a decision beforehand, it could be used against us—it could be said that we were holding him for no reason."[121] In turn, Talbott demanded Pope's release and issued a stern warning in a conversation with Russian Ambassador Ushakov when he underlined "that such a position was offensive and deeply revealing of the Russian government's cynical disregard for basic standards of humanitarian conduct. If Pope dies in Russian custody, . . . it will be a defining point for the future shape and character of our relations."[122] Eventually, Pope was released in December 2000 on Putin's orders.[123]

Russia's connections with Iran were another sensitive issue. In October 2000, Putin visited Iran and repudiated the U.S.-Russian agreements on nonproliferation by renewing Russian arms sales to Iran, including supplies of sensitive nuclear technology such as centrifuges and assistance for the completion of the Bushehr reactors.[124] There was no question that Iran tried to develop nuclear weapons with Russia's assistance. It seemed that Putin did not care about a nuclear Iran as long as it would cement Russia's position in the Middle East at the expense of the United States. In December 2000, the Clinton administration again threatened Russia with sanctions for the abrogation of the 1995 deal to halt Russian arms exports to Iran. In July 2000, at the G-8 summit meeting in Okinawa, Putin had still promised to stick to the deal and to strengthen controls on the transfer of nuclear and missile technology to Iran. Putin breached his promises, although Clinton warned him that Russia's continued assistance for Iran was "the biggest problem between us." Putin did not give in and raised commercial interests as an argument. "There's another aspect to this, which is the commercial side with regard to conventional weapons. If we weren't there [in the Iranian market], others would be. Look at the relationship between Germany and Iran. There's a lot of pressure building to reestablish relations. Russia can't stand idly to one side and let everyone else do this. I've got responsibility to protect our economic agencies and businesses."[125]

Putin's impudence signaled that he was determined to maximize his elbow room. He began to test the cohesion of the West. He tried to condition Western public opinion to get used to his assertiveness, and he used his contacts with Blair, Schröder, and Chirac to make inroads. He coopted them based on their belief in the modernization partnership with the new Russia. Western policymakers generally saw Putin as Yeltsin's legitimate heir and the guarantor of stability. Talbott was more skeptical and noted that "the West might now be paying the price for seven years of successfully turning Yeltsin's big Nyets into grudging OKs. Much had been accomplished on many fronts—on missile sales to India and Iraq, IFOR/SFOR, and NATO enlargement, among other issues. But Putin had set himself up as a departure from Yeltsin and so is more wary of saying yes to the West."[126] Putin thought it was payback time. It seemed that he used his first year in office to get even with the United States.

On the positive side, the overall security architecture seemed strong enough to project stability in the future. NATO managed to supplement its mission of collective defense with crisis management. NATO enlargement was likely to move forward, and Russia had agreed to resume its relationship with NATO, although it had not gone very far since its official inception in 1997. It would be up to the next generations of policymakers to solidify peace in Europe. Mutual trust was the critical factor for cooperation in the future. "I think we have based our relationship on a win/win premise as opposed to a win/lose framework, allowing us to manage our disagreements," Clinton told Putin during their last personal meeting in November 2000.[127]

Finally, Talbott contemplated writing a book about Clinton's Russia policy. When he published *The Russia Hand* in 2002, commentators were surprised to find that President Clinton was the Russia hand and the main character in the book. Talbott did not write it to aggrandize his own achievements. Instead, his idea was to emphasize Clinton's key contributions as a formidable hands-on negotiator and diplomat-in-chief. In the autumn of 2000, Talbott told Clinton about his plans and the book's storyline, laying out his ideas in a telephone conversation on September 28, 2000. "I tell him about my plan to write a book about him and Yeltsin," Talbott noted. "I recall how he'd once said that he trusted me not to write a memoir that made him look like an asshole and how I didn't take that as forbidding me from writing any memoir at all. He laughed and said, 'You got it!' and it sounded like a good book. I told him more than that, we had a good story to tell and how I wanted to tell it. 'Go for it,' he said," Talbott recorded in his diary.[128]

―――――――――――――

Conclusion

On President Clinton's behalf, Strobe Talbott played a vital role in the reordering of the Euro-Atlantic security architecture after the Cold War, cultivating relationships and building trust between nations. Talbott helped shape profound global transformations and remained a team player with integrity and judgment, not catching the lime-light. A broad gauge and multitalented, he was able to pursue multiple threads throughout his career in journalism, academia, and policy. As a journalist, his reporting overlapped with historical research and political analysis. As a policymaker, his leadership entailed a collaborative spirit of inquiry and investigation. The public mostly perceived him as a Russia hand, but that falls short as an attribute given his credentials as a NATO guy, arms control pundit, European Union expert, Scandinavia and especially Finland aficionado, India hand, and an authority on central and eastern Europe and especially former Yugoslavia and southeastern Europe. A driven man, Talbott saw himself as an architect and a carpenter working continuously to build a lasting Euro-Atlantic security system. Talbott used to say that "Bill Clinton came into office acutely aware that he was the first American President to be elected after the end of the Cold War. Hence he sees it as not just an opportunity but as an obligation to make sure that the United States does everything in its power to help build a Europe that is whole and free and at peace for the first time in its history. That is the goal. The means, as we see it, are largely institutional—or, as is often said, architectural. We are building a structure in which we and our children and our grandchildren will make our homes."[1]

In this endeavor, Talbott was determined to square the circle between Russia's integration, NATO's opening, and the enlargement of NATO's mission to expand the Western-led order, including both the United States as well as Russia and the new democracies in the East after the collapse of communism. After the end of the Cold War, Clinton and Talbott built security across an undivided Europe in an effort "to extend the space of stability where war simply does not happen, where democracy, freedom, and prosperity prevail."[2] President George H. W. Bush had outlined this notion in a cutting-edge speech in Mainz in May 1989 when he referred to the vision of a Europe whole and free.[3] Clinton's diplomacy was based on Bush's legacy and carried it further, although the emergence of the new Europe was in a preliminary stage when Clinton took office in 1993. "The cold war had been won," Clinton said,

> but in many ways, Europe was still divided, between the haves and have-nots, between the secure and insecure, between members of NATO and the EU and those who were not members of either body and felt left out in the cold. . . . And so we set out to do for the Eastern half of Europe what we helped to do for the Western half after World War II: to provide investment and aid, to tear down trade barriers so new democracies could stand on their feet economically; to help them overcome tensions that had festered under communism; and to stand up to the forces of aggression and hate, as we did in the Balkans; to expand our institutions, beginning with NATO, so that a Europe of shared values could become a Europe of shared responsibilities and benefits.[4]

The start of Talbott's carpenter job in 1993 was challenging. Two years after the end of the Cold War, Euro-Atlantic security was still a mess. The war in Bosnia undermined Europe's security in multiple ways. NATO could not ignore the destruction of civilization, ethnic cleansing, and genocide next to its borders. Yet, at the start of Clinton's tenure, it failed to intervene and was about to lose the peace it gained after it prevailed in the Cold War. Moreover, there was no clarity about NATO's post–Cold War mission, its role, and whether it would open up to new members. Both the

Bush and the Clinton administrations were cautious and slow to open NATO's door at a time when the countries of central and eastern Europe were determined to join given the security vacuum in the former Warsaw Pact area and the potential collapse of Russia's reform project. In 1993, Russia's stabilization was Clinton and Talbott's priority in foreign policy. They backed up Yeltsin in times of crisis, and Talbott's work was essential for the convocation of the first Clinton-Yeltsin summit in Vancouver in April 1993. It enabled Clinton and Yeltsin to pursue the kind of personal diplomacy that became a trademark of their presidencies. In addition, the Gore-Chernomyrdin Commission and Talbott's channel with his Russian counterpart Georgy Mamedov were critical in the machinery of U.S.-Russia relations, especially in times of fluidity and continued setbacks and the victory of the nationalist Vladimir Zhirinovsky in the December 1993 Duma elections.

Ukraine was another key issue in Talbott's portfolio. The potential return of nationalism in Russia threatened Ukraine's sovereignty. It triggered Kyiv's demands to obtain NATO Article 5 guarantees to protect the country against the resurrection of Russia's imperialism. In 1993, Ukraine's Deputy Foreign Minister Boris Tarasyuk conveyed Ukraine's bid for NATO membership to Talbott, although the country officially took a nonaligned position to not provoke Russia. When Ukraine agreed to abandon its inherited nuclear weapons in the trilateral agreement of January 1994, the Clinton administration was not willing to provide more robust security assurances or even NATO Article 5 guarantees because such a move would have triggered a flood of requests from the former Soviet space at a time when NATO had only begun its internal deliberations to admit a small tranche of countries from central Europe. Although the 1994 security assurances for Ukraine were inadequate and could avert neither Russia's military seizure of Ukrainian territory in Crimea and Donbas in 2014 nor Russia's full-scale war against Ukraine starting in 2022, it would not have made sense for Ukraine to keep nuclear weapons in the 1990s because the country did not have access to nuclear weapons technology—and the option of retaining the weapons meant that it would continue to rely on Russia, and thus its sovereignty would be compromised. Ukraine's partnership with the West would not have been possible had Kyiv chosen to retain nuclear arms. Ukraine paid a heavy price, however. It remained vulnerable to Russia's coercion, remained in a grey zone of insecurity, and continued to endure chaos after the end of the Cold War.

Given Europe's mess, Talbott understood that it was impossible to craft a pitch-perfect Euro–Atlantic security system from scratch. Its emergence needed patient diplomacy and extensive work in a multitude of issue areas. Time and again, crisis moments forced the Clinton administration to adapt and improvise along the way, given the scope of uncertainty, the magnitude of insecurity, and the absence of a comprehensive blueprint. The emergence of PfP in January 1994 reflected the insight that new security architecture could be built only gradually over time. PfP squared several circles to combine Russia's engagement with NATO's gradual opening and the expansion of its mission. Rather than advocating swift NATO membership, PfP emphasized bilateral cooperation programs between NATO and aspiring new member states and did not instantly extend NATO Article 5 guarantees to them. It envisaged NATO's opening at the end rather than the beginning of a long-term process. The aim was to "to revitalize NATO, to avoid antagonizing Russia by feeding nationalist tendencies, and to calm down growing fears in Central and Eastern Europe."[5]

The adoption of PfP in January 1994 signaled that President Clinton had already taken a principal decision in favor of NATO enlargement. Yet, the who, when, and how of the process had to be clarified in the years to come—and the shape of NATO's evolving partnership with Russia had to be worked out as well. Moreover, PfP offered a unique platform for expanding NATO's mission because it enabled joint peacekeeping operations with aspiring new member countries. Following his promotion to deputy secretary of state in 1994, Talbott recruited Richard Holbrooke to kickstart the efforts for Europe's transformation based on the insight that "the United States must lead in the creation of a security architecture that includes and thereby stabilizes all of Europe—the West, the former Soviet satellites of central Europe, and, most critically, Russia and the former republics of the Soviet Union. . . . Those with the ability to preserve peace have the responsibility to build lasting structures."[6] NATO's opening and the expansion of its mission played a crucial part therein, but they were not conceived as the only game in town. The transformation of the OSCE, the enlargement of the European Union, and the adoption of a new transatlantic agenda in the EU–U.S. relationship were all conceived as essential parts of the puzzle. Moreover, the Clinton administration began to set criteria by which NATO would judge the eligibility of new members based on their commitments to democracy, open markets, human rights, and fundamental freedoms to build democracies and stable societies. One of the key messages to the nations in the East was that "stability did not come solely from external guarantees; it must be built from within."[7]

Meanwhile, U.S.-Russia relations did not benefit from Talbott's promotion because he was distracted from the Russia project and preoccupied with resolving the crisis in Haiti during much of 1994, when U.S.-Russian misunderstandings began to pile up. Clinton and Yeltsin did not clarify the details of NATO enlargement and the rationale of the NATO-Russia partnership. The Clinton administration saw PfP as a waystation in the NATO enlargement process. The Russians envisaged their special relationship with NATO as a way to postpone or avoid enlargement. The gaps in conception led to the December 1994 confrontation between Clinton and Yeltsin at the Budapest CSCE Summit when Yeltsin began to demand "specific obligations" and mutual "security guarantees" that amounted to requests for a Russian veto in terms of NATO enlargement. The clash in Budapest had two immediate effects: Talbott reasserted his stewardship of the U.S.-Russia partnership, and Clinton offered Yeltsin a special NATO-Russia relationship, yet short of a Russian veto. Russia could not prevent NATO enlargement, but Yeltsin and Kozyrev wanted to define the context in which it would happen. Talbott noted that "we're not in the business of having to compensate Russia or buy it off. Russia is not doing us a favor by allowing NATO to expand."[8] Although Talbott helped mend fences in the aftermath of the Budapest confrontation, he grew more skeptical about Russia's reform trajectory after the start of the war in Chechnya.

Beginning in 1995, Talbott increasingly saw NATO enlargement as a hedge against uncertainty and a potential revival of imperialism in Russia. Talbott emphasized that the United States and Russia were not equals and would not meet halfway in reordering the Euro-Atlantic security architecture. The United States had won the Cold War. The Soviet Union had lost it, and Talbott wanted Russia to abandon its imperial notion of empire. "Fact is," Talbott noted, "we and the Soviet Union didn't meet each other halfway, and we and Russia aren't going to do so either. Russia is either coming our way, or it's not, in which case it's going to founder, as the USSR did."[9] At the same time, Clinton and Talbott emphasized the importance of the U.S.-Russia partnership to endorse Yeltsin in the 1996 presidential election campaign. Over time, Talbott evolved into a more outspoken advocate of NATO enlargement, whatever hesitations he initially harbored.

In May 1995, while in Moscow, Talbott noted, "I say that every day I ask myself if we're right about NATO+, that I think we are, that I believe our own religion, that the reason is uncertainty about what's going to happen in this place—Russia."[10] In the summer of 1995, Talbott wrote an essential *New York Review of Books* article. In it, he made a powerful argument for NATO's opening as the most promising way to build a lasting peace in post–Cold War Europe while acknowledging that an expanded NATO could be a hedge if Russia turned bad again. At the same time, he argued that fear about a return of Russian expansionism should not be the only reason for NATO's opening. "It would be far better to encourage the Central Europeans, the Russians, and the peoples of the other former Soviet states all to see NATO's enlargement as a process that can help to promote better domestic and international behavior, even as it may serve as a hedge against the worst. It should be seen as a process that has benefits for everyone and is not directed against any particular state."[11]

Starting in 1995, Talbott began to work on broader schemes for Europe's transformation to project stability to age-old conflict areas, including Ukraine, the Baltics, Turkey, the Black Sea region, and the Caucasus. He wanted to build equal security for all across Europe in an effort "to extend the Europe of the institutions to the Europe of the map," as Richard Holbrooke put it.[12] Talbott labored on all dimensions of the new Euro-Atlantic security architecture based on the assumption that NATO's opening had to be embedded in a broader overall security concept, considering the interests of the countries that did not make the first NATO enlargement round. Thus he helped establish partnership schemes with Ukraine, the Baltics, and Romania; he pushed for regional integration in the Baltic Sea area, including Finland and Sweden, worked on Turkey's rapprochement with the European Union, and was instrumental in working with Russia and European partners to end the Kosovo War. At the heart of these efforts was a postnational security concept focusing on the emergence of communities where security would be provided by a web of international institutions transcending purely national notions of stability and statehood. After the end of his tenure in 2001, Talbott was proud to say that "Europe—with all its debates and disputes, its imperfections and exasperations—is at the cutting edge of a phenomenon that is spreading—to use Euro-jargon, that is broadening and deepening—around the word. It is what might be called a benign form of proliferation: the proliferation of inclusive, integrative, cooperative structures that are working to overcome the divisions of the past and lay the predicate for collective prosperity and collective security in the future."[13]

However, Talbott's postnational concept of security was alien to Russian policymakers. Yeltsin and the new Russian foreign minister, Yevgeny Primakov, defined Russia's interest in the traditional sense of empire. They rejected the Clinton administration's liberal concept of security involving a new system of openness, supranationalism, and transparency in a networked world. In contrast, Russia's world was still the chessboard—and Russia's security policy was still based on the traditional concept of a hostile international environment and the assumption that the country needed a sphere of domination over its neighbors for its security. Russia did not abandon its great power ambitions for the sake of integration and partnership with the West. There was a permanent Russian reluctance to deal with NATO and the European Union as institutions because Yeltsin and his advisers did not sufficiently understand their inner workings. In a nutshell, Russia and the West were from different galaxies, and Russian policymakers increasingly saw the emergence of an integrated Europe as a threat. Russian policymakers had a different notion of their place in the new security system. When Yeltsin said that Russia wanted to be treated as an equal, in fact, he meant that Russia wanted to be a pivotal arbiter with a veto over the decision-making processes of the EU and NATO. This way, it was impossible to find a place for Russia, and Talbott struggled to reconcile American and Russian national security policies.

At the same time, the joint NATO-Russia peacekeeping mission in Bosnia strengthened Russia's partnership with the alliance. Talbott argued that Russia's participation in the Bosnia Implementation Force was not a problem but an opportunity to be seized. Eventually, as Russian policymakers hesitated to put their troops under NATO command, Clinton and Yeltsin found a compromise under which Russian troops would be subordinated to NATO's Supreme Allied Commander Europe, General George Joulwan, and a Russian deputy, General Leontiy Shevtsov. Joulwan wore two hats—one as SACEUR and one as head of the U.S. forces. From a political point of view, it was important for the Russian side to ensure Joulwan commanded their troops as a U.S. general and not as NATO SACEUR. Although the arrangement reflected Russia's fears over the extension of NATO's out-of-area activities, the joint IFOR mission also gave Russia a chance to participate in the emergence of the new Europe, yet under U.S. leadership. Talbott noted that the United States and Russia had contradicting interests in the Balkans. He was right when he wrote that the "U.S. sees Bosnia as way to 'save' NATO, create a vital post–Cold War mission for it. Russia fears Bosnia operation . . . as first step in NATO's dangerous transformation from a 'defensive alliance of limited post-CW importance' to an exclusive (vs. inclusive) European collective security system (w/Russia as Shirley Temple at window)."[14]

After the end of the Bosnian War, the Clinton administration went ahead with the vision to build a new Euro-Atlantic community. Clinton secured congressional support for deploying twenty thousand American troops as part of IFOR. NATO needed America's leadership and its military involvement. As Talbott said, "The Alliance can no more ignore the conflagration in the Balkans than an architect can ignore a fire raging in one wing of a building on which he is working."[15] Clinton wanted to seize "the opportunity to build a peaceful, undivided, and democratic continent."[16] A reformed and enlarged NATO and a new NATO-Russia partnership were among the key architectural components of the new security system. In the fall of 1996, Clinton underscored the vision "to build a new NATO for a new era: first, by adapting NATO with new capabilities for new missions; second, by opening its doors to Europe's emerging democracies; third, by building a strong and cooperative relationship between NATO and Russia."[17] Moreover, Clinton announced that NATO would name the first group of new members in 1997, and he identified NATO's Washington summit in the spring of 1999 as the target date for NATO's first post–Cold War enlargement round. The president's remarks conveyed his concept of the broader Euro-Atlantic security architecture that Warren Christopher laid out in a speech in Stuttgart in September 1996 when he sketched out the concept titled "A New Atlantic Community for the 21st Century," which included a specific timetable for NATO enlargement, a formal NATO-Russia charter, the addition of a political dimension to PfP, an adaption of the existing CFE Treaty provisions, an enhanced Ukraine-NATO partnership, and a free and open transatlantic marketplace.[18]

However, the negotiations on the NATO–Russia Founding Act revealed the challenges to achieve a Europe whole, free and at peace. Talbott's vision for an undivided Europe fell short. The Founding Act was a "conditional peace" and an interim security arrangement.[19] Confrontation and war between NATO and Russia could not be entirely excluded. NATO and Russia could not find consensus on the norms and rules governing the new

Euro-Atlantic security architecture. Whereas Clinton emphasized NATO's open door principle, Yeltsin saw the Founding Act as a way to enforce a new condominium over the heads of those countries that aimed to join NATO in the future. Whereas the Clinton administration made sure the Founding Act did not weaken NATO's core as a collective defense organization, the Russian side tried to use the newly established consultation mechanisms to obtain a say in NATO's decision-making process to weaken NATO's core mission. The Clinton administration defined five guiding principles to protect NATO's interests—no veto, no second-class membership, no subordination of NATO to other bodies, no dilution of or interference in the NATO command structure, and no appearance of condominium or Yalta.[20] Talbott told Primakov that "you've got to accept the premise that these countries are coming into the Alliance as genuine, equal members, including in the military dimension. If you keep trying to block or deny that, we're not going to get anywhere."[21]

Meanwhile, NATO still sought ways to make it easier for Russia to accept NATO enlargement—especially in terms of its military consequences. Although NATO reaffirmed the extension of its nuclear umbrella to the new members in the East, the alliance pledged that it had "no intention, no plan, and no reason to deploy nuclear weapons on the territory of new member states."[22] Moreover, the Russian side wanted assurances on the nonadvancement of NATO's military infrastructure to the East. The challenge for NATO was to reassure Russia yet avoid second-class membership for its new allies. Both sides struggled to find an adequate formula. Although it was impossible to have a fourth "no" on the expansion of NATO's military infrastructure, the alliance was willing to refrain from permanently deploying foreign troops in its new member states as long as Russia showed similar restraint and the partnership with Moscow was strong enough. At the same time, NATO preserved the right to deploy troops and equipment on the territory of the new member states in the future, albeit it had a hard time finding consensus about the question of what would constitute a Russian breach of the partnership. This became clear after Russia's 2014 invasion of Crimea and the start of Russia's war in Donbas, where two statelets were declared in Donetsk and Luhansk. Even after these actions, in 2016, NATO explained that its enhanced forward presence in NATO allies in the Baltics and Poland consisted of rotating rather than permanent deployments. Only after Russia's full-scale invasion of Ukraine in 2022 did NATO shift its position.

In 1997, Talbott was hopeful about the long-term prospects of the NATO-Russia relationship. As things turned out, he was mistaken in the assumption that time played to the advantage of Russia's reformers and their partnership with the West. In the remainder of Clinton's presidency, various shocks and setbacks led to a downward spiral in U.S.-Russia relations. Russia's financial collapse in 1998 destroyed Yeltsin's reform project and led to the disintegration of his presidency. The Kosovo War of 1999 led to a nationalist groundswell in Russia. Finally, starting in 1999, the second Chechen War catapulted Vladimir Putin into the president's office. The trifecta of crisis forever changed the struggle for Russia's future. Talbott's reaction to Russia's 1998 financial crisis was conditioned by strategic patience and a willingness to continue the U.S. engagement with Russia. In August 1998, he pursued a venturesome scouting expedition to Moscow, paving the way for Clinton's September visit amid crisis. By showing up, Clinton wanted to help Yeltsin make the right choices, rejecting a soft coup and ideas for the dissolution of the State Duma. While in Moscow, Clinton reiterated the need for Yeltsin to stand on principle and preserve his legacy as a reformer, yet to no avail. Yeltsin lacked the power to back a reform-oriented new administration. Instead, the new Primakov government worked with the Communists and ran a soft budget with high inflation and little regard for Western economic precepts. The era of Russia's young economic reformers was over. Talbott worked feverishly to counter the notion of Russia as a lost place. He still gave Russia the benefit of the doubt. At the same time, he had to acknowledge the limits of America's leverage over Russia's internal situation.

Although the Clinton administration managed to keep Russia on a trajectory of cooperation with the West, the 1999 Kosovo War made the partnership much more difficult and almost destroyed it. Talbott's creative Russia diplomacy helped maintain it at a crucial time. First, Talbott wanted to control the Russian reaction once NATO started bombing Yugoslavia to save Kosovo. Second, he stepped forward with creative proposals to include Russia in the diplomacy to end the war, teaming up with Finnish President Martti Ahtisaari and former Russian Prime Minister Viktor Chernomyrdin. NATO's formula for a solution in Kosovo was Yugoslav forces out, NATO in, and refugees back. NATO would only pause its bombing campaign if all refugees could return, if agreement was reached on an international security force, and if the Yugoslav army began its complete withdrawal. Eventually, Milosevic surrendered on NATO's terms.

The trick of Talbott's Kosovo statecraft was the combination of dialogue and bombing. "Diplomacy is now in support of force," he noted. "Yes, we have a diplomatic track, but no, we're not negotiating with Milosevic, directly or indirectly. We're bombing Milosevic while other people talk to him. He can stop the bombing; they can't."[23] Talbott's coercive diplomacy was essential to help NATO win the Kosovo War and to keep Russia on board. His toughness was pivotal in this endeavor. He was in favor of retaining the option of a NATO ground war in Yugoslavia and fought those in the Clinton administration who drew misguided analogies between Kosovo and the Vietnam War. After all, the Kosovo War and its Russia dimension were "about Europe and civilization—we want Russia in Europe, but we want it into a new Europe, which is civilized, not an old one, that is barbarized; and we shouldn't want a Russia into Europe that sides with Milosevic," Talbott noted.[24]

Even though Talbott's diplomacy helped to win the war and include Russia, the NATO-Russia consensus began to fall apart over the question of the international security presence in Kosovo after the withdrawal of Yugoslavian forces. NATO and Russia had to address the issue instantly to avoid renewed violence and unrest. When Talbott discussed the issue in Moscow on June 11, the revisionist forces in Russia had already gained the upper hand. The Russian military threatened to invade Kosovo unilaterally, and Vladimir Putin told Talbott lies when he promised that Russian troops would not be deployed in Kosovo unilaterally and ahead of time. Yet, while Talbott was in the air returning to the United States, he learned that the Russian peacekeeping contingent in Bosnia had started moving toward Kosovo through Yugoslavia. He therefore had his plane turn around and went back to Moscow to try to prevent a Russian incursion. Once again, Talbott met with Putin, who continued to play down what was happening. Finally, Russian troops did end up invading Kosovo, despite Putin's denials. What stuck with Talbott was the ease with which Putin had lied to him. It made him and his colleagues at the State Department wary of the ascendant Russian leader, especially given his background. Talbott was concerned that Putin would pursue foreign policy the way he operated as a mid-level KGB official—a role in which he cultivated paranoia and suspicion as a professional need. If this happened, it would be impossible for the United States to trust Russian officials. Talbott and his colleagues also worried that Putin's mindset and paranoia would produce aggression and hostility.

Although the decline of U.S.-Russia relations was not preordained, Talbott saw a variety of indicators suggesting Russia's return to its imperial past, including Putin's war in Chechnya, his moves against the free press, the revival of Russia's ambitions in its near abroad, and the comprehensive personnel changes that brought Putin's KGB entourage to positions of power. Talbott's advice to Clinton was to show reserve and to deny Putin the kind of warm relationship Clinton had been cultivating with Yeltsin. At the end of his presidency, Bill Clinton was concerned about the future of Russia's democracy. "Only time will tell what Russia's ultimate role in Europe will be," Clinton said. "We do not yet know if Russia's hard-won democratic freedoms will endure. We don't know whether it will define its greatness in yesterday's terms or tomorrow's. The Russian people will make those decisions."[25] At the same time, Clinton was optimistic about the sustainability of the transatlantic partnership and America's role as a leader in Europe. "One thing, thankfully, has not changed," Clinton said in June 2000 when he was awarded the prestigious Charlemagne Prize of Aachen for his diplomacy in the service of European unification: "Europe's security remains tied to America's security. When it is threatened, as it was in Bosnia and Kosovo, we, too, will respond. When it is being built, we, too, will always take part."[26]

This was true in the 1990s when the United States took a leadership role and helped build a new Europe in a multilateral way, working through institutions and order-building diplomacy. The Clinton administration pursued a gradual approach to open up NATO, to expand its mission, and to establish a parallel partnership with Russia. As we now know, it was impossible to square the circle. NATO enlargement and the expansion of its post–Cold War mission could not exist together with Russia's integration. The return of Russia's imperialism crashed hopes to build a Europe whole and free and at peace. Talbott's vision of an undivided Europe fell short. As we look back, it is essential to emphasize that NATO enlargement was never conceived as a threat to Russia[27] and that it did not cause Russia's war against Ukraine.[28] In fact, Russia attacked Ukraine to halt the country's evolution as a democratic, prosperous, and Western-oriented society.[29] To retain his kleptocratic tyranny at home, Putin has ordered his army to attack civilians with phosphorous bombs, killing tens of thousands, ruining towns and cities, and displacing more than ten million people inside Ukraine and beyond. Looking back, President Clinton recently expressed his regrets for having Ukraine give up nuclear weapons. "I feel a personal stake because I got them [Ukraine] to agree to give up their nuclear weapons. And none of them believe that Russia would have pulled this stunt if Ukraine still had their weapons," Clinton said. "I knew that President Putin did not support the agreement President Yeltsin made never to interfere with Ukraine's territorial boundaries."[30] Even though Clinton promoted Russia's reform, he pursued NATO's enlargement as a hedge against the revival of Russia's imperialism. In a 2022 article in *The Atlantic*, Clinton recalled his sustained effort "to help Russia make the right choice and become a great 21st-century democracy." At the same time, Clinton was aware of the potential for renewed conflict. Hence his policy "was to work for the best while expanding NATO to prepare for the worst."[31] However, NATO enlargement did not go far enough. A bigger NATO, including Ukraine, would have deterred and not provoked Russia.[32]

Acknowledgments and Note on Sources

I am grateful for Strobe Talbott's trust, generosity, and involvement in the research process. He sat down to be interviewed, read several manuscript drafts, and shared his diaries with me, a treasure trove of materials he had kept throughout his eight years in the Clinton administration. I am thankful to Strobe's wife Barbara Ascher. She and Strobe spoke with me to verify information and to share plenty of photos from the Clinton years some of which I use in this book. Thank you so very much! Strobe connected me to many of his friends and former colleagues in the United States and Europe, including former NATO Secretary General Javier Solana, who generously agreed to write a perceptive foreword. The book does not presume to be a Talbott biography that should and will be written. Although I cover a lot of new ground, the book is not an attempt to write a comprehensive study of U.S. diplomacy in the Clinton years. Over time, historians will be able to gather more information from the archives of NATO, the central and eastern European states, and additional American and western European repositories. I hope my study can provide orientation and ideas for scholars to delve through the much larger quantities of archival materials that will be released in the years to come. Future books will undoubtedly bring even more of the whole story to light.

The idea for the book emerged in 2019 when I met Strobe and many of his former colleagues at a book workshop on NATO enlargement at Johns Hopkins SAIS. Then, I worked with Daniel Hamilton and Kristina Spohr and a fantastic cohort of postdoctoral fellows as part of the multiyear project titled "The United States, Europe, and World Order," funded by the German Academic Exchange Service. Our book workshop on NATO's opening came at the right time when I sought a new project beyond the end of the Cold War. I am grateful for Daniel Hamilton's advice and support in all of this. He read several manuscript drafts, provided detailed comments on the book's design and architecture, and connected me to many of his former Clinton administration colleagues for oral history interviews. The book would not have been possible without Dan's input.

Kristina Spohr, Tina Schaller, and Ingo Trauschweizer read the manuscript at several stages and provided feedback and encouragement throughout the process—I am grateful for their support, time, and good humor. Ambassador James Goodby kindly helped me get in touch with Strobe when I began to write the book. I'm fortunate and blessed to know Jim and grateful for his support and mentorship over many years. Strobe's former colleagues at the Brookings Institution were kind and gave me feedback in a virtual book workshop. I'm grateful to Constanze Stelzenmüller. She came up with the idea, hosted the meeting, and invited many colleagues who commented, including Fiona Hill, Angela Stent, Mariana Budyerin, Ted Reinert, and Dan Hamilton.

As a child of the post–Cold War era, it was special for me to write about events that I can vividly recollect. In 1992, I was fourteen years old and became friends with new soccer teammates from Bosnia and Herzegovina and Croatia. Their families fled the war and came to southern Germany, where I grew up. They stayed for good. Our friendship triggered my curiosity, and I began to develop an interest in the places they came from. I was proud to know Bihac, Jaice, and Mostar, if only on the map. At age sixteen, I began to collect newspaper articles about Russia and the war in Chechnya, which I kept in binders. I still have them in my archive. When I was twenty and working for the Red Cross in Germany during my Civil Service time, our team had vivid discussions about the Kosovo War, especially because one of my colleagues had family in Belgrade when NATO bombed the city to stop Serbian atrocities in Kosovo. From personal experience, I knew that the post–Cold War period was conflict ridden in various ways, although I had no idea that I would be able to study these issues in such depth as I do in this book.

First, I would like to express my deepest gratitude to my family. To my wife, Valentina—my love, my life, my everything. The words in this world cannot describe how deeply I love you. You endured my absences and ups and downs with a smile. You are the anchor of my life. Your unwavering support and dedication have carried me throughout this journey. I am grateful to my parents, Erna and Günter Kieninger. They encouraged my interest in international affairs and taught me to be open and curious about the lives of the people around me. My nephew Mateo and niece Matilda provide tons of cheers and inspiration. I started this project when both were toddlers, and it's one of the greatest delights in my life to see them growing up. My in-laws, Marica and Damjan Raguz, backed me up with love and support beyond all measure. I'd like to thank my academic teachers, Oliver Bange and Gottfried Niedhart, who taught me the scholar's craft when we pursued international research projects on the Helsinki Final Act and Ostpolitik at Mannheim University.

The book was made possible by a generous fellowship from the Woodrow Wilson Center, a paradise on earth for a scholar. I'd like to express my gratitude to Christian Ostermann and his team from the center's History and Public Policy Program—Charles Kraus, Pieter Biersteker, and Kian Byrne. Their tireless support, hospitality, and contagious enthusiasm greatly helped me work on a first draft of the book manuscript during my Wilson fellowship in the academic year 2021–22. The Wilson Center is a special place for me. In 2005, I interned for Christian. Ever since, he has been a wonderful mentor and a tireless source of inspiration. At the center, I was fortunate to be affiliated with the Kennan Center as well. I benefited from the weekly meetings and the discussions with Matthew Rojanski, William Pomeranz, Joe Dresen, Izabella Tabarovsky, Victoria Pardini, and Eleanor Lopatto.

I was happy to be part of a wonderful cohort of fellows and very glad to receive feedback from them on so many occasions. Our Friday happy hour meetings were always a much-cherished opportunity to chat and to reflect on what happened during the week—with, among others, Nadia Oweidat, Sara Pangrazzi, Alla Leukavets, Hannah Chapman, Chantal de Jonge Oudraat, Daniela Campello, Cesar Zucco, Bruce Jentleson, and Sanjay Kathuria. My next-door office neighbors Lucian Kim and Nigel Gould Davies provided tons of encouragement and much-welcomed feedback. The Wilson Center's Scholars and Academic Relations Office and its entire staff were so welcoming and helpful. I am thankful for the generous support from Robert Litwak, Kim Conner, Elle Hartley, Maria-Stella Gatzoulis, Lindsay Collins, and all the others who make the Wilson Center such a fantastic place. Jonah Kaufman-Cohen worked as my research assistant. A meticulous editor, Jonah read through several drafts of the manuscript.

A heartfelt thanks goes to Barbara Wilkinson, the wife of Ronald Asmus, who granted me access to her husband's papers. Asmus got many documents declassified for his book *Opening NATO's Door.* I am fortunate to have Stephen Wesley as my editor and am grateful for his patience, diligence, and understanding when I needed more time to polish the manuscript. Stephen made the peer-review process look easy and found three reviewers who provided detailed and nuanced reports. I thank the anonymous reviewers for carefully reading the manuscript and for their insightful comments and suggestions. I'm privileged to work with Kathryn Jorge as production editor and to have Glenn Court as my copyeditor. I appreciate their careful work and would like to thank them very much. I'm blessed that the book is part of the Woodrow Wilson Center's series at Columbia, and thank Robert Litwack, Christian Ostermann, and Suzanne Naper for their encouragement. I also thank Herbert Ragan and John Keller from the William J. Clinton Presidential Library for digitizing images for the book.

Friends and colleagues in Washington, DC, provided tons of support—among them Sandra Miller, James and Sarah Goodby, Gillian and Jim Moorhead, Sarah Snyder, Daniel Fine, James Graham Wilson, Mary Barton, Fritz Bartel, Sergey Radchenko, Mary Sarotte, Hope Harrison, Klaus Larres, James Goldgeier, Joshua Shifrinson, Jason Moyer, Constanze Stelzenmüller, Bob Nurick, and Pietra Rivoli. I'm especially grateful to Charles Kraus and James Graham Wilson for their help in retrieving materials from the Paul Nitze papers at the Library of Congress, including Nitze's correspondence with Talbott and interviews of Nitze in which Talbott is featured frequently. In times of COVID, it was important for me to have online access to Strobe Talbott's papers in the State Department's Virtual Reading Room. I thank the National Security Archive (NSA) for submitting the Freedom of Information Act Request that led to the processing and the final release of Talbott's State Department papers.[1] As an NGO, the NSA does a unique job in defending and expanding public access to government information, and historians of contemporary history are all indebted to Tom Blanton, Svetlana Savranskaya, Malcolm Byrne, Bill Burr, and their colleagues.

On their request, under FOIA Case no. F-2017-13804, the State Department began to release Talbott's State Department papers in October 2019. Since then, about four thousand documents have been made available in the State Department's Virtual Reading Room—and the collection is still growing as more evidence is released.[2] This book is thus preliminary in the sense that it includes only documents released through October 2024. The materials are unique, reflecting Talbott's way of working, thinking, and writing as someone who was in constant dialogue to generate ideas and initiate new endeavors. In addition to official memos, he wrote "Strobegrams" and "Bagelgams" and all sorts of notes to colleagues and friends. He wrote extensive memos and compilations of thoughts to communicate with Warren Christopher and Madeleine Albright, which is unique in U.S. foreign policy and deserves further research. Talbott's huge paper trail reflects his mammoth capacity for analysis and his constant search for new ideas. He had always been a thinker and doer—be it as a journalist, a government official, or president of a think tank. The way Talbott worked and approached things did not change much. He usually got up between 3 and 4 a.m. to carve out enough writing time before he went to work. As a journalist and columnist, he learned to write crisply. As a policymaker and diplomat, he wrote to advocate ideas and to put things into context.

In addition to Talbott's State Department papers, I used his diaries from the Clinton years, a treasure trove of approximately five thousand pages in forty-six Microsoft Word files that Strobe shared with me in May 2022 after I interviewed him. The book is the first scholarly account to draw from them. More than twenty years ago, Talbott used them when he wrote *The Russia Hand*. The diaries are a peerless source including verbatim notes of meetings and phone conversations with President Clinton that cannot be found anywhere else. Talbott captured Clinton's remarks during private meetings at the White House, at Camp David, or at gatherings on various other occasions. Moreover, he wrote notes during their joint travels, especially during Clinton's meetings with Boris Yeltsin. Talbott's diary entries go beyond the official records of the Clinton-Yeltsin meeting in that they include observations and commentary that help put things into context. Last, but important, the diaries reveal Talbott's capacity to see things in perspective and to catch the comedy and ironies of high-stakes diplomacy. That's very much Talbott, the journalist. His writing is scholarly, racy, and quick witted at the same time. Talbott's State Department papers and his diaries complement each other in many ways. Both collections form a running tally and a throughline in the narrative. Moreover, I used newly available archival materials from the Clinton Presidential

Library's website, including President Clinton's meeting transcripts with foreign leaders and declassified materials on various issues.[3] Throughout the book, I reference the Talbott State Department papers as far as possible to allow readers to track the materials in the State Department's Virtual Reading Room. In addition to Talbott's papers, the online reading room provides a treasure trove of newly declassified materials from the post–Cold War years. I used evidence from about forty FOIA cases. Unfortunately, the titles of the FOIA listings are not available. Still, readers can locate and access the documents through the State Department's Virtual Reading Room (or any other repository) using the FOIA or MDR case numbers mentioned in the book's archive section at https://foia.state.gov/Search /Search.aspx.

In terms of archival materials from Europe, I used newly available evidence from the Helmut Kohl transcripts in the Wilson Center's Digital Archive, which feature hundreds of Helmut Kohl's conversations with world leaders after the end of the Cold War and offer tremendous insights into international diplomacy in the 1990s.[4] I helped retrieve the Kohl transcripts and am pleased I could use them in this book. The materials bear out the commonalities in Clinton's and Kohl's diplomacies focusing on the impact of institutions and international cooperation as key features in the post–Cold War world.[5] In addition, I frequently used the Prime Minister's Office files at the British National Archives in Kew featuring both the Major and Blair governments and their diplomacies on NATO enlargement and Russia relations. About ten years ago, the National Archives began its move toward releasing records when they were twenty years old rather than thirty. Today, the National Archives is one of the key repositories for researchers interested in post–Cold War history. More files will be released in the years to come. At the Clinton Presidential Library, several personal files of key actors are not yet declassified, including Coit Blacker (2016-0154-F), Nicholas Burns (2016-0159-F), Rose Gottemoeller (2016-0161-F), Daniel Fried, Richard Holbrooke, John Kornblum (2014-0088-F), Steven Pifer (2016-0153-F), Daniel Poneman (2016-0157-F), Alexander Vershbow (2016-0156-F). Finally, my research involved oral history interviews with an extensive list of former government officials. I thank all of them for their willingness to speak with me. They include Anders Aslund, John Bass, James Bindenagel, Hans Binnendijk, Joachim Bitterlich, Ian Brzezinski, Coit Blacker, Per Carlsen, Derek Chollet, Jürgen Chrobog, Bill Clinton, James Collins, Michael Dobbs, Kathleen

Doherty, William Drozdiak, Gloria Duffy, Eric Edelman, Mathea Falco, Stephen Flanagan, Daniel Fried, Grisha Freidin, Philip Goldberg, David Gompert, James Goodby, Rose Gottemoeller, Marc Grossman, Daniel Hamilton, Toomas Hendrik Ilves, Wolfgang Ischinger, Tina Kaidanow, Richard Kauzlarich, Andrei Kozyrev, Andrew Kuchins, Franklin Kramer, Anthony Lake, Stephen Larrabee, Robert Legvold, Roderic Lyne, Thomas Matussek, Shivshankar Menon, Cameron Munter, Victoria Nuland, Joseph Nye, Robert Nurick, Carlos Pascual, Steven Pifer, Itamar Rabinovich, Bruce Riedel, Jeremy Rosner, Volker Rühe, David Satter, Derek Shearer, Stephen Sestanovich, Wendy Sherman, James Sherr, Kate Schecter, Gregory Schulte, Thomas Simons, András Simonyi, Javier Solana, Rasheed Sood, Angela Stent, Thomas Szayna, Strobe Talbott, Boris Tarasyuk, Philip Taubman, William Taubman, John Thornton, James Timbie, James Townsend, Jukka Valtasaari, Alexander Vershbow, Steven Weisman, Andrew Weiss, Barbara Wilkinson, and Daniel Yergin.

$$\overline{}$$

Notes

Preface: Formative Years and Journalism

1. Strobe Talbott, *The Russia Hand: A Memoir of Presidential Diplomacy* (Random House, 2002), 42–44; Bill Clinton, *My Life* (Arrow Books, 2004), 505.

2. Talbott quoted in Rosenbaum, "U.S. Peace Negotiator Was Always a Diplomat at Heart," *New York Times*, June 7, 1999, https://archive.nytimes.com/www.ny times.com/library/world/europe/060799kosovo-talbott.html.

3. Nikita Khrushchev, *Khrushchev Remembers: With an Introduction and Commentary by Edward Crankshaw*, trans. and ed. Strobe Talbott (Little, Brown, 1970).

4. See Jerrold Schecter and Leona Schecter, *Sacred Secrets: How Soviet Intelligence Operations Changed American History* (Potomac Books, 2002); William Taubman, *Khrushchev: The Man and His Era* (Norton, 2003), 620–45.

5. Louis A. Weil III, "From the Publisher," *Time*, October 2, 1990, https://time .com/archive/6716016/from-the-publisher-oct-1-1990/.

6. Bill Clinton, interview by the author, February 2024.

7. Talbott, *Russia Hand*, 14.

8. See Svetlana Savranskaya and Tom Blanton, "The First Months of U.S. Relations with the New Russia, 1992," Briefing Book no. 819, January 30, 2023, National Security Archive, https://nsarchive.gwu.edu/briefing-book/russia -programs/2023-01-30/first-months-us-relations-new-russia-1992.

9. Notes, January 2, 1993, Talbott Diaries, 1:30.

10. See Strobe Talbott, "America and the World 1991," *Foreign Affairs* 71, no. 1 (1991/1992): 53–69. For the context, see Joseph Nye, *Bound to Lead: The Changing Nature of American Power* (Basic Books, 1990); John Ikenberry, *After Victory:*

Institutions, Strategic Restraint, and the Rebuilding of Order After Major Wars (Princeton University Press, 2001).

11. Strobe Talbott, "Hegemon and Proud of It: No Apologies Necessary for Being the Only Superpower—and Acting Like It," *Slate*, June 27, 1998, https://slate.com/news-and-politics/1998/06/hegemon-and-proud-of-it.html.

12. Talbott, "Hegemon and Proud of It."

13. Strobe Talbott, *The Great Experiment: The Story of Ancient Empires, Modern States, and the Quest for Global Governance* (Simon & Schuster, 2009), 330; for context, see Charles Krauthammer, "The Unipolar Moment," *Foreign Affairs* 70, no. 1 (1990/91), 23–33; Hal Brands, *Making the Unipolar Moment: U.S. Foreign Policy and the Rise of the Post-Cold War Order* (Cornell University Press, 2016); Philipp Zelikow and Condoleezza Rice, *To Build a Better World: Choices to End the Cold War and Create a Global Commonwealth* (Twelve, 2020).

14. Strobe Talbott, interview, PBS Putin Files, June 20, 2017, https://www.pbs.org/wgbh/frontline/interview/strobe-talbott/.

15. Talbott, *Russia Hand*, 133.

16. Anthony Lake, "From Containment to Enlargement," address at Johns Hopkins University School of Advanced International Studies, September 21, 1993, Clinton Library (CL), https://clinton.presidentiallibraries.us/items/show/9013.

17. Strobe Talbott, "Strengthening American Security Through World Leadership. Bosnia and Beyond," remarks at State Department Town Meeting, Washington, DC, November 1, 1995, https://1997-2001.state.gov/regions/eur/bosnia/bostal.html.

18. Strobe Talbott, "America Abroad: The Birth of the Global Nation," *Time*, July 20, 1992, https://content.time.com/time/subscriber/article/0,33009,976015-4,00.html; for context, see Joseph Nye, *Power in the Global Information Age: From Realism to Globalization* (Routledge, 2004).

19. See Strobe Talbott, "America Abroad. Fiddling While Dubrovnik Burns," *Time*, November 25, 1991, https://content.time.com/time/subscriber/article/0,33009,974318-2,00.html.

20. "The World: Romania's Leader Speaks," *Time*, April 2, 1973, https://content.time.com/time/subscriber/article/0,33009,907042,00.html.

21. Strobe Talbott, address at Bucharest University, Bucharest, Romania, March 18, 1998, U.S. Department of State Archives (SDA), https://1997-2001.state.gov/www/policy_remarks/1998/980319_talbott_bucharest.html.

22. Strobe Talbott, "Monnet's Brandy and Europe's Fate: A Determined Frenchman's Vision of Integration Serves as a Guide to Ending the Eurozone Crisis," Brookings Institution, 2014, http://csweb.brookings.edu/content/research/essays/2014/monnets-brandy-and-europes-fate.html.

23. Strobe Talbott, interview, Association for Diplomatic Studies and Training (ADST), July 26, 2016, https://adst.org/OH%20TOCs/Talbott-Strobe.pdf.

24. Talbott, interview, ADST.

25. John M. Broder, "An Old Russia Hand Finds Himself the Focus of Debate," *Washington Post*, September 27, 1999, https://www.nytimes.com/1999/09/27/us /public-lives-an-old-russia-hand-finds-himself-the-focus-of-debate.html.

26. John Thornton, author interview, July 2024.

27. Grisha Freidin, author interview, April 2024.

28. Daniel Yergin, author interview, June 2024.

29. David Detweiler, quoted in Marjorie Williams, "Clinton's Rhodes Warrior," *Vanity Fair*, September 1994, https://archive.vanityfair.com/article/1994/9/clin tons-rhodes-warrior.

30. Talbott, interview, ADST.

31. Talbott, quoted in Rosenbaum, "U.S. Peace Negotiator."

32. Cathy Horyn, "Strobe Talbott's Fifth Estate," *Washington Post*, July 14, 1994, https://www.washingtonpost.com/archive/lifestyle/1994/07/14/strobe-talbotts -fifth-estate/21e7c5f1-95bd-43d0-913e-443abd796e78/.

33. Talbott, *Russia Hand*, 11.

34. Talbott, *Russia Hand*, 12. For a detailed account of Clinton's trip to Scandinavia, Finland, Russia and Czechoslovakia, see David Maraniss, *First in His Class: A Biography of Bill Clinton* (Simon & Schuster, 1995).

35. Strobe Talbott, interview, William J. Clinton Presidential History Project, February 25, 2010, https://s3.amazonaws.com/web.poh.transcripts/talbott_2010_tagge dtranscript.pdf.

36. Philip Taubman, author interview, January 2024.

37. Evan Thomas, quoted in Marjorie Williams, "Clinton's Rhodes Warrior," *Vanity Fair*, September 1994, https://archive.vanityfair.com/article/1994/9/clintons -rhodes-warrior.

38. Steven Weisman, quoted in Williams, "Clinton's Rhodes Warrior."

39. Daniel Yergin, author interview, June 2024.

40. See Strobe Talbott, *Endgame: The Inside Story of Salt II* (Harper & Row 1979); James Timbie, author interview, April 2024.

41. Strobe Talbott, *Deadly Gambits: The Reagan Administration and the Stalemate in Nuclear Arms Control* (Alfred A. Knopf, 1984); Talbott, *The Russians and Reagan* (Vintage Books, 1984); Talbott, *The Master of the Game: Paul Nitze and the Nuclear Peace* (Alfred A. Knopf, 1988).

42. Bruce Jackson, quoted in Williams, "Clinton's Rhodes Warrior."

43. Talbott, *Master of the Game*, 1.

44. For a comprehensive most recent account of the context, see Susan Colbourn, *Euromissiles: The Nuclear Weapons That Nearly Destroyed NATO* (Cornell University Press, 2022).

45. Paul Nitze, interview by Stephen Rearden and Ann Smith, December 10, 1982, Paul H. Nitze Papers, Subject File, Box 118, Library of Congress (LOC). I am grateful to James Graham Wilson for sharing the transcripts of Paul Nitze's interviews.

46. Paul Nitze, interview by Stephen Rearden and Ann Smith, April 13, 1983, Subject File, Box 118, Paul H. Nitze Papers, LOC.

47. Nitze, interview, April 13, 1983.

48. *Time*, "A Letter from the Publisher," December 5, 1983, https://time.com /archive/6884080/a-letter-from-the-publisher-dec-5-1983/.

49. The Second Reagan-Mondale Presidential Debate, October, 21, 1984, Commission on Presidential Debates, https://www.debates.org/voter-education/debate -transcripts/october-21-1984-debate-transcript/.

50. Jon Draper, "Journalism, History and Journalistic History," *New York Times*, December 9, 1984, https://www.nytimes.com/1984/12/09/books/journalism -history-and-journalistic-history.html.

51. See Strobe Talbott, "Holier-Than-Thou on Star Wars," *Time*, July 1, 1985, https://time.com/archive/6704365/holier-than-thou-on-star-wars/.

52. Richard B. Thomas, "A Letter from the Publisher," *Time*, June 23, 1986, https:// time.com/archive/6706452/a-letter-from-the-publisher-jun-23-1986/.

53. Michael Mandelbaum and Strobe Talbott, "Reykjavik and Beyond," *Foreign Affairs* 65, no. 2 (1986): 215–35.

54. For an excellent biography of Nitze, see James Graham Wilson, *America's Cold Warrior: Paul Nitze and National Security from Roosevelt to Reagan* (Cornell University Press, 2024).

55. See Beth Fischer, *The Reagan Reversal: Foreign Policy and the End of the Cold War* (University of Missouri Press, 1997); Stephan Kieninger, *The Diplomacy of Détente: Cooperative Security Policies from Helmut Schmidt to George Shultz* (Routledge, 2018); Simon Miles, *Engaging the Evil Empire: Washington, Moscow, and the Beginning of the End of the Cold War* (Cornell University Press, 2020).

56. Smith, "Memorandum for the Record. Strobe Talbott," September 29, 1986, Box II-107, Folder 9, Paul H. Nitze Papers, LOC. I am grateful to Charles Kraus for sharing the Nitze-Talbott correspondence from Nitze's papers.

57. Talbott to Nitze, letter, August 23, 1986, Box I-40, Folder 10, Paul H. Nitze Papers, LOC.

58. Strobe Talbott, "Arms and the Man: Paul Nitze," *Time*, December 21, 1987, https://time.com/archive/6711116/arms-and-the-man-paul-nitze/.

59. Nitze to Talbott, letter, December 17, 1987, Box II-107, Folder 10, Paul H. Nitze Papers, LOC. For context, see Wilson, *America's Cold Warrior*, 230–31.

60. Talbott to Nitze, letter, December 15, 1987, Box I-40, Folder 10, Paul H. Nitze Papers, LOC.

61. For the context, see James Graham Wilson, *The Triumph of Improvisation: Gorbachev's Adaptability, Reagan's Engagement, and the End of the Cold War* (Cornell University Press, 2014).

62. Paul Nitze, interview by Stephen Rearden and Ann Smith, June 15, 1988, Subject File, Box 121, Paul H. Nitze Papers, LOC.

63. See Paul Nitze, *From Hiroshima to Glasnost: At the Center of Decision* (Grove Atlantic, 1989).

64. At the Council on Foreign Relations, for instance, Talbott gave papers on "Nuclear Arms Control Under Reagan" (1984) and "Star Wars and Arms Control" (1987). See Box 506, Folder 28; Box 516, Folder 15, Council on Foreign Relations Papers, Seeley G. Mudd Library, Princeton University.

65. Robert Legvold, author interview, June 2024.

66. Michael Mandelbaum and Strobe Talbott, *Reagan and Gorbachev* (Vintage Books, 1987).

67. Michael Beschloss and Strobe Talbott, *At the Highest Levels: The Inside Story of the End of the Cold War* (Little & Brown, 1993).

68. Strobe Talbott, "Rethinking the Red Menace," *Time*, January 1, 1990, https://time.com/archive/6713848/rethinking-the-red-menace/.

69. John Kohan and Strobe Talbott, Moscow, Mikhail Gorbachev, "I Want to Stay the Course," *Time*, December 23, 1991, https://time.com/archive/6719206/i-want-to-stay-the-course/.

70. Notes, n.d., August 1991–January 1993, Talbott Diaries, 1:1.

71. Notes, n.d., August 1991–January 1993, Talbott Diaries, 1:3.

72. Bill Clinton, author interview, February 2024.

73. Richard Kauzlarich, author interview, May 2024.

74. Eric Edelman, author interview, May 2024.

75. Notes, n.d., February–March 1993, Talbott Diaries, 2:1.

76. Notes, n.d., February–March 1993, Talbott Diaries, 2:1.

77. Horyn, "Strobe Talbott's Fifth Estate."

78. John Bass, author interviews, December 2023, January 2024.

79. John Bass, author interviews.

80. Victoria Nuland, author interview, December 2023.

81. See Annie Maccoby Berglof, "In his first interview at home, the former US deputy secretary of state demonstrates true kitchen-table diplomacy," *Financial Times*, December 2, 2011, https://www.ft.com/content/98a6131a-16b8-11e1-bc1d-00144feabdc0.

82. Talbott, interview, ADST.

83. Notes, February 4, 1993, Talbott Diaries, 2:3.

84. Talbott, *Russia Hand*, 46–47; Clinton, *My Life*, 505.

85. Notes, February 4, 1993, Talbott Diaries, 2:5.

86. David Hoffman, *The Oligarchs: Wealth and Power in the New Russia* (Public Affairs, 2011).

87. See Stephan Bierling, *Wirtschaftshilfe für Moskau: Motive und Strategien der Bundesrepublik Deutschland und der USA von 1990 bis 1996* (Schönigh Verlag, 1998).

88. See Margaret Shapiro, "Yeltsin Sacrifices His Reformist Premier," *Washington Post*, December 15, 1992, https://www.washingtonpost.com/archive/politics/1992/12/15

/yeltsin-sacrifices-his-reformist-premier/4d3be322-95 a.d.-4fb4-9b96-16288c0
e8c52/.

89. Michael Dobbs and Steve Coll, "Ex-Communists Are Scrambling for Quick
Cash," *Washington Post*, January 31, 1993, https://www.washingtonpost.com
/archive/politics/1993/02/01/ex-communists-are-scrambling-for-quick-cash
/00a47cf2-1f47-4051-90cd-844e3e35643b/.

90. See Anders Aslund, *How Russia Became a Market Economy* (Brookings Institution
Press, 1995).

91. See Derek Chollet and James Goldgeier, *America Between the Wars: From 11/9 to
9/11. The Misunderstood Years Between the Fall of the Berlin Wall and the Start of the
War on Terror* (Public Affairs Books, 2008); Hal Brands, *From Berlin to Baghdad.
America's Search for Purpose in the Post–Cold War World* (University Press of Ken-
tucky, 2008); Serhii Plokhy, *The Last Empire: The Final Days of the Soviet Union*
(Oneworld Publications, 2016); Kristina Spohr, *Post Wall, Post Square: Rebuilding
the World After 1989* (William Collins, 2019); Nuno Monteiro and Fritz Bartel,
eds. *Before and After the Fall: World Politics and the End of the Cold War* (Cambridge
University Press, 2021); Vladislav Zubok, *Collapse: The Fall of the Soviet Union*
(Yale University Press, 2022); Sergey Radchenko, *To Run the World: The Kremlin's
Cold War Bid for Global Power* (Cambridge University Press, 2024).

92. Strobe Talbott to George Stephanopolous, letter, February 22, 1992, Freedom of
Information Act Case no. F-2017-13804, U.S. Department of State Archives.

Introduction

1. Bill Clinton, author interview, February 2024.

2. See James E. Goodby, *Europe Undivided: The New Logic of Peace in U.S.-Russian
Relations* (United States Institute of Peace Press, 1998); James Goldgeier and
Michael McFaul, *Power, and Purpose: U.S. Policy Toward Russia After the Cold War*
(Brookings Institution Press, 2003); William Hill, *No Place for Russia: European
Security Institutions Since 1989* (Columbia University Press, 2018); William Burns,
The Back Channel: American Diplomacy in a Disordered World (Random House,
2019).

3. See Maria Snegovaya, Michael Kimmage, and Jade McGlynn, "Putin the Ideo-
logue: The Kremlin's Potent Mix of Nationalism, Grievance, and Mythmaking,"
Foreign Affairs, November 16, 2023, https://www.foreignaffairs.com/russian
-federation/putin-ideologue.

4. Mary E. Sarotte, *Not One Inch: America, Russia and the Making of the Post-Cold
War Stalemate* (Yale University Press, 2021), 2.

5. See Stephan Kieninger, "Opening NATO and Engaging Russia: NATO's Two
Tracks and the Establishment of the North Atlantic Cooperation Council," in
Open Door: NATO and Euro-Atlantic Security After the Cold War, ed. Daniel

Hamilton and Kristina Spohr (Brookings Institution Press, 2019), 57–69, https://transatlanticrelations.org/wp-content/uploads/2019/04/02-Kieninger .pdf; Liviu Horowitz, "The George H.W. Bush Administration's Policies vis-à-vis Central Europe: From Cautious Encouragement to Cracking Open NATO's Door," in Hamilton and Spohr, *Open Door*, 71–92, https://transatlanticrelations .org/wp-content/uploads/2019/04/03-Horovitz.pdf.

6. See James Goldgeier, *Not Whether but When: The U.S. Decision to Enlarge NATO* (Brookings Institution Press, 1999); Ronald Asmus, *Opening NATO's Door: How the Alliance Remade Itself for a New Era* (Columbia University Press, 2002); James Goldgeier and Joshua Itzkowitz Shifrinson, eds. *Evaluating NATO Enlargement: From Cold War Victory to the Russia-Ukraine War* (Palgrave Macmillan, 2023); Sten Rynning, *NATO: From Cold War to Ukraine. A History of the World's Most Powerful Alliance* (Yale University Press, 2024).

7. See Stephen Flanagan, "NATO from Liaison to Enlargement: A Perspective from the State Department and the National Security Council 1990–1999," in Hamilton and Spohr, *Open Door*, 93–114.

8. See Daniel Hamilton, "European Security, NATO-Russia Relations, and the Post-Cold War Order," *Journal of Cold War Studies* 26, no. 3 (2024): 204–41.

9. Sarotte, *Not One Inch*, 4.

10. See Ronald Asmus and Stephen Larrabee, "NATO and the Have-Nots: Reassurance after Enlargement," *Foreign Affairs* 75, no. 6 (1996): 13–20.

11. Sarotte, *Not One Inch*, 341.

12. Clinton and Javier Solana, memcon, February 26, 1996, Freedom of Information Act Case No. 2015-0548-M, Clinton Library (CL).

13. See Daniel Serwer, *From War to Peace in the Balkans, the Middle East and Ukraine* (Palgrave Pivot, 2019).

14. See Daniel Hamilton, "Piece of the Puzzle: NATO and Euro-Atlantic Architecture After the Cold War," in Hamilton and Spohr, *Open Door*, 3–56.

15. Strobe Talbott, "European Integration: An American Perspective. Keynote Speech by former US Deputy Secretary of State Strobe Talbott," in *The New Security Dimensions: Europe After the NATO and EU Enlargements*, ed. Adam Daniel Rotfeld (Stockholm International Peace Research Institute, June 2001), 141–42, https://www.sipri.org/sites/default/files/files/misc/SIPRI01NSD.pdf.

16. See "Euromess 2000," in Talbott, *The Great Experiment*, 321.

17. Bill Clinton, "Remarks to the American Society of Newspaper Editors in Annapolis, April 1, 1993," https://www.govinfo.gov/content/pkg/PPP-1993 -book1/pdf/PPP-1993-book1-doc-pg372.pdf.

18. Strobe Talbott, "Address at All Souls College, Oxford University, Oxford, England, January 21, 2000," U.S. Department of State, https://1997-2001.state .gov/policy_remarks/2000/000121_talbott_oxford.html.

19. Richard C. Holbrooke, "Europe Must Avoid Being Held Prisoner by Its History," Remarks Before the North Atlantic Assembly, Budapest, Hungary,

May 29, 1995, U.S. Department of State *Dispatch* 6, no. 26, https://permanent
.access.gpo.gov/gpo41448/dispatch/1995/html/Dispatchv6no26.html.

20. See Goodby, *Europe Undivided*, 173, 179; "Europe Undivided," *Washington
Quarterly* 21, no. 3 (1998): 191–207.

1. U.S. Foreign Policy and the European Security Mess

1. Daniel Hamilton and Kristina Spohr, eds., *Exiting the Cold War, Entering a New
World* (Brookings Institution Press, 2019).

2. See James Goldgeier, "NATO Expansion: Anatomy of a Decision," *Washington
Quarterly* 21, no. 1 (1998): 85–102; George Grayson, *Strange Bedfellow: NATO
Marches East* (University Press of America, 1999); Angela Stent, *Russia and Ger-
many Reborn: Unification, the Soviet Collapse, and the New Europe* (Princeton Uni-
versity Press, 2000); Mary E. Sarotte, *1989: The Struggle to Create Post-Cold War
Europe* (Princeton University Press, 2009).

3. Talbott to Clinton, letter, October 27, 1992, Talbott Diaries, 1:5.

4. Strobe Talbott, "Post-Victory Blues," *Foreign Affairs* 71, no. 1 (1991/1992): 53–69.

5. Strobe Talbott, *The Russia Hand: A Memoir of Presidential Diplomacy* (Random
House, 2002), 38.

6. Notes, November 19, 1992, Talbott Diaries, 1:9.

7. Bill Clinton, *My Life* (Arrow Books, 2004), 504.

8. Talbott to Christopher, letter, December 16, 1992, Talbott Diaries, 1:13.

9. Talbott, email to the author, February 16, 2023.

10. Notes, December 17, 1992, Talbott Diaries, 1:17.

11. Clinton and Yeltsin, telcon, January 23, 1993, Clinton Library (CL), https://
clinton.presidentiallibraries.us/items/show/101311. The eighteen Clinton-
Yeltsin memoranda of conversation (memcons) and fifty-six memoranda of telephone conversations (telcons) are available at the Clinton Digital Library
(https://clinton.presidentiallibraries.us/memcons-telcons). The documents are
in two files labeled "Declassified Documents Concerning Russian President
Boris Yeltsin." The first covers the period from January 23, 1993, to April 21,
1996 (https://clinton.presidentiallibraries.us/items/show/57568). The second
covers the period from April 21, 1996, to December 31, 1999 (https://clinton
.presidentiallibraries.us/items/show/57569). Most of the letters they sent one
another have not been declassified.

12. See Talbott to Holmes, "S/NIS Organization," March 31, 1993, Freedom of
Information Act Case No. (FOIA) F-2017-13804, U.S. Department of State
Archives (SDA).

13. Notes, n.d., Talbott Diaries, 1:1.

14. Notes, February 23, 1993, Talbott Diaries, 2:11.

15. Notes, February 23, 1993.

16. Notes, March 22, 1993, Talbott Diaries, 2:23.

17. Talbott, *Russia Hand*, 52–53.

18. See Michael Dobbs, "Yeltsin Assumes 'Special Rule' over Russia," *Washington Post*, March 21, 1993, https://www.washingtonpost.com/archive/politics/1993/03/21/yeltsin-assumes-special-rule-over-russia/94c0c908-8a95-4110-9174-9ef399a4849c/.

19. Notes, March 22, 1993, Talbott Diaries, 2:19; Talbott, *Russia Hand*, 60–61.

20. Notes, March 22, 1993, Talbott Diaries, 2:22. For context, see James Goldgeier and Michael McFaul, *Power and Purpose: U.S. Policy Toward Russia After the Cold War* (Brookings Institution Press, 2003), 123–30.

21. Notes, March 27, 1993, Talbott Diaries, 2:32.

22. Notes, March 28, 1993, Talbott Diaries, 2:34.

23. Talbott, *Russia Hand*, 59.

24. For good documentation on the commission's activities, see "Declassified Documents concerning Gore-Chernomyrdin Commission," FOIA F-2012-025789, CL, https://clinton.presidentiallibraries.us/items/show/36597. On Chernomyrdin's impact, see Anders Aslund, "Russia's Success Story: Chernomyrdin Pulls It Off," *Foreign Affairs* 73, no. 5 (1994): 58–71.

25. "Subject: Secretary Christopher's February 25 Meeting with Russian Fonmin Kozyrev," March 4, 1993, State cable 06524, FOIA M-2017-11712, SDA.

26. Mamedov agreed to have a preliminary, informal working group meeting before Talbott's confirmation. It took place on the margins of the Kozyrev visit to Washington on March 23, 1993. See "Subject: Christopher-Kozyrev Follow-Up," March 2, 1993, National Security Council cable Moscow-006191, 2016-0118-M-1, CL, https://clinton.presidentiallibraries.us/items/show/118876.

27. Talbott, *Russia Hand*, 41.

28. William J. Clinton, "Remarks to the American Society of Newspaper Editors," Annapolis, April 1, 1993, https://www.govinfo.gov/content/pkg/PPP-1993-book1/pdf/PPP-1993-book1-doc-pg372.pdf. For context, see Goldgeier and McFaul, *Power and Purpose*, 88–91.

29. See Clinton and Kohl, memcon, March 26, 1993, CL, https://clinton.presidentiallibraries.us/items/show/101319. For the German record, see "Chancellor's Meeting with U.S. President Clinton," March 29, 1993, Wilson Center Archive (WCA), https://digitalarchive.wilsoncenter.org/document/chancellors-helmut-kohls-meeting-us-president-clinton-friday-26-march-1993-washington.

30. See James Goldgeier, "Bill and Boris: A Window into a Most Important Post-Cold War Relationship," *Texas National Security Review* 4, no. 1 (August 2018): 43–54, https://tnsr.org/2018/08/bill-and-boris-a-window-into-a-most-important-post-cold-war-relationship. See Svetlana Savranskaya and Mary Elise Sarotte, eds., "The Clinton-Yeltsin Relationship in Their Own Words," Briefing Book no. 640, National Security Archive, October 2018, https://nsarchive.gwu.edu/briefing-book/russia-programs/2018-10-02/clinton-yeltsin-relationship-their-own-words.

31. Clinton, *My Life*, 508.

32. Boris Yeltsin, *Midnight Diaries* (Weidenfeld & Nicholson, 2000), 156. For context, see Leon Aron, *Boris Yeltsin: A Revolutionary Life* (Harper Collins, 2000); Timothy Colton, *Yeltsin: A Life* (Basic Books, 2008).

33. See Alexander Pavlov and Vladimir Rybachenkov, "Looking Back. The U.S.-Russian Uranium Deal: Results and Lessons," Arms Control Association, December 2013, https://www.armscontrol.org/act/2013-12/looking-back-us-russian-uranium-deal-results-lessons.

34. Notes, March 23, 1993, Talbott Diaries, 2:29.

35. Talbott, *Russia Hand*, 62.

36. Talbott, *Russia Hand*, 65.

37. Notes, March 20, 1993, Talbott Diaries, 2:20.

38. See Warren Zimmermann, *Origins of a Catastrophe: Yugoslavia and Its Destroyers* (Random House, 1999).

39. Strobe Talbott, "America Abroad: The Serbian Death Wish," *Time*, June 1, 1992, https://content.time.com/time/subscriber/article/0,33009,975621-2,00.html.

40. Strobe Talbott, "America Abroad: Why Bosnia Is Not Vietnam," *Time*, August 24, 1992, https://content.time.com/time/subscriber/article/0,33009,976295-2,00.html.

41. Notes, April 25, 1993, Talbott Diaries, 3:8.

42. Richard Holbrooke, interview, PBS, n.d., https://www.pbs.org/wgbh/pages/frontline/shows/military/guys/holbrooke.html.

43. Notes, April 25, 1993, Talbott Diaries, 3:8.

44. Notes, April 25, 1993, Talbott Diaries, 3:10–12.

45. See Richard Holbrooke, *How to End a War* (Random House, 1998); Ivo Daalder, *Getting to Dayton: The Making of America's Bosnia Policy* (Brookings Institution Press, 1999); Ivo Daalder, ed., *Beyond Preemption: Force and Legitimacy in a Changing World* (Brookings Institution Press, 2007); Derek Chollet and Samantha Power, eds., *The Unquiet American: Richard Holbrooke in the World* (Public Affairs, 2012); George Packer, *Our Man: Richard Holbrooke and the End of the American Century* (Knopf, 2019).

46. Notes, April 25, 1993, Talbott Diaries, 3:12.

47. See George Packer, "The End of the American Century," *The Atlantic*, May 2019, https://www.theatlantic.com/magazine/archive/2019/05/george-packer-pax-americana-richard-holbrooke/586042/.

48. Helmut Kohl and Warren Christopher, memcon, May 6, 1993, WCA, https://digitalarchive.wilsoncenter.org/document/chancellors-helmut-kohls-meeting-us-secretary-state-christopher-thursday-6-may-1993.

49. Talbott, *Russia Hand*, 74.

50. "Subject: Talbott/McCaffrey Bosnia Consultations in Moscow, May 7–8," telegram Moscow-013590, May 8, 1993, FOIA M-2017-11839, SDA.

51. Talbott, *Russia Hand*, 76.

52. Notes, April 25, 1993, Talbott Diaries, 3:12.

53. See Jason Deparle, "The Man Inside Bill Clinton's Foreign Policy," *New York Times Magazine*, August 20, 1995, https://www.nytimes.com/1995/08/20/maga zine/the-man-inside-bill-clinton-s-foreign-policy.html.

54. See Frank L. Jones, "Engaging the World: Anthony Lake and American Grand Strategy, 1993–1997," *The Historical Journal* 59, no. 3 (2016): 869–901.

55. Notes, mid/late November 1993, Talbott Diaries, 4:50.

56. Talbott to Lake, letter, September 30, 1993, FOIA F-2017-13804, SDA.

57. See Stephan Kieninger, "Money for Moscow: The West and the Question of Financial Assistance for Mikhail Gorbachev," in Hamilton and Spohr, *Exiting the Cold War*, 281–96, https://transatlanticrelations.org/wp-content/uploads /2019/10/11-Kieninger.pdf.

58. Talbott to Clinton, letter, July 16, 1993, FOIA F-2017-13804, SDA.

59. Talbott, *Russia Hand*, 87.

60. See Talbott, *Russia Hand*, 89; see "Statement on the Situation in Russia," September 21, 1993, Public Papers of the President, https://www.govinfo.gov /content/pkg/PPP-1993-book2/pdf/PPP-1993-book2-doc-pg1553.pdf.

61. Clinton and Yeltsin, telcon, September 21, 1993, CL, https://clinton.presidenti allibraries.us/items/show/101341.

62. For context, see Svetlana Savranskaya and Tom Blanton, eds., "Yeltsin Shelled Russian Parliament 25 Years Ago, U.S. Praised 'Superb Handling,'" Briefing Book no. 641, October 4, 2018, National Security Archive, https://nsarchive .gwu.edu/briefing-book/russia-programs/2018-10-04/yeltsin-shelled-russian -parliament-25-years-ago-us-praised-superb-handling.

63. Notes, September 21, 1993, Talbott Diaries, 4:2; Talbott, *Russia Hand*, 87.

64. "Secretary's Visit to Moscow: Domestic Political Dynamics," cable Moscow-32920, October 19, 1993, National Security Archive, https://nsarchive.gwu.edu /document/16849-document-07-cable-american-embassy-moscow.

65. See "Subject: Secretary Christopher's Meeting with Foreign Minister Kozyrev: NATO, Elections, Regional Issues," Secto-17024, October 25, 1993, National Security Archive, https://nsarchive.gwu.edu/document/16851-document-09 -secretary-christopher-s-meeting.

66. Notes, late November 1993, Talbott Diaries, 4:54; for Talbott's recollections on the weekend at Camp David, see Talbott, *Russia Hand*, 103–4.

67. See Michael McFaul, "Why Russia's Politics Matter," *Foreign Affairs* 74, no. 1 (1995): 87–99.

68. "Subject: Vice President Gore and President Yeltsin's Bilateral Meeting December 16, 1993," cable Moscow-38928, FOIA M-2017-12135, SDA.

69. Notes, December 13, 1993, Talbott Diaries, 4:65.

70. Notes, December 13, 1993.

71. See Strobe Talbott, "America Must Remain Engaged in Russian Reform," statement before the House Foreign Service Committee, January 25, 1994, https://clinton.presidentiallibraries.us/items/show/11106.

72. Clinton and Yeltsin, telcon, December 22, 1993, CL, https://clinton.presiden
tiallibraries.us/items/show/101343.

73. Yuri N. Afanasyev, "Russian Reform Is Dead. Back to Central Planning," *Foreign
Affairs* 73, no. 2 (1994): 21–22.

74. Talbott to Mamedov, letter, January 29, 1994, FOIA F-2017-13804, SDA. See
Mark Kramer, "The Soviet Legacy in Russian Foreign Policy," *Political Science
Quarterly* 134, no. 4 (2019/2020): 585–609.

75. See Serhii Plokhy, *The Gates of Europe: A History of Ukraine* (Penguin 2021).

76. For an excellent documentation and critical oral history project on Nunn and
Lugar, see National Security Archive, "The Nunn-Lugar Project. Cooperative
Threat Reduction Program with Russia, Ukraine, Belarus, and Kazakhstan,
1992–2012," https://nsarchive.gwu.edu/project/nunn-lugar.

77. Boris Tarasyuk, author interview, May 2024.

78. Notes, "Morozov in Washington at Pentagon," July 27, 1993, Talbott Diaries, 3:67.

79. Tarasyuk, author interview, May 2024.

80. See Mariana Budjeryn, *Inheriting the Bomb: The Collapse of the USSR and the
Nuclear Disarmament of Ukraine* (Johns Hopkins University Press, 2022); David
Hoffman, *The Dead Hand: The Untold Story of the Cold War Arms Race and its Dangerous Legacy* (Anchor, 2010); Togzhan Kassenova, *Atomic Steppe: How Kazakhstan Gave Up the Bomb* (Stanford University Press, 2022).

81. Notes, January 2, 1993, Talbott Diaries, 1:30.

82. See Steven Pifer, *The Eagle and the Trident: U.S.–Ukraine Relations in Turbulent
Times* (Brookings Institution Press, 2017), 25–28.

83. James E. Goodby, "Preventive Diplomacy for Nuclear Nonproliferation in the
Former Soviet Union," in *Opportunities Seized, Opportunities Missed: Preventive
Diplomacy in the Post–Cold War World*, ed. Bruce Jentleson (Rowman & Littlefield, 2000), 110, https://media.carnegie.org/filer_public/9e/43/9e435fc8-f8fd-4764
-aabd-2c8eba103b38/ccny_book_1999_opportunities.pdf.

84. See Ashton Carter and William Perry, *Preventive Defense: A New Security Strategy
for America* (Brookings Institution Press, 1999); John M. Shields and William C.
Potter, eds., *Dismantling the Cold War: U.S. and NIS Perspectives on the Nunn-
Lugar Cooperative Threat Reduction Program* (MIT Press, 1997).

85. "Subject: Talbott/Gati Consultations in Kiev: Rebuilding Bridges," cable Moscow-
13723, May 11, 1993, FOIA M-2017-11838, SDA; "Subject: Trip Report on Strobe
Talbott's Mission to the Former Soviet Union," memorandum from John A. Gordon for Secretary of Defense and Deputy Secretary, May 19, 1993, National Security
Archive, https://nsarchive.gwu.edu/document/23665-memorandum-secretary
-defense-and-deputy-secretary-defense-john-gordon-trip-report.

86. See Pifer, *Eagle and the Trident*, 27–28.

87. Clinton and Yeltsin, memcon, July 10, 1993, CL, https://clinton.presidentia
llibraries.us/items/show/101330.

88. See Stephan Kieninger, "The Bush and Clinton Administrations and Ukraine's Nuclear Dismantlement, 1991–1994," *Diplomacy & Statecraft* 33, no. 3 (2022): 566–88.

89. "Subject: London Trilateral Talks: Early Deactivation," cable State-263566, August 29, 1993, FOIA M-2017-11832, SDA.

90. See Pifer, *Eagle and the Trident*, 48–52.

91. Notes, July 23, 1993, Talbott Diaries, 3:61–62.

92. See Pifer, *Eagle and the Trident*, 73.

93. See David Yost, "The Budapest Memorandum and Russia's Intervention in Ukraine," *International Affairs* 91, no. 3 (2015): 505–38.

94. "Memorandum on Security Assurances in Connection with Ukraine's Accession to the Treaty on the Non-Proliferation of Nuclear Weapons," December 5, 1994, Volume 3007, No. 52241, United Nations Treaty Collection, https://treaties.un .org/doc/Publication/UNTS/Volume%203007/v3007.pdf.

95. Mariana Budjeryn, "The Breach: Ukraine's Territorial Integrity and the Budapest Memorandum," Nuclear Proliferation International History Project, Issue Brief no. 3, Wilson Center, September 30, 2014, https://www.wilsoncenter.org /publication/issue-brief-3-the-breach-ukraines-territorial-integrity-and-the -budapest-memorandum.

96. Mariana Budjeryn and Matthew Bunn, "Budapest Memorandum At 25: Between Past and Future," Project on Managing the Atom, Belfer Center for Science and International Affairs, Harvard Kennedy School, March 2020, https://www.belfercenter.org/sites/default/files/2020-03/budapest/BM25.pdf.

97. "Subject: Meeting of WEU SYG and WEU Presidency Rep with the Deputy Secretary," cable State-170606, June 25, 1994, FOIA F-2017-13804, SDA.

98. See Serhii Plokhy and Mary E. Sarotte, "The Shoals of Ukraine: Where American Illusions and Great-Power Politics Collide," *Foreign Affairs* 99, no. 1 (2020): 81–95.

99. Kohl and Clinton, "The Chancellor's [Helmut Kohl's] Lunch Meeting with President Clinton," memcon, January 31, 1994, WCA, https://digitalarchive.wil soncenter.org/document/chancellors-helmut-kohls-lunch-meeting-president -clinton-washington-31-january-1994; see also Helmut Kohl, *Erinnerungen 1990–1994* (Droemer und Knaur, 2007); Joachim Bitterlich, *Grenzgänger: Deutsche Interessen und Verantwortung für Europa. Erinnerungen eines Zeitzeugen* (Ibidem Verlag, 2021).

100. See Vaclav Havel, "A Call for Sacrifice: The Co-Responsibility of the West," *Foreign Affairs* 73, no. 2 (1994): 2–7; Mary E. Sarotte, "The Convincing Call from Central Europe: Let Us into NATO," *Foreign Affairs*, March 12, 2019, https://www.foreignaffairs.com/united-states/convincing-call-central-europe -let-us-nato; Liviu Horovitz and Elias Götz, "The Overlooked Importance of Economics: Why the Bush Administrations Wanted NATO Enlargement," *Journal of Strategic Studies* 43, no. 6 (2020): 847–68.

101. Bush and Havel, memcon, November 18, 1990, G. H. W. Bush Library, https:// bush41library.tamu.edu/files/memcons-telcons/1990-11-18—Havel.pdf. On Bush's account, see George H. W. Bush and Brent Scowcroft, *A World Transformed* (Alfred A. Knopf, 1998), 404–5. For context, see Simon Miles, "We All Fall Down: The Dismantling of the Warsaw Pact and the End of the Cold War in Eastern Europe," *International Security* 48, no. 3 (2024): 51–85.

102. See Joshua Itzkowitz Shifrinson, "Eastbound and Down: The United States, NATO Enlargement, and Suppressing the Soviet and Western European Alternatives, 1990–1992," *Journal of Strategic Studies* 43, no. 6 (2020), 816–46; Shifrinson, *Rising Titans, Falling Giants: How Great Powers Exploit Power Shifts* (Cornell University Press, 2018.)

103. Volker Rühe, "Shaping Euro-Atlantic Policies: A Grand Strategy for a New Era," Survival, 35, no. 2 (1993): 131; Volker Rühe, *Deutschlands Verantwortung: Perspektiven für ein neues Europa* (Ullstein, 1994); Ulrich Weisser, *Sicherheit für ganz Europa: Die Atlantische Allianz in der Bewährung* (Deutsche Verlags Anstalt, 1999); Ronald Asmus, *Opening NATO's Door: How the Alliance Remade Itself for a New Era* (Columbia University Press, 2002), 31–32; Volker Rühe, "Opening NATO's Door," in Hamilton and Spohr, *Open Door*, 217–33, https://transatlanticrelations .org/wp-content/uploads/2019/04/10-Ruhe.pdf; James Bindenagel, *Germany. From Peace to Power? Can Germany Lead in Europe Without Dominating It?* (Vandenhoeck & Ruprecht Unipress, 2020).

104. Clinton and Havel, memcon, April 20, 1993, 2009-0223-M, CL.

105. Clinton and Walesa, memcon, April 21, 1993, 2015-0780-M, CL.

106. Asmus, *Opening NATO's Door*, 29.

107. See Rebecca Moore, *NATO's New Mission: Projecting Stability in a Post-Cold War World* (Praeger, 2007).

108. See Charles Glaser, "Why NATO Is Still Best: Future Security Arrangements for Europe," *International Security* 18, no. 1 (1993): 5–50.

109. Ivo Daalder, "NATO in the 21st Century: What Purpose? What Missions?" Brookings Institution, April 1, 1999, https://www.brookings.edu/articles/nato -in-the-21st-century-what-purpose-what-missions/.

110. Richard Lugar, "NATO. Out of Area or Out of Business: A Call for U.S. Leadership to Revive and Redefine the Alliance," remarks to the Open Forum of the U.S. State Department, August 2, 1993, Indiana University Libraries, http:// collections.libraries.indiana.edu/lugar/items/show/342.

111. Lugar, "NATO."

112. See Daalder, "NATO in the 21st Century."

113. See Mary Sarotte, "How to Enlarge NATO: The Debate Inside the Clinton Administration, 1993–95," *International Security* 44, no. 1 (2019): 7–41.

114. "Subject: Woerner on Expanding NATO Membership," cable State-271405, September 3, 1993, FOIA M-2017-12017, SDA.

115. Yeltsin to Clinton, letter, September 15, 1993, FOIA M-2006-01499, SDA. On Russia's position, see Svetlana Savranskaya and Tom Blanton, eds. "NATO Expansion: What Yeltsin Heard," Briefing Book no. 621, National Security Archive, March 16, 2018, https://nsarchive.gwu.edu/briefing-book/russia-programs/2018-03-16/nato-expansion-what-yeltsin-heard.

116. See Philip Zelikow and Condoleezza Rice, *Germany Unified and Europe Transformed: A Study in Statecraft* (Harvard University Press, 1995).

117. See Peter Baker, "In Ukraine Conflict, Putin Relies on a Promise that Ultimately Wasn't," *New York Times*, January 9, 2022, https://www.nytimes.com/2022/01/09/us/politics/russia-ukraine-james-baker.html; see Philip Zelikow, "European Security, NATO-Russia Relations, and the Post-Cold War Order," *Journal of Cold War Studies* 26, no. 3 (2024): 204–41.

118. "Russian Assertions About the Two-Plus-Four-Treaty," cable State-036296, February 27, 1996, FOIA F-2008-02356, SDA.

119. See Mark Kramer, "The Myth of a No-NATO-Enlargement Pledge to Russia," *The Washington Quarterly* 32, no. 2 (2009): 39–61; Mary E. Sarotte, "Perpetuating U.S. Preeminence: The 1990 Deals to 'Bribe the Soviets Out' and Move NATO In," *International Security* 35, no. 1 (2010): 110–37. For a different view, see Joshua Itzkowitz Shifrinson, "Deal or No Deal? The End of the Cold War and the U.S. Offer to Limit NATO Expansion," *International Security* 40, no. 4 (2016): 7–44; for context, see Sergey Radchenko, Timothy Sayle, and Christian Ostermann, eds. *NATO in the Cold War and After: Contested Histories and Future Directions* (Routledge, 2022); James Goldgeier and Joshua Itzkowitz Shifrinson, "Evaluating NATO Enlargement: Scholarly Debates, Policy Implications, and Roads Not Taken," in *Evaluating NATO Enlargement: From Cold War Victory to the Russia-Ukraine War*, ed. Goldgeier and Shifrinson, 1–42 (Palgrave Macmillan, 2023).

120. See Ronald Asmus, Richard Kugler, and Stephen Larrabee, "Building a New NATO," *Foreign Affairs* 72, no. 4 (1993): 28–40.

121. Daniel Hamilton, correspondence with the author, September 2024.

122. Hamilton, correspondence, September 2024.

123. See Bastian Matteo Scannia, *Sonderzug nach Moskau. Geschichte der deutschen Russlandpolitik seit 1990* (C. H. Beck, 2024).

124. Kohl and Clinton, telcon, September 7, 1993, WCA, https://digitalarchive.wilsoncenter.org/document/chancellors-helmut-kohls-telephone-conversation-president-clinton-7-september-1993.

125. See James Goldgeier, *Not Whether But When: The U.S. Decision to Enlarge NATO* (Brookings Institution Press, 1999), 29–32; Mary E. Sarotte, *Not One Inch: America, Russia and the Making of the Post-Cold War Stalemate* (Yale University Press, 2021), 164–70.

126. Davis to Christopher "A Strategy for NATO's Expansion and Transformation," memo, September 7, 1993, National Security Archive, https://nsarchive.gwu

.edu/document/16374-document-02-strategy-nato-s-expansion-and. Stephen Flanagan of the State Department's Policy Planning Staff drafted the memo. He had already advocated a fast-track on NATO enlargement in 1992. See Stephen Flanagan, "NATO and Central and Eastern Europe: From Liaison to Security Partnership," *Washington Quarterly* 15, no. 2 (June 1992): 141–51; Flanagan, author interview.

127. Albright to Clinton, "Memorandum for the President, the Vice President and the Secretary of State and the National Security Adviser, Subject: PfP and Central and Eastern Europe," memo, January 26, 1994, 2015-0755-M, CL.

128. See Asmus, *Opening NATO's Door*, 49–52; Sarotte, *How to Enlarge NATO*, 18–21.

129. Gallucci through Davis to Christopher, "Your October 6 Lunch Meeting with Secretary Aspin and Mr. Lake," memo, October 5, 1993, National Security Archive, https://nsarchive.gwu.edu/document/16377-document-05-your-october -6-lunch-meeting.

130. See Michael Gordon, "U.S. Opposes Move to Rapidly Expand NATO Membership," *New York Times*, January 2, 1994, https://www.nytimes.com/1994/01 /02/world/us-opposes-move-to-rapidly-expand-nato-membership.html.

131. Talbott to Christopher, memo, October 17, 1993, sent by telegram to Christopher's team in Moscow, "Subject: Official-Informal—U/S Davis," cable State-317538, October 19, 1993, FOIA M-2017-11814, SDA; see Talbott, *Russia Hand*, 99–101.

132. Talbott to Christopher, memo, October 17, 1993; see Talbott, *Russia Hand*, 99–101.

133. Talbott to Christopher, memo, October 17, 1993; see Talbott, *Russia Hand*, 99–101.

134. See Sarotte, *How to Enlarge NATO*, 17.

135. Christopher and Yeltsin, memcon, October 22, 1993, National Security Archive, https://nsarchive.gwu.edu/document/16380-document-08-secretary-christopher -s-meeting. See James Goldgeier, "Promises Made, Promises Broken? What Yeltsin Was Told About NATO in 1993 and Why It Matters," *War on the Rocks*, July 12, 2016, https://warontherocks.com/2016/07/promises-made-promises -broken-what-yeltsin-was-told-about-nato-in-1993-and-why-it-matters/. See Warren Christopher, *Chances of a Lifetime: A Memoir* (Scribner, 2001).

136. Andrei Kozyrev, *The Firebird: The Elusive Fate of Russian Democracy* (University of Pittsburgh Press, 2010), 219–21.

137. "NATO Summit, U.S. Partnership for Peace Proposals," telno-74, October 21, 1993, PREM 19/4164, UK National Archives.

138. Weisser to Rühe, memo, November 29, 1993, Box 14, Ronald Asmus Papers.

139. See Zbigniew Brzezinski, "The Premature Partnership," *Foreign Affairs* 73, no. 2 (March/April 1994): 67–82.

140. Talbott to Christopher, letter, November 1, 1993, FOIA F-2017-13804, SDA.

141. See Mark Bowden, *Black Hawk Down: A Story of Modern War* (Grove Atlantic Press, 1999).

142. For context, see Samantha Power, *A Problem from Hell: America and the Age of Genocide* (Basic Books, 2002); Power, *The Education of an Idealist: A Memoir* (Dey Street Books, 2019). For a different assessment, see Michael Mandelbaum, "The Reluctance to Intervene," *Foreign Policy* 95 (1994): 3–18; Mandelbaum, "Foreign Policy as Social Work," *Foreign Affairs* 75, no. 1 (1996): 16–32.

143. Leslie H. Gelb, "Quelling the Teacup Wars: The New World's Constant Challenge," *Foreign Affairs* 73, no. 6 (1994): 2–6.

144. See Douglas Farah and Ruth Marcu, "U.S. Pulls Troops Ship Back from Haiti: Clinton Seeks Sanctions After Defiant Host Fails," *Washington Post*, October 12, 1993, https://www.washingtonpost.com/archive/politics/1993/10/13/us-pulls-troop-ship-back-from-haiti/1cbda0fe-a313-4d08-bfb6-dd1df09cc22d/.

145. Notes, November 1, 1993, Talbott Diaries, 4:23.

146. Notes, November 1, 1993, Talbott Diaries, 4:17.

147. Notes, November 1, 1993, Talbott Diaries, 4:18.

148. Notes, November 2, 1993, Talbott Diaries, 4:18.

149. Notes, November 2, 1993, Talbott Diaries, 4:19.

150. Notes, November 2, 1993, Talbott Diaries, 4:20.

151. Notes, November 3, 1993, Talbott Diaries, 4:26.

152. Notes, November 5, 1993, Talbott Diaries, 4:30.

153. Notes, November 5, 1993, Talbott Diaries, 4:30–31.

154. Elaine Sciolino, "With Foreign Policies Under Fire, Top State Dept. Deputy is Ousted," *New York Times*, November 9, 1993, https://www.nytimes.com/1993/11/09/world/with-foreign-policies-under-fire-top-state-dept-deputy-is-ousted.html.

155. Strobe Talbott, interview, William J. Clinton Presidential History Project, February 25, 2010, https://s3.amazonaws.com/web.poh.transcripts/talbott_2010_taggedtranscript.pdf.

156. William J. Clinton, "Statement on the Nomination of Strobe Talbott to Be Deputy Secretary of State," December 28, 1993, American Presidency Project, https://www.presidency.ucsb.edu/documents/statement-the-nomination-strobe-talbott-be-deputy-secretary-state.

157. Notes, late November 1993, Talbott Diaries, 4:54. For Talbott's recollections on the weekend at Camp David, see Talbott, *Russia Hand*, 103–4.

158. Talbott to William and Mary Bundy, letter, January 18, 1994, FOIA F-2017-13804, SDA.

159. See George Weigel, "Strobe Talbott's Ideas and Their Consequences: Now That His Thoughts Affect More Than Magazine Readers, the Senate Must Closely Examine His Prior Writings," *Los Angeles Times*, January 23, 1994, https://www.latimes.com/archives/la-xpm-1994-01-23-op-14514-story.html.

160. See Steven Greenhouse, "Senate Confirms Talbott as State Dept. Deputy," *New York Times*, February 23, 1994, https://www.nytimes.com/1994/02/23/world/senate-confirms-talbott-as-state-dept-deputy.html.

161. CSPAN, "Deputy Defense Secretary Confirmation Hearing," February 8, 1994, https://www.c-span.org/video/?54417-1/deputy-defense-secretary-confirmation-hearing.

162. See "Nomination of Strobe Talbott, of Ohio, to the Deputy Secretary of State," February 22, 1994, *Congressional Record* 140, no. 15, https://www.govinfo.gov/content/pkg/CREC-1994-02-22/html/CREC-1994-02-22-pt1-PgS7.htm.

163. Notes, late January 1994, Talbott Diaries, 5:20.

164. Talbott to Christopher, memo, March 11, 1994, FOIA F-2017-13804, SDA.

165. Talbott to Christopher, memo, January 2, 1994, FOIA F-2017-13804, SDA.

166. Talbott to Christopher, memo, August 21, 1994, FOIA F-2017-13804, SDA.

167. Talbott to Christopher, memo, January 2, 1994.

2. Engaging Russia and Enlarging NATO

1. William J. Clinton, "The President's News Conference with Visegrad Leaders in Prague," January 12, 1994, https://www.govinfo.gov/content/pkg/PPP-1994-book1/pdf/PPP-1994-book1-doc-pg39-2.pdf.

2. Clinton, "President's News Conference"; see also Goldgeier, *Not Whether but When: The U.S. Decision to Enlarge NATO* (Brookings Institution Press, 1999), 54–59; Mary E. Sarotte, *Not One Inch: America, Russia, and the Making of the Post-Cold War Stalemate* (Yale University Press, 2021), 182–89.

3. "Subject: Secretary's Meeting with Foreign Ministers of Hungary, Poland, Slovakia, and the Czech Republic," Secto-10020, January 16, 1994, Freedom of Information Act Case no. (FOIA) M-2017-11649, U.S. Department of State Archives (SDA).

4. Ian Brzezinski, author interview, July 2024.

5. See Simon Miles, "We All Fall Down: The Dismantling of the Warsaw Pact and the End of the Cold War in Eastern Europe," *International Security* 48, no. 3 (2024): 51–85.

6. Talbott to Lake, "Kozyrev's European Security Plan," memo, January 12, 1994, FOIA F-2017-13804, SDA.

7. Strobe Talbott, *The Russia Hand: A Memoir of Presidential Diplomacy* (Random House, 2002), 114–115; Bill Clinton, *My Life* (Arrow Books, 2004), 570; Strobe Talbott, "Bill, Boris, and NATO," in *Open Door: NATO and Euro-Atlantic Security After the Cold War*, eds. Daniel Hamilton and Kristina Spohr (Brookings Institution Press, 2019), 405–24, https://transatlanticrelations.org/wp-content/uploads/2019/04/17-talbott.pdf.

8. Talbott, *Russia Hand*, 115.

9. Talbott, *Russia Hand*, 115.

10. "Subject: Summit: Kozyrev's Views," cable Moscow-00594, January 10, 1994, FOIA M-2017-11493, SDA.

11. See John Kifner, "66 Die as Shell Wrecks Sarajevo Market," *New York Times*, February 6, 1994, https://www.nytimes.com/1994/02/06/world/66-die-as-shell-wrecks-sarajevo-market.html.

12. Under the so-called dual key system, the approval of the United Nations was required for all NATO air operations. The UN ground commanders often vetoed the use of airstrikes, however. See Mark A. Bucknam, *Responsibility of Command: How UN and NATO Commanders Influenced Airpower over Bosnia* (Air University Press, 2003).

13. See "Decisions taken at the Meeting of the North Atlantic Council in Permanent Session," North Atlantic Treaty Organization, February 9, 1994, https://www.nato.int/cps/en/natolive/official_texts_24465.htm.

14. Christopher quoted in Goldgeier, *Not Whether but When*, 98.

15. For context, see Sten Rynning, *NATO: From Cold War to Ukraine* (Yale University Press, 2024), 189–212.

16. See Nora Bensahel, "Separable but Not Separate Forces: NATO's Development of the Combined Joint Task Force," *European Security* 8, no. 2 (1999): 52–72.

17. "Subject: Deputy Secretary Talbott debriefs NAC on his trip to India, Pakistan, Poland and Slovakia," cable USNATO1505, April 21, 1994, FOIA F-2017-13804, SDA.

18. Notes, April 24, 1994, Talbott Diaries, 5:49.

19. Talbott, *Russia Hand*, 124.

20. "Subject: Secretary's Meeting with Russian Foreign Minister Andrei Kozyrev, June 22, Brussels, Belgium," cable State-169824, June 22, 1994, FOIA M-2017-11658, SDA.

21. Kozyrev, *Firebird*, 265.

22. "Subject: Peacekeeping in the Caucasus," cable Moscow-18067, June 24, 1994, FOIA F-2008-02190, SDA. For context, see Fiona Hill and Pamela Jewett, "Back in the USSR: Russia's Intervention in the Internal Affairs of the Former Soviet Republics and the Implications for United States Policy Toward Russia," Ethnic Conflict Project, Strengthening Democratic Institutions Project, John F. Kennedy School of Government, Harvard University, January 1994, https://www.brookings.edu/wp-content/uploads/2016/06/back-in-the-ussr-1994.pdf

23. Clinton and Yeltsin, telcon, July 5, 1994, Clinton Library (CL), https://clinton.presidentiallibraries.us/items/show/101388. For context, see Carl Bildt, "The Baltic Litmus Test: Revealing Russia's True Colors," *Foreign Affairs* 73, no. 5 (1994): 72–85.

24. "Subject: Deputy Secretary July 24 Bilateral with FM," cable Bangkok-25937, July 25, 1994, FOIA F-2017-13804, SDA. For context, see James Goldgeier and Michael McFaul, *Power and Purpose: U.S. Policy Toward Russia After the Cold War* (Brookings Institution Press, 2003), 171–75.

25. "Subject: Mamedov's Thoughts on your conversation with Yeltsin," cable Moscow-27484, September 23, 1994, FOIA F-2017-13804, SDA.

26. Clinton and Yeltsin, memcon, September 28, 1994, CL, https://clinton.presidentiallibraries.us/items/show/101758.

27. "Subject: US/Russian Relations: A Clinton Success?" telno 1507, October 18, 1994, PREM 19/5117, UK National Archives.

28. See "Subject: Deputy Secretary's Meeting with Presidents of Nicaragua, Guatemala, Costa Rica, and Columbian Foreign Minister," cable Caraca-04534, June 3, 1994, FOIA F-2017-13804, SDA.

29. Talbott to Christopher, memo, April 29, 1994, FOIA F-2017-13804, SDA.

30. See Morris Morley and Chris McGillion, "Disobedient Generals and the Politics of Redemocratization: The Clinton Administration and Haiti," *Political Science Quarterly* 112, no. 3 (1997): 363–84; Ambassador James Dobbins, interview, Association for Diplomatic Studies and Training, July 21, 2003, https://adst.org/OH%20TOCs/Dobbins,%20James.toc.pdf.

31. "Subject: US/Russian Relations: A Clinton Success?"

32. Strobe Talbott, "Remembering Richard Holbrooke," Brookings Institution, December 15, 2010, https://www.brookings.edu/articles/remembering-richard-holbrooke/.

33. Volker Rühe, author interviews, February 2019, October 2021.

34. Ronald Asmus, *Opening NATO's Door: How the Alliance Remade Itself for a New Era* (Columbia University Press, 2002), 77.

35. On May 12, Talbott called Holbrooke up via secure phone. He "was thinking about 2 things, 1) how to help the Pres deal w/ a growing foreign policy catastrophe, and 2, how I can get you and me to work in the same building." Richard Holbrooke Bonn/Bosnia Diary, May 12, 1994, Box 4, Richard Holbrooke Papers, Princeton University, Seeley Mudd Library.

36. Holbrooke, *To End a War*, 57.

37. Richard Holbrooke, "Marooned in the Cold War: An Exchange," *World Policy Journal* 14, no. 4 (1997/1998): 101.

38. Michael Dobbs,"Wider Alliance Would Increase U.S. Commitments," *Washington Post*, July 5, 1995, https://www.washingtonpost.com/archive/politics/1995/07/05/wider-alliance-would-increase-us-commitments/3f5c8a21-4f50-4fa9-8083-bb7d6d5b48ad/.

39. Asmus, *Opening NATO's Door*, 76.

40. Talbott to Christopher, "The Future of European Security," memo, September 12, 1994, FOIA F-2017-13804, SDA.

41. William J. Clinton, "Address to the Polish Parliament in Warsaw, July 7, 1994," https://www.govinfo.gov/content/pkg/PPP-1994-book1/pdf/PPP-1994-book1-doc-pg1208.pdf.

42. Asmus, *Opening NATO's Door*, 78.

43. Vice President Gore, "U.S.-German Relations and the Challenge of a New Europe," speech to the conference on New Traditions, Berlin, Germany, U.S. Department of State *Dispatch* 5, no. 37, September 12, 1994, https://permanent.access.gpo.gov/gpo41448/dispatch/1994/html/Dispatchv5no37.html.

44. "German Defense Minister Ruehe on NATO Expansion," cable Berlin-02794, September 10, 1994, FOIA M-2017-12044, SDA. See Gerhard Solomon, *The NATO Enlargement Debate, 1990–1997: The Blessings of Liberty* (Praeger Publishers, 1998), 65–66.

45. See "Exporting Security to the East: The Future Role of the Alliance. Research Sponsored by the German Ministry of Defense," RAND Study P386-1, 6/94, Box 14, Ronald Asmus Papers; see also Asmus, *Opening NATO's Door*, 87; David Gompert and Richard Kugler, "Free-Rider Redux: NATO Needs to Project Power," *Foreign Affairs* 74, no. 1 (1995): 7–12.

46. "NATO Expansion: Concept and Strategy," memo, September 17, 1994, SDA, https://www.archives.gov/files/declassification/iscap/pdf/2016-185-doc-2.pdf.

47. See Dobbs, "Wider Alliance"; Sarotte, *Not One Inch*, 196; Goldgeier, *Not Whether but When*, 73–76.

48. Goldgeier, *Not Whether But When*, 155; Asmus, *Opening NATO's Door*, 75–79.

49. Notes, September 29, 1994, Talbott Diaries, 8:18.

50. Notes, September 15, 16, 1994, Talbott Diaries, 7:75. See James Townsend, "In Peace and War: The Military Implications of NATO Enlargement," in *Evaluating NATO Enlargement: From Cold War Victory to the Russia-Ukraine War*, eds. James Goldgeier and Joshua Itzkowitz Shifrinson (Palgrave Macmillan, 2023), 495–530.

51. Talbott to Christopher, letter, September 11, 1994, FOIA F-2017-13804, SDA.

52. Talbott to Christopher, September 11, 1994.

53. "Subject: The Deputy Secretary's October 20 Meeting with FCO Political Director Neville-Jones," cable London-16663, FOIA F-2017-13804, SDA.

54. Talbott to Christopher, "The Future of European Security," memo, September 12, 1994, FOIA F-2017-13804, SDA.

55. Gore, "U.S.-German Relations."

56. Lake to Clinton, "NATO Expansion," memo, October 13, 1994, 2015-0755-M, CL, https://clinton.presidentiallibraries.us/items/show/57563; see Joshua Itzkowitz Shifrinson, "The NATO Enlargement Consensus and US Foreign Policy: Origins and Consequences," in Goldgeier and Shifrinson, *Evaluating NATO Enlargement*, 97–144.

57. "Subject: Memorandum of the President's Conversation with Mayor Chirac," cable State-266972, October 2, 1994, FOIA M-2017-11312, SDA.

58. Delors and Pawlak, memcon, February 3, 1994, JD-1890, Jacques Delors Papers, Historical Archives of the European Union (HAEU).

59. Delors and Clinton, memcon, January 11, 1994, JD-1866, Jacques Delors Papers, HAEU.

60. See Richard Holbrooke, "America: A European Power," *Foreign Affairs* 74, no. 2 (1995): 38–51; Strobe Talbott, "The New Geopolitics: Defending Democracy in the Post-Cold War Era," *The World Today* 51, no. 1 (January 1995), 7–10; Warren Christopher, "America's Leadership, America's Opportunity," *Foreign Policy* 98 (1995): 6–27.

61. "The President's Meeting with Chancellor Vranitzky," cable State-114595, April 30, 1994, FOIA M-2017-11516, SDA.

62. "Subject: U.S.-EU Summit in Berlin," cable USEU B-08113, July 20, 1994, FOIA M-2017-11621, SDA.

63. See Kimberly Marten, "NATO Enlargement: Evaluating Its Consequences in Russia," in Goldgeier and Shifrinson, *Evaluating NATO Enlargement*, 209–49.

64. Clinton and Kohl, memcon, December 5, 1994, CL, https://clinton.presidentialli braries.us/items/show/101377.

65. "Subject: EU preoccupied with Russia and Eastern Europe in Van den Broek-Talbott Talk," cable Brussels-04339, April 18, 1994, FOIA F-2017-13804, SDA.

66. See Alan Cowell, "Russia and European Union Sign Accord for Free Trade," *New York Times*, June 25, 1994, https://www.nytimes.com/1994/06/25/world /russia-and-european-union-sign-accord-for-free-trade.html.

67. Yeltsin's Address, excerpts, Athens News Agency Bulletin, Hellenic Resources Network, June 25, 1994, http://www.hri.org/news/greek/ana/1994/94-06-25.ana.txt.

68. Delors and Yeltsin, memcon, May 30, 1992, JD-1662, Jacques Delors Papers, HAEU.

69. See Carl Bildt, "Russia, the European Union, and the Eastern Partnership," European Council of Foreign Relations, April 14, 2015, https://ecfr.eu/archive /page/-/Riga_papers_Carl_Bildt.pdf.

70. See "European Security Architecture: The Second Track," drafted by Holbrooke's Deputy John Kornblum, October 7, 1994, PREM 19/5117, 82–89, UK National Archives.

71. Christopher to Clinton, "Night Note," memo, October 20, 1994, FOIA M-2017-12050, SDA.

72. Jonathan Dean, "OSCE and NATO: Complementary or Competitive Security Providers for Europe," *OSCE Yearbook 1999* (Nomos, 2000), 429–34.

73. Talbott to Holbrooke, "Finland and European Security," memo, August 14, 1995, FOIA FL-2017-13804, SDA.

74. Talbott to Holbrooke, "Finland and European Security."

75. Talbott to Clinton, note November 7, 1994, FOIA F-2017-13804, SDA. See also Goldgeier, *Not Whether but When*, 84–93; Goldgeier and McFaul, *Power and Purpose*, 189–97; Sarotte, *Not One Inch*, 201–10.

76. Yeltsin to Clinton, letter, November 2, 1994, FOIA F-2017-13804, SDA.

77. Communiqué NATO M-NAC-2(94)116, issued at the Ministerial Meeting of the North Atlantic Council, NATO Headquarters, Brussels, December 1, 1994, https://www.nato.int/docu/comm/49-95/c941201a.htm.

78. Clinton to Yeltsin, letter, November 28, 1994, FOIA F-2017-13804, SDA. The Clinton-Yeltsin correspondence of 1994 is also available at the Clinton Library. See 2015-0815-M-2, Declassified Documents Concerning Russian President Boris Yeltsin, https://clinton.presidentiallibraries.us/items/show /118450.

79. Talbott, *Russia Hand*, 140.

80. See Svetlana Savranskaya and Tom Blanton, eds., "NATO Expansion. The Budapest Blow Up 1994," Briefing Book no. 780, November 24, 2021, National Security Archive, https://nsarchive.gwu.edu/briefing-book/nato-russia-russia -programs/2021-11-24/nato-expansion-budapest-blow-1994.

81. Clinton to Yeltsin, letter, December 2, 1994, FOIA F-2017-13804, SDA.

82. Yeltsin to Clinton, letter, December 3, 1994, FOIA F-2017-13804, SDA. For a file on the Clinton-Yeltsin correspondence in 1994, see "Declassified Documents Concerning Russian President Boris Yeltsin," CL, https://clinton .presidentiallibraries.us/items/show/118450.

83. "Remarks to the Conference on Security and Cooperation in Europe in Budapest, Hungary," December 5, 1994, https://www.govinfo.gov/content/pkg/PPP -1994-book2/pdf/PPP-1994-book2-doc-pg2144.pdf.

84. Talbott, *Russia Hand*, 136.

85. Talbott to Fuerth, memo, December 9, 1994, Talbott Diaries, 8:77.

86. See Major and Yeltsin, memcon, December 5, 1994, PREM 19/4970, UK National Archives.

87. Talbott to Fuerth, memo, December 9, 1994, Talbott Diaries, 8:80.

88. Talbott to Christopher, memo, December 5, 1994, FOIA F-2017-13804, SDA.

89. Notes, December 13, 1994, Talbott Diaries, 8:100.

90. Notes, December 13, 1994, Talbott Diaries, 8:101.

91. Talbott to Mamedov, letter, December 12, 1994, FOIA F-2017-13804, SDA.

92. Talbott to Christopher, "Dealing with Russia," memo, December 11, 1994, FOIA F-2017-13804, SDA.

93. Talbott to Christopher, "Dealing with Russia,"

94. Clinton for Yeltsin, letter, December 12, 1994, FOIA F-2017-13804, SDA.

95. Notes, December 14, 1994, Talbott Diaries, 8:102.

96. "Gore Debrief on One-on-One w/Yeltsin," December 15, 1994, Talbott Diaries, 8:109.

97. "Gore Debrief on One-on-One w/Yeltsin," 8:111.

98. "Subject: Talbott: Ryurikov Meeting," cable Moscow-26164, December 12, 1994, FOIA F-2017-13804, SDA.

99. "Questions to Address re: Russia/NATO from ST/GEM Conversation," memo, December 15, 1994, Talbott Diaries, 8:113.

100. See "Questions to Address."

101. Goldgeier and McFaul, *Power and Purpose*, 156; see Michael McFaul, "Eurasia Letter, Russian Politics after Chechnya," *Foreign Policy* 99 (1995): 149–165.

102. Kohl and Walesa, memcon, March 11, 1995, Wilson Center Archive, https:// digitalarchive.wilsoncenter.org/document/chancellors-helmut-kohls-meeting -polish-president-walesa-copenhagen-11-march-1995.

103. Talbott to Christopher, memo, December 18, 1994, Talbott Diaries, 8:119. The passage is quoted from this "longer and entirely private version" of a memo that Talbott put into the official State Department system on December 19, 1994. See Talbott to Christopher, "The Vice President's Trip to Russia," memo, December 19, 1994, FOIA F-2017-13804, SDA.

104. Talbott to Christopher, "Subject: Your meeting with Kozyrev," memo, January 16, 1995, Talbott Diaries, 9:47.

105. William J. Clinton, "Remarks in Cleveland, Ohio, at the White House Conference on Trade and Investment in Central and Eastern Europe, January 13, 1995," https://www.govinfo.gov/content/pkg/PPP-1995-book1/pdf/PPP-1995-book1 -doc-pg41.pdf.

106. See Michael Beschloss, "Midterm Melancholy," *The New Yorker*, November 6, 1994, https://www.newyorker.com/magazine/1994/11/14/midterm-melancholy.

107. See Julian Zelizer, *Burning Down the House: Newt Gingrich, the Fall of a Speaker, and the Rise of the New Republican Party* (Penguin, 2020).

108. Talbott to Clinton, letter, November 27, 1994, Talbott Diaries, 8:65.

109. Talbott to Clinton, letter, November 27, 1994, Talbott Diaries, 8:62.

110. Clinton, Gonzalez, Santer, memcon, December 3, 1995, CL, https://clinton .presidentiallibraries.us/items/show/118881.

111. For context, see Richard Holbrooke, "America: A European Power," *Foreign Affairs* 7, no. 2 (April 1995): 38–51; Robert Art, "Why Western Europe Needs the United States and NATO," *Political Science Quarterly* 111, no. 1 (1996): 1–39.

112. Clinton and Kohl, memcon, February 9, 1995, CL, https://clinton.presidentialli braries.us/items/show/101409.

113. James Collins, interview, "The Ambassadorial Series. Deans of U.S.-Russia Diplomacy," Middlebury Institute of International Studies, January 24, 2022, https://nsarchive.gwu.edu/document/27387-transcript-ambassador-james-f-coll.

114. Talbott and Mamedov, "Mamedov-ST 1-on-1, Brussels, Jan 10, 1500–1800," memcon, January 10, 1995, FOIA FL-2017-13804, SDA.

115. Talbott to Christopher "Preparing for Geneva," memo, January 12, 1995, FOIA M-2017-11914, SDA.

116. Asmus, *Opening NATO's Door*, 108.

117. Kozyrev discussed the desiderata in a meeting with Hurd in February 1995. See Hurd and Kozyrev, memcon, February 14, PREM 19/5473, UK National Archives.

118. Talbott to Christopher, memo, March 24, 1995, Talbott Diaries, 10:51.

119. Talbott to Christopher, memo, March 24, 1995, Talbott Diaries, 10:47.

120. Notes, March 16, 1995, Talbott Diaries, 10:38.

121. Notes, February 21, 1995, Talbott Diaries, 10:20.

122. Notes, April 20, 1995, Talbott Diaries, 11:14.

123. Notes, April 20, 1995, Talbott Diaries, 11:15.

124. See Talbott to Clinton, "The Moment of Truth," memo, April 15, 1995, FOIA F-2017-13804, SDA, https://policymemos.hks.harvard.edu/files/policymemos/files/alex_dubin_memo_talbot_to_clinton_moscow.pdf?m=1655903361.

125. "Subject: Mail Call—My Lunch with Andrei," cable Moscow-11782, April 10, 1995, FOIA F-2017-13804, SDA.

126. "Subject: Official-Informal, No. 98," cable State-104841, April 28, FOIA M-2017-11863, SDA.

127. Notes, April 24, 1995, Talbott Diaries, 11:18.

128. Talbott to Christopher, "Re: Kozyrev in New York," memo, April 26, 1995, Talbott Diaries, 11:19.

129. "Subject: Secretary Christopher's Meeting with Andrei Kozyrev, 26 April 1995," cable State-106418, May 1, 1995, 2015-0792-M, CL.

130. Clinton and Yeltsin, telcon, April 27, 1995, CL, https://clinton.presidentialli braries.us/items/show/101422.

131. Talbott, *Russia Hand*, 157–58.

132. Talbott, *Russia Hand*, 158.

133. Notes, May 2, 1995, Talbott Diaries, 11:45.

134. Clinton and Yeltsin, memcon, May 10, 1995, CL, https://clinton.presidentialli braries.us/items/show/57568. For context, see Sergey Radchenko, "'Nothing but Humiliation for Russia:' Moscow and NATO's Eastern Enlargement, 1993–1995," *Journal of Strategic Studies* 43, no. 6 (2020): 769–815; Vladislav Zubok, "Myths and Realities of Putinism and NATO Expansion," in Goldgeier and Shifrinson, *Evaluating NATO Enlargement*, 145–59.

135. Clinton and Yeltsin, memcon, May 10, 1995.

136. Talbott and Mamedov, "Talbott-Mamedov Meeting in Buenos Aires on the Margins of the Menem Inaugural," memcon, July 9, 1995, FOIA F-2017-13804, SDA.

137. Notes, May 10, 1995, Talbott Diaries, 11:69.

138. Clinton and Yeltsin, memcon, June 17, 1995, CL, https://clinton.presidentialli braries.us/items/show/101432.

139. Notes, "Highlights from Mamedov Talks: Strategic Stability Talks, 20–22 September 1995," n.d., Talbott Diaries, 14:1.

140. See Ivo Daalder, *Getting to Dayton: The Making of America's Bosnia Policy* (Brookings Institution Press, 1999); Derek Chollet, *The Secret History of Dayton: A Study of American Statecraft* (Palgrave MacMillan, 2005), 1–24, https://nsarchive2.gwu.edu/NSAEBB/NSAEBB171/.

141. "Subject: Russian Ambassador Churkin on NATO Bombing," cable U.S. NATO-03531, September 10, 1995, FOIA F-2007-5000, SDA.

142. See Leontiy Shevtsov, "Russian-NATO Military Cooperation in Bosnia: A Basis for the Future?" *NATO Review* 45, no. 2 (1997): 17–21. See "Lessons and Conclusions on the Execution of IFOR Operations and Prospects for a Future Combined

Security System: The Peace and Stability of Europe after IFOR," Joint US/Russian Research Project of the Foreign Military Studies Office in Kansas and the Center for Military-Strategic Studies in Moscow, November 2000, https://apps .dtic.mil/sti/tr/pdf/ADA434985.pdf.

143. Talbott to Christopher, "Kozyrev Meeting," memo, September 15, 1995, FOIA F-2017-13804, SDA; Talbott to Mamedov, letter, October 14, 1995, FOIA F-2017-13804, SDA.

144. Coit Blacker, author interview, March 2024.

145. Clinton and Yeltsin, "Clinton-Yeltsin One-on-One," memcon, October 23, 1995, CL, https://clinton.presidentiallibraries.us/items/show/101419.

146. Strobe Talbott, "Strengthening American Security Through World Leadership: Bosnia and Beyond," remarks at the State Department Town Meeting, Washington, DC, November 1, 1995, https://1997-2001.state.gov/regions/eur/bosnia/bostal .html.

147. Daniel Hamilton, author correspondence, September 2024.

148. Notes, November 14, 1995, Talbott Diaries, 14:65.

149. See András Simonyi, "NATO Enlargement: Like Free Solo Climbing," in Hamilton and Spohr, *Open Door*, 159–71, https://transatlanticrelations.org/wp -content/uploads/2019/04/07-Simonyi.pdf

150. See Talbott to Christopher, memo, December 14, 1995, FOIA FL-2017-13804, SDA.

151. See Carl Bildt, *Peace Journey: The Struggle for Peace in Bosnia* (Weidenfeld & Nicholson, 1999).

152. See Robert H. Frowick, "The OSCE Mission to Bosnia and Herzegovina," *OSCE-Yearbook 1995/1996* (Nomos, 1997), 163–74, https://ifsh.de/file-CORE /documents/yearbook/english/95_96/Frowick.pdf.

3. Building a New Security Architecture

1. See Richard Holbrooke, "America: A European Power," *Foreign Affairs* 74, no. 2 (1995): 39.

2. See Daniel Hamilton, "Piece of the Puzzle: NATO and Euro-Atlantic Architecture After the Cold War, in *Open Door: NATO and Euro-Atlantic Security After the Cold War*, ed. Daniel Hamilton and Kristina Spohr (Brookings Institution Press, 2019), 25, https://transatlanticrelations.org/publications/open-door -nato-and-euro-atlantic-security-after-the-cold-war/.

3. See Hamilton, "Piece of the Puzzle," 29.

4. See William J. Perry, "The Enduring Dynamic Relationship That Is NATO," remarks to the Wehrkunde Conference on Security Policy, Munich, Germany, February 5, 1995; see James Goldgeier, *Not Whether but When: The U.S. Decision to Enlarge NATO* (Brookings Institution Press, 1999), 94–95; Ronald

Asmus, *Opening NATO's Door: How the Alliance Remade Itself for a New Era* (Columbia University Press, 2002), 108–9; Mary E. Sarotte, *Not One Inch: America, Russia, and the Making of the Post-Cold War Stalemate* (Yale University Press, 2021), 208.

5. Richard C. Holbrooke, "Europe Must Avoid Being Held Prisoner by Its History," remarks before the North Atlantic Assembly, Budapest, Hungary, May 29, 1995, https://permanent.access.gpo.gov/gpo41448/dispatch/1995/html/Dispatchv6no26 .html.

6. Holbrooke, "Europe Must Avoid."

7. John Kornblum, "New European Security Architecture," USIA Foreign Press Center Briefing, January 24, 1995, quoted in Hamilton, "Piece of the Puzzle," 25–26.

8. "Subject: Memorandum of Conversation between President Clinton and Georgian President Shevardnadze," cable State-142390, July 18, 1997, Freedom of Information Act Case no. (FOIA) M-2017-11613, U.S. State Department Archives (SDA).

9. "Subject: Deputy Secretary Talbott's Meeting with Moldovan President Snegur and Foreign Minister Popov," cable State-276139, October 12, 1994, FOIA F-2017-13804, SDA. For an in-depth account, see William Hill, *Russia, the Near Abroad, and the West: Lessons from the Moldova-Transdniestria Conflict* (Johns Hopkins University Press, 2012).

10. For context, see Thomas de Waal, *Black Garden. Armenia and Azerbaijan through Peace and War* (New York University Press, 2003). See Bradley Reynolds, *Alternating Visions of Europe's Post-Cold War Security Architecture: Finnish, American, and Russian Peace Mediation in Nagorno-Karabakh 1995–1997* (PhD diss., University of Helsinki).

11. "Subject: Talbott/Berger Delegation Meets with Ter-Petrossian," cable Yereva-01109, March 27, 1996, FOIA F-2017-13804, SDA.

12. See "Subject: Israeli Ambassador Rabinovich-Talbott Meeting: Israeli Proposal for Israeli-Turkish-U.S. Cooperation in the CIS," cable State-130416, May 17, 1994, FOIA F-2017-13804, SDA.

13. See Zbigniew Brzezinski, "A Geostrategy for Eurasia," *Foreign Affairs* 76, no. 5 (1997); Sabri Sayari, "Turkish Foreign Policy in the Post-Cold War Era: The Challenges of Multi-Regionalism," *Journal of International Affairs* 54, no. 1 (2000): 169–82.

14. Strobe Talbott, "Remarks to the U.S.-EU Conference 'Bridging the Atlantic: People-to-People Links,' " Washington, DC, May 6, 1997, SDA, https://1997 -2001.state.gov/regions/eur/eu/970506.html.

15. Strobe Talbott, "U.S.-Turkish Leadership in the post-Cold War World," remarks at Bilkent University, Ankara, April 11, 1995, FOIA FL-2017-13804, SDA.

16. "Subject: Official-Informal," cable Ankara-02802, March 16, 1996, FOIA F-2017-13804, SDA.

17. "Subject: Deputy Secretary Talbott's Meeting with Prime Minister Yilmaz," cable Ankara-3124, March 26, 1996, FOIA F-2017-13804, SDA.

18. Strobe Talbott, "Why NATO Should Grow," *New York Review of Books*, August 10, 1995, https://www.nybooks.com/articles/1995/08/10/why-nato-should -grow/. A reprinted PDF copy is available in FOIA F-2017-13804, SDA.

19. Onyszkiewicz quoted in Talbott, "Why NATO Should Grow."

20. Talbott, "Why NATO Should Grow."

21. See "Study on Enlargement," September 3, 1995, https://www.nato.int/cps/en /natohq/official_texts_24733.htm. See Lake to Clinton, "European Security/ NATO Enlargement Progress Report," memo, July 17, 1995, 2015-0772-M, CL.

22. See Charles Kupchan, "Reviving the West," *Foreign Affairs* 75, no. 3 (1996): 92–104.

23. See Stephen Sestanovich, "Geotherapy: Russia's Neuroses, and Ours," *The National Interest* 45 (1996): 3–13.

24. See "NATO-Russia: Objectives, Obstacles and Work Plan," memo, July 29, 1996, FOIA F-2017-13804, SDA. The memo was known as the Talbott bible. See Asmus, *Opening NATO's Door*, 171; Fried, Pifer, and Vershbow to Lake, "NATO Enlargement Game Plan: June 96 to June 97," memo, June 6, 1996, 2015-0770-M, CL.

25. Memo, July 9, 1996, Talbott Diaries, 18:36.

26. See Asmus, *Opening NATO's Door*, 169–72.

27. See Eugene Rumor, "The Primakov (Not Gerasimov) Doctrine in Action," Carnegie Endowment for International Peace, June 5, 2019, https://carnegieen dowment.org/2019/06/05/primakov-not-gerasimov-doctrine-in-action-pub -79254.

28. Strobe Talbott, *The Russia Hand: A Memoir of Presidential Diplomacy* (Random House, 2002), 194; Talbott to Christopher, note, March 16, 1996, FOIA FL-2017-13804, SDA.

29. Christopher and Primakov, "Subject: Official Informal," memcon, Moscow-08810, April 1, 1996, FOIA F-2017-13804, SDA.

30. See Talbott and Primakov, memcon, July 16, 1996, FOIA M-2017-11926, SDA.

31. Talbott and Primakov, memcon, July 16, 1996.

32. Talbott and Primakov, memcon, July 16, 1996.

33. Notes, February 21, 1996, Talbott Diaries, 16:43.

34. Notes, March 29, 1996, Talbott Diaries, 17:4.

35. Talbott, *Russia Hand*, 196.

36. "Yeltsin-Talbott Meeting, April 11, 1996," cable Moscow-10123, April 12, 1996, FOIA F-2017-13804, SDA.

37. Talbott, *Russia Hand*, 196.

38. "Yeltsin-Talbott Meeting, April 11, 1996"; see Talbott, *Russia Hand*, 196–99.

39. Clinton and Kohl, telcon, April 12, 1996, CL, https://clinton.presidentiallibraries .us/items/show/101450.

40. Kohl and Clinton, telcon, March 5, 1997, CL, https://clinton.presidentiallibraries .us/items/show/101474.

41. "Yeltsin-Talbott Meeting," April 11, 1996.

42. See Talbott, *Russia Hand*, 200–1.

43. Notes, April 19, 1996, Talbott Diaries, 17:40.

44. Strobe Talbott, interview, PBS Putin Files, June 20, 2017, https://www.pbs.org/wgbh/frontline/interview/strobe-talbott/.

45. Notes, April 20, 1996, Talbott Diaries, 17:42.

46. Notes, June 5, 1996, Talbott Diaries, 17:70.

47. See Clinton and Yeltsin, telcon, July 5, 1996, CL, https://clinton.presidentiallibraries.us/items/show/101457.

48. Talbott to Clinton, note, July 9, 1996, Talbott Diaries, 18:34, 18:35.

49. Strobe Talbott, "Russia in Turbulence and Transition," Amherst College, May 1, 1996, Draft ST, April 28, 1996, FOIA FL-2017-13804, SDA.

50. See Jack F. Matlock, "Dealing with a Russia in Turmoil," *Foreign Affairs* 75, no. 3 (1996): 38–51.

51. Notes, July 16, 1996, Talbott Diaries, 18:56.

52. Talbott and Mamedov, memcon, August 28, 1996, FOIA F-2017-13804, SDA.

53. Talbott and Mamedov, memcon, September 11, 1996, FOIA F-2017-13804, SDA.

54. William J. Clinton, "Remarks to the Community in Detroit," October 22, 1996, https://www.govinfo.gov/content/pkg/PPP-1996-book2/pdf/PPP-1996-book2-doc-pg1890.pdf.

55. Hamilton, "Piece of the Puzzle," 46.

56. Warren Christopher, "A New Atlantic Community. For the 21st Century," speech in Commemoration of Secretary of State James Byrnes' 1946 Speech of Hope, State Theater Stuttgart, September 6, 1996, printed in Warren Christopher, *In the Stream of History: Shaping U.S. Foreign Policy for a New Era* (Stanford University Press, 1998), 456–66, https://usa.usembassy.de/etexts/ga7-960906.htm.

57. Christopher, "New Atlantic Community."

58. See Joseph Harahan and John Kuhn III, *On-Site Inspections Under the CFE Treaty: A History of the On-Site Inspection Agency and CFE Treaty Implementation, 1990–1996*, U.S. Department of Defense, 1996, https://www.dtra.mil/Portals/125/Documents/History/On-Site-Inspections-CFE-Treaty-final.pdf.

59. Talbott, *Russia Hand*, 450n20. See Sarotte, *Not One Inch*, 278. For a good summary on CFE, see Christopher to Clinton, "Your Meeting with Yeltsin in Halifax," memo, June 12, 1995, FOIA F-2017-13804, SDA.

60. Talbott to Mamedov, letter, February 28, 1997, FOIA FL-2017-13804, SDA.

61. Talbott to Christopher, memo, September 24, 1996, FOIA FL-2017-13804, SDA.

62. Talbott to Christopher, memo, September 24, 1996.

63. Collins and Mamedov, "JFC/GEM Conversation September 25, 1996, JFC suite, Waldorf Astoria Hotel, NYC," memcon, September 26, 1996, FOIA F-2017-13804, SDA.

64. Christopher, Talbott, Primakov, and Mamedov, memcon, September 24, 1996, FOIA F-2017-13804, SDA.

65. Notes, January 9, 1997, Talbott Diaries, 21:2.

66. See Ronald Asmus and Stephen Larrabee, "NATO and the Have-Nots: Reassurance after Enlargement," *Foreign Affairs* 75, no. 6 (1996): 13–20.

67. See Serhii Plokhy, *The Russo-Ukrainian War. The Return of History* (W. W. Norton, 2023).

68. See Richard Pipes, "Is Russia Still an Enemy?" *Foreign Affairs* 7, no. 5 (1997): 65–78.

69. See James Sherr, "Russia and Ukraine," Seminar on Russia and the NIS, Ankara, Turkey: Ministry of Foreign Affairs Center for Strategic Research, 1996, SAM Papers No. 1, quoted in Stephen Blank, "NATO Enlargement and the Baltic States: What Can the Great Powers Do?" ETH Zürich, November 18, 1997, https://www.files.ethz.ch/isn/47654/NATO_Enlargement_Baltic.pdf. See James Sherr, *Hard Diplomacy and Soft Coercion: Russia's Influence Abroad* (Chatham House, 2013).

70. Pifer, *The Eagle and the Trident*, 91.

71. Talbott to Christopher, memo, October 17, 1993, sent by telegram to Christopher's team in Moscow, "Subject: Official-Informal—U/S Davis," cable State-317538, October 19, 1993, FOIA M-2017-11814, SDA. See also Talbott, *Russia Hand*, 99–101.

72. "Subject: Deputy Secretary's Meeting with Ukrainian Ambassador Shcherbak," cable State-226962, September 22, 1995, FOIA F-2017-13804, SDA.

73. Notes on Christopher and Kozyrev, memcon, April 27, 1995, Talbott Diaries, 11:43.

74. See John Edwin Mroz and Oleksandr Pavliuk, "Ukraine: Europe's Linchpin," *Foreign Affairs* 75, no. 3 (1996): 52–62.

75. "Subject: Ukraine FM Udovenko's Meeting with Amb. Collins," cable State-39315, February 28, 1996, FOIA F-2017-13804, SDA.

76. "Subject: DFM Tarasyuk Discusses PFP, GOU Internal Problems," cable Kyiv-001752, March 6, 1995, 2015-0792-M, CL.

77. Udovenko to Christopher, letter, August 28, 1996, FOIA M-2017-11877, SDA.

78. "Subject: Deputy Secretary's 9/16 and 9/19 Meetings with Ukrainian NSDC Secretary Horbulyn," cable State-205479, October 2, 1996, FOIA F-2017-13804, SDA.

79. See John Beyrle, "The Long Good-Bye: The Withdrawal of Russian Military Forces from the Baltic States," Institute for the Study of Diplomacy, Edmund A. Walsh School of Foreign Service, Georgetown University, 1996, https://apps.dtic.mil/sti/tr/pdf/ADA441390.pdf.

80. "Subject: Russian Troop Withdrawals: Estonian FM Luik's Meeting with the Deputy Secretary," cable State-181039, July 8, 1994, FOIA F-2017-13804, SDA.

81. "Subject: Ambassador Strobe Talbott's Visit to Estonia," cable Tallin-00868, May 17, 1993, FOIA M-2017-12156, SDA.

82. See Kristina Spohr, *Germany and the Baltic Problem After the Cold War: The Development of a New Ostpolitik, 1989–2000* (Taylor & Francis, 1997); Una Bergmane,

Politics of Uncertainty: The United States, the Baltic Question, and the Collapse of the Soviet Union (Oxford University Press, 2023).

83. Delors and Meri, memcon, November 26, 1992, JD-1490, Jacques Delors Papers, Historical Archives of the European Union (HAEU). Toomas Ilves, author interview, March 2024.

84. See Kohl and Presidents Gorbunov, Rüütel and Landsbergis, memcon, June 11, 1992, Wilson Center Archive, https://digitalarchive.wilsoncenter.org/document /chancellors-helmut-kohls-meeting-presidents-latvia-estonia-and-lithuania -margins-unced; Darius Furmonavicius, *Lithuania Transforms the West: Lithuania's Liberation from Soviet Occupation and the Enlargement of NATO (1988–2022)* (Ibidem Press, 2023).

85. See Andres Kasekamp, "An Uncertain Journey to the Promised Land: The Baltic States' Road to NATO Membership," *Journal of Strategic Studies* 43, no. 6–7 (2020): 869–96; Andris Banka, "The Breakaways: A Retrospective on the Baltic Road to NATO," *War on the Rocks*, October 4, 2019, https://warontherocks.com /2019/10/the-breakaways-a-retrospective-on-the-baltic-road-to-nato/.

86. Vitalijus Vaiksnoras, "The Role of Baltic Defence Co-operation for the Security of Estonia, Latvia and Lithuania," NATO Individual Fellowship Report 2000–2002, https://www.nato.int/acad/fellow/99-01/vaisknoro.pdf.

87. See Tony Lawrence and Tomas Jermalavičius, eds., *Apprenticeship, Partnership, Membership: Twenty Years of Defence Development in the Baltic States* (International Centre for Defence Studies, 2013), https://icds.ee/wp-content/uploads/2018/05 /RKK_Apprenticeship__Partnership__Membership_WWW.pdf.

88. "Subject: Baltic Security Issues. Deputy Secretary's June 27 Meeting with Baltic Embassy Representatives," cable State-161570, July 6, 1995, FOIA F-2017-13804, SDA.

89. See Edward Rhodes, "The American Vision of Baltic Security Architecture: Understanding the Northern Europe Initiative," *Baltic Defense Review* 4 (2000): 91–112, https://www.baltdefcol.org/files/docs/bdreview/06bdr200.pdf. Mark Kramer, "NATO, the Baltic States and Russia: A Framework for Sustainable Enlargement," *International Affairs* 78, no. 4 (2002): 731–56.

90. "Subject: Acting Secretary Talbott's Sept. 1 Meeting with Estonian P.M. Vahi: Focus on Russia and Security Concerns," cable State-219976, September 15, 1995, FOIA F-2017-13804, SDA.

91. "Subject: The Deputy Secretary's Meeting with Estonian Foreign Minister Kallas, March 25," cable State-77946, April 16, 1996, FOIA F-2017-13804, SDA.

92. "Subject: Acting Secretary Briefs Baltics on Action Plan," cable State-186058, September 7, 1996, FOIA F-2017-13804, SDA.

93. See Hamilton, "Piece of the Puzzle," 42.

94. See Asmus, *Opening NATO's Door*, 158–163.

95. Clinton, Ulmanis, Brazauskas, Meri, memcon, June 25, 1996, CL, https:// clinton.presidentiallibraries.us/items/show/101467.

96. "Subject: Acting Secretary and Lithuanian Fonmin on NATO Enlargement,"
cable State-225177, October 29, 1996, FOIA F-2017-13804, SDA.

97. See John C. Roper, "Perry: Baltic states not ready for NATO," UPI Archives,
October 6, 1996, https://www.upi.com/Archives/1996/10/06/Perry-Baltic-sta
tes-not-ready-for-NATO/7720844574400/.

98. See Ronald Asmus and Robert Nurick, "NATO Enlargement and the Baltic
States," *Survival* 38, no. 2 (1996): 121–42; Robert Nurick and Per Carlsen, author
interviews.

99. Asmus to Talbott, "The Hanseatic Strategy," memo, July 20, 1997, FOIA
M-2017-11994, SDA. The Hanseatic strategy idea came from Deputy Assistant
Secretary of State for European Affairs Ronald Asmus, Derek Shearer (the U.S.
ambassador in Helsinki), and Eric Edelman, Talbott's executive assistant. See
Asmus, *Opening NATO's Door*, 230.

100. Strobe Talbott, "A Baltic Home-Coming," Robert C. Frasure Memorial Lecture, Tallinn, Estonia, January 24, 2000, SDA, https://1997-2001.state.gov/policy
_remarks/2000/000124_talbott_tallinn.html.

101. Talbott, "Baltic Home-Coming."

102. See Daniel Hamilton, "New Members, New Missions: NATO and Euro-
Atlantic Architecture in the Second Clinton Administration," in Hamilton and
Spohr, *Open Door*, 339–84, https://transatlanticrelations.org/wp-content/up
loads/2019/04/15-Hamilton2.pdf.

103. Bureau of European Affairs, "Overview of the Northern Europe Initiative," fact
sheet, U.S. Department of State, May 1, 2000, https://1997-2001.state.gov/regions
/eur/nei/fs_000501_nei.html.

104. Clinton, Gore, Meri, Brazauskas, Ulmanis, memcon, January 16, 1998, CL,
https://clinton.presidentiallibraries.us/items/show/118565.

105. Kalnins to Talbott and Asmus, "RE: Left standing at the altar by the EC," memo,
July 24, 1997, sent as an attachment to Talbott to Asmus, note, July 29, 1997,
FOIA FL-2017-13804, SDA.

106. Notes, August 16, 1996, Talbott Diaries, 18:76, 18:77.

107. Talbott to Nelson Talbott, letter, November 8, 1996, Talbott Diaries, 20:1.

108. Talbott to Nelson Talbott, November 8, 1996.

109. Notes, November 8, 1996, Talbott Diaries, 20:7.

110. Eric Edelman, author interview, May 2024.

111. Notes, November 8, 1996, Talbott Diaries, 20:4.

112. Notes, November 8, 1996.

113. Notes, November 8, 1996, Talbott Diaries, 20:4–5.

114. Notes, November 8, 1996, Talbott Diaries, 20:6.

115. Talbott to Clinton, letter, November 11, 1996, Talbott Diaries, 20:9.

116. Notes, November 14, 1996, Talbott Diaries, 20:13.

117. Talbott to Berger, letter, November 16, 1996, Talbott Diaries, 20:16.

118. Notes, November 16, 1996, Talbott Diaries 20:21.

119. See Notes, December 4, 5, 1996, Talbott Diaries, 20:32, 20:40–41.

120. See Madeleine Albright, *Hell and Other Destinations: A 21st-Century Memoir* (Harper Collins 2020).

121. Madeleine Albright, *Madam Secretary: A Memoir* (Harper Perennial, 2003), 252; "The Testing of American Foreign Policy," *Foreign Affairs* 77, no. 6 (1998): 50–64.

4. The NATO-Russia Founding Act and Its Aftermath

1. Clinton and Kohl, telcon, September 10, 1996, Clinton Library (CL), https://clinton.presidentiallibraries.us/items/show/101452.

2. See Final Communiqué, issued at the North Atlantic Council Ministerial Meeting, held at NATO Headquarters, Brussels, December 10, 1996, https://www.nato.int/docu/pr/1996/p96-165e.htm; see also Ronald Asmus, *Opening NATO's Door: How the Alliance Remade Itself for a New Era* (Columbia University Press, 2002), 195.

3. Gore and Chernomyrdin, memcon, December 2, 1996, Freedom of Information Act Case No. (FOIA) F-2017-13804, U.S. Department of State Archives (SDA).

4. Talbott and Primakov, memcon, December 4, 1996, FOIA-F-2017-13804, SDA.

5. Talbott and Primakov, memcon, December 4, 1996.

6. "NAC Ministerial 16-plus-1 session with Russian Foreign Minister Primakov, NATO Headquarters, Brussels, Belgium," cable Secto-260007, December 11, 1996, FOIA M-2017-11708, SDA.

7. Holmes for Chilcott, "Lisbon Summit. Bilateral with Chernomyrdin [on December 2, 1996]," note, December 3, 1996, PREM 19/6243, UK National Archives.

8. See Strobe Talbott, *The Russia Hand: A Memoir of Presidential Diplomacy* (Random House, 2002), 224–26; see "Subject: Memorandum of Conversation Between Vice President Gorge and French President Jacques Chirac," cable WhiteHouse-92239, January 9, 1997, FOIA F-2017-13804, SDA.

9. Talbott and Chirac, memcon, January 14, 1997, Talbott Diaries, 21:23.

10. Talbott and Kohl, memcon, January 15, 1997, FOIA F-2017-13804, SDA.

11. Talbott, *Russia Hand*, 228.

12. Solana and Primakov, memcon, January 20, 1997, PREM 19/6144, UK National Archives; Solana, author interview.

13. See "Agreed Statement by the Secretary General of NATO and the Foreign Minister of Russia on the Visit of the Secretary-General to Moscow," NATO press release 97/8, January 20, 1997, https://www.nato.int/docu/pr/1997/p97-008e.htm.

14. Talbott and Primakov, memcon, January 26, 1997, FOIA F-2017-13804, SDA.

15. "Subject: NATO-Russia: Deputy Secretary Talbott Briefs NATO Permreps, January 13," cable USNATO-173, January 23, 1997, FOIA F-2017-13804, SDA.

16. Notes, February 5, 1997, Talbott Diaries, 22:2.

17. Clinton and Chernomyrdin, memcon, February 7, 1997, CL, https://clinton
.presidentiallibraries.us/items/show/101489.

18. "Cabinet Room, POTUS/VP Session on MKA Trip," February 12, 1997, Talbott Diaries, 22:15.

19. Talbott to Albright, "Urgent Priority. Secure Fax to Secretary Albright's Aircraft," memo, n.d., Talbott Diaries, 22:23.

20. Talbott and Pifer to Berger, Steinberg, and Fuerth, "Subject: The Prospects for Helsinki—and Beyond," memo, February 22, 1997, Talbott Diaries, 22:25.

21. Albright and Yeltsin, memcon, February 20, 1997, FOIA F-2017-13804, SDA.

22. Solana and Primakov, memcon, February 23, 1997, PREM 19/6145, UK National Archives.

23. Talbott to Albright, memo, March 5, 1997, Talbott Diaries, 22:45.

24. Portillo and Solana, memcon, March 4, 1997, PREM 19/6145, UK National Archives.

25. Asmus, *Opening NATO's Door*, 196; notes, "potentially important moment at lunch w/ solana & team at nato hq," March 5, 1997, Talbott Diaries, 22:42, 22:43.

26. See Alexander Vershbow, "Present at the Transformation: An Insider's Reflection on NATO Enlargement, NATO-Russia Relations, and Where We Go from Here," in *Open Door: NATO and Euro-Atlantic Security After the Cold War*, ed. Daniel Hamilton and Kristina Spohr (Brookings Institution Press, 2019), 435–36.

27. See Sten Rynning, "The False Promise of Continental Concert: Russia, the West and the Necessary Balance of Power," *International Affairs* 91, no. 3 (2015): 543, https://www.chathamhouse.org/sites/default/files/field/field_document/IN TA91_3_05_Rynning.pdf.

28. See Alexander Lanoszka, Christian Leuprecht, and Alexander Moens, "Lessons from the Enhanced Forward Presence, 2017–2020," NATO Defense College Research Paper, November 30, 2020, https://www.ndc.nato.int/news/news.php ?icode=1504.

29. Lodal to Talbott, memo, March 3, 1997, Talbott Diaries, 22:51.

30. Talbott and Primakov, memcon, March 6, 1997, 1930 hours, FOIA F-2017-13804, SDA.

31. Talbott and Primakov, memcon, March 6, 1997.

32. See "Statement on NATO's Conventional Force," Telno 116 UKDEL NATO to FCO, March 14, 1997, PREM 19/6146, UK National Archives.

33. Notes, March 10, 1997, Talbott Diaries, 22:87.

34. Notes, March 10, 1997.

35. Talbott to Albright, "Dealing with Central European Anxieties," memo, March 13, 1997, Talbott Diaries, 22:90.

36. George Kennan, "A Fateful Error," *New York Times*, February 1997, 5, https://
www.nytimes.com/1997/02/05/opinion/a-fateful-error.html; see Talbott, *Russia Hand*, 232; for a similarly critical view, see Michael Mandelbaum, *The Dawn of*

Peace in Europe (Twentieth Century Fund Press, 1996); Richard Sakwa, *The Lost Peace: How the West Failed to Prevent a Second Cold War* (Yale University Press, 2023); for an excellent analysis of Kennan's thinking, see Kaarel Piirimäe, "'Geopolitics of Sympathy': George F. Kennan and NATO Enlargement," *Diplomacy & Statecraft*, 35, no. 1 (2024): 182–205.

37. John Lewis Gaddis, *George F. Kennan: An American Life* (Penguin, 2012). Frank Costigliola, *Kennan: A Life Between Worlds* (Princeton University Press, 2023).

38. Talbott to Kennan, letter, February 13, 1997, FOIA FL-2017-13804, SDA; see also George F. Kennan Papers, Box 47, Folder 4, Seeley G. Mudd Library, Princeton University, https://findingaids.princeton.edu/catalog/MC076_c00583.

39. Henry Kissinger, "The Dilution of NATO," June 7, 1997, *Washington Post*, https://www.washingtonpost.com/archive/opinions/1997/06/08/the-dilution-of-nato/dad33a8c-0296-4625-9376-bc0f1013c318/.

40. Talbott notes on Kissinger Piece, n.d., FOIA FL-2017-13804, SDA.

41. Talbott to Albright, "Subject: The NATO-Russia Charter as time-released medicine," memo, March 14, 1997, Talbott Diaries, 22:92.

42. Albright and Primakov, memcon, March 15, 1997, 4:45–5:40 p.m., FOIA F-2017-13804, SDA.

43. Asmus, *Opening NATO's Door*, 198.

44. See Asmus, *Opening NATO's Door*, 199.

45. Clinton and Primakov, memcon, March 17, 1997, FOIA F-2017-13804, SDA.

46. Notes, March 17, 1997, Talbott Diaries, 22:100; Talbott, *Russia Hand*, 236–37.

47. Talbott, *Russia Hand*, 236.

48. Talbott, *Russia Hand*, 237.

49. Clinton and Yeltsin, memcon, April 21, 1996, CL, https://clinton.presidentialli braries.us/items/show/57569.

50. Clinton, Albright, Berger, Talbott, Yeltsin, Primakov, Ryurikov, and Mamedov, memcon, March 21, 1997, CL, https://clinton.presidentiallibraries.us/items /show/101480.

51. Bill Clinton, *My Life* (Arrow Books, 2004), 750.

52. Notes, March 20, 1997, Talbott Diaries, 23:1.

53. "Subject: NATO/Russia: Briefing by Talbott on Helsinki Summit," cable Telno 106 UKDEL NATO to FCO, March 22, 1997, PREM 19/6146, UK National Archives.

54. Notes, March 20, 1997, Talbott Diaries, 23:2.

55. See "Subject: NATO/Russia: Possible Paris Summit," cable Telno 155 UKDEL NATO to FCO, April 10, 1997, PREM 19/6146, UK National Archives.

56. Notes, "ST/MKA to Moscow week of May 2, 1997," April 27, 1997, Talbott Diaries, 23:43.

57. Talbott to Albright, "A Menu of Scenarios for Your May Day in Moscow: The Good, the Bad and the Ugly," memo, April 27, 1997, FOIA F-2017-13804, SDA.

58. Talbott to Albright, "A Menu of Scenarios."

59. Eventually, in 1999, under the revised CFE Treaty, the treaty parties agreed to an increase in the number of ACVs in Russia's revised northern and southern flank areas—from 580 ACVs (plus eight hundred in storage), as laid down in the 1990 CFE Treaty, to 2140 ACVs (without a storage constraint). See Zdzislaw Lachowski, "The Adapted CFE Treaty and the Admission of the Baltic States to NATO," Stockholm International Peace Research Institute, 2002, https://www.sipri.org/publications/2002/adapted-cfe-treaty-and-admission-baltic-states-nato.

60. Notes, April 30, 1997, Talbott Diaries, 23:43.

61. See "Subject: Secretary's Meeting with Russian Foreign Minister Primakov," telegram, USDEL Secretary's Aircraft to SECSTATE Washington, Immediate, May 1, 1997, FOIA F-2017-13804, SDA.

62. "Subject: Secretary's Meeting," May 6, 1997.

63. "Subject: Secretary's Telephone Conversation with Russian President Yeltsin, May 1, 1997, Moscow," cable State-084470, May 6, 1997, FOIA F-2017-13804, SDA.

64. "Subject: The Secretary's Meeting with Russian Foreign Minister Yevgeny Primakov," cable State-86872, May 9, 1997, FOIA F-2017-13804, SDA.

65. "Official-Informal," cable Moscow-11167, May 5, 1997, FOIA F-2013-08489, SDA.

66. Talbott to Mamedov, letter, May 8, 1997, FOIA FL-2017-13804, SDA.

67. Solana to the Permanent Representatives, "Subject: Meeting with the Russian Foreign Minister, Yevgeny Primakov, in Luxembourg," memo, May 7, 1997, PREM 19/149, UK National Archives.

68. "Subject: Acting Secretary's Conversation with Russian Foreign Minister Primakov," telegram, State to Moscow, May 7, 1997, FOIA F-2017-13804, SDA.

69. William J. Clinton, "Remarks on the NATO-Russia Founding Act and an Exchange with Reporters," May 14, 1997, https://www.govinfo.gov/content/pkg/PPP-1997-book1/pdf/PPP-1997-book1-doc-pg598.pdf.

70. "Subject: Official-Informal No. 41," cable State-091726, May 15, 1997, FOIA F-2013-08489, SDA.

71. Helmut Kohl, "Statement," signing ceremony of the NATO-Russia Founding Act, Paris, May 27, 1997, https://www.nato.int/docu/speech/1997/s970527k.htm.

72. Talbott, *Russia Hand*, 246–47; Mary E. Sarotte, *Not One Inch: America, Russia, and the Making of the Post–Cold War Stalemate* (Yale University Press, 2021), 272–73.

73. Boris Yeltin, "Remarks," signing ceremony of the NATO-Russia Founding Act, Paris, May 27, 1997, https://www.nato.int/docu/speech/1997/s970527e.htm.

74. See James E. Goodby, *Europe Undivided: The New Logic of Peace in U.S.-Russian Relations* (United States Institute of Peace Press, 1998), 173.

75. See Goodby, *Europe Undivided*, 179. The principle of collective defense is at the heart of NATO and means that an attack against one ally is considered an attack against all allies. Collective security pertains to the concept of a peaceful community of nations entailing security arrangements for all states in a certain region

in which all members pledge to defend each other against a broader range of potential threats. For the distinction, see Charles A. Kupchan and Clifford A. Kupchan, "Concerts, Collective Security, and the Future of Europe," *International Security* 16, no. 1 (1991): 114–61.

76. Clinton and Yeltsin, memcon, May 27, 1997, CL, https://clinton.presidentialli braries.us/items/show/101492.

77. Asmus, *Opening NATO's Door*, 216; James Goldgeier, *Not Whether but When: The U.S. Decision to Enlarge NATO* (Brookings Institution Press, 1999), 117–22; Sarotte, *Not One Inch*, 277–83.

78. Notes, "Tuesday, May 27 97 Paris, Chirac Potus bilat," Talbott Diaries, 24:1.

79. Blair and Chirac, memcon, June 12, 1997, PREM 49/78, UK National Archives.

80. Blair and Clinton, memcon, May 29, 1997, PREM 49/149, UK National Archives.

81. Clinton and Kohl, telcon, July 3, 1997, CL, https://clinton.presidentiallibraries .us/items/show/101476. Clinton took the decision on June 11. See "Subject: NATO Enlargement—U.S. Decision on New Members," cable State 111475, June 13, 1997, 2015-0771-M, CL.

82. Notes, July 5, 1997, Talbott Diaries, 24:38.

83. Notes, July 5, 1997, Talbott Diaries, 24:39.

84. See "Madrid Declaration on Euro-Atlantic Security and Cooperation. Issued by the Heads of State and Government," July 8, 1997, https://www.nato.int/docu /pr/1997/p97-081e.htm; for a detailed account, see Asmus, *Opening NATO's Door*, 238–48.

85. Notes, July 8, 1997, Talbott Diaries, 24:42.

86. See Daniel Hamilton, "New Members, New Missions: NATO and Euro-Atlantic Architecture in the Second Clinton Administration," in Hamilton and Spohr, *Open Door*, 339–84; Asmus, *Opening NATO's Door*, 248; Sarotte, *Not One Inch*, 271, 288.

87. Strobe Talbott, *The Great Experiment: The Story of Ancient Empires, Modern States, and the Quest for Global Governance* (Simon & Schuster, 2009), 289.

88. Notes, July 9, 1997, Talbott Diaries, 24:45.

89. See Igor Lukes, "Central Europe Has Joined NATO. The Continuing Search for a More Perfect Habsburg Empire," *SAIS Review* 19, no. 2 (1999): 47–59.

90. See North Atlantic Treaty Organization, "Charter on a Distinctive Partnership Between the North Atlantic Treaty Organization and Ukraine," July 9, 1997, https://www.nato.int/cps/en/natohq/official_texts_25457.htm.

91. Clinton and Kuchma, memcon, July 9, 1997, CL, https://clinton.presidentialli braries.us/items/show/101470.

92. Talbott to Asmus, note, July 14, 1997, FOIA F-2017-13804, SDA.

93. Clinton, Gore, and Kuchma, memcon, May 16, 1997, CL, https://clinton .presidentiallibraries.us/items/show/101469.

94. Gore and Kuchma, "Limousine ride of Vice President Gore with Ukrainian President Leonid Kuchma, from Andrews Air Force Base to Blair House, 5/14/97, approx time 1715–1745, reconstructed from notes of Marta Zielyk, US

interpreter, no other person in limo with VP and Kuchma," draft memcon, May 14, 1997, FOIA F-2017-13804, SDA.

95. Clinton, Gore, and Kuchma, memcon, May 16, 1997, CL, https://clinton .presidentiallibraries.us/items/show/101469.

96. See James Sherr, "Russia-Ukraine Rapprochement? The Black Sea Fleet Accords," *Survival* 39, no. 3 (1997): 33–50.

97. See Hans Binnendijk and Richard Kugler, "NATO After the First Tranche: A Strategic Rationale for Enlargement," *Strategic Forum* no. 149, October 1998, Institute for National Strategic Studies, National Defense University, https:// apps.dtic.mil/sti/pdfs/ADA394244.pdf.

98. "Subject: Talbott-Geremek Bilateral at Copenhagen Ministerial," cable USVien-00064, January 7, 1998, FOIA F-2017-13804, SDA.

99. "Subject: Deputy Secretary Talbott's April 8 Meeting with Ukraine's soon-to-be Foreign Minister Boris Tarasiuk," cable State-067506, April 15, 1998, FOIA F-2017-13804, SDA.

100. See Anders Aslund, *How Ukraine Became a Market Economy and Democracy* (Peterson Institute for International Economics, 2009).

101. "Subject: Official Informal [Memcon Kuchma and Albright]," cable Kyiv-02502, March 9, 1998, FOIA M-2017-11729, SDA.

102. "Deputy Secretary Meeting with Ukrainian Ambassador Shcherbak [June 13, 1997]," cable State-133697, July 17, 1997, FOIA F-2017-13804, SDA.

103. Strobe Talbott, "Address at the Workshop on Ukraine-NATO Relations," sponsored by the Harvard University Project on Ukrainian Security and the Stanford-Harvard Preventive Defense Project, Washington, DC, April 8, 1998, https://1997-2001.state.gov/policy_remarks/1998/980408_talbott_ukr_nato.html.

104. Slawomir Debski, "Peace Without Victory," in *Europe Whole and Free: Vision and Reality*, ed. Daniel Hamilton and Slawomir Debski (Brookings Institution Press, 2019), 15–26.

105. Clinton and Kwasniewski, memcon, July 10, 1997, FOIA F-2017-13804, SDA.

106. Clinton and Walesa, memcon, July 10, 1997, FOIA F-2017-13804, SDA.

107. See Hans Binnendijk and Jeffrey Simon, "Romania and NATO: Membership Reassessment at the July 1997 Summit," *Strategic Forum* 101, February 1997, Institute for National Strategic Studies, National Defense University, https:// apps.dtic.mil/sti/pdfs/ADA394379.pdf.

108. Clinton and Constantinescu, memcon, July 11, 1997, FOIA F-2017-13804, SDA.

109. "Subject: Romanian Prime Minister's Meeting with the Secretary, Deputy Secretary," cable State-133663, July 17, 1997, FOIA F-2017-13804, SDA.

110. "Deputy Secretary Talbott's March 18–19 Visit to Bucharest," cable Bucharest-01886, March 26, 1998, FOIA F-2017-13804, SDA.

111. See "Founding Act on Mutual Relations, Cooperations and Security between NATO and the Russian Federation," May 27, 1997, https://www.nato.int/cps/en /natohq/official_texts_25468.htm.

112. See Press Summary, "NATO-Russia Permanent Joint Council Meeting at Ministerial Level, New York, September 26, 1997," https://archives.nato.int/uploads/r/null/1/4/144367/STATEMENT_PJC_1997-09-26_ENG.pdf; "Subject: Initial Russian Reactions to PJC Upbeat," cable Moscow-24590, September 29, 1997, FOIA M-2013-08489, SDA.

113. See Notes, December 16, 1997, Talbott Diaries, 26:51.

114. Talbott to Mamedov, letter, June 19, 1997, FOIA FL-2017-13804, SDA. See James Goldgeier and Michael McFaul, *Power and Purpose: U.S. Policy Toward Russia After the Cold War* (Brookings Institution Press, 2003), 208–10; Sarotte, *Not One Inch*, 270–76.

5. Russia's Financial Crisis and the End of Reform

1. Strobe Talbott, "The Struggle for Russia's Future," *Wall Street Journal*, September 25, 1997, A22, https://www.wsj.com/articles/SB875136148358249000.

2. Strobe Talbott, "The End of the Beginning: The Emergence of a New Russia," address at Stanford University, September 19, 1997, U.S. Department of State Archives (SDA), https://1997-2001.state.gov/regions/nis/970919talbott.html. The speech is also printed in Coit Blacker, Ashton Carter, Warren Christopher, David Hamburg and Wiliam Perry, eds., *NATO After Madrid. Looking to the Future* (Stanford/Harvard Preventive Defense Project 1999), 9–18, https://www.belfercenter.org/sites/default/files/files/publication/nato_after_madrid.pdf.

3. Talbott, "The End of the Beginning."

4. See John M. Broder, "Despite a Secret Pact by Gore in '95, Russian Arms Sales to Iran Go On," *New York Times*, October 13, 2000, https://www.nytimes.com/2000/10/13/world/despite-a-secret-pact-by-gore-in-95-russian-arms-sales-to-iran-go-on.html.

5. On the modern history of Iran and its political economy, see Suzanne Maloney, *Iran's Long Reach: Iran as a Pivotal State in the Muslim World* (United States Institute of Peace Press, 2008); Suzanne Maloney, *Iran's Political Economy Since the Revolution* (Cambridge University Press, 2015).

6. Notes, December 4, 1997, Talbott Diaries, 26:47.

7. See Michael Dobbs and John M. Goshko, "Albright's Personal Odyssey Shaped Foreign Policy Beliefs," *Washington Post*, December 6, 1996, A25, https://www.washingtonpost.com/wp-srv/politics/govt/admin/stories/albright120696.htm.

8. See Michael Dobbs, *Madeleine Albright: A Twentieth-Century Odyssey* (Henry Holt Company, 1999); Madeleine Albright, *Prague Winter: A Personal Story of Remembrance and War, 1937–1948* (Harper Collins, 2012).

9. See Zbigniew Brzezinski, *The Great Chessboard: American Primacy and Its Geostrategic Imperatives* (Basic Books, 1997); Zbigniew Brzezinski, "A Geostrategy for Eurasia," *Foreign Affairs* 76, no. 5 (1997): 50–64.

10. Notes, December 1, 1997, Talbott Diaries, 26:45.

11. Notes, December 1, 1997.

12. See Zbigniew Brzezinski, Brent Scowcroft, and Richard Murphy, "Differentiated Containment: Policy Toward Iran and Iraq," *Foreign Affairs* 76, no. 3 (1997): 20–30.

13. Talbott to Craig, memo, December 30, 1997, Talbott Diaries, 27:1.

14. See Joseph Kahn and Timothy L. O'Brien, "Easy Money. A Special Report: For Russia and Its U.S. Bankers, Match Wasn't Made in Heaven," *New York Times*, October 18, 1998, https://www.nytimes.com/1998/10/18/business/easy-money -special-report-for-russia-its-us-bankers-match-wasn-t-made-heaven.html.

15. Notes, January 11, 1998, Talbott Diaries, 28:4.

16. Notes, January 11, 1998.

17. Clinton and Yeltsin, telcon, October 30, 1997, Clinton Library (CL), https:// clinton.presidentiallibraries.us/items/show/101486.

18. Higgins to Fort, "Subject: FW: Courtney relay of 10/7-8 Talbott-Mamedov talks," email, October 8, 1997, Freedom of Information Act Case no. (FOIA) F-2017-13804, U.S. Department of State Archives (SDA); Talbott to Mamedov, letter, September 30, 1997, FOIA FL-2017-13804, SDA.

19. For context, see Albert Benliot, ed., *Iran: Outlaw, Outcast or Normal Country* (Nova Publishers, 2001); Dore Gold, *The Rise of Nuclear Iran: How Tehran Defies the West* (Regnery, 2009).

20. Talbott to Albright, "Subject: Meetings with Primakov in Sweden," memo, January 20, 1998, FOIA F-2017-13804, SDA.

21. "Subject: Memorandum of Conversation between President Clinton and Prime Minister of Russia Viktor Chernomyrdin, on 03/11/1998," cable State-054451, March 27, 1998, FOIA F-2017-13804, SDA.

22. Notes for PSG meeting on March 25, 1998, Talbott Diaries, 29:10.

23. Collins to Talbott, "Meeting with Kiriyenko," memo, April 21, 1998, FOIA F-2017-13804, SDA.

24. See Anthony H. Cordesman, "Weapons of Mass Destruction in Iran: Delivery Systems, and Chemical, Biological, and Nuclear Programs," Center for Strategic International Studies, April 28, 1998, https://www.bits.de/public/documents /iran/Cordesman_WMDinIran98.pdf.

25. Clinton and Yeltsin, telcon, April 6, 1998, CL, https://clinton.presidentiallibraries .us/items/show/101525.

26. Talbott to Mamedov, letter, April 5, 1998, FOIA FL-2017-13804, SDA.

27. Notes, "Virtually identical memos to SB and MKA, Saturday, April 25, 1998," Talbott Diaries, 29:51.

28. Talbott and Yumashev, memcon, April 20, 1998, FOIA F-2017-13804, SDA.

29. "Subject: Deputy Secretary Talbott's Lunch with Secretary of the Defense Council Kokoshin [20 April]," cable Moscow-11640, May 7, 1998, FOIA F-2017-13804, SDA. See Strobe Talbott, *The Russia Hand: A Memoir of Presidential Diplomacy* (Random House, 2002), 267–68.

30. Notes, "Berger-Kokoshin Script, Version 3, Wednesday, May 6, 1998," Talbott Diaries, 29:65.

31. In October 1997, Rep. Benjamin Gilman (R–NY)-20) introduced legislation titled "The Iran Missile Proliferation Sanctions Act of 1997," https://www.congress.gov/bill/105th-congress/house-bill/2709.

32. "Subject: Official-Informal," draft memcon of the Berger Delegation Opening Meeting in Kokoshin's Kremlin Office and Parts of Luncheon at Government Guest House, cable Moscow-11871, May 8, 1998, FOIA F-2017-13804, SDA.

33. Talbott, *Russia Hand*, 267.

34. Talbott, "Report on May 7 Berger-Kokoshin Meeting," memo, May 11, 1998, FOIA F-2017-13804, SDA.

35. "Subject: Deputy Secretary Talbott's Meeting with Acting Prime Minister Kiriyenko," cable Moscow-11639, May 7, 1998, FOIA F-2017-13804, SDA.

36. See "Subject: Deputy Secretary Talbott's Meeting with Yeltsin Chief of Staff Yumashev," cable Moscow-11638, May 7, 1998, FOIA F-2017-13804, SDA.

37. Clinton and Yeltsin, telcon, May 12, 1998, CL, https://clinton.presidentiallibraries.us/items/show/101526.

38. Notes, May 12, 1998, Talbott Diaries, 29:87–88.

39. Clinton and Yeltsin, memcon, May 17, 1998, CL, https://clinton.presidentiallibraries.us/items/show/101521.

40. See Eric Schmitt, "Bill to Punish Giving Missile Help to Iran Passes in Senate," *New York Times*, May 23, 1998, https://www.nytimes.com/1998/05/23/world/bill-to-punish-giving-missile-help-to-iran-passes-in-senate.html.

41. Talbott, *Russia Hand*, 273.

42. See Walter Pincus, "Iran May Soon Gain Missile Capability," *Washington Post*, July 24, 1998, https://www.washingtonpost.com/archive/politics/1998/07/24/iran-may-soon-gain-missile-capability/053a6903-8869-4df4-843e-72c957983c4c/.

43. See Clinton and Yeltsin, memcon, June 20, 1997, CL, https://clinton.presidentiallibraries.us/items/show/101493.

44. See James M. Boughton, *Tearing Down Walls: The International Monetary Fund 1990–1999* (International Monetary Fund, 2012), https://www.imf.org/external/pubs/ft/history/2012/.

45. Blair and Yeltsin, memcon, October 6, 1997, PREM 49/160, UK National Archives.

46. Blair and Chubais/Nemtsov, memcon, October 5, 1997, PREM 49/160, UK National Archives.

47. Grigory Yavlinsky, "Russia's Phony Capitalism," *Foreign Affairs* 77, no. 3 (1998): 67–79.

48. See Braithwaite to Holmes, "Russian Economic Problems," with attached memo by Prof. Richard Layard from the London School of Economics "Russia—Current Situation and Issues," memo, December 5, 1997, PREM 49/160, UK National Archives.

49. See Parker to Chancellor, "Replacement of Chubais as Russian Finance Minister," memo, November 20, 1997, PREM 49/160, UK National Archives; Nigel Gould-Davis and Ngaire Woods, "Russia and the IMF," *International Affairs* 75, no. 1 (1999): 1–22.

50. "Subject: Deputy Secretary's Meeting with Presidential Chief of Staff Valentin Yumashev," cable State-79806, October 15, 1997, FOIA F-2017-13804, SDA.

51. See Brian Pinto and Sergei Ulatov, "Financial Globalization and the Russian Crisis of 1998," Policy Research Working Paper no. 5312 (World Bank Europe and Central Asia Region & Managing Director's Office, May 2010), https://openknowledge.worldbank.org/bitstream/handle/10986/3797/WPS5312.pdf.

52. See Anders Aslund, "Russia's Collapse," *Foreign Affairs* 78, no. 5 (1999): 64–77; Martin Gilman, *No Precedent, No Plan: Inside Russia's 1998 Default* (MIT Press, 2010).

53. See Homi Kharas, Brian Pinto and Sergei Ulatov, "An Analysis of Russia's 1998 Meltdown: Fundamentals and Market Signals," *Brookings Papers on Economic Activity*, 1:2001, https://www.brookings.edu/wp-content/uploads/2001/01/2001a_bpea_kharas.pdf.

54. Clinton and Yeltsin, telcon, May 28, 1998, CL, https://clinton.presidentiallibraries.us/items/show/101529.

55. Clinton and Yeltsin, telcon, July 10, 1998, CL, https://clinton.presidentiallibraries.us/items/show/101532.

56. See James Goldgeier and Michael McFaul, *Power and Purpose: U.S. Policy Toward Russia After the Cold War* (Brookings Institution Press, 2003), 211–46; Boughton, *Tearing Down Walls*, 323–42.

57. Robert Rubin, PBS Commanding Heights, interviews, September 26, 2000, April 4, 2001, https://www.pbs.org/wgbh/commandingheights/shared/minitext/int_robertrubin.html#6.

58. Notes, July 30, 1998, Talbott Diaries, 31:29.

59. Clinton and Yeltsin, telcon, September 12, 1998, CL, https://clinton.presidentiallibraries.us/items/show/10153.

60. See David Hoffman, "Tycoons Take the Reins in Russia," *Washington Post*, August 28, 1998, A01, https://www.washingtonpost.com/wp-srv/inatl/longterm/russiagov/stories/oligarchs082898.htm.

61. Yeltsin, *Midnight Diaries* (Weidenfeld & Nicholson, 2000), 182–83.

62. Notes, August 23, 1998, Talbott Diaries, 31:43.

63. See William J. Clinton, "Address to the Nation on Testimony Before the Independent Counsel's Grand Jury," August 17, 1998, https://www.govinfo.gov/content/pkg/PPP-1998-book2/pdf/PPP-1998-book2-doc-pg1457-2.pdf; see Peter Baker and John F. Harris, "Clinton Admits to Lewinsky Relationship, Challenges Starr to End Personal 'Prying,'" *Washington Post*, August 18, 1998, https://www.washingtonpost.com/politics/clinton-impeachment/clinton-admits-lewinsky-relationship-challenges-starr-end-personal-prying; for Clinton's account, see Clinton, *My Life* (Arrow Books, 2004), 773–76, 800–3.

64. Thomas Graham Jr., "World Without Russia," Jamestown Foundation Conference, Washington, DC, June 9, 1999, https://carnegieendowment.org/1999/06/09/world-without-russia-pub-285.

65. Talbott to Albright and Berger, "Making the Most of the Moscow Summit," memo, August 21, 1998, FOIA FL-2017-13804, SDA.

66. Notes, August 26, 1998, Talbott Diaries, 31:47.

67. Clinton and Yeltsin, telcon, August 25, 1998, CL, https://clinton.presidentiallibraries.us/items/show/101534.

68. Talbott, *Russia Hand,* 278.

69. Notes, August 23, 1998, Talbott Diaries, 31:44.

70. Notes, August 26, 1998, Talbott Diaries, 31:48.

71. Notes, September 14, 1998, Talbott Diaries, 32:64.

72. See Talbott, *Russia Hand,* 280.

73. Notes, August 27, 1998, Talbott Diaries, 31:70.

74. Notes, August 27, 1998, Talbott Diaries, 31:71; see Talbott, *Russia Hand,* 280.

75. Notes, August 27, 1998, Talbott Diaries, 31:78.

76. See Talbott, *Russia Hand,* 282.

77. See Peter Baker, "Despite Staff Debate, Clinton Plans to Attend Summit," *New York Times,* August 28, 1998, https://www.washingtonpost.com/archive/politics/1998/08/28/despite-staff-debate-clinton-still-plans-to-attend-summit/042e59e8-34ae-408d-a63c-2afbc813b5b4/.

78. Notes, August 28, 1998, Talbott Diaries, 31:81; see Talbott, *Russia Hand,* 282–83.

79. "Clinton Committed to U.S.-Russia. Expectations are low because of the turmoil," CNN, August 28, 1998, https://edition.cnn.com/ALLPOLITICS/1998/08/28/russia.summit/.

80. Freidin to Talbott, email, August 30, 1998, Talbott Diaries, 31:88.

81. See Clinton and Kohl, memcon, August 30, 1998, CL, https://clinton.presidentiallibraries.us/items/show/101516.

82. Berger and Sperling to Clinton, "Your Trip to Moscow, Russia, September 1–2, 1998," memo, August 27, 1998, CL, https://clinton.presidentiallibraries.us/items/show/101277.

83. Notes, August 31, 1998, Talbott Diaries, 32:1–2; see Talbott, *Russia Hand,* 285–86.

84. Notes, August 31, 1998, Talbott Diaries, 32:3.

85. Janine Wedel, "The Harvard Boys Do Russia," *The Nation,* May 14, 1998, https://www.thenation.com/article/world/harvard-boys-do-russia/.

86. See Janine Wedel, *Collision and Collusion: The Strange Case of Western Aid to Eastern Europe* (St. Martins's Griffin, 2000).

87. Kharas, Pinto, and Ulatov, "Analysis of Russia's 1998 Meltdown."

88. Notes, August 31, 1998, Talbott Diaries, 32:5; see Talbott, *Russia Hand,* 283–85.

89. Talbott, *Russia Hand,* 287.

90. Talbott, *Russia Hand*, 287–88.

91. Notes, September 1, 1998, Talbott Diaries, 32:21.

92. Notes, September 2, 1998, Talbott Diaries, 32:22.

93. Talbott, *Russia Hand*, 288.

94. Goldgeier and McFaul, *Power and Purpose*, 237.

95. Kennan quoted in John Lloyd, "The Russian Devolution," *New York Times Magazine*, August 15, 1999, https://archive.nytimes.com/www.nytimes.com/library/magazine/home/19990815mag-russia-crisis.html.

96. Madeleine K. Albright, address to the U.S.-Russian Business Council, Chicago, Illinois, October 2, 1998, SDA, https://1997-2001.state.gov/statements/1998/981002.html.

97. Notes, September 8, 1998, Talbott Diaries, 32:39.

98. Notes, September 10, 1998, Talbott Diaries, 32:39.

99. Talbott, *Russia Hand*, 289.

100. Clinton and Yeltsin, telcon, September 12, 1998, CL, https://clinton.presidentiallibraries.us/items/show/101535.

101. Talbott, *Russia Hand*, 289.

102. Notes, September 10, 1998, Talbott Diaries, 32:41.

103. Notes, September 11, 1998, Talbott Diaries, 32:43; see Talbott, *Russia Hand*, 289.

104. Notes, September 11, 1998, Talbott Diaries, 32:46.

105. Notes, September 14, 1998, Talbott Diaries, 32:49.

106. "Remarks by Deputy Secretary of State Strobe Talbott, G-8 meeting on Russia," Monday, September 13, 1998, FOIA FL-2017-13804, SDA.

107. "Subject: Deputy Secretary Talbott Briefing to the NAC on Moscow Summit, the Way Ahead with Russia," cable USNATO-02540, September 28, 1998, FOIA F-2017-13804, SDA.

108. Notes, September 15, 1998, Talbott Diaries, 32:64.

109. Strobe Talbott, "Gogol's Troika: The Case for Strategic Patience in a Time of Troubles," address at the conference "Russia at the End of the 20th Century," School of Humanities and Sciences, Stanford University, November 6, 1998, https://web.stanford.edu/group/Russia20/volumepdf/talbott.pdf.

110. Notes, late November/early December 1998, Talbott Diaries, 33:110.

111. Strobe Talbott, "For Carlos—My Notes on the Conversation with Larry," note to Carlos Pascual of the NSC, November 30, 1998, FOIA FL-2017-13804, SDA.

112. Notes, December 3, 1998, Talbott Diaries, 34:2.

113. "Subject: Deputy Secretary meets Malashenko," cable Moscow-33271, December 18, 1998, FOIA F-2017-13804, SDA.

114. See Peter Baker and Juliet Eilperin, "Clinton Impeached. House Approves Articles Alleging Perjury, Obstruction," *Washington Post*, December 20, 1998, https://www.washingtonpost.com/politics/clinton-impeachment/clinton-impeached-house-approves-articles-alleging-perjury-obstruction/.

115. Notes, December 18, 1998, Talbott Diaries, 34:91. On India, see Strobe Talbott, *Engaging India: Diplomacy, Democracy, and the Bomb* (Brookings Institution Press, 2006); Stephan Kieninger, "Behind the Scenes of US Nuclear Diplomacy with India," *The Diplomat*, October 12, 2024, https://thediplomat.com/2024/10/behind-the-scenes-of-us-nuclear-diplomacy-with-india/.

6. The Kosovo War as a Game Changer

1. See Louis Sell, *Slobodan Milosevic and the Destruction of Yugoslavia* (Duke University Press, 2002).

2. See Ivo Daalder and Michael O'Hanlon, *Winning Ugly: NATO's War to Save Kosovo* (Brookings Institution Press, 2000); Tim Judah, *Kosovo: War and Revenge* (Yale University Press, 2000); James Goldgeier and Michael McFaul, *Power and Purpose: U.S. Policy Toward Russia After the Cold War* (Brookings Institution Press, 2003), 247–66; Tim Judah, *Kosovo: What Everyone Needs to Know* (Oxford University Press, 2008); Christopher Hill, *Outpost: A Diplomat at Work* (Simon & Schuster, 2015).

3. See "Subject: Official Informal" [Draft Memcon of Deputy Secretary Talbott's Meeting with Macedonian Prime Minister Crvenovski and Foreign Minister Blagoj], cable Skopje-00675, March 20, 1998, Freedom of Information Act Case no. (FOIA) F-2017-13804, U.S. Department of State Archives (SDA).

4. See Helen Leigh-Phippard, "The Contact Group on (and in) Bosnia: An Exercise in Conflict Mediation?" *International Journal* 58, no. 2 (1998): 306–24.

5. "Subject: Deputy Secretary's 3/6 Meeting with Contact Group Plus Poland on Kosovo," cable State-041303, March 7, 1998, FOIA F-2017-13804, SDA.

6. "Subject: Official-Informal," cable USNATO-01167, April 22, 1998, FOIA F-2017-13804, SDA.

7. "Subject: Deputy Secretary's March 16 Meeting with Prime Minister Fatos Nano," cable Tirana-01112, March 27, 1998, FOIA F-2017-13804, SDA.

8. Strobe Talbott, *The Russia Hand: A Memoir of Presidential Diplomacy* (Random House, 2002), 300.

9. Clinton and Ivanov, memcon, September 14, 1998, Clinton Library (CL), https://clinton.presidentiallibraries.us/items/show/101522.

10. "Subject: Memorandum of Conversation between President Clinton and Russian President Yeltsin [October 5, 1998]," cable State-189900, October 14, 1998, FOIA M-2017-12151, SDA.

11. Masha Gessen, "The Undoing of Bill Clinton and Boris Yeltsin's Friendship, and How It Changed Both of Their Countries," *New Yorker*, September 5, 2018, https://www.newyorker.com/news/our-columnists/the-undoing-of-bill-clinton-and-boris-yeltsin-friendship-and-how-it-changed-both-countries.

12. See Jane Perlez, "Conflict in the Balkans: The Overview. Milosevic Accepts Kosovo Monitors, Averting Attack," *New York Times*, October 14, 1998,

https://www.nytimes.com/1998/10/14/world/conflict-balkans-overview
-milosevic-accepts-kosovo-monitors-averting-attack.html.

13. See Timothy Crawford, "Pivotal Deterrence and the Kosovo War: Why the Holbrooke Agreement Failed," *Political Science Quarterly* 116, no. 4 (2001): 499–523.

14. Talbott, *Russia Hand*, 302.

15. See Daalder and O'Hanlon, *Winning Ugly*, 63–69.

16. Holbrooke to Albright and Berger, "Kosovo: Where We Stand," memo, March 12, 1999, Box 4, Richard Holbrooke Papers, Seeley Mudd Library, Princeton University.

17. Holbrooke to Albright and Berger, "Kosovo: Where We Stand," memo, March 1999, Box 4, Richard Holbrooke Papers, Seeley Mudd Library, Princeton University.

18. Talbott, *Russia Hand*, 304–305.

19. Gore and Primakov, telcon, March 18, 1999, CL, https://clinton.presidentialli braries.us/items/show/101596.

20. Talbott, *Russia Hand*, 305.

21. Clinton and Yeltsin, telcon, March 24, 1999, CL, 208, https://clinton.presiden tiallibraries.us/items/show/58573.

22. Yeltsin, *Midnight Diaries* (Weidenfeld & Nicholson, 2000), 259.

23. Clinton and Yeltsin, telcon, March 24, 1999, CL, 211, https://clinton.presiden tiallibraries.us/items/show/58573.

24. Talbott, *Russia Hand*, 306.

25. Yeltsin, *Midnight Diaries*, 258.

26. Daalder and O'Hanlon, *Winning Ugly*, 105.

27. Clinton, Cohen, and Solana, memcon, March 15, 1999, CL, 155, https://clinton .presidentiallibraries.us/items/show/101162.

28. Massimo D'Alema, interview, Oral History Kosovo, January 16, 2019, https:// oralhistorykosovo.org/wp-content/uploads/2019/03/Massimo-DAlema-ENG.pdf.

29. See Daalder and O'Hanlon, *Winning Ugly*, 101–36.

30. See "Subject: Secretary Albright's April 12 Dinner in Brussels with Foreign Ministers and Ambassadors of Frontline States," cable State-07661, April 27, 1999, FOIA M-2017-11764, SDA.

31. See Blair and Constantinescu, telcon, May 4, 1999, PREM 49/1027, UK National Archives.

32. See Clinton and Constantinescu, telcon, April 18, 1999, FOIA F-2017-13804, SDA.

33. At the Washington summit, NATO's Head of States emphasized that "we will not tolerate threats by the Belgrade regime to the security of its neighbours. . . . We reaffirm our support for the territorial integrity and sovereignty of all countries in the region." See Statement on Kosovo Issued by the Heads of State and Government participating in the meeting of the North Atlantic Council in Washington, DC, on April 23 and 24, 1999, https://www.nato.int/docu/pr /1999/p99-062e.htm.

34. Daniel Hamilton, "New Members, New Missions: NATO and Euro-Atlantic Architecture in the Second Clinton Administration," in *Open Door: NATO and Euro-Atlantic Security After the Cold War*, ed. Daniel Hamilton and Kristina Spohr (Brookings Institution Press, 2019), 363, https://transatlanticrelations.org/wp-content/uploads/2019/04/15-Hamilton2.pdf.

35. Daniel Hamilton, email correspondence, July 2024.

36. "Subject: Deputy Secretary Talbott's Initiative on the Economic Future of South Eastern Europe," cable Athens-02242, April 9, 1999, FOIA F-2017-13804, SDA. For context, see Erhard Busek and Björn Kühne, eds., *From Stabilisation to Integration: The Stability Pact for South Eastern Europe* (Böhlau Verlag, 2010).

37. William J. Clinton, "Remarks and a Question-and-Answer Session with the American Society of Newspaper Editors in San Francisco, California, April 15, 1999," https://www.govinfo.gov/content/pkg/PPP-1999-book1/pdf/PPP-1999-book1-doc-pg551-2.pdf.

38. "Subject: SPCL. The Deputy Secretary's Meeting (and Secretary's Drop-By) with Stability Pact Coordinator Bodo Hombach," cable State-7-2622, July 26, 1999, FOIA F-2017-13804, SDA.

39. Clinton to Yeltsin, letter April 3, 1999, CL, https://clinton.presidentiallibraries.us/items/show/58573.

40. See Madeleine Albright, *Madam Secretary: A Memoir* (Harper Perennial, 2003), 416.

41. See Notes, March 31, 1999, Talbott Diaries, 36:70.

42. Notes on conversation with Javier Solana, April 6, 1999, Talbott Diaries, 36:83.

43. Talbott and Avdeyev, "First Meeting, Breakfast, Hotel Windsor Royal, Brussels Belgium," memcon, April 7, 1999," FOIA F-2017-13804, SDA.

44. Talbott and Avdeyev, "First Meeting, Breakfast, Hotel Windsor Royal, Brussels Belgium," memcon, April 7, 1999, FOIA F-2017-13804, SDA.

45. Notes, April 7, 1999, Talbott Diaries, 36:99.

46. "Secretary's Meeting with Russian FM Ivanov in Oslo, April 13," cable State-069173, April 14, 1999, FOIA M-2017-11791, SDA.

47. See Notes, April 12, 1999, Talbott Diaries, 37:133.

48. Talbott, *Russia Hand*, 308–9.

49. Talbott, *Russia Hand*, 309.

50. Clinton and Yeltsin, telcon, April 19, 1999, CL, https://clinton.presidentiallibraries.us/items/show/101600.

51. Notes, "Saturday 4/17/99, sandy, MKA, leon, dobbins, steinberg, st, 'small group' in sit room," Talbott Diaries, 37:4.

52. Holbrooke to Albright and Berger, "Subject: Kosovo: Where We Stand," memo, April 20, Box 4, Richard Holbrooke Papers, Seeley Mudd Library, Princeton University.

53. Notes, April 8, 1999, Talbott Diaries, 37:10.

54. Clinton and Yeltsin, telcon, April 25, 1999, CL, https://clinton.presidentiallibraries.us/items/show/101601.

55. Talbott, *Russia Hand*, 310.

56. Gore and Chernomyrdin, telcon, April 26, 1999, CL, https://clinton.presidentialli braries.us/items/show/101589.

57. Notes on Meeting with Clinton and Berger, April 25, 1999, Talbott Diaries, 37:18.

58. Talbott, *Russia Hand*, 313. See Christoph Zürcher, "Chechnya and Kosovo: Reflections in a Distorting Mirror," in *Mapping European Security after Kosovo*, ed. Peter van Ham and Sergei Medvedev (Manchester University Press, 2004), 179–200.

59. See "Subject: TFSR02: Deputy Secretary Talbott Briefs the NAC April 29 on Discussions with Russian Leaders," cable US NATO-01422, May 5, 1999, FOIA F-2017-13804, SDA.

60. Talbott to Albright, Berger, and Fuerth, "ST-Chernomyrdin one-on-one, April 27, 1999," memo, April 27, 1999, FOIA F-2017-13804, SDA.

61. Talbott, *Russia Hand*, 313.

62. Gore and Chernomyrdin, memcon, May 3, 1999, CL, https://clinton.presidentialli braries.us/items/show/101591.

63. Fuerth to Albright, "Readout on VP-Chernomyrdin meetings," memo, May 5, 1999, CL, https://clinton.presidentiallibraries.us/items/show/58574, 42.

64. Gore and Chernomyrdin, memcon, May 3, 1999, 8:45 p.m., CL, https://clinton .presidentiallibraries.us/items/show/101591.

65. Gore and Chernomyrdin, memcon, May 3, 1999.

66. Notes, May 4, 1999, Talbott Diaries, 37:86.

67. Gore and Chernomyrdin, memcon, May 4, 1999, CL, https://clinton.presidentialli braries.us/items/show/101592.

68. See Talbott and Ahtisaari, telcon, May 6, 1999, FOIA F-2017-13804, SDA.

69. Talbott and Chernomyrdin, telcon, May 6, 1999, FOIA F-2017-13804, SDA.

70. Strobe Talbott, interview, PBS Frontline, n.d., https://www.pbs.org/wgbh /pages/frontline/shows/kosovo/interviews/talbott.html.

71. Talbott, *Russia Hand*, 317–19.

72. Edelman, author interview, May 2024; see Edelman and Ahtisaari, memcon, May 15, 1999, FOIA FL-2017-13804, SDA.

73. Notes, May 15, 1999, Talbott Diaries, 37:120.

74. Notes, May 17, 1999, Talbott Diaries, 38:1.

75. Notes, "6:30 p.m., meet with POTUS in cabinet room," May 17, 1999, Talbott Diaries, 38:5.

76. Talbott, *Russia Hand*, 318–19.

77. Talbott, Chernomyrdin, and Ahtisaari, "Memorandum to Sec. Albright, APNSA, Berger, OVP Fuerth from Strobe Talbott, Trip Report No. 2 (from Moscow)," memcon, May 21, 1999, FOIA M-2017-12144, SDA.

78. Notes, May 23, 1999, Talbott Diaries, 38:28.

79. Talbott, *Russia Hand*, 318–23.

80. Viktor Chernomyrdin, interview, PBS Frontline, n.d., https://www.pbs.org /wgbh/pages/frontline/shows/kosovo/interviews/chernomyrdin.html.

81. Notes, June 1 and 2, 1999, Talbott Diaries, 38:62.

82. Talbott, *Russia Hand*, 325.

83. Talbott, *Russia Hand*, 325.

84. Notes, June 3, 1999, Talbott Diaries, 38:79.

85. Talbott, *Russia Hand*, 328.

86. See Norris Chrono, June 3, 1999, Talbott Diaries, 38:69.

87. Notes, June 3, 1999, Talbott Diaries, 38:81.

88. See Notes, June 3, 1999, Talbott Diaries, 38:80–82.

89. Notes, June 3, 1999, Talbott Diaries, 38:82.

90. "Press Point of Mr. Strobe Talbott, US Deputy Secretary of State," NATO HQ Brussels, June 3, 1999, https://www.nato.int/docu/speech/1999/s990603b.htm; see Talbott, *Russia Hand*, 329.

91. Notes, June 3, 1999, Talbott Diaries, 38:86.

92. Notes, June 3, 1999, Talbott Diaries, 38:87.

93. See Talbott, *Russia Hand*, 330.

94. See "Secretary's Participation in G-8 Foreign Ministers meeting on Kosovo, June 7, 1999, Bonn, Germany, and June 8, 1999, Cologne, Germany," cable State-120246, June 26, 1999, FOIA M-2017-11772, SDA.

95. Clinton and Yeltsin, telcon, June 7, 1999, CL, https://clinton.presidentiallibraries.us/items/show/101603.

96. Clinton and Yeltsin, telcon, June 8, 1999, CL, https://clinton.presidentiallibraries.us/items/show/101604.

97. See United Nations, "Resolution 1244 (1999), Adopted by the Security Council at its 4011th meeting, on 10 June 1999," https://digitallibrary.un.org/record/274488.

98. Clinton and Yeltsin, June 10, 1999, CL, https://clinton.presidentiallibraries.us/items/show/101605.

99. Talbott, *Russia Hand*, 332–36.

100. Norris Chrono, June 10, 1999, Talbott Diaries, 39:3.

101. Talbott, *Russia Hand*, 335–36; Strobe Talbott, interview, PBS Putin Files, June 20, 2017, https://www.pbs.org/wgbh/frontline/interview/strobe-talbott; Strobe Talbott, "The Making of Vladimir Putin," *Politico*, August 19, 2014, https://www.politico.com/magazine/story/2014/08/putin-the-backstory-110151/.

102. Talbott, *Russia Hand*, 336. Following Talbott's meetings with Putin, National Security Advisor Sandy Berger worked with Putin at the National Security Advisor level. See 2017-0222-M: Declassified Documents Concerning Russian President Vladimir Putin, CL, https://clinton.presidentiallibraries.us/items/show/100505.

103. Talbott, *Russia Hand*, 336.

104. Talbott, *Russia Hand*, 337.

105. Talbott, Russia Hand, 338–42.

106. Talbott, *Russia Hand*, 343.

107. See Notes, June 12, 1999, Talbott Diaries, 39:71–75.

108. Yeltsin, *Midnight Diaries*, 266.

109. Talbott, *Russia Hand*, 344.

110. See Mike Jackson, *Soldier* (Bantam Press, 2007), 318. For Clark's account, see Wesley Clark, *Waging Modern War: Bosnia, Kosovo and the Future of Combat* (Public Affairs, 2001), 375–403.

111. See Jackson, *Soldier*, 336.

112. See Gore and Stepashin, telcon, June 12, 1999, CL, https://clinton.presidentialli braries.us/items/show/101594.

113. Clinton and Yeltsin, telcon, June 13, 1999, CL, https://clinton.presidentialli braries.us/items/show/101608.

114. Gore and Stepashin, telcon, June 14, 1999, CL, https://clinton.presidentiallibraries .us/items/show/101595.

115. Notes, June 13, 1999, Talbott Diaries, 39:83.

116. See Clinton and Yeltsin, telcon, June 14, 1999, CL, https://clinton.presidentialli braries.us/items/show/101607.

117. Notes, June 18, 1999, Talbott Diaries, 39:89.

118. See William Drozdiak, "U.S., Russia Reach Military Agreement," *Washington Post*, June 19, 1999, https://www.washingtonpost.com/wp-srv/inatl/longterm /balkans/stories/helsinki061999.htm; see "Remarks by the President on Agreement from Helsinki," June 18, 1999, https://clintonwhitehouse4.archives.gov /WH/New/Europe-9906/html/Speeches/990618c.html.

119. Notes, June 20, Talbott Diaries, 39:91.

120. Clinton and Yeltsin, memcon, April 20, 1999, CL, https://clinton.presidentialli braries.us/items/show/101606.

121. Notes, June 20, 1999, Talbott Diaries, 39:95.

122. Notes, June 20, 1999, Talbott Diaries, 39:95.

123. Notes, June 20, 1999, Talbott Diaries, 39:98.

124. See Notes, July 26, 1999, Talbott Diaries, 40:7–8; Talbott, *Russia Hand*, 353–54.

125. Talbott, *Russia Hand*, 354.

126. Notes, August 7, 1999, Talbott Diaries, 40:18.

127. See Mark Tran, "Yeltsin sacks prime minister. Political novice appointed as president's heir apparent," *The Guardian*, August 9, 1999, https://www.theguardian .com/world/1999/aug/09/russia.marktran.

128. Talbott, *Russia Hand*, 355.

129. Berger and Putin, telcon, August 12, 1999, CL, https://clinton.presidentialli braries.us/items/show/10158512.

7. Putin and the Crisis of U.S.-Russia Relations

1. Catherine Belton, "Did Vladimir Putin Support Anti-Western Terrorists as a Young KGB Officer?" *Politico*, June 20, 2020, https://www.politico.com/news /magazine/2020/06/20/vladimir-putin-dresden-kgb-330203; Belton, *Putin's*

People: How the KGB Took Back Russia and Then Took on the West (William Collins, 2021).

2. At the time, Marina Salye, a deputy of the legislative assembly of St. Petersburg, headed a special commission to investigate Putin's activities. For the context, see Karen Dawisha, *Putin's Kleptocracy. Who Owns Russia?* (Simon & Schuster, 2015). The Havighurst Center for Russian and Post-Soviet Studies at Miami University published some of Salye's findings online: https://www.miamioh.edu/cas /academics/centers/havighurst/additional-resources/putins-russia/salye-com mission-landing/index.html.

3. James Collins, interview, PBS Putin Files, June 14, 2017, https://www.pbs.org /wgbh/frontline/interview/james-collins/.

4. To assess the underlying factors for Putin's appointment, see Memo Barrow to Tatham, "Russia. Government Changes," August 9, 1999, PREM 49/1033, UK National Archives.

5. See Celeste Bohlen, "Yeltsin Resigns, Naming Putin as Acting President To Run in March Election," *New York Times*, January 1, 2000, https://www.ny times.com/2000/01/01/world/yeltsin-resigns-overview-yeltsin-resigns-naming -putin-acting-president-run-march.html.

6. Strobe Talbott, interview, PBS Putin Files, June 20, 2017, https://www.pbs.org /wgbh/frontline/interview/strobe-talbott/.

7. Barrow to Sawers, "Russia," memo, September 3, 1999, PREM 49/1033, UK National Archives.

8. Clinton and Yeltsin, telcon, September 8, 1999, Clinton Library (CL), https:// clinton.presidentiallibraries.us/items/show/101609.

9. Clinton and Putin, memcon, September 12, 1999, CL, https://clinton.presidentialli braries.us/items/show/101587.

10. Clinton, *My Life* (Arrow Books, 2004), 869–70.

11. See Carlotta Gall and Thomas de Waal, *Chechnya: Calamity in the Caucasus* (New York University Press, 1999); Emma Gilligan, *Terror in Chechnya: Russia and the Tragedy of Civilians in War* (Princeton University Press, 2009).

12. Strobe Talbott, *The Russia Hand: A Memoir of Presidential Diplomacy* (Random House, 2002), 356.

13. See Daniel Treisman, "Presidential Popularity in a Hybrid Regime: Russia under Yeltsin and Putin," *American Journal of Political Science* 55, no. 3 (2011): 590–609.

14. See Mike Eckel, "Two Decades On, Smoldering Questions About the Russian President's Vault to Power," Radio Free Europe, August 7, 2019, https://www.rferl .org/a/putin-russia-president-1999-chechnya-apartment-bombings/30097551.html.

15. Albright and Ivanov, memcon, September 20, 1999, Freedom of Information Act Case no. (FOIA) F-2017-13804, U.S. Department of State Archives (SDA).

16. See Gleb Pavlovsky, "Putin and Yumashev: Survivors of the Nineties," Carnegie Endowment for International Peace, June 29, 2018, https://carnegiemoscow .org/commentary/76716.

17. "Subject: Lunch with Yumashev," cable Moscow-23684, September 27, 1999, FOIA F-2017-13804, SDA.

18. See Matthew Evangelista, *The Chechen Wars: Will Russia Go the Way of the Soviet Union?* (Brookings Institution Press, 2002).

19. Talbott interview, quoted in James Goldgeier and Michael McFaul, *Power and Purpose: U.S. Policy Toward Russia After the Cold War* (Brookings Institution Press, 2003), 271.

20. Talbott to Albright, note, October 24, 1999, Talbott Diaries, 41:6.

21. See "Remarks at the Opening of the Organization for Security and Cooperation in Europe Summit in Istanbul," November 18, 1999, https://www.govinfo.gov/content/pkg/PPP-1999-book2/pdf/PPP-1999-book2-doc-pg2105.pdf.

22. Clinton and Yeltsin, memcon, November 19, 1999, CL, https://clinton.presidentiallibraries.us/items/show/101582.

23. Clinton and Yeltsin, memcon, November 19, 1999.

24. Notes, November 21, 1999, Talbott Diaries, 41:61.

25. See "Istanbul Document, Organization for Security and Co-operation in Europe," November 19, 1999, https://www.osce.org/mc/39569.

26. See "Subject: Mamedov on Chechnya and CFE," cable Moscow-No. 136, October 15, 1999, FOIA F-2017-13804, CL.

27. Blair and Clinton, telcon, December 16, 1999, PREM 49/1683, UK National Archives.

28. Clinton and Putin, memcon, November 2, 1999, CL, https://clinton.presidentiallibraries.us/items/show/101586.

29. Talbott, *Russia Hand*, 361.

30. Clinton and Shevardnadze, memcon, September 23, 1999, FOIA F-2017-13804, SDA.

31. Notes, October 28, 1999, Talbott Diaries, 41:9.

32. See Andrew Tully, "Economy: Gore Adviser Says Russian Corruption Hard to Fight," Radio Free Europe, July 7, 2000, https://www.rferl.org/a/1094418.html.

33. See Amelia Gentleman, "Scandals challenge to Yeltsin," *The Guardian*, September 5, 1999, https://www.theguardian.com/world/1999/sep/05/russia.ameliagentleman.

34. See Janet Perlez, "Russian Corruption Leads to Questions for White House," *New York Times*, September 1, 1999, https://archive.nytimes.com/www.nytimes.com/library/world/europe/090199russia-us.html.

35. See Thomas Graham Jr., "World Without Russia?" testimony at Jamestown Foundation Conference, Washington, DC, Carnegie Endowment for International Peace, June 9, 1999, https://carnegieendowment.org/1999/06/09/world-without-russia-pub-285.

36. See John Lloyd, "The Russian Devolution," *New York Times Magazine*, August 15, 1999, https://archive.nytimes.com/www.nytimes.com/library/magazine/home/19990815mag-russia-crisis.html.

37. Victoria Nuland to Talbott, "Subj: Re: your lunch with Condi Rice, etc.," email, September 14, 1999, Talbott Diaries, 40:67.

38. See Ivo H. Daalder, James M. Goldgeier, and James M. Lindsay, "Deploying NMD: Not Whether, But How," *Survival* 42, no. 1 (2000): 6–28, https://www.brookings.edu/wp-content/uploads/2016/06/2000survival.pdf; John Newhouse, "The Missile Defense Debate," *Foreign Affairs* 80, no. 4 (July/August 2000): 97–109.

39. See Igor Ivanov, "The Missile-Defense Mistake: Undermining Strategic Stability and the ABM Treaty," *Foreign Affairs* 79, no. 5 (2000): 15–20.

40. Notes, July 27, 1999, Talbott Diaries, 40:10–11.

41. Notes, July 27, 1999, Talbott Diaries, 40:11.

42. Notes, January 22, 2000, Talbott Diaries, 43:8.

43. Notes, January 25, 2000, Talbott Diaries, 43:9.

44. "Subject: Memorandum of Conversation. Meeting Between the Deputy Secretary and Russian Prime Minister Putin, Moscow," cable State-244337, December 22, 1999, FOIA M-2017-11844, SDA; see Talbott, *Russia Hand*, 367–69.

45. Talbott, *Russia Hand*, 369.

46. Boris Yeltin, "Statement," December 31, 1999, http://en.kremlin.ru/events/president/transcripts/24080; see Talbott, *Russia Hand*, 371.

47. Clinton and Yeltsin, telcon, December 31, 1999, CL, https://clinton.presidentiallibraries.us/items/show/101611.

48. Clinton, *My Life*, 882; see Boris Yeltsin, *Midnight Diaries* (Weidenfeld & Nicholson, 2000), 14.

49. Clinton and Yeltsin, telcon, January 1, 2000, CL, https://clinton.presidentiallibraries.us/items/show/101655.

50. See Svetlana Savranskaya, Tom Blanton with Natalie Sherman, eds., "Putin's First Election, March 2000," Briefing Book no. 854, National Security Archive, March 21, 2024, https://nsarchive.gwu.edu/briefing-book/russia-programs/2024-03-21/putins-first-election-march-2000.

51. "Subject: Secretary's Meeting with Russian Politician Grigory Yavlinsky," cable State-028923, February 17, 2000, FOIA M-2017-11776, SDA.

52. In his diaries, Talbott noted that "Jim Collins secure Jan 5 00, after his session with GEM . . . 1:15 minutes, Putin will not go to Davos; got a CIS summit and can't go." Notes, January 5, 2000, Talbott Diaries, 42:80.

53. See "Excerpts from a news conference with Vladimir Putin and Alexander Lukashenko after a meeting of the Supreme State Council of the Union State of Russia and Belarus," January 26, 2000, http://en.kremlin.ru/events/president/transcripts/24118.

54. "Subject: POTUS December 21 Meeting with President Nazarbaev," cable State-014531, January 27, 2000, FOIA M-2017-11577, SDA.

55. "Subject: Deputy Secretary's Meeting with Belarusian Parliamentarians," cable State-030955, February 19, 2000, FOIA F-2017-13804, SDA.

56. Vladimir Putin, *First Person* (Public Affairs, 2000), 69, 80.

57. William Safire, "Putinism Looms," *New York Times*, January 31, 2000, https://archive.nytimes.com/www.nytimes.com/library/opinion/safire/013100safi.html.

58. Clinton and Schröder, telcon, January 7, 2000, CL, https://clinton.presidentialli
braries.us/items/show/101681.

59. Clinton and Schröder, telcon, January 7, 2000.

60. Christopher Meyer, "Gore and Foreign Policy. Conversation with Leon
Fuerth," note, March 3, 2000, PREM 49/1684, UK National Archives.

61. Blair and Cheney, memcon, February 23, 2001, PREM 49/2353, UK National
Archives. For context, see Jonathan Haslam, "Russia's Seat at the Table: A Place
Denied or a Place Delayed?" *International Affairs* 74, no. 1 (January 1998): 119–30.

62. Talbott and Ivanov, memcon, February 19, 2000, FOIA F-2017-13804, SDA. On
the rise of Russia's post–Cold War imperialism, see Sergey Medvedev, *The
Return of the Russian Leviathan* (Polity Books 2019).

63. Notes, February 10, 2000, Talbott Diaries, 43:55.

64. Notes, February 26, 2000, Talbott Diaries, 43:75.

65. Notes, February 19, 2000, Talbott Diaries, 43:68.

66. See Daniel Williams, "Babitsky Reveals Russian Abuses," *Washington Post*, February 29, 2000, https://www.washingtonpost.com/wp-srv/pmextra/feb00/29
/A48891–2000Feb29.html.

67. "Subject: Foreign Secretary Cook's Visit to Moscow," cable Moscow-00453,
February 24, 2000, FOIA F-2017-13804, SDA.

68. See Anna Politkovskaya, *A Small Corner of Hell: Dispatches from Chechnya* (University of Chicago Press, 2007).

69. Talbott and Ivanov, memcon, February 19, 2000, FOIA F-2017-13804, SDA.

70. "Subject: Secretary's February 2 Meeting with Russian Acting President
Putin," cable State-029384, February 17, 2000, FOIA M-2017-11776, SDA.

71. See Ian Traynor and Michael White, "Blair courts outrage with Putin visit," *The
Guardian*, March 11, 2000, https://www.theguardian.com/world/2000/mar/11
/russia.ethicalforeignpolicy.

72. "Subject: The Deputy Secretary's Meeting with UK Amb. Meyer," cable State-
049876, March 16, 2000, FOIA F-2017-13804, SDA.

73. Jennifer Rankin, "Ex-Nato head says Putin wanted to join alliance early on in
his rule," *The Guardian*, November 4, 2021, https://www.theguardian.com
/world/2021/nov/04/ex-nato-head-says-putin-wanted-to-join-alliance-early
-on-in-his-rule.

74. See "Joint statement on the occasion of the visit of the Secretary-General of
NATO, Lord Robertson, in Moscow on February 16, 2000," https://www.nato
.int/docu/pr/2000/p000216e.htm.

75. Notes, February 19, 2000, Talbott Diaries, 43:68.

76. "Subject: NATO-Russia: Kislyak on Mitrovica, Upcoming PJC," cable
USNATO-00445, February 24, 2000, FOIA F-2017-13804, SDA.

77. "BBC Breakfast with Frost Interview: Vladimir Putin," March 5, 2000, http://
news.bbc.co.uk/hi/english/static/audio_video/programmes/breakfast_with
_frost/transcripts/putin5.mar.txt.

78. See David Hoffman, "Putin Says 'Why Not?' to Russia Joining NATO," *Washington Post*, March 6, 2000, https://www.washingtonpost.com/archive/politics/2000/03/06/putin-says-why-not-to-russia-joining-nato/c1973032-c10f-4bff-9174-8cae673790cd/.

79. "BBC Breakfast with Frost Interview: Vladimir Putin," March 5, 2000, http://news.bbc.co.uk/hi/english/static/audio_video/programmes/breakfast_with_frost/transcripts/putin5.mar.txt.

80. "Subject: Acting Secretary's March 6, 2000 Meeting with Latvian FM Berzins," cable State-047857, March 14, 2000, FOIA F-2017-13804, SDA.

81. See Peter Rutland, "Putin's Path to Power," *Post-Soviet Affairs* 16, no. 4 (2000): 313–54.

82. Michael McFaul, "Russia's 2000 Presidential Elections. Implications for Russian Democracy and U.S.-Russian Relations," testimony before the US Senate Committee on Foreign Relations, Washington, DC, April 12, 2000, https://carnegieendowment.org/2000/04/01/russia-s-2000-presidential-elections-implications-for-russian-democracy-and-u.s.-russian-relations-pub-421.

83. CSPAN, "Chechnya, Russia, and U.S. Policy and Aid Programs," April 4, 2000, https://www.c-span.org/video/?156388-1/chechnya-russia-us-policy-aid-programs.

84. See Peter Baker and Susan Glasser, *Kremlin Rising: Vladimir Putin's Russia and the End of Revolution* (Scribner, 2005); Masha Gessen, *The Man Without a Face: The Unlikely Rise of Vladimir Putin* (Riverhead, 2012); Angela Stent, *Putin's World: Russia Against the West and with the Rest* (Twelve, 2019); Andrew Weiss, *Accidental Czar: The Life and Lies of Vladimir Putin* (First Second Books, 2022); Philip Short, *Putin. His Life and Times* (Bodley Head, 2022); Alex Bellamy, *Warmonger: Vladimir Putin's Imperial Wars* (Agenda Publishing, 2024).

85. Clinton and Putin, memcon, March 27, 2000, CL, https://clinton.presidentiallibraries.us/items/show/101657.

86. For the context of U.S. strategic arms control policy after the Cold War, see James E. Goodby, *At the Borderline of Armageddon: How American President Managed the Atom Bomb* (Rowman & Littlefield, 2006), 155–78.

87. Talbott, *Russia Hand*, 384.

88. Talbott, *Russia Hand*, 391.

89. See Dean Mathew "A Failure Revisited: A Closer Look at the Jan 2000 NMD Test," *Strategic Analysis* 24, no. 1 (2008): 97–110.

90. See Wade Boese, "Crucial NMD Test Misses; Booster Failure Responsible," Arms Control Association, July/August 2000, https://www.armscontrol.org/act/2000-07/news/crucial-nmd-test-misses-booster-failure-responsible.

91. Notes, third week of April 2000, Talbott Diaries, 44:14.

92. Notes, April 24, 2000, Talbott Diaries, 44:26.

93. Talbott, *Russia Hand*, 390.

94. Notes, April 30, 2000, Talbott Diaries, 44:49.

95. Notes, June 2, 2000, Talbott Diaries, 45:12; see Angela Stent, *The Limits of Partnership: U.S.-Russian Relations in the Twenty-First Century* (Princeton University Press, 2015).

96. Clinton and Putin, telcon, April 15, 2000, CL, https://clinton.presidentiallibraries .us/items/show/101656.

97. See Talbott, *Russia Hand*, 392–95.

98. Stephen Sestanovich, author interview, June 2024.

99. Talbott, *Russia Hand*, 6.

100. Talbott, *Russia Hand*, 7–8.

101. Notes, June 5, 2000, Talbott Diaries, 45:40.

102. Clinton and Kuchma, memcon, June 5, 2000, CL, https://clinton.presidentialli braries.us/items/show/101662.

103. "Subject: Secretary's Meeting with Leonid Kuchma, President, Kyiv, Ukraine," cable Tashke 01476, April 17, 2000, FOIA M-2017-11777, SDA.

104. Clinton and Kuchma, memcon, June 5, 2000, CL, https://clinton.presidentialli braries.us/items/show/101663.

105. See Michael McFaul, "U.S. Foreign Policy and Chechnya," Century Foundation and Stanley Foundation, March 2003, https://fsi-live.s3.us-west-1.amazonaws .com/s3fs-public/US_Foreign_Policy_and_Chechnya.pdf.

106. Talbott to Albright, memo, July 14, 2000, FOIA FL-2017-13804, SDA.

107. Talbott to Albright, memo, July 14, 2000.

108. "Subject: Overview from the First Session of the G-8 Foreign Ministers: Political and Security Issues," cable State-153745, August 11, 2000, FOIA F-2017-13804, SDA.

109. "Subject: The Deputy Secretary's Meeting with EU Commissioner Patten: G8 Ministerial Miyazaki, Japan," cable State-153746, August 11, 2000, FOIA, F-2017-13804, SDA.

110. "Subject: Deputy Secretary's Meeting with French Foreign Minister Vedrine at the G8 Ministerial," cable State-153744, August 11, 2000, FOIA F-2017-13804, SDA.

111. Boris Yeltsin, annual address to the Federal Assembly of the Russian Federation, July 8, 2000, http://en.kremlin.ru/events/president/transcripts/21480.

112. Talbott to Berger, note, August 4, 2000, Talbott Diaries, 46:66.

113. William J. Clinton, "Remarks at Georgetown University," September 1, 2000, https://www.govinfo.gov/content/pkg/PPP-2000-book2/pdf/PPP-2000-book2 -doc-pg1744-2.pdf.

114. See Erik Schmitt, "Clinton's Missile Decision: The Overview: President Decides to Put Off Work on Missile Shield," *New York Times*, September 2, 2000, https:// www.nytimes.com/2000/09/02/world/clinton-s-missile-decision-overview -president-decides-put-off-work-missile.html.

115. Notes, September 1, 2000, Talbott Diaries, 46:72.

116. Clinton and Putin, memcon, September 6, 2000, CL, https://clinton .presidentiallibraries.us/items/show/101653; see Talbott, *Russia Hand*, 399–400.

117. "Subject: Deputy Secretary's Meeting with Russian Foreign Minister Ivanov at the G8 Ministerial," cable State-153114, August 11, 2000, FOIA F-2017-13804, SDA.

118. Notes, September 6, 2000, Talbott Diaries, 46:78.

119. See Sabrina Tavernise with Christopher Drew, "Frantic Russian Effort To Rescue Crew of Sub," *New York Times,* August 15, 2000, https://www.nytimes.com/2000/08/15/world/frantic-russian-effort-to-rescue-crew-of-sub.html.

120. See Peter Truscott, *Kursk: Russia's Lost Pride* (Simon & Schuster, 2002); Robert Moore, *A Time to Die: The Kursk Disaster* (Doubleday, 2002).

121. Clinton and Putin, memcon, September 6, 2000, CL, https://clinton.presidentiallibraries.us/items/show/101653.

122. "Subject: Deputy Secretary Discusses Pope Case with Russian Ambassador," cable State-212407, November 4, 2000, FOIA F-2017-13804, SDA.

123. See Sabrina Tavernise, "American Jailed as Spy in Moscow Is Freed on Putin's Orders. U.S. Welcomes Gesture," *New York Times,* December 15, 2000, https://www.nytimes.com/2000/12/15/world/american-jailed-as-spy-in-moscow-is-freed-on-putin-s-orders-us-welcomes-gesture.html.

124. See John M. Broder, "Despite a Secret Pact by Gore in '95, Russian Arms Sales to Iran Go On," *New York Times,* October 13, 2000, https://www.nytimes.com/2000/10/13/world/despite-a-secret-pact-by-gore-in-95-russian-arms-sales-to-iran-go-on.html.

125. Clinton and Putin, memcon, July 21, 2000, Talbott Diaries, 46:16.

126. "Subject: The Deputy Secretary's November 7 meeting with UK NATO Ambassador Designate David Manning," cable State-219498, November 16, 2000, FOIA F-2017-13804, CL.

127. Clinton and Putin, memcon, November 15, 2000, CL, https://clinton.presidentiallibraries.us/items/show/101654.

128. Notes, September 28, 2000, Talbott Diaries, 46:87.

Conclusion

1. Strobe Talbott, "Address to the Paasikivi Society, Helsinki, Finland. Opening Doors and Building Bridges in the New Europe," January 21, 1998, U.S. Department of State Archives (SDA), https://1997-2001.state.gov/policy_remarks/1998/980121_talbott_eursecurity.html.

2. Daniel Hamilton, "Europe. Whole and Free or Fractured and Anxious?," in *Europe Whole and Free: Vision and Reality,* ed. Slawomir Debski and Daniel Hamilton (Brookings Institution Press, 2019), 346, https://transatlanticrelations.org/wp-content/uploads/2019/11/Hamilton.pdf.

3. George W. Bush, "A Europe Whole and Free," remarks to the citizens in Mainz, Federal Republic of Germany, May 31, 1989, https://usa.usembassy.de/etexts/ga6-890531.htm.

4. William J. Clinton, "Remarks at Georgetown University," November 8, 1999, https://www.govinfo.gov/content/pkg/PPP-1999-book2/pdf/PPP-1999 -book2-doc-pg2008.pdf.

5. Albright to Clinton, "Memorandum for the President, the Vice President and the Secretary of State and the National Security Adviser, Subject: PfP and Central and Eastern Europe," January 26, 1994, 2015-0755-M, Clinton Library (CL).

6. See Richard Holbrooke, "America: A European Power," *Foreign Affairs* 74, no. 2 (1995): 39.

7. Daniel Hamilton, "Piece of the Puzzle: NATO and Euro-Atlantic Architecture After the Cold War," in *Open Door. NATO and Euro-Atlantic Security After the Cold War*, eds. Daniel Hamilton and Kristina Spohr (Brookings Institution Press, 2019), 29, https://transatlanticrelations.org/publications/open-door-nato -and-euro-atlantic-security-after-the-cold-war.

8. Talbott to Christopher, "Preparing for Geneva," memo, January 12, 1995, Freedom of Information Act Case no. (FOIA) M-2017-11914, SDA.

9. Talbott to Christopher, memo, March 24, 1995, Talbott Diaries, 10:51.

10. Notes, May 10, 1995, Talbott Diaries, 11:69.

11. Strobe Talbott, "Why NATO Should Grow," *New York Review of Books*, August 10, 1995, https://www.nybooks.com/articles/1995/08/10/why-nato -should-grow/. A reprinted PDF file is available in FOIA F-2017-13804, SDA.

12. Richard C. Holbrooke, "Europe Must Avoid Being Held Prisoner by Its History," remarks before the North Atlantic Assembly, Budapest, Hungary, May 29, 1995, https://permanent.access.gpo.gov/gpo41448/dispatch/1995/html/Dispatchv6no26 .html.

13. Strobe Talbott, "European Integration: An American Perspective. Keynote Speech by former US Deputy Secretary of State Strobe Talbott," in *The New Security Dimensions: Europe after the NATO and EU Enlargements*, ed. Adam Daniel Rotfeld (Stockholm International Peace Research Institute, June 2001), 141–42, https://www.sipri.org/sites/default/files/files/misc/SIPRI01NSD.pdf.

14. Notes, "Highlights from Mamedov Talks: Strategic Stability Talks, 20–22 September 1995," Talbott Diaries, 14:1.

15. Strobe Talbott, "Strengthening American Security Through World Leadership: Bosnia and Beyond," remarks at the State Department Town Meeting, Washington, DC, November 1, 1995, https://1997-2001.state.gov/regions/eur/bosnia /bostal.html.

16. William J. Clinton, "Remarks to the Community in Detroit, October 22, 1996," https://www.govinfo.gov/content/pkg/PPP-1996-book2/pdf/PPP-1996 -book2-doc-pg1890.pdf.

17. Clinton, "Remarks to the Community in Detroit."

18. See Warren Christopher, "A New Atlantic Community for the 21st Century," State Theater Stuttgart, September 6, 1996, printed in Warren Christopher, *In*

the Stream of History: Shaping U.S. Foreign Policy for a New Era (Stanford University Press, 1998), 456–66, https://usa.usembassy.de/etexts/ga7-960906.htm.

19. See James E. Goodby, *Europe Undivided: The New Logic of Peace in U.S.-Russian Relations* (United States Institute of Peace Press, 1998), 173, 179.

20. See "NATO-Russia. Objectives, Obstacles and Work Plan," memo, July 19, 1996, FOIA F-2017-13804, SDA. The memo was known as the "Talbott bible." See Ronald Asmus, *Opening NATO's Door: How the Alliance Remade Itself for a New Era* (Columbia University Press, 2002), 171; see also Fried, Pifer, and Vershbow to Lake, "NATO Enlargement Game Plan: June 96 to June 97," memo, June 6, 1996, 2015-0770-M, CL.

21. Talbott and Primakov, memcon, March 6, 1997, 1930 hours, FOIA F-2017-13804, SDA.

22. See Final Communiqué, North Atlantic Council Ministerial Meeting, NATO Headquarters, Brussels, December 10, 1996, https://www.nato.int/docu/pr /1996/p96-165e.htm. See also Asmus, *Opening NATO's Door*, 195.

23. Talbott to Albright, Berger, and Fuerth, "Trip Report No. 4 (Shannon-Andrews)," memo, May 21, 1999, Talbott Diaries, 38:21.

24. Notes on conversation with Javier Solana, April 6, 1999, Talbott Diaries, 36:83.

25. William J. Clinton, "Remarks on Receiving the International Charlemagne Prize," Aachen, Germany, June 2, 2000, https://www.karlspreis.de/en/laureates /william-jefferson-bill-clinton-2000/speech-by-bill-clinton.

26. Clinton, "Remarks on Receiving the International Charlemagne Prize."

27. See Ian Brzezinski, Daniel Fried, and Alexander Vershbow, "A Rebuttal to Russia's Narrative About the West, Grounded in History," Atlantic Council, March 4, 2021, https://www.atlanticcouncil.org/blogs/new-atlanticist/a -rebuttal-to-russias-narrative-about-the-west-grounded-in-history/.

28. See James Goldgeier, "NATO Enlargement Didn't Cause Russia's Aggression," commentary, Carnegie Endowment for International Peace, July 31, 2023, https://carnegieendowment.org/2023/07/31/nato-enlargement-didn-t-cause -russia-s-aggression-pub-90300.

29. See Stephen Kotkin, "What Putin Got Wrong About Ukraine, Russia, and the West: A Conversation with Stephen Kotkin," *Foreign Affairs*, May 26, 2022, https://www.foreignaffairs.com/podcasts/what-putin-got-wrong-about -ukraine-russia-and-west.

30. "Clinton regrets persuading Ukraine to give up nuclear weapons," *RTE*, April 4, 2023, https://www.rte.ie/news/primetime/2023/0404/1374162-clinton-ukraine/.

31. Bill Clinton, "I Tried to Put Russia on Another Path," *The Atlantic*, April 7, 2022, https://www.theatlantic.com/ideas/archive/2022/04/bill-clinton-nato -expansion-ukraine/629499/.

32. Dan Williams, "Ivo Daalder says NATO enlargement didn't go far enough," *The Economist*, April 9, 2022, https://www.economist.com/by-invitation/2022 /04/09/ivo-daalder-says-nato-enlargement-didnt-go-far-enough.

Acknowledgments and Note on Sources

1. See National Security Archive, "FOIA Suit seeks Strobe Talbott Files," September 12, 2018, https://nsarchive.gwu.edu/document/23755-foia-suit-seeks-strobe-talbott-files.

2. U.S. Department of State, Virtual Reading Room, Case no. F-2017-13804, n.d., https://foia.state.gov/Search/Results.aspx?caseNumber=F-2017-13804; see Stephan Kieninger, "The Strobe Talbott Papers at the State Department's Virtual Reading Room," Woodrow Wilson Center, February 2, 2022, https://www.wilsoncenter.org/blog-post/strobe-talbott-papers-state-departments-virtual-reading-room.

3. See Clinton Library, "Memcons & Telcons," n.d., https://clinton.presidentiallibraries.us/memcons-telcons; Clinton Library, "Declassified Documents," https://clinton.presidentiallibraries.us/collections/show/36.

4. Wilson Center Digital Archive, "Helmut Kohl Transcripts," n.d., https://digitalarchive.wilsoncenter.org/topics/helmut-kohl-transcripts.

5. See Stephan Kieninger, "The Helmut Kohl Transcripts. A New Resource for Post-Cold War History," Woodrow Wilson Center, January 30, 2024, https://www.wilsoncenter.org/blog-post/helmut-kohl-collection-new-resource-post-cold-war-history.

Archives and Interviews

Asmus, Ronald. Papers. Box 14, Europe. Private collection.

Blair, Tony. Prime Minister's Office Papers. PREM 49. UK National Archives, Kew.

Bush, George Herbert Walker. Presidential Library. Memcons and telcons. https://bush41library.tamu.edu/archives/memcons-telcons.

Clinton, William Jefferson. Presidential Library. Memcons and telcons. https://clinton.presidentiallibraries.us/memcons-telcons.

2009-0223-M: Declassified Documents Concerning President Vaclav Havel of the Czech Republic and President Lech Walesa of Poland, https://clinton.presidentiallibraries.us/items/show/101110.

2015-0755-M: Declassified Documents Concerning NATO Expansion, https://clinton.presidentiallibraries.us/items/show/57563.

2015-0770-M: Declassified Documents Concerning NATO Expansion, https://clinton.presidentiallibraries.us/items/show/57565.

2015-0771-M: Declassified Documents Concerning NATO Expansion, https://clinton.presidentiallibraries.us/items/show/100538.

2015-0772-M: Declassified Documents Related to the North Atlantic Treaty Organization (NATO), https://clinton.presidentiallibraries.us/items/show/101137.

2015-0782-M-1: Declassified Documents Concerning Russian President Boris Yeltsin, https://clinton.presidentiallibraries.us/items/show/57568.

2015-0782-M-2: Declassified Documents Concerning Russian President Boris Yeltsin, https://clinton.presidentiallibraries.us/items/show/57569.

2015-0815-M-2: Declassified Documents Concerning Russian President Boris Yeltsin, https://clinton.presidentiallibraries.us/items/show/118450.

2015-0792-M: Declassified Documents Concerning NATO Expansion, https://clinton.presidentiallibraries.us/items/show/101829.

2016-0143-M: Declassified Documents Regarding President Clinton's Trip to Russia, September 1–2, 1998, https://clinton.presidentiallibraries.us/items/show/101277

2017-0222-M: Declassified Documents Concerning Russian President Vladimir Putin, https://clinton.presidentiallibraries.us/items/show/100505.

Council on Foreign Relations. Papers. Seeley G. Mudd Library, Princeton University.

Delors, Jacques. Papers. Historical Archives of the European Union. https://archives.eui.eu/en/fonds/235128?item=JD.

Holbrooke, Richard. Papers. Seeley G. Mudd Library, Princeton University.

Kennan, George. Papers. Seeley G. Mudd Library, Princeton University.

Kohl, Helmut. Transcript. History and Public Policy Program Digital Archives. Woodrow Wilson Center. https://digitalarchive.wilsoncenter.org/topics/helmut-kohl-transcripts.

Major, John. Prime Minister's Office Papers. PREM 19. UK National Archives, Kew.

Nitze, Paul H. Papers. Library of Congress.

Talbott, Strobe. Diaries. Vols. 1–46, 1991–2000. Private collection.

U.S Department of State. Freedom of Information Act. Various document collections.

F-2017-13804 and FL-2017-13804, submitted by Svetlana Savranskaya and the National Security Archive, Strobe Talbott Files, Lot 05D292, Office of the Deputy Secretary, September 12, 2018, https://nsarchive.gwu.edu/document/23755-foia-suit-seeks-strobe-talbott-files.

F-2007-5000, F-2008-02190, F-2013-08489, M-2006-01499, M-2013-08489, M-2017-11312, M-2017-11493, M-2017-11516, M-2017-11577, M-2017-11621, M-2017-11641, M-2017-11649, M-2017-11708, M-2017-11712, M-2017-11729, M-2017-11732, M-2017-11760, M-2017-11764, M-2017-11772, M-2017-11776, M-2017-11776, M-2017-11777, M-2017-11791, M-2017-11814, M-2017-11832, M-2017-11838, M-2017-11839, M-2017-11863, M-2017-11877, M-2017-11914, M-2017-11926, M-2017-11994, M-2017-12017, M-2017-12022, M-2017-12044, M-2017-12050, M-2017-12135, M-2017-12144, M-2017-12151, M-2017-12156.

Author Interviews

Anders Aslund, July 2024

John Bass, December 2023, February 2024

James Bindenagel, May 2024

Hans Binnendijk, April 2020

Joachim Bitterlich, November 2023

Coit Blacker, March 2024

Ian Brzezinski, July 2024

Per Carlsen, May 2020

Derek Chollet, January 2024

Jürgen Chrobog, July 2024

Bill Clinton, February 2024

James Collins, October 2021

Michael Dobbs, May 2024

Kathleen Doherty, May 2024

William Drozdiak, June 2024

Gloria Duffy, January 2024

Eric Edelman, May 2024

Mathea Falco, April 2024

Stephen Flanagan, May 2020

Daniel Fried, March 2024

Grisha Freidin, April 2024

Philip Goldberg, March 2024

David Gompert, April 2020

James Goodby, September 2022

Rose Gottemoeller, October 2023

Marc Grossman, January 2024, April 2024

Daniel Hamilton, October 2023

Toomas Hendrik Ilves, March 2024

Wolfgang Ischinger, June 2022

Tina Kaidanow, May 2024

Richard Kauzlarich, May 2024

Andrei Kozyrev, October 2021

Franklin Kramer, March 2024

Andrew Kuchins, July 2024

Anthony Lake, June 2024

Stephen Larrabee, May 2020

Robert Legvold, June 2024

Roderic Lyne, September 2020

Thomas Matussek, July 2024

Shivshankar Menon, April 2024

Cameron Munter, August 2024

Victoria Nuland, December 2023

Joseph Nye, May 2024

Robert Nurick, May 2020

Carlos Pascual, June 2023

Steven Pifer, October 2023

Itamar Rabinovich, March 2024

Bruce Riedel, April 2024

Jeremy Rosner, March 2024

Volker Rühe, February 2019 and October 2021

David Satter, January 2024

Derek Shearer, January 2024

Stephen Sestanovich, June 2024

Wendy Sherman, April 2024

James Sherr, May 2024

Kate Schecter, June 2024

Gregory Schulte, February 2024

Thomas Simons, June 2024

András Simonyi, August 2024

Javier Solana, June 2022 and November 2023

Rasheed Sood, April 2024

Angela Stent, January 2024

Thomas Szayna, September 2020

Strobe Talbott, April 2022

Boris Tarasyuk, May 2024

Philip Taubman, January 2024

William Taubman, January 2024

John Thornton, June 2024

James Timbie, April 2024

James Townsend, March 2024

Jukka Valtasaari, January 2024

Alexander Vershbow, December 2023

Steven Weisman, January 2024

Andrew Weiss, November 2023

Barbara Wilkinson, May 2022

Daniel Yergin, June 2024

Miscellaneous Interviews

Chernomyrdin, Viktor. PBS Frontline. n.d. https://www.pbs.org/wgbh/pages
/frontline/shows/kosovo/interviews/chernomyrdin.html.

Collins, James. "The Ambassadorial Series. Deans of U.S.-Russia Diplomacy,"
Middlebury Institute of International Studies, January 24, 2022. https://nsarchive
.gwu.edu/document/27387-transcript-ambassador-james-f-coll.

——. PBS Putin Files. June 14, 2017. https://www.pbs.org/wgbh/frontline/interview
/james-collins/.

D'Alema, Massimo. Oral History Kosovo. January 16, 2019. https://oralhistorykosovo
.org/wp-content/uploads/2019/03/Massimo-DAlema-ENG.pdf.

Dobbins, James, Ambassadro. Association for Diplomatic Studies and Training. July 21, 2003. https://adst.org/OH%20TOCs/Dobbins,%20James.toc.pdf.

Rubin, Robert. PBS Commanding Heights. September 26, 2000, April 4, 2001. https://www.pbs.org/wgbh/commandingheights/shared/minitext/int_robertrubin.html#6.

Talbott, Strobe. The Association for Diplomatic Studies and Training. July 26, 2016. https://adst.org/OH%20TOCs/Talbott-Strobe.pdf.

——. PBS Putin Files. June 20, 2017. https://www.pbs.org/wgbh/frontline/interview/strobe-talbott/.

——. William J. Clinton Presidential History Project. February 25, 2010. https://s3.amazonaws.com/web.poh.transcripts/talbott_2010_taggedtranscript.pdf.

Bibliography

Strobe Talbott's Writings and Speeches

Khrushchev, Nikita. *Khrushchev Remembers: The Glasnost Tapes.* With a foreword by Strobe Talbott. Trans. and ed. Jerrold Schecter and Vyacheslav Luchkov. Little, Brown, 1990.

——. *Khrushchev Remembers: The Last Testament.* Introduction by Edward Crankshaw and Jerrold Schecter. Trans and ed. Strobe Talbott. Harper Collins, 1974.

——. *Khrushchev Remembers: With an Introduction and Commentary by Edward Crankshaw.* Trans. and ed. Strobe Talbott. Little, Brown, 1970.

Kohan, John, and Strobe Talbott. "Mikhail Gorbachev, 'I Want To Stay the Course.'" *Time,* December 23, 1991. https://time.com/archive/6719206/i-want-to-stay-the-course/.

Mandelbaum, Michael, and Strobe Talbott. *Reagan and Gorbachev.* Vintage Books, 1987.

Talbott, Strobe. "Address at All Souls College, Oxford University, Oxford, England, January 21, 2000." U.S. Department of State Archives. https://1997-2001.state.gov/policy_remarks/2000/000121_talbott_oxford.html.

——. "Address at Bucharest University, Bucharest, Romania, March 19, 1998." U.S. Department of State Archives. https://1997-2001.state.gov/www/policy_remarks/1998/980319_talbott_bucharest.html.

——. "Address to the New Traditions Conference, Berlin, Germany, March 20, 1998." U.S. Department of State Archives. https://1997-2001.state.gov/policy_remarks/1998/980320_talbott_berlin.html.

———. "Address at the Workshop on Ukraine-NATO Relations sponsored by the Harvard University Project on Ukrainian Security and the Stanford-Harvard Preventive Defense Project, Washington, DC, April 8, 1998." U.S. Department of State Archives. https://1997-2001.state.gov/policy_remarks/1998/980408_talbott_ukr_nato.html.

———. "America Abroad. The Birth of the Global Nation." *Time*, July 20, 1992. https://content.time.com/time/subscriber/article/0,33009,976015-4,00.html.

———. "America Abroad. Fiddling While Dubrovnik Burns." *Time*, November 25, 1991. https://content.time.com/time/subscriber/article/0,33009,974318-2,00.html.

———. "America Abroad. The Serbian Death Wish." *Time*, June 1, 1992. https://content.time.com/time/subscriber/article/0,33009,975621-2,00.html.

———. "America Abroad. Why Bosnia Is Not Vietnam." *Time*, August 24, 1992. https://content.time.com/time/subscriber/article/0,33009,976295-2.

———. "America Must Remain Engaged in Russian Reform." Statement Before the House Foreign Service Committee. 103rd Cong., 2nd sess. (January 25, 1994).

———. "America and Russia in a Changing World, Address on the 50th Anniversary of the Harriman Institute." October 29, 1996. U.S. Department of State. https://1997-2001.state.gov/regions/nis/1029talb.html.

———. "America's Stake in a Strong Europe." October 7, 1999. U.S. Department of State Archives. https://1997-2001.state.gov/policy_remarks/1999/991007_talbott_london.html.

———. "A Baltic Home-Coming. Robert C. Frasure Memorial Lecture, Tallinn, Estonia, January 24, 2000." U.S. Department of State Archives. https://1997-2001.state.gov/policy_remarks/2000/000124_talbott_tallinn.html.

———. "Bill, Boris, and NATO." In *Open Door: NATO and Euro-Atlantic Security After the Cold War*, ed. Daniel Hamilton and Kristina Spohr, 405–24. Brookings Institution Press, 2019. https://transatlanticrelations.org/wp-content/uploads/2019/04/17-talbott.pdf.

———. "The Crisis in Africa: Local War and Regional Peace." *World Policy Journal* 17, no. 2 (2000): 21–25.

———. *Deadly Gambits: The Reagan Administration and the Stalemate in Nuclear Arms Control*. Alfred A. Knopf, 1984.

———. "Democracy and the National Interest." *Foreign Affairs* 75, no. 6 (1996): 47–63.

———. "Hegemon and Proud of It: No Apologies Necessary for Being the Only Superpower—and Acting Like It." *Slate*, June 27, 1998. https://slate.com/news-and-politics/1998/06/hegemon-and-proud-of-it.html.

———. "The End of the Beginning: The Emergence of a New Russia." Address at Stanford University, Stanford, California, September 19, 1997. U.S. Department of State Archives. https://1997-2001.state.gov/regions/nis/970919talbott.html.

———. *Endgame: The Inside Story of Salt II*. Harper & Row, 1979.

———. *Engaging India: Diplomacy, Democracy, and the Bomb*. Brookings Institution Press, 2006.

———. "Gogol's Troika: The Case for Strategic Patience in a Time of Troubles." Address at the Conference "Russia at the End of the 20th Century." School of Humanities and Sciences, Stanford University, November 6, 1998. htps://web .stanford.edu/group/Russia20/volumepdf/talbott.pdf.

———. *The Great Experiment: The Story of Ancient Empires, Modern States, and the Quest for Global Governance.* Simon & Schuster, 2009.

———. "Holier-Than-Thou on Star Wars." *Time*, July 1, 1985. https://time.com /archive/6704365/holier-than-thou-on-star-wars/.

———. "The Making of Vladimir Putin." *Politico*, August 19, 2014. https://www .politico.com/magazine/story/2014/08/putin-the-backstory-110151/.

———. "Monnet's Brandy and Europe's Fate: A Determined Frenchman's Vision of Integration Serves as a Guide to Ending the Eurozone Crisis." Brookings Institution, 2014. http://csweb.brookings.edu/content/research/essays/2014/monnets -brandy-and-europes-fate.html.

———. *The Master of the Game. Paul Nitze and the Nuclear Peace.* Alfred A. Knopf, 1988.

———. "The New Geopolitics. Defending Democracy in the Post-Cold War Era." *The World Today* 51, no. 1 (January 1995): 7–10.

———. "Opening Doors and Building Bridges in the New Europe." Address to the Paasikivi Society, Helsinki, Finland, January 21, 1998. U.S. Department of State Archives. https://1997-2001.state.gov/policy_remarks/1998/980121_talbott_eursecurity.html.

———. "Post-Victory Blues." *Foreign Affairs* 71, no. 1 (1991/1992): 53–69.

———. "Remarks at the Signing Ceremony for the Baltic Nations-United States Charter of Partnership, January 16, 1998." Administration of William J. Clinton, 1998. https://www.govinfo.gov/content/pkg/PPP-1998-book1/pdf/PPP-1998-book1 -doc-pg68.pdf.

———. "Remarks to the U.S.-EU Conference 'Bridging the Atlantic: People-to-People Links.' " Washington, DC, May 6, 1997. U.S. Department of State Archives. https://1997-2001.state.gov/regions/eur/eu/970506.html.

———. "Rethinking the Red Menace." *Time*, January 1, 1990. https://time.com /archive/6713848/rethinking-the-red-menace/.

———. *The Russia Hand: A Memoir of Presidential Diplomacy.* Random House, 2002.

———. "Russia Has Nothing to Fear." *New York Times*, February 18, 1997, A25.

———. "But Russia Is a Special Case." *Slate*, June 11, 2002. https://slate.com/culture /2002/06/but-russia-is-a-special-case.html.

———. "Russia in Turbulence and Transition." Address at Amherst College, May 1, 1996.

———. *The Russians and Reagan.* Vintage Books, 1984.

———. "Strengthening American Security Through World Leadership: Bosnia and Beyond." Remarks at State Department Town Meeting, Washington DC, November 1, 1995. U.S. Department of State Archives. https://1997-2001.state .gov/regions/eur/bosnia/bostal.html.

——. "The Struggle for Russia's Future." *Wall Street Journal*, September 25, 1997, A22. https://www.wsj.com/articles/SB875136148358249000.

——. "U.S.-Turkish leadership in the post-Cold War World." Remarks at Bilkent University, Ankara, April 11, 1995. Telegram. Case no. FL-2017-13804, Document no. C06703280. U.S. Department of State Archives.

——. "Why NATO Should Grow." *New York Review of Books*, August 10, 1995. https://www.nybooks.com/articles/1995/08/10/why-nato-should-grow/.

——. "War in Europe." Interview with PBS Frontline. n.d. https://www.pbs.org/wgbh/pages/frontline/shows/kosovo/interviews/talbott.html.

——, and Michael Beschloss. *At the Highest Levels: The Inside Story of the End of the Cold War*. Little, Brown, 1993.

Literature

Afanasyev, Yuri. "Russian Reform Is Dead." *Foreign Affairs* 73, no. 2 (1994): 21–26.

Albright, Madeleine, "The Testing of American Foreign Policy." *Foreign Affairs* 77, no. 6 (1998): 50–64.

Albright, Madeleine. *Madam Secretary: A Memoir*. Harper Perennial, 2003.

——. *Prague Winter: A Personal Story of Remembrance and War, 1937–1948*. Harper Collins, 2012.

Albright, Madeleine. *Hell and Other Destinations: A 21st-Century Memoir*. Harper Collins 2020.

Arnold, John-Michael, "NATO's Readiness Action Plan: Strategic Benefits and Outstanding Challenges." *Strategic Studies Quarterly* 10, no. 1 (2016): 74–105.

Aron, Leon, *Boris Yeltsin: A Revolutionary Life*. Harper Collins, 2000.

Art, Robert. "Why Western Europe Needs the United States and NATO." *Political Science Quarterly* 111, no. 1 (1996): 1–39.

Aslund, Anders. *How Russia Became a Market Economy*. Brookings Institution Press, 1995.

——. *How Ukraine Became a Market Economy and Democracy*. Peterson Institute for International Economics, 2009.

——. "Russia's Collapse." *Foreign Affairs* 78, no. 5 (1999): 64–77.

——. "Russia's Success Story: Chernomyrdin Pulls It Off." *Foreign Affairs* 73, no. 5 (1994): 58–71.

Asmus, Ronald, Richard L. Kugler, and Stephen Larrabee, "Building a New NATO." *Foreign Affairs* 72, no 4 (1993): 28–40.

Asmus, Ronald, and Robert Nurick. "NATO Enlargement and the Baltic States." *Survival* 38, no. 2 (1996): 121–42.

Asmus, Ronald, and Stephen Larrabee. "NATO and the Have-Nots: Reassurance After Enlargement." *Foreign Affairs* 75, no. (1996): 13–20.

Asmus, Ronald. *Opening NATO's Door: How the Alliance Remade Itself for a New Era.* Columbia University Press, 2002.

Baker, Peter. "In Ukraine Conflict, Putin Relies on a Promise That Ultimately Wasn't." *New York Times*, January 9, 2022. https://www.nytimes.com/2022/01/09/us/politics/russia-ukraine-james-baker.html.

Baker, Peter, and Susan Glasser. *Kremlin Rising: Vladimir Putin's Russia and the End of Revolution.* Scribner, 2005.

Banka, Andris. "The Breakaways. A Retrospective on the Baltic Road to NATO." *War on the Rocks*, October 4, 2019.

Bellamy, Alex J. *Warmonger: Vladimir Putin's Imperial Wars.* Agenda Publishing, 2024.

Belton, Catherine. "Did Vladimir Putin Support Anti-Western Terrorists as a Young KGB Officer?" *Politico*, June 20, 2020. https://www.politico.com/news/magazine/2020/06/20/vladimir-putin-dresden-kgb-330203.

——. *Putin's People: How the KGB Took Back Russia and Then Took on the West.* William Collins, 2021.

Benliot, Albert, ed. *Iran: Outlaw, Outcast or Normal Country.* Nova Publishers, 2001.

Bensahel, Nora. "Separable but not Separate Forces: NATO's Development of the Combined Joint Task Force." *European Security* 8, no. 2 (1999): 52–72.

Bergmane, Una. *Politics of Uncertainty: The United States, the Baltic Question, and the Collapse of the Soviet Union.* Oxford University Press, 2023.

Beyrle, John. "The Long Good-Bye: The Withdrawal of Russian Military Forces from the Baltic States." Institute for the Study of Diplomacy, Edmund A. Walsh School of Foreign Service, Georgetown University, 1996.

Bierling, Stephan. *Wirtschaftshilfe für Moskau: Motive und Strategien der Bundesrepublik Deutschland und der USA von 1990 bis 1996.* Schönigh Verlag, 1998.

Bildt, Carl. "The Baltic Litmus Test: Revealing Russia's True Colors." *Foreign Affairs* 73, no. 5 (1994): 72–85.

——. *Peace Journey: The Struggle for Peace in Bosnia.* Weidenfeld & Nicholson, 1999.

——. "Russia, the European Union, and the Eastern Partnership." European Council of Foreign Relations, April 14, 2015. https://ecfr.eu/archive/page/-/Riga_papers_Carl_Bildt.pdf.

Bindenagel. James. *Germany. From Peace to Power? Can Germany Lead in Europe Without Dominating It?* Vandenhoeck & Ruprecht Unipress, 2020.

Binnendijk, Hans. "The Emerging European Security Order." *Washington Quarterly* 14, no. 4 (1991): 67–81.

Binnendijk, Hans, and Jeffrey Simon. "Romania and NATO. Membership Reassessment at the July 1997 Summit." *Strategic Forum* 101 (1997). https://apps.dtic.mil/sti/pdfs/ADA394379.pdf.

Binnendijk, Hans, and Richard L. Kugler. "NATO After the First Tranche: A Strategic Rationale for Enlargement." *Strategic Forum* 149 (1998).

——. *Seeing the Elephant. The U.S. Role in Global Security.* National Defense University Press and Potomac Books, 2006.

Bitterlich, Joachim. *Grenzgänger: Deutsche Interessen und Verantwortung für Europa. Erinnerungen eines Zeitzeugen.* Ibidem Verlag, 2021.

Blacker, Coit, Ashton Carter, Warren Christopher, David Hamburg, and William Perry, eds. *NATO After Madrid. Looking to the Future.* Stanford/Harvard Preventive Defense Project, 1999.

Blank, Stephen. "NATO Enlargement and the Baltic States: What Can the Great Powers Do?" ETH Zürich, November 18, 1997. https://www.files.ethz.ch/isn/47654/NATO_Enlargement_Baltic.pdf.

Blanton, Tom, and Emily Willard. "Srebrenica Conference Documents Detail Path to Genocide from 1993 to 1995." Electronic Briefing Book no. 519, July 1, 2015. National Security Archive. https://nsarchive2.gwu.edu/NSAEBB/NSAEBB519-Srebrenica-conference-documents-detail-path-to-genocide-from-1993-to-1995/.

Bowden, Mark. *Black Hawk Down. A Story of Modern War.* Grove Atlantic Press, 1999.

Brands, Hal. *From Berlin to Baghdad. America's Search for Purpose in the Post-Cold War World.* University Press of Kentucky, 2008.

——. *Making the Unipolar Moment. U.S. Foreign Policy and the Rise of the Post-Cold War Order.* Cornell University Press, 2016.

——. *War in Ukraine: Conflict, Strategy, and the Return of a Fractured World.* Johns Hopkins University Press, 2024.

Brzezinski, Zbigniew. "A Geostrategy for Eurasia." *Foreign Affairs* 76, no.5 (1997): 50–64.

——. *The Grand Chessboard: American Primacy and Its Geostrategic Imperatives.* Basic Books, 1997.

——. "A Plan for Europe." *Foreign Affairs* 74, no. 1 (1995): 26–42.

——. "The Premature Partnership." *Foreign Affairs* 73, no. 2 (1994): 67–82.

——, Brent Scowcroft, and Richard Murphy. "Differentiated Containment: Policy Toward Iran and Iraq." *Foreign Affairs* 76, no. 3 (1997): 20–30.

Brzezinski, Ian, Daniel Fried, and Alexander Vershbow, "A Rebuttal to Russia's Narrative about the West, Grounded in History." Atlantic Council, March 4, 2021. https://www.atlanticcouncil.org/blogs/new-atlanticist/a-rebuttal-to-russias-narrative-about-the-west-grounded-in-history/.

Boughton, James. *Tearing Down Walls: The International Monetary Fund 1990–1999.* International Monetary Fund, 2012.

Bucknam, Mark A. *Responsibility of Command: How UN and NATO Commanders Influenced Airpower over Bosnia.* Air University Press, 2003.

Budjeryn, Mariana. "The Breach. Ukraine's Territorial Integrity and the Budapest Memorandum." Issue Brief no. 3. Woodrow Wilson Center, Nuclear Proliferation International History Project. https://www.wilsoncenter.org/publication/issue-brief-3-the-breach-ukraines-territorial-integrity-and-the-budapest-memorandum.

——. *Inheriting the Bomb: The Collapse of the USSR and the Nuclear Disarmament of Ukraine.* Johns Hopkins University Press, 2022.

———. "Ukraine and the Treaty on the Non-Proliferation of Nuclear Weapons." Woodrow Wilson Center, October 15, 2018. https://www.wilsoncenter.org /blog-post/ukraine-and-the-treaty-the-non-proliferation-nuclear-weapons.

Budjeryn, Mariana, and Matthew Bunn. "Budapest Memorandum At 25: Between Past and Future." Project on Managing the Atom, Belfer Center for Science and International Affairs, Harvard Kennedy School, March 2020. https://www .belfercenter.org/publication/budapest-memorandum-25-between-past-and -future.

Burns, William. *The Back Channel: American Diplomacy in a Disordered World*. Random House, 2019.

Bush, George H. W., and Brent Scowcroft. *A World Transformed*. Alfred A. Knopf, 1998.

Carter, Ashton, and William Perry. *Preventive Defense: A New Security Strategy for America*. Brookings Institution Press, 1999.

Chaudhuri, Rudra. *Forged in Crisis: India and the United States Since 1947*. Hurst, 2014.

Chollet, Derek, and James Goldgeier. *America Between the Wars: From 11/9 to 9/11. The Misunderstood Years Between the Fall of the Berlin Wall and the Start of the War on Terror*. Public Affairs Books, 2008.

Chollet, Derek. *The Secret History of Dayton*. National Security Archive, 2005.

———, and Samantha Power, eds. *The Unquiet American: Richard Holbrooke in the World*. Public Affairs, 2012.

Christopher, Warren. "America's Leadership, America's Opportunity." *Foreign Policy* 98 (1995), 6–27.

———. *Chances of a Lifetime*. Scribner, 2001.

———. *In the Stream of History: Shaping U.S. Foreign Policy for a New Era*. Stanford University Press, 1998.

Clark, Wesley. *Waging Modern War: Bosnia, Kosovo and the Future of Combat*. Public Affairs, 2001.

Clinton, Bill. "I Tried to Put Russia on a Different Path." *The Atlantic*, April 7, 2022. https://www.theatlantic.com/ideas/archive/2022/04/bill-clinton-nato-expan sion-ukraine/629499/.

———. *My Life*. Alfred A. Knopf, 2004.

Colton, Timothy, *Yeltsin: A Life*. Basic Books, 2008.

Cordesman, Anthony. "Weapons of Mass Destruction in Iran: Delivery Systems, and Chemical, Biological, and Nuclear Programs." Center for Strategic International Studies, April 28,1998. https://www.bits.de/public/documents/iran/Cordesman _WMDinIran98.pdf.

Costigliola, Frank. *Kennan: A Life Between Worlds*. Princeton University Press, 2023.

Crawford, Timothy. "Pivotal Deterrence and the Kosovo War: Why the Holbrooke Agreement Failed." *Political Science Quarterly* 116, no. 4 (2001): 499–523.

Daalder, Ivo. *Getting to Dayton: The Making of America's Bosnia Policy*. Brookings Institution Press, 1999.

———. "NATO in the 21st Century: What Purpose? What Missions?" Brookings Institution, April 1, 1999. https://www.brookings.edu/articles/nato-in-the-21st-century-what-purpose-what-missions/.

———, and Michael O'Hanlon. *Winning Ugly: NATO's War to Save Kosovo.* Brookings Institution Press, 2000.

———, James Goldgeier, and James Lindsay. "Deploying NMD. Not Whether, But How." *Survival* 42, no.1 (2000): 6–28.

Dawisha, Karen. *Putin's Kleptocracy: Who Owns Russia?* Simon & Schuster, 2015.

Debski, Slawomir. "Peace Without Victory." In Debski and Hamilton, *Europe Whole and Free: Vision and Reality,* 15–26.

———, and Daniel Hamilton, eds., *Europe Whole and Free: Vision and Reality.* Brookings Institution Press, 2019.

Dean, Jonathan. "OSCE and NATO: Complementary or Competitive Security Providers for Europe." *OSCE Yearbook 1999.* Nomos, 2000, 429–34.

Dobbs, Michael. *Madeleine Albright: A Twentieth-Century Odyssey.* Henry Holt, 1999.

Dobbs, Michael. "Strobe Talbott and the 'Cursed Questions.'" *Washington Post,* June 9, 1996. https://www.washingtonpost.com/archive/lifestyle/magazine/1996/06/09/strobe-talbott-and-the-cursed-questions/bd8dbc3c-019d-4884-abac-b6bf91f22955/.

Dobbs, Michael. "Wider Alliance Would Increase U.S. Commitments." *Washington Post,* July 5, 1995. https://www.washingtonpost.com/archive/politics/1995/07/05/wider-alliance-would-increase-us-commitments/3f5c8a21-4f50-4fa9-8083-bb7d6d5b48ad/.

Dobbs Michael, and Steve Coll. "Ex-Communists Are Scrambling for Quick Cash," *Washington Post,* January 31, 1993. https://www.washingtonpost.com/archive/politics/1993/02/01/ex-communists-are-scrambling-for-quick-cash/00a47cf2-1f47-4051-90cd-844e3e35643b/.

Dobbs, Michael, and John M. Goshko. "Albright's Personal Odyssey Shaped Foreign Policy Beliefs." *Washington Post,* December 6, 1996, A25. https://www.washingtonpost.com/wp-srv/politics/govt/admin/stories/albright120696.htm.

Evangelista, Matthew. *The Chechen Wars: Will Russia Go the Way of the Soviet Union?* Brookings Institution Press, 2002.

Fawn, Rick, and Stephen White, eds. *Russia After Communism.* Routledge, 2002.

Fischer, Beth. *The Reagan Reversal: Foreign Policy and the End of the Cold War.* University of Missouri Press, 1997.

Flanagan, Stephen. "NATO and Central and Eastern Europe: From Liaison to Security Partnership." *Washington Quarterly* 15, no. 2 (1992): 141–51.

———. "NATO from Liaison to Enlargement: A Perspective from the State Department and the National Security Council 1990–1999." In Hamilton and Spohr, *Open Door,* 93–114.

———. "Sustaining the Promise of Mainz." In Debski and Hamilton, *Europe Whole and Free: Vision and Reality,* 93–114.

Flockhart, Trine. "The Dynamics of Expansion: NATO, WEU, and EU." *European Security* 5, no. 2 (1996): 196–218.

Fukuyama, Francis. *The End of the History and the Last Man*. Free Press, 1992.

Furmonavicius, Darius. *Lithuania Transforms the West: Lithuania's Liberation from Soviet Occupation and the Enlargement of NATO (1988–2022)*. Ibidem Press, 2023.

Gaddis, John Lewis. *George F. Kennan: An American Life*. Penguin, 2012.

Gall, Carlotta, and Thomas de Waal. *Chechnya: Calamity in the Caucasus*. New York University Press, 1999.

Gelb, Leslie H. "Quelling the Teacup Wars. The New World's Constant Challenge." *Foreign Affairs* 73, no. 6 (1994): 2–6.

Gessen, Masha. *The Man Without a Face: The Unlikely Rise of Vladimir Putin*. Riverhead, 2012.

Gilman, Martin. *No Precedent, No Plan: Inside Russia's 1998 Default*. MIT Press, 2010.

Gilligan, Emma. *Terror in Chechnya: Russia and the Tragedy of Civilians in War*. Princeton University Press, 2009.

Glaser, Charles. "Why NATO Is Still Best: Future Security Arrangements for Europe." *International Security* 18, no. 1 (1993): 5–50.

Götz, Elias, ed. *Russia, the West, and the Ukraine Crisis*. Routledge, 2017.

Götz, Elias, and Camille-Renaud Merlen, eds. *Russia and the Question of World Order*. Routledge, 2021.

Gold, Dore. *The Rise of Nuclear Iran: How Tehran Defies the West*. Regnery, 2009.

Goldgeier, James. "Bill and Boris: A Window into a Most Important Post-Cold War Relationship." *Texas National Security Review* 4, no. 1 (2018): 43–54.

——. "NATO Enlargement and the Problem of Value Complexity." *Journal of Cold War Studies* 22, no. 4 (2020): 146–74.

——. "NATO Expansion. Anatomy of a Decision." *Washington Quarterly* 21, no. 1 (1998): 85–102.

——. *Not Whether but When: The U.S. Decision to Enlarge NATO*. Brookings Institution Press, 1999.

——. "Promises Made, Promises Broken? What Yeltsin Was Told About NATO in 1993 and Why It Matters." *War on the Rocks*, July 12, 2016. https://warontherocks .com/2016/07/promises-made-promises-broken-what-yeltsin-was-told-about -nato-in-1993-and-why-it-matters/.

——, and Michael McFaul. *Power and Purpose: U.S. Policy Toward Russia After the End of the Cold War*. Brookings Institution Press, 2003.

——, and Joshua Itzkowitz Shifrinson. "The United States and NATO After the End of the Cold War." In *Before and After the Wall: World Politics and the End of the Cold War*, ed. Nuno Monteiro and Fritz Barthel, 265–85. Cambridge University Press, 2022.

——, eds. *Evaluating NATO Enlargement: From Cold War Victory to the Russia-Ukraine War*. Palgrave Macmillan, 2023.

——. "Evaluating NATO Enlargement. Scholarly Debates, Policy Implications, and Roads not Taken." In Goldgeier and Shifrinson, *Evaluating NATO Enlargement*, 1–42.

Gompert, David and Richard Kugler. "Free-Rider Redux: NATO Needs to Project Power." *Foreign Affairs* 74, no. 1 (1995): 7–12.

Gompert, David, and Stephen Larrabee, eds. *America and Europe*. Cambridge University Press, 1997.

Goodby, James E. *At the Borderline of Armageddon: How American President Managed the Atom Bomb*. Rowman & Littlefield, 2006.

——. "Diplomatic Cathedral Building." *Foreign Service Journal*, September 2002: 71–75.

——. "Europe Undivided." *Washington Quarterly* 21, no. 3 (1998): 191–207.

——. *Europe Undivided: The New Logic of Peace in U.S.-Russian Relations*. United States Institute of Peace Press, 1998.

——. "Preventive Diplomacy for Nuclear Nonproliferation in the Former Soviet Union." In *Opportunities Seized, Opportunities Missed: Preventive Diplomacy in the Post-Cold War World*, ed. Bruce Jentleson, 108–132. Rowman & Littlefield, 2000.

Gould-Davis, Nigel, and Ngaire Woods. "Russia and the IMF." *International Affairs* 75, no. 1 (1999): 1–22.

Grayson, George. *Strange Bedfellow: NATO Marches East*. University Press of America, 1999.

Hamilton, Daniel. "Europe. Whole and Free or Fractured and Anxious?" In Debski and Hamilton, *Europe Whole and Free*, 339–52. https://transatlanticrelations.org/wp-content/uploads/2019/11/Hamilton.pdf.

——. "New Members, New Missions: NATO and Euro-Atlantic Architecture in the Second Clinton Administration." In Hamilton and Spohr, *Open Door*, 339–84.

——. "Piece of the Puzzle: NATO and Euro-Atlantic Architecture After the Cold War." In Hamilton and Spohr, *Open Door*, 3–56.

Hamilton, Daniel, and Kristina Spohr, eds. *Exiting the Cold War. Entering a New World*. Brookings Institution Press, 2019.

——. *Open Door: NATO and Euro-Atlantic Security After the Cold War*. Brookings Institution Press, 2019.

Harahan, Joseph, and John Kuhn III. *On-Site Inspections Under the CFE Treaty: A History of the On-Site Inspection Agency and CFE Treaty Implementation, 1990–1996*. U.S. Department of Defense, 1996. https://archive.org/details/onsiteinspectionoohara_0/page/n7/mode/2up.

Harris, John F. *The Survivor: Bill Clinton in the White House*. Random House, 2005.

Haslam, Jonathan. "Russia's Seat at the Table: A Place Denied or a Place Delayed?" *International Affairs* 74, no. 1 (1998): 119–30.

Havel, Vaclav. "A Call for Sacrifice: The Co-Responsibility of the West." *Foreign Affairs* 73, no. 2 (1994): 2–7.

Headley, Jim. "Sarajevo, February 1994: The First Russia-NATO Crisis of the Post-Cold War Era." *Review of International Studies* 29, no. 2 (2003): 209–27.

Herbst, John E., Philip D. Zelikow, Charles Gati, Daniel S. Hamilton, and Petr Lunák. "European Security, NATO-Russia Relations, and the Post–Cold War Order." *Journal of Cold War Studies* 26, no. 3 (2024): 204–41.

Hill, Christopher. *Outpost: Life on the Frontlines of American Diplomacy. A Memoir.* Simon & Schuster, 2014.

Hill, Fiona, and Pamela Jewett. "Back in the USSR: Russia's Intervention in the Internal Affairs of the Former Soviet Republics and the Implications for United States Policy Toward Russia." Ethnic Conflict Project, Strengthening Democratic Institutions Project, John F. Kennedy School of Government, Harvard University, January 1994. https://www.brookings.edu/wp-content/uploads/2016/06/back-in-the-ussr-1994.pdf.

Hill, William. *No Place for Russia: European Security Institutions Since 1989.* Columbia University Press, 2018.

——. *Russia, the Near Abroad, and the West: Lessons from the Moldova-Transdniestria Conflict.* Johns Hopkins University Press, 2012.

Hoffman, David. *The Dead Hand: The Untold Story of the Cold War Arms Race and its Dangerous Legacy.* Anchor, 2010.

——. *The Oligarchs: Wealth and Power in the New Russia.* Public Affairs, 2010.

Holbrooke, Richard. "America: A European Power." *Foreign Affairs* 74, no. 2 (1995): 38–51.

——. *To End a War.* Random House, 1998.

——. "Europe Must Avoid Being Held Prisoner by Its History." Remarks Before the North Atlantic Assembly, Budapest, Hungary, May 29, 1995. *U.S. Department of State Dispatch* 6, no. 26. https://permanent.access.gpo.gov/gpo41448/dispatch/1995/html/Dispatchv6no26.html.

——. "Marooned in the Cold War: An Exchange," *World Policy Journal* 14, no. 4 (1997/1998): 100–102.

Horovitz, Liviu and Elias Götz. "The Overlooked Importance of Economics: Why the Bush Administrations Wanted NATO Enlargement." *Journal of Strategic Studies* 43, no. 6 (2020): 847–68.

Horovitz, Liviu. "The George H.W. Bush Administration's Policies vis-à-vis Central Europe: From Cautious Encouragement to Cracking Open NATO's Door." In Hamilton and Spohr, *Open Door,* 71–92.

Horyn, Cathy. "Strobe Talbott's Fifth Estate." *Washington Post,* July 14, 1994. https://www.washingtonpost.com/archive/lifestyle/1994/07/14/strobe-talbotts-fifth-estate/21e7c5f1-95bd-43d0-913e-443abd796e78/.

Ikenberry, John. *After Victory: Institutions, Strategic Restraint, and the Rebuilding of Order After Major Wars.* Princeton University Press, 2001.

Ivanov, Igor. "The Missile-Defense Mistake: Undermining Strategic Stability and the ABM Treaty." *Foreign Affairs* 79, no. 5 (2000): 15–20.

Jackson, Mike. *Soldier.* Bantam Press, 2007.

Jentleson, Bruce, ed., *Opportunities Seized, Opportunities Missed: Preventive Diplomacy in the Post–Cold War World.* Rowman & Littlefield, 2000.

Johnston, Seth. *How NATO Adapts: Strategy and Organization in the Atlantic Alliance Since 1950.* Johns Hopkins University Press, 2017.

Jones, Frank. "Engaging the World: Anthony Lake and American Grand Strategy, 1993–1997." *The Historical Journal* 59, no. 3 (2016): 869–901.

Judah, Tim. *Kosovo: War and Revenge.* Yale University Press, 2000.

Judah, Tim. *Kosovo: What Everyone Needs to Know.* Oxford University Press, 2008.

Jung, Carsten. *Contemporary Concert Diplomacy: A New Mechanism for Great Power Crisis Management in the Post-Cold War World.* Tectum Wissenschaftsverlag, 2016.

Kasekamp, Andres. "An Uncertain Journey to the Promised Land: The Baltic States' Road to NATO Membership." *Journal of Strategic Studies* 43, no. 6–7 (2020): 869–96.

Kassenova, Togzhan. *Atomic Steppe: How Kazakhstan Gave Up the Bomb.* Stanford University Press, 2022.

Kennan, George. "A Fateful Error." *New York Times,* February 5, 1997. https://www.nytimes.com/1997/02/05/opinion/a-fateful-error.html.

Kharas, Homi, Brian Pinto, and Sergei Ulatov. "An Analysis of Russia's 1998 Meltdown: Fundamentals and Market Signals." *Brookings Papers on Economic Activity,* 1:2001. https://www.brookings.edu/wp-content/uploads/2001/01/2001a_bpea_kharas.pdf.

Kieninger, Stephan. "Behind the Scenes of US Nuclear Diplomacy with India." *The Diplomat,* October 12, 2024. https://thediplomat.com/2024/10/behind-the-scenes-of-us-nuclear-diplomacy-with-india/.

———. "The Bush and Clinton Administrations and Ukraine's Nuclear Dismantlement, 1991–1994." *Diplomacy & Statecraft* 33, no. 3 (2022): 566–88.

———. *The Diplomacy of Détente: Cooperative Security Policies from Helmut Schmidt to George Shultz.* Routledge, 2018.

———. "The Helmut Kohl Transcripts: A New Resource for Post-Cold War History." *Woodrow Wilson Center* (blog), January 30, 2024. https://www.wilsoncenter.org/blog-post/helmut-kohl-collection-new-resource-post-cold-war-history.

———. "Money for Moscow: The West and the Question of Financial Assistance for Mikhail Gorbachev." In Hamilton and Spohr, *Exiting the Cold War,* 281–96.

———. "The 1999 Kosovo War and the Crisis in U.S.-Russia Relations." *International History Review* 43, no. 4 (2021): 781–95.

———. "Opening NATO and Engaging Russia: NATO's Two Tracks and the Establishment of the North Atlantic Cooperation Council." In Hamilton and Spohr, *Open Door,* 57–69.

———. "The Strobe Talbott Papers at the State Department's Virtual Reading Room." Woodrow Wilson Center, February 2, 2022. https://www.wilsoncenter.org/blog-post/strobe-talbott-papers-state-departments-virtual-reading-room.

Kissinger, Henry. "Expand NATO Now." *Washington Post,* December 18, 1994. https://www.washingtonpost.com/archive/opinions/1994/12/19/expand-nato-now/f1f0b4ed-56ee-4e5b-84ba-ae19a07a9997.

———. "It's an Alliance, Not a Relic." *Washington Post*, August 15, 1994. https://www
.washingtonpost.com/archive/opinions/1994/08/16/its-an-alliance-not-a-relic
/d8fd82b9-66bd-415b-a2d5-82f8f3c08a67.

Kohl, Helmut. *Erinnerungen 1990–1994*. Droemer und Knaur, 2007.

Kolesnikov, Andrei. "Caught Between Reform and Revanche. Russia's Struggle to
Modernize." Carnegie Moscow Center, February 2016. https://carnegie-production
-assets.s3.amazonaws.com/static/files/Article_Kolesnikov2016_Eng.pdf.

Kotkin, Steven. *Armageddon Averted: The Soviet Collapse, 1970–2000*. Oxford University Press, 2001.

Kozyrev, Andrei. *The Firebird: The Elusive Fate of Russian Democracy*. University of
Pittsburgh Press, 2010.

Kramer, Mark. "The Myth of a No-NATO-Enlargement Pledge to Russia." *Washington Quarterly* 32, no. 2 (2009): 39–61.

———. "NATO, the Baltic States and Russia: A Framework for Sustainable Enlargement." *International Affairs* 78, no. 4 (2002): 731–56.

———. "The Soviet Legacy in Russian Foreign Policy." *Political Science Quarterly* 134,
no. 4, (2019/2020): 585–609.

Krauthammer, Charles. "The Unipolar Moment." *Foreign Affairs* 70, no. 1 (1990/91):
23–33.

Kupchan, Charles. "Reviving the West." *Foreign Affairs* 75, no. 3 (1996): 92–104.

Kupchan, Charles, and Clifford A. Kupchan. "Concerts, Collective Security, and the
Future of Europe." *International Security* 16, no. 1 (1991): 114–61.

Lachowski, Zdzislaw. "The Adapted CFE Treaty and the Admission of the Baltic States
to NATO." Stockholm International Peace Research Institute, 2002. https://www
.sipri.org/publications/2002/adapted-cfe-treaty-and-admission-baltic-states-nato.

Lanoszka, Alexander, Christian Leuprecht, and Alexander Moens. "Lessons from the
Enhanced Forward Presence, 2017–2020." NATO Defense College Research
Paper. North Atlantic Treaty Organization, November 30, 2020. https://www
.ndc.nato.int/news/news.php?icode=1504.

Larrabee, Stephen. "*NATO Enlargement After the First Round*." Study no. P-786.
RAND Corporation, 1999.

———. "*NATO Enlargement and the Post-Madrid Agenda*." Study no. P-7999. RAND
Corporation, 1997.

———. "Russia, Ukraine and Central Europe: The Return of Geopolitics." *Journal of
International Affairs* 63, no. 2 (2010): 33–52.

Lawrence, Tony, and Tomas Jermalavičius, eds. *Apprenticeship, Partnership, Membership:
Twenty Years of Defence Development in the Baltic States*. International Centre for
Defence Studies, 2013.

Leigh-Phippard, Helen. "The Contact Group on (and in) Bosnia: An Exercise in
Conflict Mediation?" *International Journal* 58, no. 2 (1998): 306–24.

Lukes, Igor. "Central Europe Has Joined NATO: The Continuing Search for a More
Perfect Habsburg Empire." *SAIS Review* 19, no. 2 (1999): 47–59.

Maccoby Berglof, Annie. "In His First Interview at Home, the Former US Deputy Secretary of State Demonstrates True Kitchen-Table Diplomacy." *Financial Times*, December 2, 2011. https://www.ft.com/content/98a6131a-16b8-11e1-bc1d-00144 feabdc0.

Maloney, Suzanne. *Iran's Long Reach: Iran as a Pivotal State in the Muslim World*. United States Institute of Peace Press, 2008.

———. *Iran's Political Economy Since the Revolution*. Cambridge University Press, 2015.

Mandelbaum, Michael. *The Dawn of Peace in Europe*. Twentieth Century Fund Press, 1996.

———. "Foreign Policy as Social Work." *Foreign Affairs* 75, no. 1 (1996): 16–32.

———. *Mission Failure: America and the World in the Post-Cold War Era*. Oxford University Press, 2016.

———. "Preserving the New Peace: The Case Against NATO Expansion," *Foreign Affairs* 74, no. 3 (1995): 9–13.

———. "The Reluctance to Intervene." *Foreign Policy* 95 (Summer 1994): 3–18.

Maraniss, David. *First in His Class: A Biography of Bill Clinton*. Simon & Schuster, 1995.

Marten, Kimberly. "NATO Enlargement: Evaluating Its Consequences in Russia." In Goldgeier and Shifrinson, *Evaluating NATO Enlargement*, 209–49.

Mathew, Dean. "A Failure Revisited: A Closer Look at the Jan 2000 NMD Test." *Strategic Analysis* 24, no. 1 (2008): 97–110.

Matlock, Jack F. "Dealing with a Russia in Turmoil." *Foreign Affairs* 75, no. 3 (1996): 38–51.

McFaul, Michael. "Eurasia Letter, Russian Politics After Chechnya." *Foreign Policy* 99 (Summer 1995): 149–65.

———. "U.S. Foreign Policy and Chechnya." Century Foundation and the Stanley Foundation, March 2003. https://fsi-live.s3.us-west-1.amazonaws.com/s3fs-public /US_Foreign_Policy_and_Chechnya.pdf.

———. "Why Russia's Politics Matter." *Foreign Affairs* 74, no. 1 (1995): 87–99.

Medvedev, Sergey. *The Return of the Russian Leviathan*. Polity Books, 2019.

Miles, Simon. *Engaging the Evil Empire: Washington, Moscow, and the Beginning of the End of the Cold War*. Cornell University Press, 2020.

Miles, Simon. "We All Fall Down: The Dismantling of the Warsaw Pact and the End of the Cold War in Eastern Europe." *International Security* 48, no. 3 (2024): 51–85.

Moore, Robert. *A Time to Die: The Kursk Disaster*. Doubleday, 2002.

Moore, Rebecca. *NATO's New Mission: Projecting Stability in a Post-Cold War World*. Praeger, 2007.

Monteiro, Nuno, and Fritz Bartel, eds. *Before and After the Fall. World Politics and the End of the Cold War*. Cambridge University Press, 2021.

Morley, Morris, and Chris McGillion. "Disobedient Generals and the Politics of Redemocratization: The Clinton Administration and Haiti." *Political Science Quarterly* 112, no. 3 (1997): 363–84.

Mroz John Edwin, and Oleksandr Pavliuk. "Ukraine: Europe's Linchpin." *Foreign Affairs* 75, no. 3 (1996): 52–62.

National Security Archive. "The Nunn-Lugar Project. Cooperative Threat Reduction Program with Russia, Ukraine, Belarus and Kazakhstan, 1992–2012." The George Washington University. https://nsarchive.gwu.edu/project/nunn-lugar.

Norris, John. *Collision Course. NATO, Russia, and Kosovo.* Praeger Books, 2005.

Newhouse, John. "The Missile Defense Debate." *Foreign Affairs* 80, no. 4 (2000): 97–109.

Nye, Joseph. *Bound to Lead: The Changing Nature of American Power.* Basic Books, 1990.

Nye, Joseph. *Power in the Global Information Age: From Realism to Globalization.* Routledge, 2004.

Packer, George. "The End of the American Century," *The Atlantic,* May 2019, https://www.theatlantic.com/magazine/archive/2019/05/george-packer-pax-americana-richard-holbrooke/586042/.

——. *Our Man: Richard Holbrooke and the End of the American Century.* Knopf, 2019.

Parker, David. *U.S. Foreign Policy Toward Russia in the Post-Cold War Era: Ideational Legacies and Institutionalized Conflict and Cooperation.* Routledge, 2019.

Pavlov, Alexander, and Vladimir Rybachenkov. "Looking Back. The U.S.-Russian Uranium Deal. Results and Lessons." Arms Control Association, December 2013. https://www.armscontrol.org/act/2013-12/looking-back-us-russian-uranium-deal-results-and-lessons.

Pavlovsky, Gleb. "Putin and Yumashev: Survivors of the Nineties." Carnegie Endowment for International Peace, June 29, 2018. https://carnegieendowment.org/posts/2018/06/putin-and-yumashev-survivors-of-the-nineties.

Perry, William. *My Journey at the Nuclear Brink.* Stanford University Press, 2015.

Pifer, Steven. *The Eagle and the Trident: U.S.–Ukraine Relations in Turbulent Times.* Brookings Institution Press, 2017.

——. "The Trilateral Process. The United States, Ukraine, Russia and Nuclear Weapons." Brookings Institution Press. 2011. https://www.brookings.edu/articles/the-trilateral-process-the-united-states-ukraine-russia-and-nuclear-weapons/.

Piirimäe, Kaarel. "'Geopolitics of Sympathy:' George F. Kennan and NATO Enlargement." *Diplomacy & Statecraft,* 35, no. 1 (2024): 182–205.

Pipes, Richard. "Is Russia Still an Enemy? *Foreign Affairs* 76, no. 5 (1997): 65–78.

Plokhy Serhii. *The Gates of Europe: A History of Ukraine.* Penguin, 2021.

——. *The Last Empire: The Final Days of the Soviet Union.* Oneworld Publications, 2016.

——. *The Russo-Ukrainian War: The Return of History.* Norton, 2023.

——, and Mary Elise Sarotte. "The Shoals of Ukraine: Where American Illusions and Great-Power Politics Collide." *Foreign Affairs* 99, no. 1 (2020): 81–95.

Power, Samantha. *The Education of an Idealist: A Memoir.* Dey Street Books, 2019.

——. *A Problem from Hell: America and the Age of Genocide.* Basic Books, 2002.

Primakov, Yevgeny. *Russian Crossroads: Toward the New Millennium.* Yale University Press, 2004.

Politkovskaya, Anna. *A Small Corner of Hell: Dispatches from Chechnya.* University of Chicago Press, 2007.

Putin, Vladimir. *First Person.* Public Affairs, 2000.

Radchenko, Sergey. "'Nothing but Humiliation for Russia:' Moscow and NATO's Eastern Enlargement, 1993–1995." *Journal of Strategic Studies* 43, no. 6 (2020): 769–815.

Radchenko, Sergey, Timothy Sayle, and Christian Ostermann, eds. *NATO in the Cold War and After: Contested Histories and Future Directions.* Routledge, 2022.

Radchenko, Sergey. *To Run the World: The Kremlin's Cold War Bid for Global Power.* Cambridge University Press, 2024.

Reynolds, Bradley. *Alternating Visions of Europe's Post-Cold War Security Architecture: Finnish, American, and Russian Peace Mediation in Nagorno-Karabakh 1995–1997.* PhD diss., University of Helsinki.

Rice, Condoleezza. "Campaign 2000. Promoting the National Interest." *Foreign Affairs* 79, no. 1 (2000): 45–62.

Rosenbaum, David. "U.S. Peace Negotiator Was Always a Diplomat at Heart." *New York Times*, June 7, 1999. https://archive.nytimes.com/www.nytimes.com/library /world/europe/060799kosovo-talbott.html.

Rühe, Volker. *Deutschlands Verantwortung: Perspektiven für ein neues Europa.* Ullstein, 1994.

——. "Opening NATO's Door." In Hamilton and Spohr, *Open Door*, 217–33.

——. "Shaping Euro-Atlantic Policies. A Grand Strategy for a New Era." *Survival* 35, no. 2 (1993): 129–37.

Rynning, Sten. "The False Promise of Continental Concert: Russia, the West and the Necessary Balance of Power." *International Affairs* 91, no. 3 (2015): 539–52.

——. *NATO: From Cold War to Ukraine, A History of the World's Most Powerful Alliance.* Yale University Press, 2024.

Safire, William. "Putinism Looms." *New York Times*, January 31, 2000.

Sakwa, Richard, *The Lost Peace: How the West Failed to Prevent a Second Cold War.* Yale University Press, 2023.

Sayari, Sabri. "Turkish Foreign Policy in the Post-Cold War Era: The Challenges of Multi-Regionalism." *Journal of International Affairs* 54, no. 1 (2000): 169–82.

Sarotte, Mary Elise. "A Broken Promise? What the West Really Told Moscow About NATO Expansion." *Foreign Affairs* 93, no. 5 (2014): 90–97.

——. "The Convincing Call from Central Europe. Let Us into NATO," *Foreign Affairs*, March 12, 2019. https://www.foreignaffairs.com/united-states/convincing -call-central-europe-let-us-nato.

——. "How to Enlarge NATO: The Debate Inside the Clinton Administration, 1993–95." *International Security* 44, no. 1 (2019): 7–44.

——. *Not One Inch: America, Russia, and the Making of the Post-Cold War Stalemate.* Yale University Press, 2021.

——. *1989: The Struggle to Create Post-Cold War Europe.* Princeton University Press, 2009.

———. "Perpetuating U.S. Preeminence: The 1990 Deals to 'Bribe the Soviets Out' and Move NATO In." *International Security* 35, no. 1 (2010): 110–37.

——— and Tom Blanton, eds. "The End of the Soviet Union 1991." Briefing Book no. 576. National Security Archive, December 2016. https://nsarchive.gwu.edu /briefing-book/russia-programs/2021-12-21/end-soviet-union-1991.

———. *The Last Superpower Summits: Reagan, Gorbachev and Bush. Conversations that Ended the Cold War.* Central European University Press, 2016.

———. "NATO Expansion. The Budapest Blow Up 1994." Briefing Book no. 780. National Security Archive, November 24, 2021. https://nsarchive.gwu.edu/brief ing-book/nato-russia-russia-programs/2021-11-24/nato-expansion-budapest -blow-1994.

———. "NATO Expansion. What Gorbachev Heard." Briefing Book no. 613. National Security Archive, December 12, 2017. https://nsarchive.gwu.edu /briefing-book/russia-programs/2017-12-12/nato-expansion-what-gorbachev -heard-western-leaders-early

———. "NATO Expansion. What Yeltsin Heard," Briefing Book no. 621. National Security Archive, March 16, 2018. https://nsarchive.gwu.edu/briefing-book /russia-programs/2018-03-16/nato-expansion-what-yeltsin-heard.

———. "Yeltsin Shelled Russian Parliament 25 Years Ago, U.S. Praised 'Superb Handling.'" Briefing Book no. 641. National Security Archive, October 4, 2018. https://nsarchive.gwu.edu/briefing-book/russia-programs/2018-10-04/yeltsin -shelled-russian-parliament-25-years-ago-us-praised-superb-handling.

Savranskaya, Svetlana, and Tom Blanton, with Natalie Sherman, eds. "Putin's First Election, March 2000." Briefing Book no. 854. National Security Archive, March 21, 2024. https://nsarchive.gwu.edu/briefing-book/russia-programs/2024 -03-21/putins-first-election-march-2000.

Savranskaya, Svetlana, and Mary Elise Sarotte, eds. "The Clinton-Yeltsin Relationship in Their Own Words." Briefing Book no. 640. National Security Archive, October 2018. https://nsarchive.gwu.edu/briefing-book/russia-programs/2018 -10-02/clinton-yeltsin-relationship-their-own-words.

Sayle, Timothy. *Enduring Alliance: A History of NATO and the Postwar Global Order.* Cornell University Press, 2019.

———. "Patterns of Continuity in NATO's Long History." *International Politics* 57, no. 3 (2020): 322–41.

Scannia, Bastian Matteo. *Sonderzug nach Moskau. Geschichte der deutschen Russlandpolitik seit 1990.* C. H. Beck, 2024.

Schecter, Jarrold, and Leona Schecter. *Sacred Secrets: How Soviet Intelligence Operations Changed American History.* Potomac Books, 2002.

Schmies, Oxana, ed. *NATO's Enlargement and Russia: A Strategic Challenge in the Past and Future.* Ibidem, 2021.

Scott, James, ed. *After the End: Making U.S. Foreign Policy in the Post-Cold War World.* Duke University Press, 1999.

Sell, Louis. *Slobodan Milosevic and the Destruction of Yugoslavia.* Duke University Press, 2002.

Serwer, Daniel. *From War to Peace in the Balkans, the Middle East and Ukraine.* Palgrave Pivot, 2019.

Sestanovich, Stephen. "Geotherapy. Russia's Neuroses, and Ours." *The National Interest* 45 (Fall 1996): 3–13.

Shapiro, Ian and Adam Tooze, eds. *Charter of the North Atlantic Treaty Organization.* Yale University Press, 2018.

Sherr, James. *Hard Diplomacy and Soft Coercion: Russia's Influence Abroad.* Chatham House, 2013.

——. "Russia-Ukraine Rapprochement? The Black Sea Fleet Accords." *Survival* 39, no. 3 (1997): 33–50.

Shevtsov, Leontiy. "Russian-NATO Military Cooperation in Bosnia: A Basis for the Future?" *NATO Review* 45, no. 2 (1997): 17–21.

Shields, John, and William Potter, eds. *Dismantling the Cold War: U.S. and NIS Perspectives on the Nunn-Lugar Cooperative Threat Reduction Program.* MIT Press, 1997.

Shifrinson, Joshua Itzkowitz. "Deal or No Deal? The End of the Cold War and the U.S. Offer to Limit NATO Expansion." *International Security* 40, no. 4 (2016): 7–44.

——. "Eastbound and Down: The United States, NATO Enlargement, and Suppressing the Soviet and Western European Alternatives, 1990–1992." *Journal of Strategic Studies* 43, no. 6 (2020): 816–46.

——. *Rising Titans, Falling Giants. How Great Powers Exploit Power Shifts.* Cornell University Press, 2018.

Short, Philip. *Putin: His Life and Times.* Bodley Head, 2022.

Simonyi, András. "NATO Enlargement: Like Free Solo Climbing." In Hamilton and Spohr, *Open Door,* 159–71. https://transatlanticrelations.org/wp-content/uploads/2019/04/07-Simonyi.pdf.

Slaughter, Ann-Marie. *The Chessboard and the Web: Strategies of Connection in a Networked World.* Yale University Press, 2017.

Solomon, Gerald. *The NATO Enlargement Debate, 1990–1997: The Blessings of Liberty.* Praeger Publishers, 1998.

Spohr Kristina. *Germany and the Baltic Problem After the Cold War: The Development of a New Ostpolitik, 1989–2000.* Routledge, 2004.

——. *Post Wall, Post Square: Rebuilding the World After 1989.* William Collins, 2019.

—— and Kaarel Piirimae. "With or without Russia? The Boris, Bill and Helmut Bromance and the Harsh Realities of Securing Europe in the Post-Wall World, 1990–1994." *Diplomacy & Statecraft* 33, no. 1 (2022): 158–93.

Stent, Angela. *The Limits of Partnership: U.S.-Russian Relations in the Twenty-First Century.* Princeton University Press, 2015.

——. *Putin's World: Russia against the West and with the Rest.* Twelve, 2019.

——. *Russia and Germany Reborn: Unification, the Soviet Collapse, and the New Europe.* Princeton University Press, 2000.

Taubman, William. *Khrushchev: The Man and His Era*. W. W. Norton, 2003.

Townsend, James. "In Peace and War: The Military Implications of NATO Enlargement." In Goldgeier and Shifrinson, *Evaluating NATO Enlargement* 495–530.

Treisman, Daniel. "Loans for Shares Revisited." *Post-Soviet Affairs* 26, no. 3 (2010): 207–27.

——. "Presidential Popularity in a Hybrid Regime: Russia Under Yeltsin and Putin," *American Journal of Political Science* 55, no.3 (2011): 590–609.

Truscott, Peter. *Kursk: Russia's Lost Pride*. Simon & Schuster, 2002.

Vaiksnoras, Vitalijus. "The Role of Baltic Defence Co-operation for the Security of Estonia, Latvia and Lithuania." NATO Individual Fellowship Report 2000–2002. North Atlantic Treaty Organization, 2002. https://www.nato.int/acad/fellow/99 -01/vaisknoro.pdf.

Van Ham, Peter, and Sergei Medvedev, eds. *Mapping European Security After Kosovo*. Manchester University Press, 2004.

Vershbow, Alexander. "Present at the Transformation: An Insider's Reflection on NATO Enlargement, NATO-Russia Relations and Where We Go from Here." In Hamilton and Spohr, *Open Door*, 425–47.

De Waal, Thomas. *Black Garden: Armenia and Azerbaijan Through Peace and War*. New York University Press, 2003.

Wedel, Janine. "The Harvard Boys Do Russia." *The Nation*, May 14, 1998. https:// www.thenation.com/article/world/harvard-boys-do-russia/.

Wedel, Janine. *Collision and Collusion: The Strange Case of Western Aid to Eastern Europe*. St. Martins's Griffin, 2000.

Weiss, Andrew. *Accidental Czar: The Life and Lies of Vladimir Putin*. First Second Books, 2022.

Weisser, Ulrich. *Sicherheit für ganz Europa: Die Atlantische Allianz in der Bewährung*. Deutsche Verlags Anstalt, 1999.

Williams, Marjorie. "Clinton's Rhodes Warrior." *Vanity Fair*, September 1994. https://archive.vanityfair.com/article/1994/9/clintons-rhodes-warrior.

Wilson, James Graham. *America's Cold Warrior: Paul Nitze and National Security from Roosevelt to Reagan*. Cornell University Press, 2024.

——. *The Triumph of Improvisation: Gorbachev's Adaptability, Reagan's Engagement, and the End of the Cold War*. Cornell University Press, 2014.

Wolczuk, Kataryna, and Rilka Dragneva. "Russia's Longstanding Problem with Ukraine's Borders." Chatham House, August 24, 2022. https://www.chatham house.org/2022/08/russias-longstanding-problem-ukraines-borders

Yavlinsky, Grigory. "Russia's Phony Capitalism." *Foreign Affairs* 77, no. 3 (1998): 67–79.

Yeltsin, Boris. *Midnight Diaries*. Weidenfeld & Nicholson, 2000.

Yost, David. "The Budapest Memorandum and Russia's Intervention in Ukraine." *International Affairs* 91, no. 3 (2015): 505–38.

Zelikow, Philip. "European Security, NATO-Russia Relations, and the Post–Cold War Order." *Journal of Cold War Studies* 26, no. 3 (2024): 204–41.

Zelikow, Philip and Condoleezza Rice. *To Build a Better World: Choices to End the Cold War and Create a Global Commonwealth.* Twelve, 2020.

———. *Germany Unified and Europe Transformed: A Study in Statecraft.* Harvard University Press, 1995.

Zelizer, Julian. *Burning Down the House: Newt Gingrich, the Fall of a Speaker, and the Rise of the New Republican Party.* Penguin, 2020.

Zimmermann, Warren. *Origins of a Catastrophe: Yugoslavia and Its Destroyers.* Random House, 1999.

Zubok, Vladislav. *Collapse: The Fall of the Soviet Union.* Yale University Press, 2022.

———. "Myths and Realities of Putinism and NATO Expansion." In Goldgeier and Shifrinson, *Evaluating NATO Enlargement,* 145–59.

Zürcher, Christoph. "Chechnya and Kosovo: Reflections in a Distorting Mirror." In *Mapping European Security After Kosovo,* ed. Peter van Ham and Sergei Medvedev, 179–200. Manchester University Press, 2004.

Index

Abkhazia, 26, 48, 209

ABM Treaty. *See* Anti-Ballistic Missiles Treaty

Abramson, James, xxiv

Ahtisaari, Martti, 8, 123, 178–185

Albania, 161, 163, 166

Albright Madeleine, 197, 207, 209, 241; background of, 110–11, 137; Baltics and NATO enlargement, 106; Kosovo conflict and, 165–69, 178–81, 190–91; NATO-Russia charter and, 116, 120–125; Russia and, 116, 135–39, 147–48, 150, 153, 155, 160; Talbott and, 110–11, 137, 139

Annan, Kofi, 178

Anti-Ballistic Missles Treaty, 202, 212, 214; NMD and, 202, 212, 214, 219

Armenia, 81

Ascher, Barbara, 94, 237

Asian financial crisis (1997), 144

Asmus, Ronald, 33, 51, 52, 53, 100, 105, 106, 240

Aspin, Les, 19, 26, 34, 35, 37–40

August Coup (Moscow, 1991), xxvi, 83

Avdeyev, Alexander, 167–68

Azerbaijan, 80, 81, 215

Baker, James A., III, 16, 33

Balkans, 2, 3, 19–21, 47, 59, 73–74, 81, 135, 156, 160, 162, 166, 178

Baltic states, xxx, 55, 65, 96, 99, 100, 118, 203, 228, 231; NATO enlargement and, 6, 7, 22, 65, 78, 83–84, 103–06, 121–22, 130–31; Russian troop withdrawals from, 48, 103

Barak, Ehud, 193

Bass, John, 119, 242

Belarus, 26, 30, 36, 95, 101, 131–32, 171, 205–06

Berezovsky, Boris, 157, 195, 205

Berger, Sandy, 150, 152, 156, 170, 174, 176, 179, 190, 193, 213; Bosnia conflict, and, 20; Kosovo conflict and, 170, 174, 176, 17, 183, 186–87; at Moscow summit (1998), 146–148,

Berger, Sandy (*continued*)
150, 152; at Moscow summit (2000),
213; NATO enlargement and, 53–54,
118–19, 121, 129; Putin and, 186, 193;
Russia-Iran issue and, 141–42,
146–48; Talbott and, 107–09, 142
Bildt, Carl, 58, 76, 173, 178
Birmingham G-8 summit, 141–42
Bitterlich, Joachim, 306
Blair, Tony, 143, 199, 207, 209, 221, 242
Bordyuzha, Nikolai, 156
Bosnia conflict, 32, 180, 186–87,
189–90, 224, 229, 230, 233–34, 238;
Dayton Accords and, 160, 174;
lift-and-strike-proposal, 21; Lugar,
Richard, and, 32; NATO and, 18–22,
47–48, 51, 53, 55, 74–78; Russia and,
74–76, 180, 186; Talbott and, xv,
xvii, xxix, 2, 5, 6, 10, 18–22, 38, 41,
42, 47–48, 51, 53, 55
Brzezinski, Zbigniew, 37, 110, 120,
138–39
Budapest Summit (1994), ii, 6, 28–29, 35,
59–63, 65, 69–70, 73, 180, 227
Bulgaria, 59, 129–32, 134–35, 166
Burns, Nick, 171, 242
Bush, George H. W., xvii, xxvi, 2, 15,
27, 28, 30, 39, 224–25
Bushehr project, 221

Canada, 86, 172
Carter administration, xx, xxi, 12, 13,
85, 110, 139
CFE. *See* Treaty on Conventional
Forces in Europe
Chechnya: Chechen War (1994), 65–66,
70, 78, 99, 138; Chechen War (1999),
159, 176, 194, 196–99, 200–205,
207–10, 216–19, 227, 234, 238;
Georgia and, 200, 202; Putin and,
194, 196–99

Chernomyrdin Viktor, xxx, 8, 15, 63,
69, 115, 137, 140, 146, 154, 169, 192,
225, 232; "catchall" regulation
announced by, 140–41; Gore-
Chernomyrdin Commission and, 15,
63, 140, 176, 225; in Hammer-and-
Anvil Plan, 178, 180; Kosovo conflict
and, 8, 175–82, 184–85; NATO
enlargement and, 112–13, 115;
Yeltsin's appointment of, xxx, 69,
146, 148–152, 154; Yeltsin's dismissal
of, 140
Chirac, Jacques, 114, 125, 128–29, 221
Christopher, Warren, 18, 19, 21, 24, 31,
53, 55, 63, 85, 111; Bosnia conflict
and, 20–22; Kozyrev and, 15–16, 37,
48–50, 60, 68–69, 71–72; NATO
enlargement and, 42–47, 96–99;
Russia and, 68–72, 101–2; Primakov
and, 97–99; Talbott and, xv, xxvi, 5,
11–16, 38–43, 107; Vancouver summit
and, 14–16
Chubais Anatoly, 143–44, 146–47, 158,
Clark, Wesley, 54, 189–90
Clinton, Bill; at Birmingham G-8
summit (1998), 141–42; Bosnia
conflict and, 19–22, 32, 47–48,
74–78, 122; Chechen conflict and,
196–200, 202–05, 207–10, 216–19;
CSCE Budapest summit and, 60–63;
EAPC meeting and, 130–31; first
Moscow visit of, 45–46; Helsinki
summit and, 116, 121, 123;
impeachment of, 147, 158; Kosovo
conflict and, 166, 169–85; Lewinsky
affair and, 147, 153, 158; Madrid
summit and, 129–30; NATO
enlargement and, 33, 37, 44–46,
53–63; 1992 election and, xxvi–xxvii;
NMD issue and, 202, 212, 214, 219;
at Oxford, xiii, xiv–xx, 12, 92, 109;

Putin and, 199, 213–15; Putin's
Auckland encounter with, 196;
Russia aid issue and, xxx, 13, 17, 22,
66, 151; Russian parliamentary crisis
and, 14–15, 23–25; Russia's 1996
election and, 87–88; St. Petersburg
1996 visit and, 86–87; Talbott's first
meeting with, xix–xx; Talbott's first
memorandum to, 13–14; at Tokyo
summit, 22, 28; at Vancouver
summit, 5, 15–18
Clinton, Hillary Rodham, xxix, 41
Clinton-Talbott conversations; on
Bosnian conflict, 18–22; on
democracy in Russia, xiv, xxvi,
11–18, 143–54; on foreign policy, xiv,
11–18, 38–42; on G-7, 86, 116–17,
141–42; on Russian economy, xiv,
10–18, 143–54; on U.S.-Russia
relations, xiii–xv, xix–xx, 10–18,
13–25, 70–71; on Yeltsin-parliament
relations, 22–26, 42, 83, 145–47,
152, 154
Clinton-Yeltsin meetings and
exchanges; on Bosnia conflict,
47–48, 74–76; on Chechen conflict,
198–200; on IMF loans, 143–46,
151–52; on Kosovo conflict, 162–64,
167–69, 175–76, 179–80, 184–85,
187–91; on NATO enlargement and,
45–46, 49–50, 60–65, 69–76, 121–30;
on non-proliferation, 23, 141–42; on
Putin, 196, 198, 204–5, 214–15; on
Russia-Iran issue, 137–43; on Russian
economy, 143–154; Russian rocket
part sales to India, 23; on Russia-
Ukraine warheads dispute, 26–30; on
U.S.-Russia relations, 15–18, 45–46,
49–50, 60–65, 69–76, 121–30,
167–69, 175–76, 179–80, 184–85,
187–91

Cohen, William, 165, 179, 189–91
Cold War: arms control and, xxi, xxiv,
xxvi; Cuban Missile Crisis, xviii;
legacies of, xxx, 3–11, 16–22; Talbott
and, xviii, xx
Collins, Jim, 24, 67, 146–47, 195, 239,
242
Communist Party of the Russian
Federation, xiv, 8, 14, 24, 83–84,
86–87, 146, 150, 152–55, 205,
211, 232
Conference on Security and
Cooperation (CSCE), 58–60, 227
Congress, U.S., 7, 15, 23, 42, 60, 71,
75–76, 139–41, 143, 151, 157, 230, 247;
Bosnia and, 75–76; Russia-Iran issue
in, 139–41, 143
Contact Group on Bosnia, 161–63, 168
Contract with America, 66
Czechoslovakia, 30, 110, 137
Czech Republic, 7, 30–31, 33–34, 36, 45,
65, 76, 99, 114, 128, 130, 133–34

Davis, Lynn, 34
Defense Department, U.S., xxi, 20, 34,
35, 51, 54, 179, 220
Deliberate Force, Operation, 74
Denver G-7 summit, 136–37
Detweiler, David, xx
Deutch, John, 54
Donilon, Thomas, 39–40
Duma, Russian, 8, 24–25, 42, 83,
145–46, 152, 154, 169, 203, 217,
225, 232

Edelman, Eric, xxvii, 12, 37, 123,
179, 243
Ely, Clint, xviii
Estonia, 48–49, 102–06, 203
European Atlantic Partnership Council
(EAPC), 130–31

European Union, 3, 6, 33–34, 53, 56–58, 76, 80–81, 96, 100, 143, 166, 173, 223, 226, 228–29

Federal Security Service (FSB), 158, 195
Finland, 57, 223, 228
Foglesong, Robert "Doc," 183, 186–87
Foreign Affairs, 38, 77, 96, 100
France, 20–21, 31, 84, 98, 113–14, 161, 220
Freidin, Gregory, xix, 150, 243
Fuerth, Leon, 54, 63, 69, 158, 177, 207
Fyodorov, Boris, 25, 146

G-7 enlargement and Group of Eight (G-8), 23, 28, 48, 64, 74, 86, 116, 122, 136, 139, 141–42, 158, 167, 169, 179–80, 189–90, 216–17, 221
Gaidar, Yegor, xxx, 14, 24–25, 146
Gati, Toby, 171
Georgia, xxix, 26, 48, 59, 79, 199, 200, 202, 204, 207, 209, 215, 219; Chechen conflict and, 199, 200, 202, 204, 207
Germany, unification of, 151; NATO enlargement and, 32, 33
Gingrich, Newt, 66, 155
Goldberg, Phil, 243
Gorbachev, Mikhail, xxiv, xxvi, 14, 23, 103
Gore, Al: Gore-Chernomyrdin commission and, 15, 63, 112–13, 115; Gore-Chernomyrdin meeting, 112–13, 140, 176–77, 225; Holbrooke and, 109–10; Kosovo conflict and, 175–78, 190, 193; NATO enlargement and, 53–56, 112–16; Primakov exchanges with, 112–13, 163–64; Russia and, 15, 25, 53–56, 59, 84, 112–16, 137, 219; Russia's financial crisis, 149–50, 154; Russia-Iran issue, 140–41; Ukraine

and, 132; Yeltsin's beside meeting with, 63–64
Gottemoeller Rose, 242–43
Grachev, Pavel, 21, 177
Great Britain, xx, 21, 50, 68, 113, 117, 143, 184, 189, 199, 208–9, 242
Grunwald, Henry, xxii

Haiti, xxviii, 5,6, 38, 50–51, 62, 76, 227
Halifax G-7 summit, 74
Havel, Vaclav, 2, 30–31, 139
Hayward, Max, xx
Helms, Jesse, 42, 71
Helsinki Final Act, 79, 203
Hitler, Adolf, 79, 203
Holbrooke, Richard, xxvi, 6, 12, 19, 51–55, 76–79, 96, 99, 108–10, 162–63, 167, 173–74, 226, 228, 242–43; Bosnian conflict and; NATO enlargement and, 6, 19, 51–55, 76–79, 96, 99, 226, 228; Kosovo crisis and, 162–63, 167, 173–74; Talbott and, xxvi, 12, 108–10
Hungary, 7, 30, 34, 36, 56, 76, 99, 128, 133–34; Bosnia conflict and, 76; NATO enlargement and, 7, 30, 34, 36, 56, 99, 128, 133–34

IMF. *See* International Monetary Fund
Implementation Force (IFOR), in Bosnia, 75–76, 177, 187, 189–90, 222, 229–30
India, 23, 159, 222–23
International Monetary Fund, 143–46, 150–52, 158
International War Crimes Tribunal, 181
Iran, 7,76, 135–43, 154, 202, 219–21; Russian catchall regulation and, 140–41; Russian nuclear program and, 135–43, 219–21
Iraq, 202, 220, 222

Ischinger, 243

Israel, 80, 220

Istanbul OSCE summit (1999), 198–99

Italy, 119, 128, 161, 165

Ivanov, Igor, 148, 156, 16–62,
    167–68, 176, 180–81, 184,
    186–88, 190–91, 197

Ivanov, Sergei, 207–8, 210

Ivashov, Leonid, 182, 185–86, 193

Jackson, General Mike, 184–85, 189–90

Japan, 41, 67

Joint Chiefs of Staff, U.S., 5, 35,
    38, 54, 187

Joulwan, George, 75, 229

Kasyanov, Mikhail, 156

Kazakhstan, 17, 26, 36, 87, 101, 205, 207

Kennan, George, 119, 153; NATO
    enlargement opposition of, 119

Khrushchev, Nikita, xiii, xx, 213;
    memoirs of, xiii, xx

KFOR. See Kosovo Force

KGB, 83, 156, 158, 194–96, 200, 208,
    233–34

Khasbulatov, Ruslan, 14, 23

Kiriyenko, Sergey, 8, 140, 142,
    145–46, 150

Kissinger, Henry, xxvi, 37–38,
    51, 62, 120

Kohl Helmut, 21, 29, 34, 57, 67, 112–14,
    125–27, 129, 242; NATO
    enlargement and, 29, 34, 112–14,
    125–27

Kokoshin, Andrei, 141–42, 148–49, 152,
    156, 186

Kosovo conflict; Ahtisaari-
    Chernomyrdin initiative in, 8,
    178–85, 232; Cohen-Sergeyev talks
    in, 190–91; ethnic cleansing in, 160,
    163, 165–68; Gore-Chernomyrdin

commission and, 176–78; Holbrooke
    and, 162–63, 167, 174; Milosevic and,
    8, 160–65, 167–70, 176–84; NATO
    "at the core" principle in, 180;
    NATO bombing campaign in, 8,
    164–70, 177–81, 184, 192, 232–33;
    peacekeeping mission debate in,
    182–85, 187–92; Primakov's "turn-
    around" flight and, 164; Pristina
    air-field crisis in, 188–92, 204;
    Rambouillet agreement in, 163;
    Russian diplomacy in, 8, 178–85,
    232; Russian forces in, 187–88; Serb
    atrocities in, 160, 163, 165–68;
    U.S.-Russia relations and, 8, 164–70,
    177–81, 184, 189–92, 232–33

Kosovo Liberation Army, 160, 170

Kosovo Force, 182, 185–87, 189–91,
    202, 210

Kozyrev, Andrei, 15–16, 21–22, 37,
    45–46, 48–50, 60–61, 64–65, 67–69,
    71–72, 101, 156, 227, 243; Christopher
    and, 15–16, 21; NATO enlargement
    debate and, 37, 45–46, 60–61, 64–65,
    67–69,71–72; PfP and, 48–50, 60–61,
    64–65, 71–72; Talbott and, 21–22, 101

Kravchuk, Leonid, 27

Kuchma, Leonid, 101, 131–33, 173, 215

Lake, Anthony, xvi, 15, 22, 34–35, 53,
    70, 171, 243

Latvia, 48–49, 102, 104, 106

Lavrov, Sergey, 184

Lebed, Alexander, 70, 152

Lewinsky, Monica, 8, 147, 153, 158

Lithuania, 103–04, 106

Lugar, Richard, 27, 32–33

Luzhkov, Yuri, 152, 203

Madrid NATO summit, 7, 67, 111, 115,
    124, 128–31, 133

Major, John, 242

Mamedov, Georgy: ABM treaty and, 202–4, 219; background of, 16; CFE treaty and, 97, 199; Iran and, 135, 140, 142; Kosovo conflict and, 169, 188, 192; NATO enlargement and, 49, 55, 59, 62–64, 68, 73, 95, 121, 124–25, 135, 192; Talbott and, 25, 70, 97–98, 147–48, 154–56, 216, 219, 225; Ukraine denuclearization of, 28

Marshall Plan, xxx, 17, 151

Mayakowsky, Vladimir, xx, 186

Meri, Lennart, 103, 203

Milosevic, Slobodan, 8, 21, 48, 160–70, 174, 176–84, 210, 219, 232–33; background of, 160–61; Kosovo conflict and, 160–70, 174, 176–84, 210, 219, 232–33; NATO ultimatum accepted, 182–83

Mondale, Walter, xxiii

Montenegro, 168, 219

Moscow summit (1994), 45–46

Moscow summit (1995), 72–73

Moscow summit (1998), 147–54

Moscow summit (2000), 212–15

NAFTA (North American Free Trade Agreement), xxvii

Nagorno-Karabakh, 59, 78–80

Naples G-7 summit, 48–50

National Missile Defense (NMD), 202, 212, 214, 219

NATO. *See* North Atlantic Treaty Organization

NATO-Russia Founding Act, xv, v, 88, 91, 95, 96–98, 111–28, 132, 137, 141, 156, 177

NATO-Russia partnership, 5–7, 35, 45–47, 49, 60–61, 63–64, 67–68, 72, 74, 82–83, 229–30, 232–33

NATO-Russia Permanent Joint Council, 135, 165, 186–87, 209, 210, 227

Nemtsov, Boris, 8, 143–44,

Nitze, Paul, xx–xxv, 240

Nixon, Richard, 13

North Atlantic Treaty Organization (NATO): Bosnian conflict and, xv, xxix, 2, 5–6, 10, 18–22, 41–42, 47–48, 74–78, 81, 101, 122, 224, 229–30, 324, 238; enlargement of, x–xi, xv–xvi, xvii, 1–7, 16, 30–38, 44–61, 63–77, 81–83, 95–106, 112–31, 134–35, 148, 166, 201, 212, 222, 224, 226–31, 234, 237, 242; Kosovo conflict and, 8, 160–70, 174–93, 201–2, 204, 209–10, 212, 219, 232–34; Madrid summit of, 7, 67, 111, 115, 124, 128–31, 133; opening of, 2–3, 5–6, 31, 33–35, 45–47, 51, 53–56, 58, 61, 66, 71, 74, 81–85, 95, 102, 114, 119, 122, 127, 130, 224; nuclear weapons deployment issue and, 54, 68, 82, 84–85, 95, 102, 112–13, 116, 123–24, 127, 231; Paris summit of, 124–27; PfP and, 3–6, 35–37, 44–46, 48, 50, 53, 56, 60, 61, 71–74, 96, 104, 227, 230; Washington summit of, 230

Nuland, Victoria, xxvii, xxviii, 12, 71, 201, 243

Olsen, Bill, xviii

Organization for Security and Cooperation in Europe (OSCE), 3–4, 6, 59, 76, 80, 96, 112, 131, 192, 198–99, 226

Ottoman Empire, 78, 163

Pakistan, 159

Partnership for Peace (PfP), 3–6, 35–37, 44–46, 48, 50, 53, 56, 60, 61, 71–74, 96, 104, 227, 230

Perle, Richard, xxiii, xxiv
Perry, Bill, 34, 53–54, 78, 105, 177
Poland, xx, 7, 30–34, 76, 103, 114;
    NATO enlargement and, 30–34, 36,
    55–56, 99, 117–18, 123, 128, 130,
    132–34, 231
post–Cold War, 3–11, 16–22; NATO
    enlargement and, 32, 45–47, 57,
    66–69, 74–78; security system,
    61, 69, 77–78, 83, 88, 96, 100, 114,
    119, 122, 133, 160, 167, 203, 223–24,
    227, 238
Primakov, Yevgeny: Albright and, 137;
    Christopher and, 85–86; diplomatic
    style of, 83–84; Kosovo conflict and,
    163–64, 169, 176; NATO
    enlargement and, x–xi, 91, 96–98,
    113–18, 120–26, 135; as prime
    minister, 8, 154–157, 162, 185, 232;
    Russia's financial crisis and, 154–157,
    162; Talbott and, 142, 147–49,
    229, 231
Putin, Vladimir, xi, xvi, 1, 8–9, 86–87,
    135, 158–59, 185–90, 196–99, 201–5,
    211–14, 218–22; as acting president,
    159, 195, 204, 209–11; Berger and,
    186, 193; career of, 86–87, 194;
    Chechen conflict and, 194, 196–99;
    Clinton's encounters with, 196–99,
    201–5, 211–14, 218–22; Clinton's
    St. Petersburg visit and, 86–87;
    Kosovo conflict and, 185–190; in
    Moscow Summit (2000), 147–54;
    NATO enlargement and, 210; NMD
    issue and, 202, 212, 214, 219;
    personality and style of, 9, 194–96,
    203, 220; Russian election of 2000,
    197–205

Racak massacre, 163
Ralston, Joe, 187

Rambouillet Agreement (1999), 163
RAND Corporation, 33, 105
Reagan, Ronald, xx–xxvi
Reich, Robert, 12, 109
Republican Party, 42, 60, 66, 70–71,
    107, 109, 141, 200
Reston, James, xix
Rodionov, Igor, 97
Roosevelt, Franklin, 155–56
Ross, Dennis, 16
Rubin, Robert, 145, 158
Russia: Asian financial crisis and,
    144–46; August coup in 1991 and,
    xxvi, 14, 83, 150; Bosnia conflict
    and, 18–22, 47–48, 74–76; catchall
    regulation of, 140–41; economy of,
    xxix–xxx, 5, 4–8, 21, 25–26, 83–86,
    99–106, 143–59; G-7 enlargement
    and Group of Eight (G-8), 23, 28, 48,
    64, 74, 86, 116, 122, 136, 139, 141–42,
    158, 167, 169, 179–80, 189–90,
    216–17, 221; IMF loans and, 143–46,
    150–52, 158; NATO enlargement and
    (see North Atlantic Treaty
    Organization)
Rutskoi, Alexander, 23
Ryurikov, Dimitri, 64

Safire, William, 206
Sergeyev, Igor, 187–91
Schecter, Jerrold, xiii
Schröder, Gerhard, 206, 221
Senate, U.S., 27–28, 66, 71, 107, 141,
    143, 158, 211
Serbia, 19, 21, 47, 163, 169, 189, 219, 238
Shearer, Brooke, xiii, xix, xxix, xxviii,
    62, 91–92, 94, 107–10
Shearer, Derek, xix, 243
Shevardnadze, Eduard, 79, 199–200,
    209, 220
Sobchak, Anatoly, 86–87, 194–95

Solana, Javier, xi, 113–18, 124–26,
    156–57, 167, 173, 177, 183, 237, 243
Soviet Union, 96, 100, 103, 122, 154,
    226–27; collapse of, ix; former
    republics of, xi, xv, xxx, 11–17, 27,
    49, 77–80, 85–87; Gorbachev and,
    xxvi; Putin and, 203–207; Talbott
    perception of, xviii, xix, xxi, xxii,
    xxiii, xxiv, xxv; Talbott's first visit,
    xix–xx; Ukraine and, 26–31
State Department, ix, xx, xi, xiii,
    xv, xxi, xxiv, xxvii, 9, 12, 33–35,
    40–41, 108–9, 138, 154, 179, 183,
    233, 240–42
Stepashin, Sergey, 185, 190, 192–93,
    196, 198
Strategic Arms Limitation Talks
    (SALT), xx, xxv
Strategic Arms Reduction Talks
    (START I, II, III), xxv, 219
Strategic Defense Initiative (SDI),
    xxiii, xxiv
Strategic Stability Group, 16
Summer, Larry, 151–52, 154, 158
Supreme Soviet, xiv, 14, 23

Talbott, Adrian, xxviii, 62, 92
Talbott, Devin, xxviii, 62, 92
Talbott, Josephine, xviii
Talbott, Nelson, xviii
Talbott, Strobe: background of,
    xviii–xxi; Clinton's first meeting
    with, xix, xx; joins State
    Department, 11–13; Holbrooke and,
    xxvi, 12, 108–10; Mamedov and, xi,
    16, 25, 28, 49, 55, 59, 62–64, 68, 70,
    73, 95, 97–98, 121, 124–25, 135, 140,
    142, 147–48, 154, 169, 188, 192, 199,
    202–4, 216, 219, 225; named deputy
    secretary of state, 40–43; at Oxford,

xiii–xx; Nitze and, xx–xxv, 240;
    Primakov and, 142, 147–49, 229, 231;
    Shearer and, xiii, xix, xxix, xxviii,
    62, 91–92, 94, 107–10; as *Time*
    correspondent, xx, xxviii, 93; Yeltsin
    and, 86–87, 148–52
Tarasyuk, Boris, 26, 28, 100–101, 132,
    173, 225, 243
Taubman, Philipp, xx, 243
Thomas, Evan, xx
Time (magazine), x, xiii, xvi, xvii, xx,
    xxiv, xviii, 12, 19, 42, 93
Tyutchev, Fyodor, xix, 186

Ukraine, xi, xv, 2, 3, 5, 6, 7, 17, 26–31,
    34, 36, 38, 55, 59, 65, 67, 78; NATO
    enlargement and, 83–84, 95–96,
    99–105, 131–35, 228, 230; Soviet
    warheads dispute and, 26–31, 225;
    Ukraine-Russia relations, 26–31,
    131–35, 215–16
United Kingdom, xix, 20–21, 28, 84,
    113, 143, 161, 208, 220
United Nations, xiv, 74–75, 110, 177–78,
    184–85, 210, 214
Ushakov, Yuri, 221

Vance, Cyrus, xx–xxi
Vancouver summit (1993), 5, 10–18, 225
Védrine, Hubert, 216–17
Vershbow, Alexander, 117, 174, 183,
    242–43
Vietnam War, xix, 19, 167, 170, 233

Walesa, Lech, 2, 31–32, 65, 134
Warsaw Pact, ix, xxx, 33, 45, 73,
    96–97, 130, 225
Weisman, Steven, xx, 243
Wharton, Clifton, 41, 171
White House Fellows, xxix, 108

Yavlinsky, Grigory, 144, 205, 211
Yalta Conference (1945), 82, 231
Yeltsin, Boris; Albright and, 116;
    August 1991 coup and, xxvi, 83, 152;
    Baltic withdrawal issue, 48–49;
    Bosnia conflict and, 47–48, 74–76;
    Clinton's meetings with, 17–22,
    60–69, 73–75, 85–87, 120–28,
    146–54, 166–69, 175–76, 179–80,
    184–85, 187–91, 214–15; "cold peace"
    remarks of, 6, 61; depression of, 88,
    154; drinking habit of, 18, 69, 123;
    Gore's bedside meeting with, 63–64;
    health of, 69, 113, 123, 149, 196, 204;
    Kosovo conflict and, 161–65, 167–69,
    175–76, 178–80, 182, 184–93;
    Moscow summit 1994, 45–46;
    Moscow summit 1995, 72–73;
    Moscow summit 1998, 147–54;
    NATO enlargement and, 45–46,
    49–50, 60–65, 69–76, 121–30;
    parliamentary opposition to, xiv,
    14–18, 23–25; resignation, 204;
    Russian election of 1996, 85–88;
    Talbott's meetings with, 85–86,
    149–50; Ukraine-Russia warheads
    dispute and, 26–30; Vancouver
    summit, 15–18
Yergin, Daniel, xix, 243
Yugoslav Federal Republic of; Kosovo
    conflict and, 160–69, 174–77,
    180–81, 185, 187–88, 192, 232–33
Yugoslavia, xvii, xxx, 210, 219, 223;
    Bosnian war and, 8 10, 18, 20, 26, 67,
    74, 81, 135
Yumashev, Valentin, 141–42, 144, 197

Zhirinovsky, Vladimir, 24–25, 70, 203,
    207, 225
Zlenko, Anatoly, 101
Zyuganov, Gennady, 24, 84–87,
    123, 211

Printed and bound by CPI Group (UK) Ltd, Croydon, CR0 4YY

07/07/2026

14916230-0001